THE HISTORICAL DEVELOPMENT OF THE BHAKTI MOVEMENT IN INDIA

The Japanese Association for South Asian Studies
Established in 1988

- **Office Bearers as of 1 October 2009**

  President
  Haruka Yanagisawa, Professor Emeritus, University of Tokyo

  General Secretary
  Hisayoshi Miyamoto, Toyo University

  Members of the Board of Executive Directors
  Toshie Awaya, Tokyo University of Foreign Studies
  Hideki Esho, Hosei University
  Kouichi Fujita, Kyoto University
  Takako Hirose, Senshu University
  Takako Inoue, Daito Bunka University
  Norio Kondo, Institute of Developing Economies
  Hiroyuki Miyake, University of Kitakyushu
  Fumiko Oshikawa, Kyoto University
  Takanobu Takahashi, University of Tokyo
  Masayuki Usuda, Tokai University

- **Head Office** (until September 2012)
  c/o Department of Indian Philosophy, Faculty of Letters, Toyo University
  5-28-20 Hakusan, Bunkyo-ku, Tokyo 112-8606, Japan
  E-mail: jasas@toyonet.toyo.ac.jp
  http://wwwsoc.nii.ac.jp/jasas/index_e.html

- **Publications in English**

  1 *JJASAS (Journal of the Japanese Association for South Asian Studies),* (annual publication in Japanese and English, the current issue: No. 18)

  2 Japanese Studies on South Asia Series

  No. 1: H. Kotani, ed., *Caste System, Untouchability and the Depressed*, Manohar, New Delhi, 1997.
  No. 2: N. Karashima, ed., *Kingship in Indian History*, Manohar, New Delhi, 1999.
  No. 3: S. Mayeda, ed., *The Way to Liberation*, Manohar, New Delhi, 2000.
  No. 4: S. Einoo and J. Takashima, eds., *From Material to Deity*, Manohar, New Delhi, 2005.
  No. 5: H. Okahashi, ed., *Emerging New Industrial Spaces and Regional Developments in India*, Manohar, New Delhi, 2007.
  No. 6: H. Ishii, D.N. Gellner and K. Nawa, eds., *Social Dynamics in Northern South Asia,* Vol. 1: *Nepalis Inside and Outside Nepal*, Manohar, New Delhi, 2007.
  No. 7: H. Ishii, D.N. Gellner and K. Nawa, eds., *Social Dynamics in Northern South Asia,* Vol. 2: *Political and Social Transformations in North India and Nepal*, Manohar, New Delhi, 2007.
  No. 8: Iwao Shima, Teiji Sakata and Katsuyuki Ida, eds., *The Historical Development of the Bhakti Movement in India: Theory and Practice*, Manohar, New Delhi, 2010.

Japanese Studies on South Asia No. 8

The Historical Development of the Bhakti Movement in India
Theory and Practice

Edited by
IWAO SHIMA
TEIJI SAKATA
KATSUYUKI IDA

MANOHAR
2026

First published 2011
Reprinted 2026

ISBN 978-81-7304-884-5

Published by

Ajay Kumar Jain *for*
Manohar Publishers & Distributors
4753/23 Ansari Road, Daryaganj
New Delhi 110 002

Typeset at

Digigrafics
New Delhi 110 049

Printed and bound in India

Contents

Preface 7

List of Contributors 13

PART I: THE THEORETICAL FRAMEWORK OF BHAKTI AND ITS HISTORICAL DEVELOPMENT

1. Reflections on Bhakti as a Type of Indian Mysticism
Yoshitsugu Sawai 19

2. The Use of Bhakti/Bhakta in the Pāñcarātra Scriptures
Hiromichi Hikita 35

3. Rāmānuja's Theory of Bhakti Based on the Vedānta Philosophy
Bunki Kimura 51

4. Theories of Salvation in the Teṅgalai and Vaḍagalai Schools
Sadanori Ishitobi 75

5. Some Sources of Madhva's Bhakti Theory
Hiroaki Ikebe 95

6. The Concept of Bhakti in the Tantric Tradition
Katsuyuki Ida 113

7. Realization of Inner Divinity: Nātha Yogins in the Medieval Bhakti Movement
Kazuyo Sakaki 131

PART II: THE PHILOSOPHICAL INFLUENCE OF BHAKTI AND ITS POPULAR ACCEPTANCE

8. The Atmosphere of Bhakti in Literature: A Buddhist *Stotra*, a *Kathā*, and a Folk Tale
Yoshifumi Mizuno 159

9. Jñāneśvar's Interpretation of the *Bhagavad-gītā* I–VI
Iwao Shima 183

10. The Bhakti in Tukārām's *Abhaṅgas*
Chihiro Koiso 197

11. A Study of an Aspect of Kabīr's Bhakti with the Text and Translation of the *Gyāna Cauṁtīsā* in the *Bījak*
Taigen Hashimoto 213

12. Analytical Study of *Bhaktirasa* as a Religious Sentiment Established by the Gauḍīya Vaiṣṇava School
Masaru Tonguu 223

13. Rāma in the Eyes of his Consort, Sītā: A Study of Tulsīdās's *Rāmcaritmānas*
Teiji Sakata 251

14. Saint Ramalingar and the Exemplification of God as Effulgence
Hiroshi Yamashita 265

Postscript 289

Index 291

Preface

This book is the eighth volume of the series, 'Japanese Studies on South Asia', published by the Japanese Association for South Asian Studies. The main purpose of this series is to illustrate Japan's contribution to South Asian studies in the international academic world. This volume, entitled *Historical Development of Bhakti Movement in India: Theory and Practice*, is an attempt to elucidate the meanings of bhakti in various religious traditions.

In India, bhakti or devotion to God by devotees has been an important part of religious life since the early medieval period. When a devotee humbly worships God, he/she is embraced by divine grace; thus, a devotee can be united with God through bhakti. Taking into consideration the importance of religious commitment of bhakti among the Hindus, we organized this research group to work on its various phases in India and continued researching it from perspectives such as Indian philosophy, Hindu literatures, and modern Indian literatures. As a result, the source materials for our studies are written in various languages, not only in classical Sanskrit but also in such medieval and modern languages as Bengālī, Marāṭhī, Hindī, and Tamil.

In order to share our academic efforts and results, several seminars were held at Kanazawa University in Kanazawa City and Takushoku University in Tokyo. At these seminars, all the contributors to this volume presented their draft papers and later revised them on the basis of the suggestions given by the participants. our academic research was financially supported by a Grants-in-Aid for Scientific Research (Grant 13301-B-17320014), awarded by the Japan Society for the Promotion of Science during the period 2005–8.

This volume consists of two parts: Part I, entitled 'The Theoretical Framework of Bhakti and Its Historical Development', contains seven papers, mainly discussing the various theories of bhakti and its development in Indian religious traditions. Part II, entitled 'The Philosophical Influence of Bhakti and Its Popular Acceptance', also contains seven papers, focusing on how the philosophies of bhakti influenced Indian religious traditions, or how bhakti was popularly accepted in the Indian cultural context. Here is a brief introduction to the main themes and contents of this volume.

In 'Reflections on Bhakti as a Type of Indian Mysticism', Yoshitsugu Sawai presents a general discussion on the meaning of bhakti, comparing it with 'mysticism' in Indian religious contexts. In his semantic analysis, focusing on the theories of bhakti demonstrated by two scholars—Surendranath Dasgupta and Rudolf Otto—he argues that the ascetic dimensions of bhakti correspond to the religious phenomena covered by mysticism, although it may be preferable to use the term 'faith' or 'practice' when referring to the concept of bhakti in its popular dimension. In the second paper, 'The Use of Bhakti/Bhakta in the Pāñcarātra Scriptures', Hiromichi Hikita analyses the usage of the words bhakti (devotion) and bhakta (devotees) found in the 'three jewels', the early Pāñcarātra scriptures. Through his careful analysis of the usage of these terms, he concludes that only those who receive initiation into the Pāñcarātra sect are authorized to worship Viṣṇu with bhakti in daily ritual and that Viṣṇu thus grants various favours to his devotees in this world and absolute happiness in the next world.

The following two articles focus on the Śrīvaiṣṇava philosophy. First, Bunki Kimura's paper, 'Rāmānuja's Theory of Bhakti Based on the Vedānta Philosophy', attempts to clarify how, on the basis of the authority of the Upaniṣads, Rāmānuja introduces bhakti to the Brahman as the indispensable means for *mokṣa* in the Vedānta philosophical tradition. According to his research, Rāmānuja succeeded in establishing the theory that a Brahman's knowledge (*vidyā*) is interchangeable with bliss (*ānanda*), and constructed the basis of the later Vedānta philosophy connected to the bhakti cult. For his part Sadanori Ishitobi discusses the theory of salvation in the Śrīvaiṣṇava tradition, especially in its two sub-sects, the Teṅgalai (southern school) and the Vaḍagalai (northern school) in 'Theories of Salvation in the Teṅgalai and Vaḍagalai Schools'. Through analysis of the meanings of bhakti and *prapatti* expounded by Piḷḷai Lokācārya and Vedānta Deśika, Ishitobi concludes that the signs of antagonism between Teṅgalai's populism and Vaḍagalai's traditionalism are evident in the difference of these two thoughts.

In 'Some Sources of Madhva's Bhakti Theory', Hiroaki Ikebe philologically examines Madhva's concepts of bhakti and *mokṣa* in the Nārāyaṇīya section of the *Mahābhārata*, the *Ahirbudhnya-Saṃhitā*, the *Lakṣmī-Tantra*, and the *Bhāgavata-Purāṇa*, for he supposes that these texts constitute the source of Madhva's theory of salvation. Clarifying the similarities between Madhva's concept of bhakti or *mokṣa* and with that of these texts, Ikebe suggests that Madhva must have had his own source of thought. Regarding the concept of bhakti in Hindu Tantric philosophy, Katsuyuki Ida's paper, 'The Concept of Bhakti in the Tantric Tradition', examines how the concept of bhakti was accepted in the Hindu Tantric tradition. Ida concludes that 'instead of bhakti to the divinity, bhakti to the *guru* is remarkably emphasized in the Tantric scriptures, particularly in the Śāktas'. Moreover, he emphasizes that bhakti to the *guru* may be traced back to the Brahmanical tradition, as typically found in the Dharmaśāstras.

The last paper of Part I is the 'Realization of Inner Divinity: Nātha Yogins in the Medieval Bhakti Movement', by Kazuyo Sakaki. By limiting her study to the Nātha tradition, which developed physical techniques for gaining complete control over *prāṇa*, Sakaki investigates how the Nāthas, as the result of their interiorized bhakti, become God themselves. They formulated spiritual practices for spiritual death and rebirth through the processes of purification. Thus, these seven articles trace the development of the theories of bhakti and also examine them along with some other theories in the Bhakti movements, including those pertaining to the Tantric and Nātha traditions.

Part II also contains seven articles that examine the development of the Bhakti movement in various areas in later medieval India. The first article, 'The Atmosphere of Bhakti in Literature: A Buddhist *Stotra*, One Work of *Kathā* Literature, and a Folk Tale' is written by Yoshifumi Mizuno. He investigates how the atmosphere of bhakti is exhibited in other literary works. According to him, it is self-evident that bhakti literatures such as the *Bhagavad-gītā* and *Bhāgavata-Purāṇa* characterize the atmosphere of bhakti, but aspects of bhakti can also be detected some Buddhist *stotra*s, in *kathā* literature in Sanskrit, and in folk tales in modern vernacular languages.

In 'Jñāneśvar's Interpretation of the *Bhagavad-gītā* I–VI', Iwao

Shima points out that Jñāneśvar's philosophy, written in Marāṭhī , represents the earliest stage of the development of bhakti. After his careful examination of the first six chapters of Jñāneśvar's commentary on the *Bhagavad-gītā*, Shima clarifies that Jñāneśvar's interpretation is strongly influenced by Śaṅkara's thought and that it also accepts the style of the Tantric meditation developed mainly in the Nāthas. Considering this fact, he argues that bhakti and Tantrism, which constitute the two main currents in medieval Hindu tradition, bear overlapping aspects. Like Shima's paper, Chihiro Koiso's paper, 'The Bhakti of Tukārām in His *Abhaṅga*s', also examines the meaning of bhakti in the Marāṭhī-speaking area. In her analysis of Tukārām's poetical compositions (The *Abhaṅga*s), she concludes that his approach to bhakti can be summarized as follows: 'Make God the centre of your life. Walk the Path of Love. Serve mankind, and thus, see God in all.'

Moreover, Kabīr's theory of bhakti is discussed by Taigen Hashimoto in his paper 'A Study of an Aspect of Kabīr's Bhakti: With the Text and Translation of the Gyāna Cauṁtīsā in Kabīr's *Bījak*'. As the title suggests, Hashimoto gives the full text along with the English translation of the Gyāna Cauṁtīsā in Kabīr's *Bījak*. This is important research material in Hindi for examining the popular acceptance of bhakti. The theory of bhakti in the eastern part of India is argued in Masaru Tonguu's paper, 'Analytical Study of *Bhaktirasa* as a Religious Sentiment Established by the Gauḍīya Vaiṣṇava School'. According to Tonguu's research, the Gauḍīya Vaiṣṇava School places bhakti toward Kṛṣṇa above all the other types of bhakti, and subordinates the traditional rasa theory to that of the Gauḍīya Vaiṣṇava school in order to emphasize the excellence of *bhakti rasa*.

In Teiji Sakata's paper, 'Rāma in the Eyes of His Consort, Sītā: A Study of Tulsīdās's *Rāmcaritmānas*', the region where Rāma has been the Supreme God for centuries is argued. Sakata focuses on the characteristics of Rāma through the eyes of his consort, Sītā, with reference to the Hindī epics in the sixteenth century. According to his research, from Sītā's perspective, Rāma has three phases: Rāma as Sītā's beloved husband, the lord of Kosala kingdom, and the Supreme God, born as an incarnation of Viṣṇu. In this case, one may identify devotion the Supreme God integrated into human love. The last paper of the volume brings us to south India in the nineteenth century. Hiroshi Yamashita's paper entitled 'Saint Ramalingar and the Exemplification of God as Effulgence' sheds light on the aspect of bhakti in the case of Saint Ramalingar, one of the central figures in the Hindu reform movement. Yamashita focuses on the devotion and practices of the saint.

By compiling these papers we would like to convey a message to the international academic community. Needless to say, we realize that considerable research remains to be completed in order to satisfactorily clarify the characteristics of bhakti in Indian religious traditions.

Tokyo EDITORS
19 July 2010

Contributors

TAIGEN HASHIMOTO is Professor of Indology at the Department of Indian Philosophy, Faculty of Literature, Tokyo University, Tokyo, Japan. His major area of research is the *bhakti* movement in the northern India, especially the Nirguṇa traditions started by Kabīr. He has recently published the Japanese translation of the whole Bījak which is the basic canon of the Kabīr Caurā Maṭh in Banāras, in his *A Study of Folk Religious Thoughts in the Northern Medieval India* (in Japanese, 2006).

HIROMICHI HIKITA is Professor of Buddhism at the Department of Religious and Buddhist Studies, Aichi Gakuin University, Nisshin, Japan. He is the author of *The Study of Hindu Tantrism* (in Japanese, 1997) and 'Consecration of Divine Images in a Temple' in *From Material to Deity: Indian Ritual of Consecration* (2005). He is specializing the *Sātvata Saṃhitā*, one of the oldest texts in the Pāñcarātra Sect.

KATSUYUKI IDA is Lecturer of South Asian Studies at Kanazawa University, Ishikawa, Japan. He has been working on medieval Hinduism, focusing mainly on the Tantric practices. His 'Cakrapūjā in the Śrīkula Sect' (in Japanese) is published in *Journal of Religious Studies,* 79.3 (2006).

HIROAKI IKEBE is Teacher of Social Studies at Futaba High School, Hokkaido, Japan. He is the author of 'Madhva's Salvation Theory' in S. Mayeda, ed., *The Way to Liberation: Indological Studies in Japan,* Japanese Studies on South Asia No. 3 (2000) and 'A Study of Madhva's Salvation Theory' (in Japanese, doctoral dissertation submitted to Hokkaido University, 2001).

SADANORI ISHITOBI is Lecturer of Philosophy at Rakuno Gakuen University, Ebetsu, Japan. He is the author of 'Vedānta Deśika and Īśvarānumāna' (in Japanese) in *Hokkaido Journal of Indological and Buddhist Studies*, 17 (2002), and 'Is God Beyond

Description? Rāmānuja's Concept of God' (in Japanese, *Kokugakuin Zasshi*, 106.3 (2005).

BUNKI KIMURA is Associate Professor of the History of Religions at the Division of General Education, Aichi Gakuin University, Nisshin, Aichi, Japan. He is the author of 'Rāmānuja's Theory of Three *Yoga*s: The Way to *Mokṣa'* in S. Hino and T. Wada, eds., *Three Mountains and Seven Rivers,* Musashi Tachikawa Felicitation Volume (2004).

CHIHIRO KOISO is Lecturer of Hyogo University of Health Science, Kobe, Japan. She is the author of 'Bhakti-Mārga of Jñāneśvar: Social Aspect of Advaita-bhakti' in H. Kotani et al., eds., *Mārga* (2007). She is a co-author of *Food Culture of the World: India* (in Japanese, 2006).

YOSHIFUMI MIZUNO is Professor of Hindi and Sanskrit, South and West Asian Studies, Institute of Global Studies, Tokyo University of Foreign Studies, Tokyo, Japan. He is the author of 'The Letter of Death Motif: To the East or to the West?' (in Japanese) in *Trans-Cultural Studies*, 10 (2007). He has published articles on ancient and medieval Indian literature and poetics in academic books and journals in Japanese.

KAZUYO SAKAKI is Lecturer of Hokkaido Musashi Women's Junior College, Sapporo, Japan. She is the author of 'Yogavāsiṣṭha and the Medieval Islamic Intellectuals in India' in *Yogavāsiṣṭha Mahārāmāyaṇa: A Perspective,* ed. Manjula Sahdev (2004) and 'Yogico-Tantric Traditions in the Ḥawḍ al-Ḥayāt', *Journal of the Japanese Association for South Asian Studies*, 17 (2005). She specializes in medieval Hindu-Muslim inter-cultural relations in religious and philosophical aspects.

TEIJI SAKATA is Professor Emeritus of Hindi, Takushoku University, Tokyo, Japan. He is the author of 'The Exchange of Services and Gifts at the Birth of Hindu Boys as Described in Hindi *Bhakti* Literature and Folk Songs' in M. Horstmann, ed., *Bhakti in Current Research* (2006). He edited with I. Shima *The Saints of India* (in Japanese, 2000). He has a plan to translate major parts of *Rāmcaritmānas* by Tulsīdās into Japanese.

YOSHITSUGU SAWAI is Professor of the History of Religions at the Department of Religious Studies, Tenri University, Nara, Japan. He is the author of *The Faith of Ascetics and Lay Smārtas: A Study of the Śaṅkaran Tradition of Śṛṅgeri* (1992) and 'The Structure of Consciousness in Śaṅkara's Philosophy' in *Consciousness and Reality: Studies in Memory of Toshihiko Izutsu* (1998).

IWAO SHIMA is late Professor of Kanazawa University, Kanazawa, Japan. He is the author of *A Philological Study of Bhāmatī* (in Japanese, a doctoral dissertation submitted to Kanazawa University in 2001), *Śaṅkara* (in Japanese, 2002), and *The Relationship of Bhakti and Tantrism in the Jñāneśvarī* (Kanazawa University, 2006).

MASARU TONGUU is Associate Professor, Nara University of Education, Nara, Japan. He translated the *Caitanya-caritāmṛta* written by Kṛṣṇadāsa Kavirāja into Japanese and published it as *The Biography of Caitanya*, 2 vols. (2000 and 2001). He is the author of 'What Existed between Kṛṣṇa Legend and Vaiṣṇava Sect in Bengal' in *Folk-Literature and Traditions*, vol. 10 (2002).

HIROSHI YAMASHITA is Professor at the Graduate School of International Cultural Studies, Tohoku University, Sendai, Japan. His main interest lies in the historical development of Hinduism in the Tamil-speaking area of southern India. His recent publications include 'God as Warrior King' in N. Karashima, ed., *Kingship in Indian History* (1999), and 'The Forms and Functions of the Aiyaṉār Temple Complex' in Y. Ikari and Y. Nagano, eds., *From Vedic Altar to Village Shrine* (1993).

PART I

THE THEORETICAL FRAMEWORK OF BHAKTI AND ITS HISTORICAL DEVELOPMENT

1

Reflections on Bhakti as a Type of Indian Mysticism

YOSHITSUGU SAWAI

India has been regarded by scholars of religious studies as the place where mysticism flowered in the past and continues to do so in the present. Derived from the Western cultural context, the term 'mysticism' was considered appropriate for the Indian religious traditions, although its meaning is still ambiguous. In fact, this term could be applied to describe Indian religious phenomena both from the monistic and theistic aspects. As John Carman points out, the applicability of the Western category of 'mysticism' to Indian religious phenomena is not self-evident.[1]

With special reference to comparative religion which compares the Hindu concept of bhakti with the religious concept of mysticism, the aim of this paper is to clarify the extent to which the Hindu concept of bhakti can be understood as mysticism. In this sense, this paper makes a semantic attempt to examine the meanings of bhakti and mysticism. In the Western academic world, elaborate studies on mysticism were undertaken by such scholars of religious studies as William James, Evelyn Underhill, Wayne Proudfoot, and Grace Jantzen; however, no scholar can be considered as representative, except for Rudolf Otto who specialized in Indian religious traditions. On the other hand, Surendranath Dasgupta, a scholar of Hindu thought, was familiar both with Western philosophy and with Hindu thought; his five-volume *A History of Indian Philosophy* reflects his deep understanding of Indian philosophy. Thus, in this paper, I would like to focus on the two scholars who discuss the meanings of bhakti and mysticism in Indian religious contexts: Rudolf Otto (1869–1937), whose perspective provides a

Western standpoint on 'Indian mysticism', and is found in his classical works on religious studies such as *Das Heilige, West-östliche Mystik* and *Die Gnadenreligion des Indiens und das Christentum*, and Surendranath Dasgupta (1885–1952), who is known by his popular books *A History of Indian Philosophy* and *Hindu Mysticism*, and who, from the Indian viewpoint of 'mysticism', attempted to elucidate the meaning of bhakti as a theistic form of mysticism.

THE DEFINITION OF MYSTICISM

Mysticism is a religious concept derived from specific historical contexts in the West. Scholars have used the term to describe an intuitive or ecstatic union with the ultimate reality through contemplation, communion, or other mental experiences. In other words, it implies the potential union of the human soul with the ultimate reality.

In *Hindu Mysticism*, Dasgupta defines mysticism as 'a theory, doctrine, or view that considers reason to be incapable of discovering or of realizing the nature of ultimate truth, whatever be the nature of this ultimate truth, but at the same time believes in the certitude of some other means of arriving at it'.[2] In his definition of mysticism, he suggests that the ultimate truth is realized through mysticism or through an ecstatic communion that human reason cannot achieve. According to Dasgupta, like the Islamic and Christian mystics, the 'devotional mystics or bhaktas of India' also hold the view that 'the vision of God and His grace is attained through devotional communion or devotional rapture of various kinds'.[3] The thoughts of all mystics are thus characterized by 'a keen sense of the necessity of purity of mind, contentment, ever alert striving for moral goodness, self-abnegation, and one-pointedness to God'.[4] In such a perspective, mysticism is 'the basis of all religions'. This view is shared by Otto.

In *West-östliche Mystik*, Otto mentions mysticism as an 'experience of the immanence of the divine, and of unification or unity in essence with it' (*Erfahrung der Immanenz des Göttlichen, Wesenseinigung oder Wesenseinheit mit dem Göttlichem*). It is generally considered that mysticism is based on one's union with the transcendent, as is suggested by the term *unio mystica.* For Otto, a mystic experience, characterized by 'the experience of the divine as transcendent' (*Erfahrung des Göttlichen als des Transzendenten*) is a contrast to other forms of religious experience.[5] Instead of emphasizing the infinite gap between the transcendent and the human, one is united with the divine. Thus, the relationship between the human and the transcendent differs between mysticism and general religious experience, and this depends upon the two types of religious commitment.

For Otto, the nature of mysticism is different from what has been generally understood as his theory of mysticism. First, when clarifying the differences between mysticism and general religious experience with regard to one's relationship with the divine, Otto focuses on the implication of the term 'the divine' (*das Göttliche*) in both cases. In the case of mysticism, the same term means Godhead as an immanent principle (*'Gottheit' als immanentes Prinzip*), while in the case of general religious experience, the divine implies 'the transcendent God' (*der transzendente Gott*), or the object of religious commitment for adherents. This suggests that both mystic and general religious experiences contain fundamentally different structures of the human and the divine; the difference of the object of religious commitment influences the corresponding difference in the relationship between the human and the divine.

Moreover, Otto emphasizes that mysticism is not first of all an act of union, but predominantly the life lived in the wonder of this 'wholly other' God (*nicht erst die Einigung, sondern schon und ganz überwiegend das Leben in dem Wunder dieses 'Ganz Anderen' Gottes ist Mystik*).[6] Man is a mystic as soon as he has this conception of God, even when the element of union recedes or remains unemphasized, which can easily happen in mysticism. It is the wholly non-rational character of this conception of God with its divergence from the intimate, personal, modified God of simple theism, which makes the mystic'.[7] The general understanding of Otto's perspective on mysticism must be revised, for he emphasizes 'the life lived in the wonder of this "wholly other" God' as the fundamental characteristic of mysticism, rather than 'an act of union', or *unio mystica*, generally accepted as its essential characteristic. However, such an understanding might lead to an ambiguity with regard to the boundary between mysticism and general religious experience. At the least it can be stated that such ambiguity of boundary represents the essential argument of Otto's theory of religion, the core of which is characterized by mystical experience.

In any case, Otto and Dasgupta share a perspective on mysticism in that both consider it as constituting the core of religion. Combining their perspectives, it can be stated that mysticism as a religious phenomenon is recognized when the ultimate truth or the 'wholly other' God is seen as being in a non-rational dimension of reality. While the applicability of the concept of mysticism to Indian religious traditions must be carefully examined, two modern Hindu scholars who belong to a devotional community already transcend the issue of such an applicability, for they maintain that 'only the mysticism of union with the personal Lord is true mysticism'.[8]

TYPES OF INDIAN MYSTICISM

Otto and Dasgupta find it quite adequate to apply the concept of mysticism to Indian religious phenomena. This implies that for both of them, mysticism is a universal category. When mysticism is applied to Indian contexts, however, different types of Indian mysticism might be encountered. Bhakti can be included as one of the Indian forms of mysticism.

Dasgupta's Perspective on Indian Mysticism

With special focus on bhakti, we would now like to discuss the main characteristics of Indian mysticism, according to Dasgupta's typology. This is the sacrificial type of mysticism, the source of the four fundamental types of Indian mysticism. The sacrificial type, characterized by the ritualistic thought of the Vedas, is the earliest. Dasgupta argues that 'the assumption of the mysterious omnipotence of sacrifices, performed by following the authoritative injunctions of the Vedas independently of reason or logical and discursive thought, forms the chief trait of the mysticism of the Vedic type'.[9]

Dasgupta maintains that Indian mysticism consists of the Upaniṣadic, Yogic, Buddhistic and bhakti types; in reality, some concrete examples of mysticism are 'of a syncretistic nature', and others represent the combinations of such distinct types of mysticism.[10] It is well known that the Upaniṣads, which form the concluding portions of the Vedas, are referred to as Vedānta, but were not composed systematically and logically; rather, they represent the 'mystical experiences of the soul gushing forth from within us' to which Dasgupta refers at a later point. Different philosophers proposed different systems of Vedānta philosophy, based on their different interpretations of the Upaniṣadic texts.[11] The main features of Upaniṣadic mysticism are characterized by the earnest and sincere quest for the highest reality, known as *brahman* or *ātman*, which is 'a totality of partless, simple and undifferentiated experience' and which is 'the ultimate essence of our self and the highest principle of the universe'. However, it is noteworthy that there is another current of thought in the Upaniṣads, in which *brahman* is regarded as the theistic God. In this religious context, Dasgupta points out that two of the earlier Upaniṣads—the *Muṇḍaka* (3.1.1) and the *Śvetāśvatara* (4.6)—express the 'duality between the individual and God'.[12]

In order to examine the point of contact between bhakti and mysticism, it is imperative to ascertain that the Upaniṣadic texts reveal different strains of thought. On the one hand, in his Advaita Vedānta philosophy, Śaṅkara contends that the Upaniṣads teach that *brahman* alone exists. On the other hand, Rāmānuja, in his Viśiṣṭādvaita Vedānta philosophy, holds that the Upaniṣads favour the doctrine of modified duality. Madhva is another commentator who maintains in his Dvaita Vedānta philosophy that the Upaniṣads provide a doctrine of uncompromising duality. With regard to these differences in the interpretations of the Upaniṣads, Dasgupta argues that 'all these interpretations are biased and one-sided, and therefore inexact'; although the Upaniṣads provide knowledge about 'different phases of thought and experience', he maintains that all these different phases are considered as 'different stages of development in the experience of minds seeking to grasp a sublime, ultimate but inexpressible truth'.[13]

Otto's Perspective on Indian Mysticism

According to Otto, mysticism appears in religious experience to the extent to which the hidden, non-rational and numinous elements of the object of religious feelings predominate and determine emotional life. The word 'mystica' is originally an adjective qualifying the substantive 'theologia', and Otto's view of Indian mysticism is thus based on the theistic model. However, he argues that mysticism can also exist where there is absolutely no conception of God. He classifies the contents of mysticism into 'soul-mysticism' (*Seelenmystik*) and 'God-mysticism' (*Gottesmystik*).[14] 'Soul-mysticism' arises when the hidden characteristic of the soul becomes vital and active, while God-mysticism arises when the *Deus sine modis*, God in complete non-rationality, is predominant. In the Indian philosophical context, Otto mentions that soul-mysticism can be referred to as *ātman*-mysticism. Yoga and Buddhist teachings are regarded as concrete examples of soul-mysticism, while Śaṅkara's philosophy of non-duality is viewed as combining soul-mysticism with God-mysticism. As Otto discusses in *West-östliche Mystik*, Śaṅkara's mysticism has a particular emphasis through its relation to Indian theism. Thus, although Otto himself personally sympathizes with the bhakti type of Indian mysticism, which is related to a personal God, the combination of these two types in Śaṅkara, being distinct from theistic mysticism, provides the possibility of transcending the bhakti type of Indian mysticism; this can be likened to the 'lower knowledge' (*aparavidyā*) of truth in Śaṅkara, which corresponds with bhakti to the personal God, as emphasized by Rāmānuja.

Apart from distinguishing soul-mysticism and God-mysticism, Otto classifies them as 'the mysticism of introspection' (*Mystik der Selbstversenkung*) and 'the mysticism of unifying vision' (*Mystik der Einheitsschau*) respectively.[15] The former is characterized by withdrawal from all outward things and events, retreat into one's soul and its depth, the knowledge of mystical depth and of the possibility of reflecting upon one's soul. Although this mysticism necessarily has its own doctrine of the soul, it largely remains soul-mysticism. In contrast, though closely related to the mysticism of introspection, the mysticism of unifying vision does not require such a soul-mysticism. This mysticism looks upon the world of things and events in its multiplicity and leaps to the unifying vision as opposed to their multiplicity.

And so, not only Upaniṣadic mysticism but also Indian mysticism in general could be classified into two main types: the *jñāna* type which is non-theistic, and the bhakti type which is theistic. Particularly with regard to the Upaniṣadic mysticism, the *jñāna* type of Indian mysticism corresponds to the soul-mysticism of Otto; its perspective is shared with the non-dual interpretation of the Upaniṣads, represented by Śaṅkara. The bhakti type corresponds to the God-mysticism of Otto; its perspective is shared with the theistic interpretations of the Upaniṣads, which is represented by Rāmānuja and Madhva.

BHAKTI AND ITS IMPLICATION

Let us now turn to the main issue—the extent to which bhakti is a theistic type of mysticism. In Hindu religious tradition, bhakti is one of its fundamental religious commitments, the premise of which is the distinction between a devotee and God or gods. The Sanskrit term bhakti, often translated as 'devotion', is derived from the verbal root √ *bhaj*, which means 'to share in', 'to belong to', or 'to worship'. Bhakti is generally used in a broad sense: the objects of bhakti are divine or human figures, both individually and communally. Thus, the religious commitment of bhakti has a theistic structure, and its forms are many and diverse. It can be traced back to a few classical Upaniṣads and to large sections of the epics, including the *Bhagavadgītā*, which culminates in a vision of the divine.

For most Hindus, bhakti is both the goal of religious life and the means to such a goal. The grace of the divine can be obtained through it, and ultimately the promise of *mokṣa* or salvation. The meaning of bhakti includes the range of devotional commitment to God or gods—from devotional meditation, called *upāsanā*, to passionate attachment. For example, Rāmānuja's *Bhagavadgītā-bhāṣya* states that upāsanā is equivalent to bhakti: 'It is, however, established in the passages of the Vedānta that only upāsanā which has taken the form of bhakti is the means of attaining the highest (*brahman*)' (*upāsanaṃ tu bhakti-rūpāpannam eva para-prāpty-upāya-bhūtam iti vedānta-vākya-siddham*).[16] When passionate commitment is emphasized, bhakti may be a striking contrast to yoga and other ascetic commitments, which are characterized by detachment from worldly preoccupation. Thus, since the meaning of bhakti is ambiguous, passionate commitment known as *prapatti* (complete surrender to God), being distinct from bhakti, came to be emphasized in the Śrī Vaiṣṇava tradition.

As John Carman points out in *The Theology of Rāmānuja*, later Śrī Vaiṣṇavas came to believe that in his *Gadyatraya,* Rāmānuja expounds the doctrine that one is saved if one simply and completely surrenders the self to God, even though one has not practised any of the recognized means to salvation, *karma*, *jñāna*, or bhakti. In John Carman's words, the Vaḍagalais, one of the two Śrī Vaiṣṇava schools, maintain that 'it is only in the *Gadyas* and the *Nityagrantha* that *prapatti* is unambiguously expounded as an independent means to salvation, for in his other writings Rāmānuja teaches the more difficult path of repeated devotional meditation, called bhakti or upāsanā'.[17] In this regard, both Dasgupta and Otto argue that in the *Bhagavadgītā*, bhakti does not merely contain the meaning of contemplation, but it also implies that of 'complete surrender to God' or *prapatti*.

Dasgupta on Bhakti as a Theistic Type of Mysticism

Dasgupta classifies the bhakti type of Hindu mysticism into two categories: 'classical forms of devotional mysticism' and 'popular devotional mysticism'. With regard to the former he points out that the concept of 'self-abnegation and self-surrender to God' is characteristic of the *Bhagavadgītā*, where 'contemplative union with God' is mentioned. He maintains that the idea of 'love for God' was known from very early times in India, although it was not prominent in early Sanskrit literature. The doctrine of bhakti, however, can hardly be found in the Upaniṣads except for faint traces. In contrast, 'the *Gītā* is steeped in the mystic consciousness of an intimate personal relation with God'.[18] According to the story of Prahlāda in the *Viṣṇupurāṇa*, he is cast into the depths of the ocean by his unbelieving father on account of his faith in Viṣṇu; however, he remains firmly true to his faith. With regard to this story, Dasgupta argues that Prahlāda's devotion was 'a concentration on God and a serene contemplation in which he became one, as it were, with the Lord'; further, 'he desired not only contemplative union but longed also to taste God's love as one tastes the pleasures of the senses'.[19] Moreover, according to Dasgupta, in the *Bhāgavatapurāṇa* (probably dated to the eleventh century CE), devotion is the 'supreme source of a bliss or spiritual enjoyment'; this type of bhakti, denoted in the *Bhāgavatapurāṇa* is well illustrated in the life of Caitanya (1486–1534).

With regard to popular devotional mysticism, Dasgupta focuses on the mysticism of divine love, portrayed not only in Sanskrit literature but also in the languages of north and south India. As concrete examples of such a popular devotional mysticism, he chooses the bhakti movement of the Āḻvār saints and such saints as Nāmdev and Tukārām in the South, and also the bhakti movement of north India, represented by Kabīr, Nānak and others—which, Dasgupta says, 'followed the line traced by the Gītā and the Bhāgavata'. According to Dasgupta, 'the new religious ideal of bhakti, in all its enthusiastic circles, dispensed with the consideration of caste, creed, and social status'; therefore, for example, Kabīr, who fought against the prevailing superstitions, rituals, and litanies of all religious sects, 'dived deep in the depth of God's love' and 'beheld nothing but God on all sides, becoming as it were one with Him in spiritual union'.[20] Finally, Dasgupta says,

> Through oral instruction, tradition, and the example of great men who renounced the world in pursuance of the high ideals of philosophy, the essence of these different systems, with their spiritual longings and their yearnings after salvation and the cessation of rebirth, has gradually been filtering down into the minds of the masses of the population. The tiller of the soil and the grocer in the shop may be uneducated and often wholly illiterate, but even they, while tilling the ground, driving a bullock cart or resting after the work of the day, will be singing full of mystical meaning, and for the moment transporting themselves to regions beyond the touch of material gains and comforts.[21]

It is thus obvious that for Dasgupta, bhakti is synonymous with 'religion' and 'faith'. It is theoretically possible to regard bhakti as a theistic type of mysticism; however, this might restrict its implication to a theistic type of mysticism, which is derived from the Western religious context. Bearing this issue in mind, let us proceed to discuss Otto's interpretation.

OTTO ON BHAKTI AS A THEISTIC TYPE OF MYSTICISM

Otto's theory of religion doubtlessly owes much to a theistic model. John Carman points out that his work shows more 'sympathy' with 'the devotional movements related to a personal Lord than with the monistic philosophy of Śaṅkara'.[22] Thus, in *West-östliche Mystik*, Otto argues that although Śaṅkara's mysticism is certainly 'cool' (*kühl*) and 'unimpassioned' (*unleidenschaftlich*), 'it [Śaṅkara's mysticism] is distinguished by that it is indeed not neutral to theism, out of which it emerges, but however far it rises above theism, it at the same time maintains a fixed relationship to Indian *theism*, particularly to that of the *Gītā*, and this relationship gives it a special character'.[23] Moreover, in Śaṅkara's philosophy, the relationship between *brahman* and *parameśvara* is shifting and interpenetrating. Since Otto makes use of Śaṅkara's terminology, it is noteworthy that from the Indological point of view, Paul Hacker also elucidates that the terms (*param*) *brahma* or *paramātman* are almost always interchangeable with *īśvara* and that *īśvara* can in most cases be replaced by (*param*) *brahma* or *paramātman*.[24]

With regard to the story of Prahlāda in the *Viṣṇupurāṇa*, Otto maintains that upāsanā gradually passes into mystical experience; the mystical experience arises from a determined act of bhakti. Further, the personal, beloved, and trusted Lord expands into the mystical 'all-being' (*Allwesen*), who is 'the one being' (*das eine Wesen*). Although this mystical experience slips back into ordinary bhakti, this personal intercourse with Viṣṇu is equal in value to the mystical experience. According to Otto, from Prahlāda's point of view, the religious experience of Śaṅkara would be 'one-sided' and also poorer; the religious experience of Prahlāda is 'more consistent' (*konsequenter*) than that of Śaṅkara.[25] Comparing the type of Prahlāda with that of Caitanya, Otto maintains that within 'bhakti-mysticism' there are differentiations that can lead to sharp emotional antitheses. In the case of Caitanya, bhakti becomes *prema* (love), characterized by 'Krishna-eroticism' in which union with the beloved is desired; in the case of Prahlāda, bhakti is the stilling of the soul before God, and complete faith as *fiducia*, a trustful, concentrated 'contemplation' (*Sinnen*) leads to 'the loss of self' (*Sichverlieren*) and to 'becoming one' (*Einswerden*) with God.[26]

As a result of his comparative study of mysticism, Otto argues that one can find Christian analogies for all, or almost all, the forms of Indian mysticism and that despite the 'convergence of types' between Indian and Western mysticism, 'the inner "spirit" differs' between both.

RECONSIDERATION OF BHAKTI AS A FORM OF MYSTICISM

Since the latter part of the nineteenth century, when the area of the history of religions began to be studied, the theme of mysticism in the history of religions has been a dominant part of the study of Indian religions. The application of the Western concept of mysticism to Indian religions has led to its being interpreted as representing Indian types of mysticism. Thus, bhakti was also understood as a theistic type of Hindu mysticism. With regard to the theories of bhakti demonstrated by Dasgupta and Otto, we clarified that both scholars treat bhakti as mysticism; further, their theories of bhakti as a theistic form of Indian mysticism certainly makes sense.

At the same time, however, we must pay attention to the fact that bhakti has often been understood as 'faith'. In his book *Die Gnadenreligion des Indiens und das Christentum*, Otto compared bhakti in the Śrī Vaiṣṇava tradition with faith in Christian tradition.[27] For him, Indian religious thought was not metaphysics or mere philosophical speculation, but a 'theory of faith' (*Glaubenslehre*) or a 'theory of salvation' (*Heilslehre*), which was based on the experiences of the holy or the divine. A certain Hindu tradition that, like the Śrī Vaiṣṇava tradition, emphasized the significance of bhakti for the attainment of salvation was regarded as a 'religion of grace' (*Gnadenreligion*) in the Indian religious context. Thus, it is evident that Otto's perspective on Indian religions considers the concept of bhakti as being similar to that of faith. In Wilfred C. Smith's words, 'bhakti is definitely one of the Hindu forms of faith'.[28] In that case we must question the extent to which bhakti is a Hindu form of mysticism.

In proportion to one's religious commitment to the object of bhakti, there could be some dimensions of bhakti, irrespective of whether it is a form of mysticism or faith. The nature of bhakti varies according to an adherent's psychological attitudes and practices. The bhakti of the Śrī Vaiṣṇava tradition, which Otto attempted to clarify in his comparative study of Indian and Christian religions, includes the broad range of religious commitment, varying from a popular Hindu's dimension of faith to that of mysticism. Although the meanings of bhakti and mysticism overlap to a fair extent in Hindu religious tradition, the semantic aspect of bhakti naturally shifts from that of mysticism in the light of the reality of Hindu religious tradition. Swaying between the ascetic and popular poles, it implies both the ascetic and popular dimensions of religious commitment. For example, in Śaṅkara's Advaita Vedānta philosophy, bhakti almost seems to represent the ascetic pole of religious practice; here bhakti, which indirectly leads to *mokṣa*, is concerned with *saguṇa-brahman* and is a personal attachment to gods. It may suffice to note that Śaṅkara speaks of bhakti in two ways: as a gradual preparation for *mokṣa*, and as characterized by *jñāna*. At the concrete level of religious phenomena, however, the Jagadguru in the modern Śaṅkaran religious tradition of Śṛṅgeri interprets bhakti as a 'continuous contemplation of one's own real nature'.[29] Such an implication may represent the Upaniṣadic or Yogic mysticism, to which Dasgupta refers.

Moreover, in bhakti movements, the devotees or bhaktas used various regional languages in their religious practice, directing themselves towards different deities. These movements developed various forms of devotional yoga, techniques for evoking the relationship with God. They all shared their religious attitude in that they commonly had devotional love to God. Irrespective of whether they directed themselves towards Śiva, Kṛṣṇa, Rāma, or the goddess Kālī, the bhaktas always sought a personal relationship with that divine figure. For example, according to the sixteenth-century devotional theologian Rūpa Gosvāmī, one can enjoy various relationships with God; in Richard H. Davis's words, 'one may relate to God as an insignificant human relates to the Supreme Deity, as a respectful servant relates to his lord and master, as a mother relates to her child, as a friend relates to his friend, or as a lover relates to her beloved.' Devotional groups explore 'these modes of relationship, and particularly the latter three, through their poetic and ritual practices'.[30] In *Bhaktirasāmṛtasindhu*, Rūpa Gosvāmī classifies bhakti into *sādhanā-bhakti*, which is instrumental to generate true bhakti, *bhāva-bhakti*, which is a permanent mental state of the devotee's love for God, and *prema-bhakti*, that is, ecstatic love for God, the ultimate goal.[31] The second and the third categories of bhakti to which he refers constitute two aspects of *sādhyā-bhakti*, or their soteriological goal. Such an expression may represent a certain theorization of the popular religious practice. As mentioned above, one has to admit that the sphere of bhakti is much broader than the semantic area of the term mysticism.

CONCLUSION

In the light of the above-mentioned relationship between bhakti and mysticism or faith, it is true that some aspects of bhakti correspond to a theistic form of mysticism, while others correspond to a popular form of faith. Accordingly, it may be adequate to maintain that Hindu bhakti does not necessarily imply a theistic type of mysticism alone; it also implies a theistic type of religion or a form of faith. It is noteworthy that in popular Hindu tradition, bhakti is often found in the ritual of *pūjā*, or the worship of the an image of the deity with such offerings as flower and food, performed at home or in local temples.

On the basis of the semantic research of the relationship between bhakti and mysticism, one may argue that the ascetic dimensions of bhakti correspond to the religious phenomena covered by mysticism. While translating the popular dimension of bhakti into English, however, it may be preferable to use the term 'faith' or 'practice' rather than the term 'mysticism', although Dasgupta attempted to explain this in his phrase, 'popular devotional mysticism'.

NOTES

1. John B. Carman, 'Conceiving Hindu "Bhakti" as Theistic Mysticism', *Mysticism and Religious Traditions*, ed. Steven T. Katz, Oxford: Oxford University Press, 1983, p. 194. Cf. John B. Carman, *Majesty and Meekness: A Comparative Study of Contrast and Harmony in the Concept of God*, Michigan: William B. Eerdmans, 1994, pp. 347–9.
2. Surendranath Dasgupta, *Hindu Mysticism*, Chicago: The Open Court, 1927, p. 17.
3. Ibid., p. viii.
4. Ibid.
5. Rudolf Otto, *West-östliche Mystik*, Gotha: L. Klotz, 1926; München: Verlag C.H. Beck, Dritte Auflage, 1971, S.162; Rudolf Otto, *Mysticism East and West*, tr. Bertha L. Bracey and Richenda C. Payne, New York: Macmillan, 1932, p. 158. In this article, the English translation has been partly modified.

6. Rudolf Otto, *West-östliche Mystik*, S. 163; *Mysticism East and West*, p. 159.
7. Ibid., pp. 158–9.
8. The two scholars, mentioned by John B. Carman, are A. Govindacharya and P. N. Srinivasachari. Cf. John B. Carman, 'Conceiving Hindu "Bhakti", as Theistic Mysticism', *Mysticism and Religious Traditions*, pp. 195, 222 (note 3).
9. Surendranath Dasgupta, *Hindu Mysticism*, p. 18.
10. Ibid., pp. x–xi.
11. Ibid., p. 29.
12. Ibid., pp. 51–2.
13. Ibid., pp. 53–4. In *Hindu Mysticism*, Dasgupta states the following:

> The various commentators upon the Upanishads belonging to different schools of thought and yet each interested to secure for himself the support of the Upanishads, have been fighting with one another for the last twelve hundred years or more to prove that the Upanishads are exclusively in favour of one party as against the others. Thus some contend that the Upanishads teach that Brahman alone exists and all the rest that appears is false and illusory. Others hold that the Upanishads favor the doctrine of modified duality of man in God and of God in man. Still others maintain that the Upanishads give us exclusively a doctrine of uncompromising duality.

On different interpretations of the Upaniṣad texts in Vedānta philosophical traditions, see Yoshitsugu Sawai, 'Rāmānuja's Hermeneutics of the Upaniṣads in Comparison with Śaṅkara's Interpretation', *Journal of Indian Philosophy*, vol. 19, no. 1, 1991, pp. 89–98; Yoshitsugu Sawai, 'The Scriptural Interpretation of Madhva's Vedānta Theology', *Journal of Vaishnava Studies*, vol. 10, no. 2, 2002, pp. 99–109.

14. Rudolf Otto, *West-östliche Mystik*, S. 164–7; *Mysticism East and West*, pp. 159–61.
15. Ibid., S. 43–60; *Mysticism East and West*, pp. 57–72.
16. Rāmānuja, *Bhagavadgītābhāṣya,* in *Śrī-bhagavad-rāmānuja-grantha-mālā*, p. 62. Cf. Rāmānuja, *Śrī-bhāṣya*, Bombay Sanskrit and Prakrit Series, no. LXVIII, Bombay: Government Central Press, 1914, I.iv.6, p. 348.
17. John B. Carman, *The Theology of Rāmānuja: An Essay in Interreligious Understanding*, New Haven: Yale University Press, 1974, p. 214.
18. Surendranath Dasgupta, *A History of Indian Philosophy,* vol. II, Delhi: Motilal Banarsidass, 1975, p. 534. Cf. Dasgupta, *Hindu Mysticism*, p. 119.
19. Surendranath Dasgupta, *Hindu Mysticism*, pp. 121–2.
20. Ibid., pp. 158–61.
21. Ibid., pp. 165–6.
22. John B. Carman, 'Conceiving Hindu "Bhakti" as Theistic Mysticism', p. 195.

23. Rudolf Otto, *West-östliche Mystik*, S. 176–7; *Mysticism East and West*, pp. 168–9.
24. Paul Hacker, 'Eigentümlichkeiten der Lehre und Terminologie Śaṅkaras: Avidyā, Nāmarūpa, Māyā, Īśvara', *Kleine Schriften*, Wiesbaden: Franz Steiner, 1978, S. 107–9.
25. Rudolf Otto, *West-östliche Mystik*, S. 187–9; *Mysticism East and West*, pp. 176–8.
26. Ibid., S. 190; *Mysticism East and West*, pp. 178–9.
27. Rudolf Otto, *Die Gnadenreligion des Indiens und das Christentum*, Gotha: L. Klotz, 1930.
28. Wilfred C. Smith, *Faith and Belief*, Princeton: Princeton University Press, 1979, p. 219.
29. Yoshitsugu Sawai, *The Faith of Ascetics and Lay Smārtas: A Study of the Śaṅkaran Tradition of Śṛṅgeri*, Vienna: Sammlung de Nobili, 1992, pp. 46–8.
30. Richard H. Davis, 'Introduction', in *Religions of India in Practice*, ed. Donald S. Lopez, Jr., Princeton: Princeton University Press, 1995, p. 39.
31. Rūpa Gosvāmī, *Bhakti-rasāmṛta-sindhu*, I.2.1. Cf. Sanjukta Gupta, *Advaita Vedānta and Vaiṣṇavism: The Philosophy of Madhusūdana Sarasvatī*, London: Routledge, 2006, p. 122.

2

The Use of Bhakti/Bhakta in the Pāñcarātra Scriptures

HIROMICHI HIKITA

A couple of years ago, I wrote an article entitled 'Contemplation and Worship' based on the *Paramasaṃhitā*,[1] a later portion of the Pāñcarātra.[2] There are 'eight elements of bhakti' (*aṣṭāṅgā bhaktir uddiṣṭā*: 4.72c) in the *Paramasaṃhitā*, namely 'daily worship of the god' (*devasyārādhanaṃ nityaṃ*: 4.73c), 'adhering to rules' (*samayasya ca rakṣaṇam*: 4.73d), 'trust in Vaiṣṇava devotees' (*vaiṣṇavasya ca viśvāsaḥ*: 7.74a), 'great concern for reverential worship' (*pūjāyām ādaro mahān*: 4.74b), 'effort to worship by oneself' (*svayam ārādhane yatnam*: 4.74c), 'willingness to hear Viṣṇu's legends' (*tatkathāśravaṇādaraḥ*: 4.74d), 'indifference to injuring others' (*parabādhāsv anāsthā ca*: 4.75a), and 'not living on the reverential worship of the god' (*tatpūjānupajīvanam*: 4.75b). The text also insists that bhakti should increase perpetually (30. 28–31). This insistence on bhakti and its complicated systematization were noted by Dr. Czerniak-Drożdżowicz.[3]

The primary objective of this article is to understand the usage of the words bhakti (devotion)[4] or bhakta (devotees) in the early instead of later parts of the Pāñcarātra. In order to achieve this, I consult the 'three jewels' of the Pāñcarātra, *Sātvatasaṃhitā*, *Jayākhyasaṃhitā* and *Pauṣkarasaṃhitā*, considered to have been compiled in the early period. Further, I investigate the usage of terms which express devotional feeling to god, such as *śraddhā*[5] and *prapatti*.[6]

SĀTVATASAṂHITĀ

The word *sātvata*, which might mean *Sātvatasaṃhitā*, finds mention in the *Lakṣmītantra* (2.59b and 11.28c); therefore, we can easily infer that the former was used before the latter, which is assumed to have been compiled in the sixth century.[7] In this work, the terms bhakti and *śraddhā* appear frequently.

Bhakti, which is steady and can end the cycle of rebirth,[8] appears mostly in connection with reverential worship and worship. For example, we come across such expressions as 'one should worship him with devotion' (*tasya vai pūjanaṃ bhaktyā kuryāt*: 8.52ab). Similar expressions are also seen in 6.50c (*samabhyarcya*); 6.51c (*samālabhya*); 7.77d (*yajet*); 7.87a (*ārādhya*); 8.82c (*pūjanaṃ kuryāt*); 8.88d (*samarcayet*); 8.96d (*pūjanīyaś*); 8.100c (*kṛtvaivaṃ prīṇanaṃ*); 8.118a (*tadarcanaṃ kṛtvā*); 10.39d (*iṣṭvā*); 13.63d (*arcanīyam*); 14.17d (*yajāmy*); 14.24d (*pūjayāmy*); 17.64a (*dadyāc*); 25.282c (*santarpitaṃ*); 25.365a (*balipīṭhaṃ bahiḥ kuryād*); 25.375a (*dadāti*) and 25.378b (*pradīyate*).

Bhakti is connected with observance (*vrata*) in 7.10, 37, 56, 62 and 8.128. It also appears in connection with 'purification of mind' as well as *śraddhā*. We see such expressions as 'with the mind joined with bhakti' (*cetasā bhaktiyuktena*: 6.25a), 'one should fix the object of meditation with bhakti' (*baddhalakṣyo bhaved bhaktyā*: 7.109a), 'with the mind tranquillized with bhakti' (*bhaktyā prasannenāntarātmanā*: 8.79ab) and 'his mind is purified with bhakti for the Lord now' (*bhagavadbhaktyā pavitrīkṛtamānasaḥ*: 16.11cd). This word plays the most important role in the process of initiation (*dīkṣā*).

> When the preceptor recognizes the eligibilities for initiation according to the disciples' feelings of devotion, he should give them initiations such as the impetuous one (*tīvra*) and the dull one (*manda*)[9] (17.118).[10]

In the eighteenth chapter, this feeling of devotion is described in detail as 'the characteristics of devotion' (*bhaktilakṣaṇa*), namely 'hair erect with joy' (*romāñca*), 'ardent desire' (*autsukya*), 'joy' (*harṣa*), and 'shedding tears with delight' (*ānandāśru*) (18.120ab). This text also says that, having purified their minds (*bhāvitātmanām*), disciples awash with bhakti can be authorized to take the initiation ceremonies (19.5). One of the sixty-two rules given to the *putraka*-initiated disciples prior to or while receiving these scriptures is bhakti to five objects, namely the sacred fire, the preceptor, the mantra, the sacred scriptures and the authorized people (21.62).

Further, bhakta and bhakti are, respectively, connected with 'worshipper' (*upāsakānāṃ*: 2.2c and 9.11c) and 'worship' (*gṛhītakusumāṃs*: 17.116b; *balivāhakān*: 17.283b; *kriyāratānāṃ*: 17. 334a; *nityakriyāparāṇāṃ*: 17.458a; *yāgasādhane*: 19.56d). The idea is also connected with the 'purification of the mind' (*bhāvitātmanām*: 6.224d; 7.103b; 17.407d; 20.40b and 25.381d). God bestows compassion upon such devotees (*bhaktānugrahakāmyayā*: 12.5b and 24.165d; *bhaktānām anukampayā*: 12.10b; *abhayapradam:* 8.55b). Similarly, the preceptor too wants to grant favours to his devoted disciples (*anugrahadhiyā*: 18.48b and 22.47c).

A devotee may belong to any of the four castes. By dedication to duty and devotion to the highest god, even those who do not have the right discrimination (wisdom) and are hindered by selfishness can be authorized to perform worship with the mantras of Vibhava deities.[11] Since god loves his devotees (*bhaktavatsalam*: 12.78d), he is benevolent to those who devote themselves to him even if they are attached to worldly desires. Even though the devotees are filled with ignorance (*avidyā*) (12.27), god guides them towards the attainment of the right states. He uproots the tree of deeds (*karma-vṛkṣa*) that bears the fruits of delusion (*moha*) and illusion (*māyā*) of the devotees tied down by restraints (*prabandhapratipannānāṃ*) (12.99–100). He also pacifies the delusions of devotees who have been burned by the fire of transmigration (17.420). Needless to say, he saves the devotees who have pure wisdom (*śuddhajñānānuviddhaṃ*: 12.78a), those who have an intense dislike for transmigration (*saṃsārodvignacetasām*: 17.458b), and those with purified minds (*śuddhāśayānāṃ*: 18.210c). The only condition for a preceptor to accept a candidate as his disciple (*saṃgraha*) is that the latter should have devoted himself to Viṣṇu (22.43). It is strictly forbidden for such a disciple to approach non-devotees, impart sacred teachings to them, or receive alms from them (21.15–19).

In addition to bhakti, the word *śraddhā* (loyalty) appears several times in this text (8.140b; 16.23d and 25.377b). We find the expression 'with the mind purified with loyalty' (*śraddhāpūtena cetasā*: 14.2d and 20.35d; *śraddhāpūtena manasā*: 17.370a). The verbal form *śraddadhāna* appears with bhakta (22.2). The most frequently appearing form of this word is *bhakti-śraddhā* (with devotion and loyalty), seen in 2.38d; 6.221d; 8.9d; 12.16a; 16.13c; 24.18b and 90a. We can also find *śraddhā-bhakti* (5.110d) and *bhaktiśraddhā-vrata* (13.61c) which combines bhakti and *śraddhā* with a vow. While the word *prapatti* cannot be found in this text, the word *prapanna* (one who surrenders himself to god) is mentioned on several occasions. With the exception of the conversation with saint Nārada (1.16ab), this word is linked to sin. For example, this appears in passages enumerating methods to escape evils (*duṣkṛtāt*: 16.16d and *svaduṣkṛtaśāntaye*: 17.399d) and delusions (*vyāmoha*: 1.24cd and *avidyāpaṅka*: 12.48d). Anybody from the four castes can be a *prapanna* (2.9cd and 17.399a).

JAYĀKHYASAṂHITĀ

The *Jayākhyasaṃhitā*, one of the three jewels like the *Sātvatasaṃhitā*, is considered a manual of rituals with mantras. It begins with the statement 'Without knowing the highest truth (*paratattva*) that only those who dedicate themselves to Viṣṇu will be able to transgress the transmigration and attain Viṣṇu,[12] no ritual is fruitful'. Thus, it also focuses on bhakti.

Bhakti is the feeling that necessarily accompanies worship of the highest god. The god residing in the void of the cave of a lotus-heart becomes the object of meditation for those who know the *yoga* connected with bhakti.[13] The most interesting aspect of this text is that it insists on bhakti towards a preceptor. It is one of the bhaktis to a preceptor (*guru*) that involves the sacrificial fire (*agni*) and the teaching of mantras (*mantraśāstra*) (16.305ab).[14] Jagannātha creates mortal bodies, and with a weapon in his hand, he compassionately saves the people in such bodies who are sunk in the sea of transmigration. Since the preceptor is considered the incarnation of the god who could save people in this world, those fearful of transmigration should have devotion to their preceptors.[15] Hence, a devotee of Viṣṇu should devote himself to similar devotees, particularly the preceptor (16.307). In any circumstance, without devotion to the preceptor, it is impossible to even know his name.[16]

Next, the bhakta is defined as 'he who is intent on meditating on god and is versed in his worship' (*bhaktas taddhyānaniṣṭhaś ca tatkriyāparamo mahān*: 5.11cd) and 'he who has purified his mind and is intent on the worship of mantra' (*bhaktas tadbhāvitātmā ca yadi mantrakriyāparaḥ*: 6.107ab). In particular, such expressions as 'he who has purified his mind' are found in the *Jayākhyasaṃhitā* (4.

24d; 6.200d; 10.100a; 12.136d and 13.202d). Some tremble with the fear of transmigration (*saṃsārabhayabhītasya*: 2.25c; 16.5c; 18.69c and 33.84c) and seek emancipation (*nirvāṇabhāg*: 6.234b); they dedicate themselves to Viṣṇu (*viṣṇubhaktasya*: 21.105b) or to God (*bhagavadbhaktān*: 23.111a). Such people are also known as Vaiṣṇava people (*vaiṣṇavānāṃ sadbhaktānāṃ*: 24.71); they dedicate themselves not only to god but also to their preceptor (*gurubhaktaṃ*: 18.2a). In addition, Vaiṣṇava people are categorized as four types of pupils: *samayajña, putraka*, *sādhaka* and *guru*. They know what is implied by good disposition; they are kind-hearted and do not harbour any feelings of jealousy; their focus is on true teaching; they possess good behaviour and follow the required rules.[17] This work does not specify the relationship between the devotees and the four castes, but only mentions that a *śrotriya* is a devotee (*bhaktānāṃ śrotriyāṇāṃ*: 9.8a).

The god grants favours to such devotees (*anugraha*: 4.24cd). For instance, he grants them desires (*abhīpsitapradas*: 6.200c), leads them to emancipation (*nirvāṇabhāg*: 6.234b) and unites them with its course (*mokṣamārge niyojayet*: 31.21d). The most remarkable among his many kinds of favours is his manifestation before his devotees.

> O Lord of gods, I am (your) devotee, desiring the Omniscient. I am afraid of the terror of transmigration. Please show your own highest form to me.[18]

Moreover, the *Jayākhyasaṃhitā* insists that as a way of bestowing favours (*anugrahārthaṃ*), the preceptor should disclose this secret (*idaṃ rahasyaṃ*) to those devotees with purified minds after examining their righteous dispositions (13.202). Therefore, this teaching of the secret should not be imparted to non-devotees (*abhaktānāṃ*), liars (*śaṭhānāṃ*), atheists (*nāstikānām*), the ill-behaved (*asādhūnāṃ*), the knavish (*dhūrtānāṃ*), and the cunning (*chadmacāriṇām*) (7.116).[19] There is a clear difference between those with Vishnuite characteristics (*vaiṣṇavānāṃ ca lakṣaṇam*: 22.56d) and those without them.

Such expressions as 'following the loyalty and restraint' (*śraddhāsaṃyamasevinām*) occur in several places in *Jayākhyasaṃhitā* (7.117b; 15.240b and 22.4b). This might convey a meaning more rational than emotional. Another such example of a meaning that is more rational than emotional is the phrase, 'a holder of sacred knowledge' (*śāstradhāraka*)[20] who collects traditional doctrines with loyalty, meditates on *brahman* and retains it carefully in memory.

Next, there are two types of expressions on the usage of *prapanna*. The first comprises examples such as 'those who ever surrender themselves to me' (*sadaiva madprapannānāṃ*: 12.34a) and 'I surrender myself to you' (*tvāṃ prapanno 'smi*: 21.124a). The other is seen in 'those who surrender themselves to your doctrine' (*tvacchāsanaprapannānām*: 18.55c) and 'those who surrender themselves to my doctrine' (*macchāsanaprapannānāṃ*: 33.85a). The former denotes that the object to whom they surrender themselves is god himself and the latter denotes that the object to which they surrender is god's doctrine. The word *prapatti* has also been mentioned in this text. However, such an expression as 'both of those who are well versed in the doctrine of *prapatti*' (*prapattiśāstraniṣṇātau*: 1*.109c)[21] seems to be a late insertion because it is based on an earlier philosophical discussion; this expression is found in the additional part of the first chapter as the editor has indicated.

PAUṢKARASAṂHITĀ[22]

The term bhakti appears together with the worship of god, for example 'after worshipping with the highest devotion' (*saṃpūjya parayā bhaktyā*: 19.116c). Further, there is also an expression that is joined by the verb to worship: 'After the period of sleep, when I am awake, I will worship you with devotion' (*tvām arcayāmy ahaṃ bhaktyā suptyatīte tu jāgare*: 30.107cd). There are also expressions that contain a reference to bhakti such as 'reverent worship with devotion' (*ārādhanaṃ bhaktyā*: 32.119a) and 'it should be sacrificed with the highest devotion' (*yaṣṭavyaṃ parayā bhaktyā*: 40.105c). There is also an expression mentioned in combination with sacrificial fire: 'after offering to the sacrificial fire with devotion' (*hutvāgniṃ bhaktyā*: 32.27a). This devotion is considered indispensable to devotees who worship god without deceit or dishonesty.[23]

Bhakti also appears in expressions that make a reference to the mind, such as 'a disposition combined with devotion' (*bhāvabhakti-*:

27.185d; 31.174a, 188a, 309b; 32.122b; 36.63a, 259a and 421d) and 'with the mind joined by devotion' (*bhaktiyuktena cetasā*: 31. 271b). There are more mentions of bhakti in expressions like 'devotion to the Lord' (*bhagavadbhakti*: 27.327c and 37.63b), 'devotees of the Lord' (*bhagavadbhakta*: 27.176c and 31.49c), 'devotion to me' (*bhaktir māṃ prati*: 30.209c) and 'with the right devotion to Acyuta' (*samyagacyutabhaktyā*: 32.51a).

What is the reward of worshipping god with devotion? The reward is bestowed upon the worshipper not only in this world, 'the worshipper acquires what he desires in this world without asking god'[24] but also in the next world, 'The worshipper receives a memorial service like Viṣṇu as long as he lives, and after death, he arrives at the White Island (*śvetadvīpa*) the ideal world'.[25] The progression of the relationship between the devotee's worship and its reward can be outlined as follows: worship god with devotion—satisfy him and earn his favour (*prasāda*)—receive rewards both in this and the next world. The following verse lucidly expresses this relationship.

> Please impart me the highest devotion with which you will be satisfied. O Lord of gods, when you will be satisfied, there will be nothing in this world that is not acquired by me. (31.152)[26]
>
> This devotion is directed not only to god but also to the preceptor since he is considered as equal to god. (1.28)

We now proceed to investigate the use of the term bhakta. This term is in conjunction with *pūjā* (1.12a; 8.10c and 37.60c), *yāga* (1.28c; 4.200b and 9.91d) and *ārādhana* (38.42c) as well as in such expressions as 'those who are intent on the worship of the Lord' (*bhagavat-karmaniṣṭhānāṃ*: 31.64a), 'those who sacrifice the mantra' (*mantrayājinām*: 38.132b), and 'those who are intent on worship' (*kriyāparais*: 38.75c). Further, this term appears in conjunction with 'those have recourse on' (*āśrita*: 8.5a), 'those who bow down' (*praṇatānāṃ*: 8.41c), 'those who have purified their minds' (*bhāvitātmanām*: 31.62b and 82b), and 'those who believe in god' (*āstikānāṃ*: 31.90c).

To what caste do these devotees belong? Given such expressions as 'the Brahmin, etc.' (*viprādīnāṃ*: 32.33c), 'kings' (*nṛpāṇāṃ*: 37.45d and 43.124b) and 'three kinds of Lord-worshippers such as the kṣatriya, the vaiśya and the śūdra' (*traividyaiḥ kṣatriyair vaiśyaiś śūdrair vā bhagavanmayaiḥ*: 38.26cd), it appears that a member of any caste can be authorized to become a devotee. However, in the case of expiation rituals, the devotees of the upper caste should chant more repetitions of mantras for atonement than those of the lower caste even though they may be equally devoted.[27] In addition, there is no discrimination among devotees based on gender: a devotee can be either male or female.[28] There are two types of devotees: 'true devotees' (*bhaktās tattvato*: 36.260d) and 'those pretending to be devotees who perform various forms of worship' (*vyāmiśrayājinaś cānye bhaktābhāsās*: 36.262cd). The former are known as *ekāyana* (27.210d; 36.260c and 42.147a), *ekāntin* (36.261a) and *ekacittaḥ* (27.103b). They perform worship without expectation and attain the state of Vāsudeva (*vāsudevatvam*) after death (36.261–2ab). On the other hand, devotees who belong to the latter type are those who carry out various kinds of worship. After having received the initiation, they worship Viṣṇu and go to his abode after death. Thereafter, they will be reborn in this world in a superior life form (*janma cāsādya cotkṛṣṭam*); in their next life, they will be intent on the worship of the Lord without desiring any fruit (*bhagavatkarmaniṣṇātas*); and after their demise, they will be freed from the cycle of birth and death (36.263–6). These two types of devotees are also described on other occasions in expressions such as 'dull and middle rank devotees' (*mandamadhya-bhaktānāṃ*: 38.62a), 'dull devotion' (*mandabhakti*: 36.428a), 'those who perform various kinds of worship' (*vyāmiśrayājinām*: 36.429b), 'intensive devotion' (*tīvrabhakty*: 36.452d) and so on. Any confusion between the two types of bhakti (*bhaktisāṃkarya*) is strictly forbidden (36.259cd).

Devotees are categorized into four kinds, a son (*putraka*), an upholder of rules (*samayajña*), a mantra achiever (*sādhaka*) and a preceptor (*deśika*) (27.426ab). The man who wants to acquire a purified life and succeed in attracting the attention of a mantra-god is known as a son; one who desires prosperity by adherence to the right rules is a keeper of rules; one who achieves the favour of god by chanting any mantra is known as a mantra achiever (27.6ab–7cd). In addition, those who live through the four stages of life (*āśrama*) are considered as devotees.[29] A devotee in the last stage, desiring the feet of the Lord, receives a final initiation ceremony that leads him to emancipation (*nirvāṇadīkṣā*) without taking any indicated step.[30]

There is a strict difference between a devotee and a non-devotee. In order to uphold the values of a community of devotees, it is essential that any instruction unique to this sect is maintained in secrecy from non-devotees. For instance, one should not impart knowledge of the secret to non-devotees, liars, or hostile individuals.[31] A devotee must not receive any initiation ceremony (*dīkṣaṇīyaḥ*) that is performed by a non-devotee (30.210cd). The following points are mentioned with regard to non-devotees: he should not know the right worship (*satkriyāṃ*); he is not required to know the scriptures (*śāstravid*); he should not be allowed to perform worship (*arcāṃ*), sacrifice (*yāgaṃ*) or fire-offering (*vahnim*); he should not be trained to know how to bind fingers; and he should not be taught the rules of devotees (*samayān*). If a preceptor imparts knowledge to a non-devotee, by mistake or out of avarice, on any of the above-mentioned subjects, he is on the road to perdition. This is because a non-devotee does not have any devotion to god, has inverted knowledge, and is discourteous and rude to his fellowmen (30.217–19).

Next, on most occasions, the term *śraddhā*, appears in this text along with bhakti. Two types of instances are seen here: the first type is 'on account of devotion and loyalty' (*bhaktiśraddhāvaśāc*: 26.5c) and the second type is 'with loyalty and highest devotion' (*śraddhayā parayā bhaktyā*: 43.35c). The latter type of usage is also seen in 1.53a; 23.7c; 27.640a; 30.19a; 30.134a; 31.230c; 32.63a; 32.158a; 33.84c; 38.60a; 38.140d; 38.230c; 40.68a and so on. The latter one appears also in 26.2cd; 27.636b; 28.8d; 31.236c; 32.30b; 36.456c; 38.172d and so on. We also come across such expressions as 'with the mind purified by loyalty' (*śraddhāpūtena cetasā*: 27.226b; 32.25d and 38.238d) and 'when the mantra is recited with loyalty as before during the performance of worship' (*prāgvad ārādhite mantre śraddhayā*: 27.433cd). The term *prapanna* appears in connection with worship and knowledge that are joined by devotion.[32] Although the term *bhagavanmaya* (27.161d) appears frequently in the *Pauṣkarasaṃhitā*, terms such as *tanmayātmanām* (36.21d) and *śaraṇāgatabhūtaṃ* (36.33a) are seldom mentioned.

LAKṢMĪTANTRA

Finally, I would like to investigate the *Lakṣmītantra*, considered a later work of the twelfth and thirteenth centuries. This work deals with Goddess Lakṣmī, the source of universal energy (*śakti*). It is also believed that it elaborates on the Vyūha theory of the *Sātvatasaṃhitā* and is influenced by goddess worship stated in the *Jayākhyasaṃhitā*.

Several use of bhakti can be noticed in this work. First, this term appears in association with yogic practice. As stated in the *Lakṣmītantra*, with the highest devotion to Viṣṇu, he who is intent on Vedānta and Sāṃkhya-yoga will be freed from the chains of bondages and become the highest *brahman* who is none other than Lakṣmī-nārāyaṇa (13.12). A *yogin* who earnestly practices meditation will be devoted to Lakṣmī and thus reach her abode (31.71). *Yogin*s bind (*badhnanti*) the goddess with their devotion (50.43). In this context, there is also an expression that describes a *yogin* as 'the one who is completely free from worldly desires (*nivṛtta-viṣayasya*)' (14.32).

Next, this term is used in reference to daily worship. In this case, too, it is connected with meditative practice. For instance, in an ablution ritual, one should devote oneself to the lineage of Hari and Lakṣmī and perform their worship internally by applying wisdom with utmost concentration (*jñānasamādhinā*) (34.136–7). In another instance of such usage (48.13),[33] it is mentioned that one should bow down to Hari with devotion while reciting one's own mantra. Further, one should be loyal in one's faith in the unique god Hari; one should be moderate in diet and should meditate in silence. In addition, as expected, bhakti also appears in the mention of a fire-offering which is not connected with meditation (40.81 and 48.9).

Third, this term appears in the description of an initiation ceremony. 'A firm devotion' is enumerated as one of the qualities required to become a preceptor (21.34). In 41.12–13ab, the phrase 'those who are devoted to the Lord' (*bhagavadbhaktān*) specifies the above-mentioned quality as one of the conditions to become a disciple in the initiation ceremony.

In the *Lakṣmītantra*, the term bhakta signifies a simple devotee. These are some instances of this usage: 'from the protection of devotees' (*bhaktarakṣāvidher*: 4.46d), 'desiring to grant favours to devotees' (*bhaktānugrahakāmyayā*: 10.11d and *anugrahāya bhaktānām*: 11.42c), 'the state of Viṣṇu to the devotees' (*bhaktānāṃ vaiṣṇavaṃ*: 49.57ab) and so on.[34] A condition required to be a devotee is explained as follows:

O Slayer of Bala, there is no difference in the results of one who performs his duties five times a day and one who is intent on the mantra of Lakṣmī. Both are approved as devotees and will arrive unto me (=Lakṣmī). (28.52–3ab)[35]

The text explains the relationship between devotion (bhakti) and the *Bhāgavata*. It states that only the one who is devoted to Hari can be known as a *Bhāgavata*, and that this title cannot be earned by merely worshipping Hari and the goddess Śrī.[36] In conclusion (50.235–6), this text maintains that Lakṣmī, the highest tantra among tantric works (*tantrāṇāṃ paramaṃ tantraṃ mudritaṃ matsamākhyayā*: 50.233cd), should not be revealed either to those who do not devote themselves to Vāsudeva or to atheists; instead, it should be disclosed only to those who devote themselves to Lakṣmī or Vāsudeva.[37]

The term *śraddhā* seldom appears in this work; this implies that its purport is not important. It appears with bhakti, denoting 'devotion and loyalty' (*bhaktiśraddhā*: 9.51cd), with an etymological explanation of Goddess Śrī (50.80) and with *soma, anna* and *vīrya* which are offerings to god (50.119–20ab and 124cd–5ab). In 27.7 and 50.213d, the term *śraddadhāna*, a present participle of *śraddhā*, appears connected with the term *prapanna*. However, greater emphasis is laid on the latter. With regard to the term *prapanna*, we can come across some interesting expressions in the text:

I have abandoned the performance of unpleasant actions (*pratikūlya*) to the living and have committed helpful deeds (*ānukūlya*) unto them. (28. 11cd–12ab)
Since I am lazy, incompetent and bereft of the power of right discrimination, these methods (*upāyāḥ*), even though executed well, might not emancipate me. (12cd–13ab)
So, I am depressed and miserable, and I do not have any food or property. All the established texts (*siddhānta*) and Upaniṣads (*vedānta*) acclaim to praise Hṛṣīkeśa as a protector as well as Goddess Lakṣmī (*rakṣaka*). (13cd–14)
O Husband of Śrī, I will entrust (*nyasta*) at your feet everything that I possess such as my son, wife and work, although it is very difficult for me to abandon them. (15)
O Lord of gods, O Ruler, O Husband of Lakṣmī, be my refuge (*śaraṇa*). (16ab)
To such a man who prostrated before god saying 'thus once' (*prapannasya*), is expected no other obligation. (16cd)

There are many expressions wherein the term *prapanna* refers to 'a simple devotee' in a context that is roughly similar to that of bhakta. This word is used with *prasīda* (9.24d), *śraddadhāna* (27.7c), and *śaraṇaṃ* (27.41c). The verbal forms of *prapanna* such as *prapadyeta* and *prapadyate* are used to convey the meaning of 'prostrating oneself before the highest god or the goddess or both'.[38] In 36.12, a term *sāntvayet*, which means 'to appease', conveys the same meaning as *prapanna*. The entity that the word *prapadyeta* refers to is god who assumes 'the pleasant form' (*prasanna*) (36. 122 and 124). There is an expression that one should prostrate oneself before Hṛṣīkeśa, the husband of Śrī, Hari as an object of protection.[39]

A characteristic feature of this text is the occurrence of expressions similar to those in the *Bhagavadgītā*. For instance, 'abandonment of all' (*sarvatyāga*) in 15.17 is synonymous with 'take refuge in me alone' (*mām ekāṃ śaraṇaṃ vrajet*) after abandoning all kinds of *dharma*s, high and low. The goddess (meaning I), provides refuge (*śaraṇaṃ prāptā*) to those whose minds are inclined to nothing; she unifies with herself those who have rid themselves of all imperfections (16.42cd–4). As already indicated by Tokunaga, this expression appears to be based on the *Bhagavadgītā* 18.66 (*sarvadharmān parityajya mām ekaṃ śaraṇaṃ vraja*).[40] Moreover, as indicated by Gupta,[41] the concept of 'consignment' (*nyāsa*), which implies consigning the results of deeds to the highest god and thereby pleasing him,[42] appears to be strongly influenced by *Bhagavadgītā* 3.30 and 4.20.

CONCLUSION

According to the three jewels compiled in the early times, bhakti is a prerequisite for the devoted to belong to the Pāñcarātra sect. Only he who has received initiation as part of this sect is authorized to worship Viṣṇu with bhakti in the daily rituals. Viṣṇu, when pleased with such a worship, in return grants to the devotees favours such as fulfilment in this world and absolute happiness in the next world. Therefore, as emphasized on several occasions in these texts, the teachings of Viṣṇu should not be disclosed to those outside the sect, for example those who do not believe in these teachings or atheists.

NOTES

* This article is based on my work 'Devotional Sentiments as Seen in the Early Pāñcarātra Scriptures' (in Japanese). *Bungakubukiyo*, vol. 36, Aichigakuin University, 2007, pp. 99–109.

1. *Paramasaṃhitā*, edited critically and tr. S. Krishnaswami Aiyangar. *Gaekwad's Oriental Series*, no. 86, Baroda: Oriental Institute, 1940.
2. Meisou to Saishi in *Azuma Ryushin Seventy year Felicitation Volume, Zen no Shinri to Jissen*, Tokyo: Shunjusha, 2005, pp. 349–62.
3. Marzenna Czerniak-Drożdżowicz, *Pāñcarātra Scripture in the Process of Change: A Study of the Paramasaṃhitā*, Vienna: De Nobili Research Library, vol. 31, 2003, pp. 172–4. She says that these 'eight elements of bhakti' might be the substitution of 'worship' in 'eight kinds of daily worship' (*vidhir aṣṭadhā*) with bhakti. According to her, this work was compiled before CE 1000 (p. 28).
4. See J. Gonda, *Medieval Religious Literature in Sanskrit: A History of Indian Literature*, vol. 2, fasc. 1, Wiesbaden: Otto Harrassowitz, 1977, pp. 10–39.
5. On the meaning of bhakti and *śraddhā*. see Minoru Hara, 'Notes on Two Sanskrit Religious Terms: Bhakti and Śraddhā', *Indo-Iranian Journal,* vol. 7, pp. 124–45.
6. On the difference between bhakti and *prapatti* in the Pāñcarātra sect, see S. Gupta, 'From Bhakti to Prapatti: The Theory of Grace in the Pāñcarātra System', *Sanskrit and World Culture*, SCHR. OR. 18, Berlin, 1986, pp. 537–42. See also Muneo Tokunaga, Prapatti Shisou no Rekishiteki Tenkai (in Japanese). *Shukyou Kenkyu*, vol. 45 no. 4 (1972), pp. 77–9.
7. See H. Hikita, *Hindu Tantorizumu no Kenkyu* (in Japanse), Tokyo: Sankibobusshorin, 1997, p. 11.
8. *tavāsti bhaktir acalā janmabījakṣayaṅkarī* / (1.5cd)
9. The words *tīvra* and *manda* also mean that the disciple's feelings are in conjunction with bhakti. See 18.199cd.
10. *tatkālaṃ bhaktibhāvena vijñātā yogyatā yadā* /
tīvramandādikāṃ teṣāṃ tadā dīkṣāṃ samācaret // (17.118)
11. *sakriye mantracakre tu vaibhavīye 'vivekinām* // (2.10cd)
mamatāsannirastānāṃ svakarmaniratātmanām /
karmavāṅmanasaiḥ samyag bhaktānāṃ parameśvare // (11)
caturṇām adhikāro vai prāpte dīkṣākrame sati / (12ab)
12. *ye saṃśrayanti taṃ bhaktyā sūkṣmam adhyātmacintakāḥ* /
te yānti vai padaṃ viṣṇor jarāmaraṇavarjitāḥ // (1.24). See J. Gonda, op. cit., p. 89.
13. *hṛdambujaguhāvāsaparavyomāntaśāyine* /
bhaktiyogavidabhyāsagrāhyāya khalu te namaḥ // (2.10)
14. See *Sātvatasaṃhitā* 21.62.
15. *hetunā 'nena vai viprā gurur gurutamaḥ smṛtaḥ* /

yasmād devo jagannāthaḥ kṛtvā martyamayīṃ tanum // (1.63)
magnān uddharate lokān kāruṇyāc chastrapāṇinā /
tasmād bhaktir gurau kāryā saṃsārabhayabhīruṇā // (64)

16. *yathā yathā yatra tatra na gṛhnīyāc ca kevalam /*
abhaktyā tu guror nāma gṛhṇīyāt prayatātmanā // (16.302)
17. *sadbhāvajñe tu vaktavyaṃ samayajñe 'tha putrake //* (15.263cd)
sādhake tu guror vāpi bhakte snigdhe vimatsare /
satyadharmapare vāpi sācāre samayasthite // (264)
18. *mama bhaktasya deveśa paraṃ jñānātmakāṃkṣiṇaḥ /*
saṃsārabhayabhītasya rūpaṃ vai svaṃ pradarśaya // (2.25)
19. Similar expressions are seen in 15.262cd–263ab; 16.369ab; 29.184cd–5 and 33.81–3.
20. *śraddhayā yaḥ samuccitya yatra kutracid āgamam /*
brahma dhyāyaṃs tathā paścāt saṃdhārayati yatnataḥ // (22.54)
21. This asterisk (*) signifies the additional first chapter.
22. There are two texts. The first is *Pauṣkara Saṃhitā*, ed. P.P. Apte, Tirupati: Rashtriya Sanskrit Vidyapeetha, 1991. This text is the critical edition with the English translation of the first twenty-six chapters, which delineate how to make *maṇḍalas* and worship them. The second text is *Sree Poushkara Samhita*: *One of the Three Gems in Pancharatra*, ed. His Holiness Sree Yatiraja Sampathkumara Ramanuja Muni of Melkote, Bangalore, 1934. I refer to the latter in this article. Neither of these texts are clearly understandable and they are expected to be critically emended in the near future.
23. *bhaktyā saṃpratipannānāṃ vinā śāṭhyena māyayā /* (31.301ab)
24. *yo 'rcayaty acyutaṃ bhaktyā vane vā parvatāntare /*
bahavo 'bhimatān kāmān prāpnoty aprārthitāṃs tu vai // (31.211)
25. *pūjāṃ viṣṇuvad āpnoti yāvaj jīvāvadhiṃ tu saḥ //* (31.208cd)
dehāvasānasamaye śvetadvīpaṃ prayāti ca / (209ab)
26. *mama yaccha parāṃ bhaktiṃ yayā tvaṃ me prasīdasi /*
tvayi prasanne deveśa kiṃ na prāptaṃ mayā bhuvi // (31.152)
27. *sati vai bhaktisāmye tu prāyaścittam idaṃ smṛtam /*
sāmānyaṃ sarvavarṇānāṃ manacchaḥ prakaṭe tu vai // (43.159)
uttarottaram ādhikyaṃ japakarmaṇi vai smṛtam /
śūdraviṭkṣatraviprāṇāṃ bhaktānāṃ nānyayājinām // (160)
28. *tadbhaktā sā satī sādhvī karmaṇā manasā girā /* (30.187ab)
29. *putrakān samayajñān vā sādhakān atha deśikān /*
gṛhasthān brahmacārīn vā vanasthān vā yatīn // (27.426)
30. *nirvāṇadīkṣitānāṃ ca bhaktānām api cābjaja //* (27.4cd)
anirdiṣṭakramāṇāṃ ca caturthāśramiṇāṃ tu vai /
bhagavatpadalipsūnāṃ jñāninām ca tathaiva hi // (5)
31. *tad avācyam abhaktānāṃ śaṭhānāṃ cātmavairiṇām //* (18.56cd)
32. See 32.61–2, 114.

33. *praṇipatya hariṃ bhaktyā prāk svamantreṇa vāsava* /
ekāntaśīlo laghvāśī maunī dhyānaparāyaṇaḥ // (48.13)
The term *ekāntabhāva* occurs in 1.54. On the meanings of the *ekānta* and *ekāntin*, see J. Gonda, op. cit., 1977, p. 10.
34. See also 50.54, 102.
35. *dīkṣitaḥ pañcakālajño lakṣmīmantraparāyaṇaḥ* /
antaraṃ nānayoḥ kiṃcin niṣṭhāyāṃ balasūdana // (28.52)
ubhāv etau matau bhaktau viśato māṃ tanukṣaye / (53ab)
36. *ete bhaktā mama hareḥ viprā bhāgavatā ime* // (41.73cd)
anye bhāgavatā naiva pūjāyām āvayor dvayoḥ /
bhaktyā bhāgavatāś cānye yad vā bhagavato hareḥ // (74)
subhaktās cetare loke proktā bhāgavatā iti / (75ab)
37. Among the 57 chapters, the last 7 were incorporated later and can be found in the abridged version of the earlier chapters. See S. Gupta, *Lakṣmī Tantra: A Pāñcarātra Text, Translation and Notes*, Leiden: E.J. Brill, 1972, p. 356, n. 1. See also *Lakṣmītantra* 57.46cd–47ab.
38. See, for instance 50.211–13.
39. *prapadyeta hṛṣīkeśaṃ śaraṇyaṃ śrīpatiṃ harim* // (28.8cd)
40. See M. Tokunaga, op. cit., p. 79.
41. *Lakṣmī Tantra,* tr. S. Gupta, p. 256, n. 1.
42. For instance, we see statements such as 'After accomplishing chanting rightly, one should consign the results of chanting to me' (*japaṃ samāpya vidhivan nyasyen mayi japaṃ kṛtam*: 40.18ab), 'One should consign the deeds to me staying in an image' (*mayi nyasyed arcāsthāyāṃ kṛtiṃ*: 40. 77cd) and 'One should consign results of *anuyāga* to me' (*nyasyed anuyāgaṃ tato mayi*: 40.99cd).

3

Rāmānuja's Theory of Bhakti Based on the Vedānta Philosophy

BUNKI KIMURA

THE THINKING OF RĀMĀNUJA

The purpose of this paper is to consider how Rāmānuja introduces bhakti into the system of the Vedānta school and establishes it as the means of *mokṣa*. The discussion will rely mainly on his three major works: the *Vedārthasaṃgraha*, the *Śrībhāṣya* and the *Bhagavadgītābhāṣya*.

The history of Hinduism in the last one thousand years is characterized by the bhakti cult in which a person completely devotes oneself to praying for salvation by worshipping the personal God with love. Although the meanings of bhakti and the styles to manifest it have changed in various ways with the times and within the sects, the bhakti cult has performed an important role in both Śaivism and Vaiṣṇavism, and, in particular, the bhakti cult in Vaiṣṇavism has been based on the theory of the Vedānta school. The concept of bhakti was first clearly mentioned in the *Bhagavadgītā* which was completed in around the first century, and has been nourished afterwards both in the *Pāñcarātrasaṃhitā*s of Vaiṣṇavism and in the *Āgama*s of Śaivaism. Moreover, since around the seventh or eighth century, the bhakti movement has spread among the people in south India through the influence of the poet-saints called Āḻvārs who worship Viṣṇu, and Nāyaṉārs who worship Śiva.

Before the tenth century, however, brahmins carrying on the Vedic tradition scarcely recognized bhakti as a means of attaining *mokṣa*.[1] Śaṅkara (*c*. 700–50), who was the contemporary Vedānta master with the poet-saints in the south, making the oldest extant commentary on the *Bhagavadgītā*, did not approve of bhakti.[2] He affirmed that *Brahman* is the only real existence having no attributes (*nirguṇa*) and is the impersonal consciousness (*caitanya*) identical with an *ātman*, and that the phenomenal and multiple world is unreal existence caused by *avidyā* (the nescience). Thought of this kind might explode the theoretical basis of the bhakti cult, because bhakti should be devoted to a personal God with attributes (*saguṇa*), because one who is devoted to bhakti should be different from one who devotes bhakti, and because the phenomenal world should be regarded as the real existence in which a devotee practices several activities to express bhakti.

The Advaita school following the teachings of Śaṅkara became dominant in the Vedānta school, and masters of the school despised brahmins belonging to the Bhāgavata sect because of their worship of God, Viṣṇu=Nārāyaṇa, with devoting bhakti.[3] It was, therefore, of great concern to the Bhāgavata brahmins to prove bhakti as the effective means of attaining *mokṣa* on the authority of the Veda, or the Upaniṣads. Yāmuna (916–1036) wrestled with the problem, and Rāmānuja (1017–1137) succeeded him and accomplished Yāmuna's task to establish a new type of Vedānta philosophy supporting the bhakti cult.[4]

First, Rāmānuja identifies *Brahman* with the personal God, Nārāyaṇa, having countless auspicious attributes (*saguṇa*) and no evil ones (*nirguṇa*). Second, he compares the relation between an *ātman* and *Brahman* to the relation between a body and an *ātman* (*śarīra-ātma-bhāva*) to affirm that, although both are not one and the same, the former is a dependent entity which cannot exist separately from the latter as the substratum (*apṛthaksiddha*).[5] In this manner, he shows that *Brahman* to be devoted to bhakti and the *ātman* to devote bhakti are not identical. Yet he adheres to the principle of the Vedānta school that *Brahman* is one without a second (*advitīya*). Third, he establishes the reality of the phenomenal world as a body, or a dependent entity, of *Brahman*.[6]

On the basis of this theistic view of the world, Rāmānuja regards attaining *mokṣa* as to arrive at *Brahman* identified with God, and explains the steps for it as follows:

> We have already declared that the means of arriving at *Brahman* is only *parabhakti* (higher bhakti). It is to be acquired by the complete practice of bhakti which is furthered by the performance of one's proper acts

(*svakarman*) preceded by knowledge of the truth as learned from the scriptures.[7]

It shows that one wishing to attain *mokṣa*, after studying the Veda, should perform his proper acts assigned by the Veda as the practice of *karma-yoga*, in which he is required to renounce the agency of those activities (*kartṛtva*), the sense of possession of those activities (*mamatā*) and the desire for the fruits of those activities (*phala*). His will to devote bhakti to God would be improved through the practice, and lastly originate *parabhakti* as the direct means of *mokṣa*.[8]

For the sake of stating these steps from the standpoint of the Vedānta school, Rāmānuja had two points to clarify. The first point to be made is that the steps are in conformity with the orthodox means of *mokṣa* approved by the Vedānta school. In order to show this, he identifies *parabhakti* with knowledge (*vidyā*) of *Brahman*, which has traditionally been accepted as the direct means of *mokṣa* in the school. At the same time, it is necessary to prove that the type of knowledge of *Brahman* defined as the direct means of *mokṣa* by Śaṅkara and his followers is not suitable, and to also clarify the character of the knowledge which Rāmānuja proposes as the means of *mokṣa*.

The second point to be made is that bhakti is indispensable for *mokṣa* even in the doctrine of the Vedānta school. For the purpose of explaining this, he has to give his definition of bhakti and to show the reason why bhakti is able to stop the power of *karman* which is the cause of *saṃsāra*.

KNOWLEDGE IDENTIFIED WITH *PARABHAKTI*

KNOWLEDGE AS THE DIRECT MEANS OF *MOKṢA*

First of all, we will examine the reason declared by Rāmānuja why the knowledge approved by Śaṅkara and his followers is not suitable for the direct means of *mokṣa*. Before starting his declaration in the *Śrībhāṣya*, Rāmānuja acknowledges the following point affirmed by the masters of the Advaita school as the principle of the Vedānta school.

It is stated [by you] that the cessation of *avidyā* in itself is *mokṣa*, and only results from the knowledge of *Brahman* (*brahmavijñāna*). It is admitted by us.[9]

And he goes on to say: 'It should be discriminated of what form the knowledge is, which is, for the sake of the cessation of *avidyā*, intended to be enjoined by the passages of the Vedānta.' Rāmānuja classifies knowledge into two types, one is 'mere knowledge of the sense of passages [of the sacred scriptures] which originates from the passages' and the other is 'knowledge in the form of meditation (*upāsanā*) based on it'.[10] The former is, in other words, 'knowledge of indirect (*parokṣa*) form obtained by means of the scriptures', and the latter is 'knowledge of direct (*aparokṣa*) form obtained by means of yoga'.[11] In the beginning of the *Śrībhāṣya*, Rāmānuja argues with Śaṅkara and his followers as opponents about the form of knowledge as the direct means of *mokṣa*.

According to Śaṅkara, the knowledge as the direct means of the cessation of *avidyā* is the spiritual awakening to the essential identity of *Brahman* with an *ātman*, which is acquired by means of just hearing the sacred passage: 'That You Are (*tat tvam asi*).' Śaṅkara defines it as 'knowledge of direct form',[12] and refers to it as 'complete realization (*saṃyakdarśana*)', 'direct realization (*anubhava*)' and 'intuitive realization (*sākṣātkāra*)'. Meditation is, on the other hand, never knowledge but an activity performed in the unreal phenomenal world (*vyavahāra*) caused by *avidyā*. Furthermore, it is not possible in the highest truth (*paramārtha*) for an *ātman* to practice the meditation of *Brahman* because of the identity of *Brahman* with an *ātman*.

Rāmānuja, on the contrary, defines the meditation of some particular object as 'knowledge of direct form', and, accordingly, concludes that the knowledge approved by Śaṅkara is 'mere knowledge of the sense of passages'.[13] Moreover, he supposes the views of an opponent on the knowledge which is to be confuted. First, he considers the following point:

Unless the innate impression of differences (*bhedavāsanā*) has been removed, the passages [of the sacred scriptures] would not produce the knowledge being destructive of *avidyā*.[14]

Śaṅkara states in his *Brahmasūtrabhāṣya* that a variety of innate impressions (*nānārūpā vāsanā*) are caused by the perception of [a variety of] objects in every case.[15] In the highest truth affirmed by him, however, there is no difference, since the real existence is only *Brahman* of no attributes. Therefore, both the perception and the innate impression caused by it are unreal, caused by *avidyā*.[16] It follows from this, says the opponent, that the knowledge of *Brahman* would not be originated, even after hearing the passages, as long as the innate impression remains.

Rāmānuja disproves this statement on the following grounds:

> Even if the innate impression opposed [to the knowledge] exists, it is seen that the knowledge to stultify [the innate impression] is originated by means of instruction from the authority and logical inference and others.[17]

In this passage, Rāmānuja affirms that the origination of knowledge is not prevented by the innate impression, an unreal thing to be removed by the knowledge; 'mere knowledge of the sense of passages' results not only from the passages of the sacred scriptures but also from teachings of the trustworthy preceptors and others even in existing innate impression.

In addition to this, Rāmānuja declares that if the theory of the opponent were accepted, there would never be the origination of knowledge. He explains the reason as follows:

> The innate impression of differences is immeasurable, since it has been accumulated from the beginningless time. And the meditation (*bhāvanā*) opposed to it is weak. The removal of it is, therefore, not possible by means of this (meditation).[18]

Śaṅkara agrees that meditation is an effective measure to remove the obstacles to the origination of knowledge, although he never accepts it as the direct means of *mokṣa* in itself.[19] Rāmānuja, however, points out in this passage that, even if so, the power of meditation approved by Śaṅkara is too weak to completely remove the whole of immeasurable innate impression. Thus, Rāmānuja concludes: 'The origination of knowledge could never take place in ones who admit that it results from the removal of the innate impression of differences.'[20]

Next, Rāmānuja takes up the following statement of an opponent to disprove:

> It is not wrong that, even if the knowledge is originated, the cessation of

perception of differences in the case of all does not arise at once. It is similar to the case that, even if the oneness of the moon is known, the cessation of perception of two moons [because of an eye disease] does not arise. Even if the cessation [of the perception of differences] does not arise, it (the perception of differences) does not bind [an *ātman*] because of its root (*avidyā*) being already cut.[21]

According to Śaṅkara, as soon as knowledge is originated, the cessation of *avidyā* arises and *mokṣa* is attained. At that time, however, the *karman* whose effects have already begun to operate (*ārabdhakarman*) continues to exist up to the time of it becoming powerless, while the whole *karman* whose effects have not yet begun to operate (*anārabdhakarman*) disappears. Due to the operating power of the former *karman*, the lives in the phenomenal world and the perception of difference of an *ātman* also continue to exist even after its attainment of *mokṣa*, although they would not cause the *ātman* to be binded in *saṃsāra*.[22]

Rāmānuja disproves this declaration on the following grounds:

Because the innate impressions constituting the means of the perception of differences are also of the nature of unreality (*mithyārūpatva*), they would be surely removed by the origination of knowledge. If there is, even after the origination of the knowledge, no removal of the [innate impressions], which are of the nature of unreality, there would never be the removal of these innate impressions because of the absence of any other means [but the knowledge] to remove [them]. It is a childish statement that the perception of differences caused by the innate impressions still continues to exist even after its roots have been cut.[23]

Śaṅkara insists that everything but *Brahman*, which is unreal and caused by *avidyā*, would vanish as soon as the knowledge as the sole means of the removal of *avidyā* is originated. Yet he admits, as mentioned above, the continuous existence of some particular *karman* and the perception of differences based on it even after the removal of *avidyā*. Rāmānuja points to this contradiction to confirm that the theory of *avidyā* declared by Śaṅkara and his followers is inconsistent, and, consequently, denies the efficacy of the knowledge affirmed by them. In this manner, Rāmānuja demonstrates that knowledge as the direct means of *mokṣa* is not 'mere knowledge of the sense of passages' advocated by Śaṅkara and his followers, but knowledge as meditation.

MEDITATION WITH THE NATURE OF BHAKTI

Let us now look more carefully into the characteristics of knowledge (*vidyā*) in the form of meditation approved by Rāmānuja. The first question is why he is able to identify knowledge (*vidyā=jñāna*) as the direct means of *mokṣa* with meditation (*upāsanā, dhyāna*). The authority on which he depends is the usage of the Upaniṣads where the words √*vid*, *upa*-√*ās* and √*dhyai* are used synonymously.[24] And the synonymy of these words appears to have been common knowledge in the Vedānta school in those days,[25] accepted by Taṅka (*c.* 500–50) and by Śaṅkara.[26] Rāmānuja follows the traditional usage of the school to use the terms *vidyā*, *upāsanā* and *dhyāna* in the same sense as meditation.

Furthermore, he describes it as follows:

> Knowledge (*vedana*) is denoted by the word *dhyāyati*. Meditation (*dhyāna*) is contemplation (*cintana*). Contemplation is of the nature of a continuity of remembrance (*smṛtisaṃtatirūpa*). It is not mere remembrance (*smṛtimātra*). The word *upāsti* has the same meaning with it, because it is seen that the word is used to denote an uninterrupted series of activities of the mind fixing on one object. As both of these words have the same meaning, the continuous remembrance repeated frequently (*asakṛdāvṛttasaṃtatasmṛti*) is here denoted by the words such as *vedana* and others in some scriptures.[27]

Rāmānuja explains in other places that meditation is 'of the nature of an uninterrupted continuity of remembrance like a stream of oil (*tailadhārāvad avicchinnasmṛtisaṃtanarūpa*)'.[28] It is clear that this definition also follows the passage of Taṅka that 'meditation would be a firm memory (*dhruvānusmṛti*)',[29] and Śaṅkara's explanation that the meditation (*dhyāna*) is 'a continuity of uninterrupted consciousness like a stream of oil (*tailadhārāvat saṃtato-'vicchinnapratyaya*)'.[30]

The next question is what the remembrance (*smṛti*) is. According to Rāmānuja, it is 'of the nature of seeing (*darśanarūpa*)' or 'of the nature of the intuitive realization (*sākṣātkārarūpa*)', and possessing this nature is the same as 'having acquired the nature of immediate perception (*pratyakṣatāpatti*)'.[31] We may say, therefore, that knowledge declared by the term of remembrance (*smṛti*) is the intuitive realization of God identified with *Brahman*. Moreover, remembrance (*smṛti*) is explained as 'knowledge whose object is what has been formerly experienced and which arises only from the subtle impressions of the experiences (*anubhavasaṃskāra*)'.[32] It indicates that to acquire knowledge is to rediscover the essential nature of God which was once experienced and then lost by an *ātman*.

The perception of God would never be clear when it is first acquired. It would gradually become clear through continuous repetition of the remembrance. This is supported by his declaration: 'Knowledge, which becomes more perfect through practice up to death, is to originate day by day.'[33] Rāmānuja thus emphasizes the importance of repetition of the meditation.

Rāmānuja refers to this knowledge (*vidyā*) as *parabhakti* and explains it as 'the meditation which possesses the nature of bhakti (*bhaktirūpāpannadhyāna*)'. This drives us to the third question of what the nature of bhakti is. Rāmānuja states in the *Vedārthasaṃgraha*:

> [God] is grasped only through the meditation which possesses the nature of bhakti. . . . In other words, when one wishing for *mokṣa* is devoted to the meditation (*dhyāna*) possessing the nature of the knowledge (*vedana*) enjoined by passages of the Upaniṣads, unlimited and unsurpassed love (*niravadhikātiśaya prīti*) is originated in him in the midst of that meditation (*anudhyāna*). At the same time, the Supreme Person is grasped through it [by him].[34]

From this we may say that the 'nature of bhakti' is 'unlimited and unsurpassed love [for God]' and that it is to be acquired by the devotion to the meditation of God. There are, on the other hand, some examples showing that the unsurpassed love for God is presupposed by the repetition of the remembrance of God, which are such phrases as 'the repeated practice of remembrance filled with unsurpassed love (*niratiśayapreman*) to Me (God)'[35] and 'the practice of the remembrance [of God] which is difficult on account of the lack of exceeding love (*atyarthaprīti*) [for God]'.[36] The coexistence of these two types of expression is a reflection of the characteristic of *parabhakti* consisting of two elements: the knowledge as the repeated remembrance and the exceeding love. Both elements are combined inseparably in *parabhakti* and improve each other. It is fully expressed in the following passage of the *Vedārthasaṃgraha*: 'The word bhakti has the sense of a certain kind of love (*prītivi-*

śeṣa), and this love again that of a certain kind of knowledge (*jñānaviśeṣa*).'[37] And, when *parabhakti* comes to perfection, it 'becomes of no other object [but God], uninterrupted and unsurpassed love (*ananyaprayojanānavarataniratiśayapriya*), and possesses the nature of the meditation attaining the highest degree of immediate perception (*viśadatamapratyakṣatāpannānudhyānarūpa*)'.[38] At that time, *mokṣa* is attained.

The fourth question then arises about the reason why knowledge and love are inseparably combined. Rāmānuja answers this question as follows: 'On account of the object to be remembered being unsurpassably pleasant/beloved one (*priya*), the continuity of remembrance is in itself also unsurpassably pleasant/beloved one (*priya*).'[39] He explains this in further detail in the following passage:

> When it is admitted that the knowledge particularized by some particular object originates pleasure (*sukha*), the knowledge having that object is of itself pleasure (*sukha*). . . . It depends on its object [whether the knowledge is of the nature of pleasure or not]. Therefore, since the knowledge [having Brahman as its object] is of the nature of pleasure (*sukha*), Brahman itself is [of the nature of] pleasure (*sukha*). . . . The Supreme Person (God) is by himself and in himself [of the nature of] unlimited and unsurpassed pleasure (*sukha*), and is also [of the nature of] pleasure for other ones, because there is no difference in regard to the nature of pleasure [of God]. It means that one who has Brahman as the object of his knowledge becomes one having pleasure (*sukhin*).[40]

It is safe to say that the word *priya*, which Rāmānuja sometimes replaces with *prīti*, is interchangeable with the word *sukha*. The word *sukha* is again interchangeable with *ānanda*, since Rāmānuja cites the passage '*Brahman* is Bliss (*ānanda*)' from the *Taittirīya Upaniṣad* III.6 as the authority for maintaining that *Brahman* is of the nature of pleasure (*sukha*). We may, therefore, reasonably conclude that the knowledge of God is in itself of the nature of love (*prīti*) identical with pleasure (*sukha*) and bliss (*ānanda*), because God is of the nature of Bliss (*ānanda*) for both Himself and others. And, accordingly, one who acquires the knowledge of God is filled with pleasure. Since then, he would not be able to sustain himself even for a moment in the separation from God, or without devoting *parabhakti* to God,[41] and longs for the eternal union with Him, owing to 'his nature that the union with Me (God) and the separation from Me (God) are only his pleasure and pain'.[42]

THE MEANING OF BHAKTI

The Element of Love in Bhakti

Parabhakti approved by Rāmānuja, as mentioned above, consists of two elements: knowledge and love. We have considered the characteristic of the knowledge in the previous section, and now, we will go on to examine his definition of love. Rāmānuja expresses the element of love in bhakti not by the words *sneha* nor [*anu-*] *rāga*, which are preferred by the later masters,[43] but by the words *priya*, *prīti* and *preman*, all of which are derivatives of √*prī*. It is likely that his choice of words follows the diction of the *Bhagavadgītā*.[44] At the same time, it is a manifestation of his definition of love. Both *sneha* and *rāga* have the meaning of 'to be adhesive' and 'to be passionate'. On the other hand, √*prī*, which acquires the meaning of 'to love' afterwards, originally means 'to make one pleased'.[45] The characteristic of love in bhakti approved by Rāmānuja is derived from this original meaning of √*prī* in two senses.

The first sense is that bhakti itself, of which the object is God having the nature of Bliss, makes an *ātman* pleased, which we have discussed. The second sense is that an *ātman* devoting bhakti makes God pleased, which is represented in the phrase 'My bhaktas are ones whose only purpose is to please Me (*matprīṇana*).'[46] Furthermore, Rāmānuja often states that the meditation of God and other activities performed in behalf of God are 'of the nature of pleasing (*prīṇanarūpa, ārādhanarūpa*) God',[47] and also describes them as 'forms of pleasing (*ārādhanaveṣa*)'.[48] Here Rāmānuja uses *prīṇana* and *ārādhana* interchangeably.

The question that now arises is why the meditation and other activities are able to pleased God. What has to be noticed here is that they are enjoined to be performed by 'My commandment known as the Veda (*vedākhyaṃ madanuśāsanam*)'.[49] It follows from this that God is pleased by His commandment being obeyed, and, accordingly, that to please God is to obey Him. This assumption is supported by the statements that 'pleasing (*ārādhanā*)' is 'the behaviour of a complete subordinate (*paripūrṇaśeṣavṛtti*)'[50] and that 'those determining to be My servants practise meditation'.[51]

For further understanding of this point, it is useful to observe the following passage on the relation between an *ātman* and *Brahman*, or God:

The Supreme Brahman is the principal (*śeṣin*) of all things, and an *ātman* is a subordinate (*śeṣa*). Therefore, the Supreme Brahman, who is to be meditated as one being accompanied [by an *ātman*] and who is the object of unlimited and unsurpassed love, makes this *ātman* attain [Himself].[52]

What the passage makes clear is that the basis on which an *ātman* devotes bhakti to God is the relation between an *ātman* and God compared to the relation between a subordinate and the principal (*śeṣa-śeṣī-bhāva*). This relation is, as mentioned before, also compared to the relation between a body and an *ātman* (*śarīra-ātma-bhāva*), explained in the following passage:

A substance, which a sentient being (*cetana*) is capable of completely controlling and supporting for its own purposes, and whose essential nature is solely to be subservient (*śeṣatā*) to it (the sentient being), is the body (*śarīra*) of it (the sentient being). . . . All things are completely controlled and supported by the Supreme Person for His own purpose, and their essential natures are solely to be subservient to Him. Thus, all sentient and non-sentient beings constitute His body.[53]

This shows that an *ātman* as a subordinate to God constitutes the body of God. In other words, an *ātman* has its essential nature (*svarūpa*), existence (*sthiti*) and activities (*vṛtti*) depending on God,[54] and, therefore, to be subservient to God is not only its essential nature (*svabhāva/svarūpa*) but also the sole delight (*rati*) for an *ātman*.[55] Rāmānuja describes in the *Vedārthasaṃgraha* that 'there is no mutual relationship between a subordinate and the principal among anyone other than the Supreme Person', and, accordingly, that 'only the Supreme Person is worthy to be served by all who know the true nature of an ātman'. This description is based on his other definition of the relation as that between a slave and his master.[56] And he goes on to say that such a service being of the nature of bhakti is denoted by the term of *vedana* in the scriptures.[57] In other words, Rāmānuja considers that pleasing (*ārādhana*) God is to be performed by His subordinate as the service (*sevā*), and he regards it as the manifestation of love in bhakti compared to the love of a slave to his master.

What has to be noticed here is that pleasing God is the essential element, not only of *parabhakti* but also of the practice of bhakti which is to be furthered by the practice of *karma-yoga* as the means of acquiring *parabhakti*. All wishing to attain *mokṣa* should devote bhakti to God without any exception. Still, it is likely that the strength of the will to please God is not the same between an *ātman* who has acquired *parabhakti* and one who has not. The reason is that the realization of the relation between an *ātman* and God improves the element of love in bhakti to the higher level. Thus only an *ātman* having acquired *parabhakti* can perform the service of God with complete understanding of the reason. Rāmānuja says, '*parabhakti* to Me will arise by itself (*svayam eva*) when an individual *ātman* (*jīvātman*) is intuitively realized as of the nature of being solely subservient (*śeṣatā*) to Me'.[58]

There is another point to be noted. Rāmānuja sometimes uses *pra-√pad* meaning 'to take refuge in' and its synonyms like (*sam-*) *ā-√śri* and *śaraṇam (upa-)√gam*[59] to refer to the sense of bhakti.[60] He explains that to take refuge in God is 'to follow (*anu-√vṛt*) God'[61] and also 'to attribute the agency and others to God' in practising *karma-yoga*.[62] There is a suggestion here that to take refuge in God is to obey His commandments and attribute oneself and everything of one's possession to God, that is to say, to completely concentrate one's mind on God. Thus he urges one wishing to attain *mokṣa* 'to practice *karma-yoga* and others presupposing to take refuge in Me (*matprapatti*)'[63] and 'to devote bhakti to Me alone after taking refuge in Me (*śaraṇam upa-√gam*)'.[64] When the practices are conducted in this manner, according to Rāmānuja, several obstacles, such as stains of an internal organ (*antaḥkaraṇa*) preventing the completion of *karma-yoga*, and Māyā of God concealing His nature to prevent the meditation, would be removed.[65] We may, therefore, say that taking refuge in God is another essence of the element of love in bhakti, which is, as mentioned above, to be compared to the love of a slave to his master.

It is, again, likely that the strength of the will to take refuge in God is not the same between an *ātman* who has realized the relation with God and one who has not. This is confirmed by the expression that it is only one with knowledge (*jñānavat*) who takes refuge in God based on the knowledge of the real essence of an *ātman* possessing its essential nature/delight (*rasa*) in the subservience to God.[66] To put it another way, only one having acquired *parabhakti* can take refuge in God with a complete understanding: 'Vāsudeva alone is my highest goal and also the means [of its attainment]. Even if any other desire arises, He alone is all that to me.'[67]

In this section, we have examined the element of love in bhakti approved by Rāmānuja, and come to the conclusion that it is characterized by the desire to please God after taking refuge in Him; it is theoretically based on the relation between an *ātman* and God as a subordinate and the principal. It is, therefore, to be improved more exceedingly, as the relation is realized more clearly by an *ātman*.

KARMAN AND THE GRACE OF GOD

There is a further point that needs to be considered: the reason why bhakti is the efficient and indispensable means of attaining *mokṣa*. The question is, in other words, why bhakti is capable of stopping the power of *karman* as the cause of *saṃsāra*. In order to examine this question, it is useful to observe his explanation on the origination of *saṃsāra*.

> Individual *ātmans* (*jīvātman*) are essentially of the nature of uncontracted, unlimited and spotless knowledge. When they are enveloped by *avidyā* which has the nature of *karman* (*karmarūpāvidyā*), however, they become ones whose knowledge are contracted in proportion to their *karman*. They enter into bodies of various kinds from Brahmā to tuft of grass, and obtain knowledge whose range is limited in accordance with their own bodies. These *ātmans* [are deluded to] identify themselves with their own bodies, and perform activities in accordance with their bodies. Then, they get into a stream of *saṃsāra* with the nature of experience of the pleasure and pain correlated with their activities.[68]

In this passage, we should notice the phrase '*avidyā* which has the nature of *karman*'. Rāmānuja also uses, in other places, the phrase '*karman* which has the nature of *avidyā* (*avidyārūpaṃ karman*)',[69] and explains that *avidyā* is '*karman* being of the nature of concealing knowledge (*jñānāvaraṇarūpaṃ karman*)'.[70] These phrases make it clear that *karman* approved by Rāmānuja is not an unreal thing caused by *avidyā*, as defined by Śaṅkara, but real and identical with *avidyā*. With the knowledge concealed (*āvṛtta*) or contracted (*saṃkucita*) by such *karman*, or *avidyā*, an *ātman* loses both the nature of itself and the nature of God, and becomes embodied to fall into *saṃsāra*, in which it performs several activities to originate innumerable *karman*.

Rāmānuja explains the nature of activities performed by an embodied *ātman* in the following passage:

> And that (the Veda) declares that good and evil activities have respectively the nature of pleasing the Supreme Person and the opposite, and that pleasure and pain, which are the results of those activities, depend on His grace (*anugraha*) and wrath (*nigraha*). . . . Then, recognizing a person who performs activities of a good nature as one who follows His commandments, He blesses him with piety, riches, worldly pleasures and *mokṣa*. He, on the contrary, makes a person who does not follow His commandments experience the opposites of these.[71]

Pleasing God by obeying His commandment is, as we have seen, the expression of love for Him, while displeasing God by disobeying is the reverse. We may, therefore, say that performing good or evil activity is the manifestation of one's love or hate for God, and becomes the cause of His pleasure or displeasure. Depending on it, God gives several types of fruits, including attainment of *mokṣa* and lives in *saṃsāra*, as His grace or wrath to one who performs activities. Thus, it is safe to say that Rāmānuja considers the real nature of *karman* as the manifestation of the pleasure and displeasure of God.[72] Assuming this to be true, we can conclude that the contraction of the knowledge of an *ātman* caused by *karman* also reflects the pleasure or displeasure of God. It is supported by the following passage: 'Their knowledge given by Me (God) is limited in proportion to their good [*karman*] which is the cause of their being gods, divine sages and others.'[73] Here, Rāmānuja clearly declares that the contracted knowledge of an *ātman* is given by God.

We can be fairly certain, however, that God is not heartily pleased with one obeying His commandments with an earthly desire. According to Rāmānuja, *karman* is identical with *avidyā* and of the nature of concealing knowledge. Both good and evil *karman* are equally the cause of *saṃsāra*. For one wishing for *mokṣa*, therefore, even good *karman* is not desirable, and is to be regarded as the manifestation of His displeasure.

God is, on the other hand, exceedingly pleased with one who devotes himself to please Him by obeying His commandment without attachment to worldly matters after taking refuge in Him. Rāmānuja describes that such an *ātman* is 'the most beloved one (*priyatama*)' for God,[74] and that He becomes unable to endure separation from the *ātman*.[75] For the sake of dissolving the separation from it, therefore, God makes the *ātman* arrive at Him. To put it in detail, God rids the *ātman* of all *karman*, and grants it the direct means of *mokṣa*, that is the uncontracted knowledge, as the manifestation of His supreme pleasure. Rāmānuja states:

> When the activities thus done for the purpose of sacrifices and others by one who is free from any attachment, the Supreme Person, who is pleased with the sacrifices and other activities, grants him the undisturbed intuition of the *ātman* (*ātmāvalokana*), after eradicating his subtle impressions of *karman* (*karmavāsanā*) which have continued from the beginningless time.[76]

He also describes:

> One to whom the essential nature of an ātman has become manifest as of the sole form (*ākāra*) consisting of the infinite knowledge and as of the essential character (*svabhāva*) of being subservient (*śeṣatā*) to Me (God) . . . acquires bhakti to Me (God), which is of the nature of direct realization with the superme love.[77]

To sum it up, according to Rāmānuja, 'such meditation (*dhyāna*)' as *parabhakti* 'is originated through the grace of the Supreme Person [pleased] with daily and occasional rituals, which are practiced day by day and which are of the nature of pleasing the Supreme Person'.[78]

We are now ready to consider the final question of what the function of the knowledge as *parabhakti* is. It has, according to Rāmānuja, 'the ability to destroy the power of *karman* (*pāpman*), which has been produced before, to bring forth the fruits, and also the ability to cause obstruction to the production of the power of [*karman*], which would be hereafter produced, to bring forth the fruits'.[79] Knowledge as *parabhakti* is, as discussed above, the manifestation of the supreme pleasure of God, while both good and evil *karman* are, strictly speaking, the manifestation of His displeasure. Rāmānuja, accordingly, changes an expression to show the grounds of the removal of *karman* from the viewpoint of the pleasure and displeasure of God as follows:

> [Knowledge is] of the nature of pleasing the Supreme Person who is the object of knowledge. It destroys the displeasure of the Supreme Person, which has been produced by an accumulation of *karman* (or activities) made before. And the same knowledge obstructs the origination of the displeasure of the Supreme Person caused by *karman* (or activities) which would be made after the origination of [knowledge] itself.[80]

It is clear from this passage that the supreme pleasure of God caused by *parabhakti* transcends the whole of His displeasure caused by immeasurable activities, and that it is powerful enough to stop all *karman* as the manifestation of His displeasure, whichever has been produced before or would be produced in future. It means that the *ātman* who has acquired *parabhakti* would never have new *karman* given by God, and it is surely destined to attain *mokṣa* when its *karman* whose effects have already begun to operate (*ārabdhakarman*) becomes powerless.[81]

Let me summarize the main points that have been made in this section. Rāmānuja considers that God gives an *ātman* either the lives in *saṃsāra* or the attainment of *mokṣa* depending on His displeasure or supreme pleasure. To put it in detail, God gives an *ātman* either *karman* (or *avidyā*) to contract its knowledge or the uncontracted knowledge (or *vidyā*) freed from *karman* as His wrath or grace, and, in accordance with them, an *ātman* is determined to live in *saṃsāra* or to attain *mokṣa*. Therefore, an *ātman* either living in *saṃsāra* due to its *karman* or attaining *mokṣa* owing to the knowledge, is ruled by God. On the grounds of this theory, Rāmānuja establishes that God is the sole master possessing all *ātman*s both in *saṃsāra* and in *mokṣa*, as His subordinates, and is the administrator of their *karman*. This is why Rāmānuja affirms that devoting bhakti is the only effective and indispensable means for pleasing God enough to grant an *ātman* the termination of the power of *karman* and, after that, the attainment of *mokṣa* as His grace.

KNOWLEDGE AND PLEASURE: ESSENTIAL ELEMENTS OF BHAKTI

Śaṅkara defines *Brahman* as the impersonal existence only of the nature of True Being and Knowledge (*saccinmātra*), although he does not deny that *Brahman* is also Bliss (*ānanda*). Among the followers of Śaṅkara, however, this Bliss has gradually acquired greater importance, so that the nature of *Brahman* came to be 'True Being, Knowledge and Bliss (*saccidānanda*)'.

Rāmānuja, on the other hand, identifies *Brahman* with the personal God and finds that it has five essential natures: True Being (*satya*), Knowledge (*jñāna*), Bliss (*ānanda*), Stainlessness (*amalatva*) and Infinity (*anantatva*).[82] He regards Knowledge and Bliss as the principal natures among the five, and, moreover, considers that both of them are one and the same. He says: 'The attribute defining the essential nature of *Brahman* is solely Knowledge of the nature of Bliss in opposition to impurities.'[83] Furthermore, Rāmānuja declares that an *ātman* freed from all *karman* or *avidyā* possesses, in principal, the same essential nature as *Brahman*.[84] It follows from this that 'Knowledge of the nature of Bliss' is also the essential nature of an *ātman*.

The definition of the essential natures of *Brahman* and an *ātman* in this manner is derived from a will to establish the authenticity of bhakti to God on the Upaniṣadic tradition of 'knowledge'. In other words, Rāmānuja intends to prove that the knowledge (*vidyā*) as direct means of *mokṣa* is of the nature of love identical with Bliss or pleasure. For this purpose, he demonstrates the following points.

First, because God possesses the nature of Bliss, or supreme pleasure, for Himself and others, one having the knowledge of God would acquire the love for Him as the supreme pleasure. Second, because an *ātman* possesses the nature as a subordinate to God, the *ātman* with knowledge of Him would acquire unsurpassed love for Him who is the only principal of the *ātman*, and would be supremely pleased with the subservience to Him. Third, because one with knowledge of God has been freed from *karman* to conceal the knowledge, the *ātman* is destined to be released from *saṃsāra* caused by *karman*, and to enjoy the Supreme Bliss in *mokṣa* after leaving its body. On account of these points, Rāmānuja declares that 'the nature of possessing Knowledge (*jñātṛtva*)' is 'the nature of possessing Bliss (*ānanditva*)',[85] and demonstrates that the uncontracted knowledge is identical with the supreme pleasure.

Parabhakti possessing such characteristic is, according to Rāmānuja, granted by God to one devoting bhakti by means of pleasing God after taking refuge in Him. And, God supremely pleased with the devotion of *parabhakti* by an *ātman* would stop all the *karman* that has been given, or would be given, to the *ātman* as the manifestation of His displeasure. That is to say, God would completely rid the *ātman* of the cause of *saṃsāra* and let it attain *mokṣa*. In this manner, Rāmānuja demonstrates that devoting bhakti to God is the indispensable means of *mokṣa* and that the personal God is the absolute ruler of all *ātman*s, on the grounds of his theory that the attainment of *mokṣa* and existence in *saṃsāra* of an *ātman* is determined by the grace and wrath of God as the manifestation of His pleasure and displeasure.

Owing to the success of Rāmānuja in proving that bhakti is an effective path to *mokṣa* on the authority of the Upaniṣads, the worship of the personal God with devoting bhakti has become widely accepted by brahmins and the later masters of the Vedānta school after Rāmānuja such as Madhva (1238–76), Vallabha (1479–1531) and Caitanya (1486–1533), who constructed their theistic theories of worshipping God with bhakti. We may, therefore, say that Rāmānuja established the basis of the connections between theories of the Vedānta school and the bhakti cult in later ages.

These masters were able to form the theory of bhakti with less restriction than Rāmānuja, since they were freed of the task to demonstrate the authenticity of bhakti as the true means of *mokṣa*. Moreover, they used the *Bhāgavata-purāṇa* as the authority of bhakti cult as well as the *Bhagavadgītā*, or rather, much more than the latter text.[86] The *Bhāgavata-purāṇa* was edited in the tenth century under the influence of the Āḻvārs to express the emotional and passionate bhakti similar to the love of an ardent woman for her lover. In the theory of bhakti advocated by these masters, consequently, the element of knowledge gradually weakened, while that of pleasure, or Bliss, strengthened. And, since the time of Rāmānuja, masters of the Vedānta school not only made investigations into the passages of the Upaniṣads, but also gave the mass of people a lead of worshipping God with devoting bhakti.

In sum, Rāmānuja succeeded in establishing the theory that knowledge as the nature of *Brahman* and an *ātman*—is interchangeable with Bliss. He played an important role in changing the history of the Vedānta school from practising direct realization of the Real Being with heavy dependence on knowledge, to fervent devotion to the personal God with considerable stress on pleasure or Bliss. Further, Rāmānuja played an important part in change from intellectual investigations of doctrine to emotional worship of God as the master, or rather, of God as the lover.

ABBREVIATIONS

BhG	:	*Bhagavadgītā.*
BhP	:	*Bhāgavatapurāṇa.*
GBh	:	Rāmānuja's *Gītābhāṣya* ad *Bhagavadgītā*, in *Śrī Bhagavad Rāmānuja Granthamālā*, ed. Sri Kanchi P.B. Annangaracharya Swami, Kancheepuram: Granthamala Office, 1956.
ŚBh	:	Rāmānuja's *Śrībhāṣya* ad *Brahmasūtras*, in *Śrībhāṣya of Rāmānuja*, ed. R.D. Karmarkar, 3 parts, Vol. 1 in University of Poona Sanskrit and Prakrit Series, Poona: University of Poona, 1959–64.
Ś.BSBh	:	Śaṅkara's *Bhāṣya* ad *Brahmasūtras*, in *Brahmasūtra-Śāṅkarabhāṣyam with the Commentaries*, ed. J.L. Shastri, Delhi: Motilal Banarsidass, 1988 (rpt).
Ś.GBh	:	Śaṅkara's *Gītābhāṣya* ad *Bhagavadgītā*, in *Śrīmad Bhagavadgītā with Śaṅkara's Bhāṣya*, ed. H. N. Apte, No. 34 in Ānandāśrama Saṃskṛt Series, Poona: Ānandāśrama, 1908.
VAS	:	*Rāmānuja's Vedārthasaṃgraha*, ed. J.A.B. van Buitenen, No. 16 in Deccan College Monograph Series, Poona: Deccan College Postgraduate and Research Institute, 1956.

NOTES

1. Nakamura points out that it would be only Dramiḍa in the sixth century (?) who accepted the bhakti cult among masters in the early Vedānta school. (H. Nakamura, *Śaṅkara no Shisou* [*Thought of Śaṅkara*], in Japanese, Tokyo: Iwanami Shoten, 1989, pp. 836, 842 n. 34.)

2. Shima points out that Śaṅkara, in *Ś.GBh*, explains the word 'bhakti' used in *BhG* only literally as *bhajana* in some cases, and defines it as knowledge (*jñāna*) in other cases. (I. Shima, 'Śaṅkara's Interpretation of the *Bhagavadgītā*', *Journal of Indian and Buddhist Studies*, vol. 39, no. 1, 1990, p. 496.)
3. Yāmuna records the contempt of the masters of the Advaita school or the Smārta sect toward the brahmins of the Bhāgavata Sect in his *Āgamaprāmāṇya* (*Āgamaprāmāṇya of Yāmunācārya*, ed. M. Narasimhachary, No. 160 in Gaekwad's Oriental Series, Baroda: Oriental Institute, 1976, pp. 11–17). Hacker makes clear, however, that although the Smārta sect belongs to Śaivism in the present day, almost all masters of the Advaita school, including Śaṅkara, up to the end of the tenth century worshipped the personal God, Viṣṇu=Nārāyaṇa in their daily lives as in the case of the Bhāgavata sect. (P. Hacker, 'Relations of Early Advaitins to Vaiṣṇavism,' WZKSO, vol. 9, 1965, pp. 147–54.)
4. In the Śrī-Vaiṣṇava sect, or the Bhāgavata sect in Tamil, Nāthamuni, Yāmuna and Rāmānuja have been traditionally honoured as the first, second and third head of the sect.
5. *VAS* §. 76, p. 114, l. 1.
6. The theory of Rāmānuja has been named 'qualified non-dualism (Viśiṣṭādvaita)' since *Brahman* is qualified by sentient and non-sentient existences as qualifying attributes (viśeṣaṇa).
7. *VAS* §. 141, p. 170, ll. 10–11.
8. For details of the steps for attaining *mokṣa* affirmed by Rāmānuja, see B. Kimura, 'Rāmānuja's Theory of Three *Yoga*s: The Way to *Mokṣa*,' in *Three Mountains and Seven Rivers: Prof. Musashi Tachikawa Felicitation Volume*, ed. S. Hino and T. Wada, Delhi: Motilal Banarsidass, 2004, pp. 645–68.
9. *ŚBh* I.1.1, p. 12, ll. 5-6. The word *vijñāna* in this quotation has the same meaning as the word *jñāna*.
10. *ŚBh* I.1.1, p. 12, ll. 6–7.
11. *ŚBh* I.2.23, p. 373, l. 8.
12. Hatae points out that Śaṅkara himself does not use both terms of *parokṣajñāna* and *aparokṣajñāna* though commentators on his *Upadeśasāhasrī* often use them. (H. Hatae, 'Kakennamono-toshiteno-Chi ni tsuite' ('On Knowledge as the Visible'), in Japanese, *Journal of Indian and Buddhist Studies*, vol. 31, no. 2, 1983, pp. 126–7.) Śaṅkara, however, describes clearly that *ātman=Brahman* should not be realized indirectly (*parokṣa*) but only directly (*aparokṣa*) in *Ś.BSBh*. III.3.2 and IV.1.13 and other parts.
13. Before the following discussion, Rāmānuja insists that 'mere knowledge of the sense of passages' is not the effective means of *mokṣa* 'because of that knowledge resulting from the passages even without an injunction of the Veda (*vidhāna*)' (*ŚBh* I.1.1, p. 12, l. 8). It is, however, in vain, since

Śaṅkara declares that the knowledge as the means of *mokṣa* 'depends entirely on the real existence (*vastu*), and neither on the Vedic rules (*codanā*) nor on a man.' (*Ś.BSBh* I.1.4, p. 83, ll. 5–6.)

14. *ŚBh* I.1.1, p. 12, l. 9.
15. *Ś.BSBh* II.2.30, p. 477, ll. 7–8.
16. Nakamura points out that Śaṅkara uses the phrase of 'being made up of innate impression (*nānārūpā vāsanā*)' as the contradictory meaning of 'in the highest truth (*paramārthika*)' (Nakamura, op. cit., p. 212).
17. *ŚBh* I.1.1, p. 12, l. 12-p. 13, l. 1.
18. *ŚBh* I.1.1, p. 13, ll. 9–10. The word *bhāvana* in this quotation means *nididhyāsana*, which is the meditation approved by the Advaita masters, according to the comment in Sudarśana Sūri's *Śrutaprakāśikā* (*Brahmasūtra-Śribhāṣya with Śrutaprakāśikā*, ed. T. Viraraghavacharya, Madras: Ubhaya Vedanta Granthamala, 1967 (rpt. Madras: Visishtadvaita Pracharini Sabha, 1989), vol. 1, p. 52, ll. 23–6).
19. Śaṅkara states in *Ś.BSBh* IV.1.13 (p. 847, l. 6): 'It is settled that the fruit of it (the meditation (*vidyā*) of *Brahman* having attributes) is acquisition of the divine power (*aiśvarya*) preceded by the eradication of sins (*pāpman*).' The sins to be eradicated are the obstacles of the origination of knowledge as the direct means of *mokṣa*.
20. *ŚBh* I.1.1, p. 13, ll. 8–9.
21. *ŚBh* I.1.1, p. 12, ll. 10–11. This statement is based on the description in *Ś.BSBh* IV.1.15.
22. See *Ś.BSBh* IV.1.15.
23. *ŚBh* I.1.1, p. 13, ll. 2–5. In addition, Rāmānuja insists in *ŚBh* I.1.1 (p. 13, ll. 6–8) that the perception of two moons is not effective as a similar example in this case since it is caused by an eye disease irrelevant to the acquisition of knowledge.
24. *ŚBh* I.1.1, p. 15, ll. 4-5, *ŚBh* IV.1.1, p. 977, ll. 6-7.
25. Nakamura points out that the terms *vidyā*, *upāsana* and *dhyāna* have already been used synonymously in the *Brahmasūtras*. (H. Nakamura, *Brahmasūtra no Tetsugaku* (*The Philosophy in Brahmasūtras*), in Japanese, Tokyo: Iwanami Shoten, 1951 (rpt. 1981), p. 476.)
26. The passage of Taṅka in the sixth century (?), 'vedana would be upāsana' is quoted in *ŚBh* I.1.1 (p. 16, l. 9). Śaṅkara declares in *Ś.BSBh* IV.1.1 (p. 826, l. 12) that the words √*vid* and *upa*-√*ās* have been used without any distinction in the Upaniṣads, and he uses the terms of *upa*-√*ās* and √*dhyai* synonymously in *Ś.BSBh* IV.1.1 and 8. Notice, however, that Śaṅkara stresses that the meditation denoted by *upāsana* and *dhyāna* is not knowledge but an activity caused by *avidyā*.
27. *ŚBh* IV.1.1, p. 978, ll. 7–12.
28. *ŚBh* I.1.1, p. 15, l. 15.
29. This passage is quoted in *ŚBh* I.1.1, p. 16, l. 15.
30. *Ś.GBh* XIII. 24, p. 199, l. 28.

31. *ŚBh* I.1.1, p. 17, l. 2, p. 18, l. 1.
32. *GBh* XV.15, p. 138, l. 7.
33. *ŚBh* IV.1.16, p. 992, l. 15–p. 993, l. 1.
34. *VAS* §§. 91–2, p. 127, ll. 9–13.
35. *GBh* XII.9, p. 111, l. 10.
36. *GBh* XII.12, p. 112, l. 3.
37. *VAS* §. 141, p. 170, ll. 11–12.
38. *VAS* §. 91, p. 126, ll. 11–12.
39. *GBh* VII. intro., p. 62, l. 15.
40. *VAS* §§. 142, p. 170, l. 16–p. 171, l. 5.
41. See *GBh* VII.1, IX.13–14, 22, XI.55, XII.6–8.
42. *GBh* XI.55, p. 109, l. 1.
43. Both Madhva in the thirteenth century and Vallabha in the sixteenth use the term of *sneha* and Caitanya in the sixteenth century uses *rāga* for the sake of defining bhakti. On this point, see Kimura, op. cit., p. 665 n. 14.
44. In *BhG*, there are no examples for the words *anurāga* nor *sneha*, and *rāga* is used only in the sense of desire to be forsaken, while the derivatives of √*prī* are used for the sake of expressing bhakti.
45. O. Böhtlingk and R. Roth, *Sanskrit Wörterbuch*, vol. IV, St. Petersburg, 1862–5, (rpt. Delhi: Motilal Banarsidass, 1990), pp. 1166–7.
46. *GBh* VII.23, p. 68, ll. 17–18.
47. On the examples of the statements of the nature of meditation, see *ŚBh* I.3.39, p. 467, l.3, IV.1.1, p. 977, l. 1, IV.1.13, p. 989, l. 10 and others. On the examples of that of other activities, see *ŚBh* III.4.26, p. 953, l. 10, *GBh* IX.28, p. 85, l. 7, XVI.24, p. 145, l. 16 and others. Most of the examples use the term *ārādhana*.
48. *VAS* §. 91, p. 126, l. 8, *GBh* III.3, p. 24, l. 8.
49. *GBh* XVI.23, p. 145, l. 8
50. *GBh* XVIII.65, p. 169, l. 10.
51. *GBh* IX.14, p. 81, l. 5.
52. *VAS* §. 142, p. 171, ll. 6-9. For further details on *śeṣa*, see J.B. Carman, *The Theology of Rāmānuja: An Essay in Interreligious Understanding*, New Haven: Yale University Press, 1974, pp. 147–57.
53. *ŚBh* II.1.9, p. 575, ll. 2–8.
54. Also see *GBh* intro., p. 1, l. 14, VII.19, p. 67, ll. 10–11, IX.27, p. 85, ll. 1–2 and others.
55. An example of *śeṣataika-svabhāva-* is in *GBh* XVIII.54, p. 166, l. 9, that of *-svarūpa-* is in *GBh* XII.11, p. 111, l. 24 and that of *-rati-* in *GBh* intro., p. 1, l. 14. In addition, there are examples of *-rasa-* in *GBh* VII.16, p. 66, l.18 and in *VAS* §. 78, p. 116, l. 10. van Buitenen explains this term indicating both meanings of *-svabhāva / svarūpa-* and *-rati-*. (J.A.B. van Buitenen, *Rāmānuja's Vedārthasaṃgraha*, No. 16 in Deccan College Monograph Series, Poona: Deccan College Postgraduate and Research Institute, 1956, p. 238 n. 349.)

56. *VAS* §. 122, p. 151, ll. 4–6.
57. *VAS* §. 144, p. 173, ll. 3–10.
58. *GBh* XII.11, p. 111, ll. 24–5.
59. The synonymy of these words has already been pointed out by J.A.B. van Buitenen, *Rāmānuja on the Bhagavadgītā*, 2nd ed., Delhi: Motilal Banarsidass, 1968, p. 25 n. 66.
60. The word *prapatti* is a derivative of *pra-√pad*. Note that Rāmānuja does not mention the doctrine of *prapatti*, 'the complete self-surrender to God without any other efforts', which had become so important in the later Viśiṣṭādvaita school, especially in the southern school. For a discussion on the doctrine of *prapatti* in later ages, see P.N. Srinivasachari, *The Philosophy of Viśiṣṭādvaita*, vol. 39 in the Adyar Library Series, Madras: The Adyar Library and Research Centre, 1943, pp. 382–413; N.S. Anantharangachar, *The Philosophy of Sādhana in Viśiṣṭādvaita*, Mysore: University of Mysore, 1967, pp. 190–238; Carman, op. cit., pp. 214–37.
61. *GBh* XVIII.62, p. 168, l.13. Also see *GBh* IV.11, p. 37, ll. 18–19.
62. *GBh* XVIII.56, p. 167, ll. 1–2. Rāmānuja requires one practising *karma-yoga* to attribute the agency of one's activities (*kartṛtva*), the sense of possession of those (*mamatā*) and the desire for the fruits of those (*phala*) to God. On this point, see Kimura, op. cit., pp. 647–9.
63. *GBh* XV.11, p. 137, l. 3.
64. *GBh* VII.16, p. 66, l. 14. Also see *GBh* VII.14, 15, 28, IX.13, XVIII.66 and others.
65. On removing stains of an internal organ, see *GBh* II.61–8, VI.15, XV.5, 11 and others, and on removing Māyā of God, see *GBh* VII.14. We may note here that Māyā of God maintained by Rāmānuja is not 'false existence (*mithyārtha*)' or *avidyā*, as insisted by Śaṅkara, but 'what is made up of the guṇas and of the highest reality' (*GBh* VII.14, p. 65, l. 23.).
66. *GBh* VII.19, p. 67, ll. 9–10. My interpretation of the word *rasa* follows the explanation of van Buitenen mentioned above.
67. *GBh* VII.19, p. 67, ll. 11–12.
68. *VAS* §. 78, p. 116, ll. 5–8.
69. *VAS* §. 43, p. 98, l. 8.
70. *GBh* V.15, p. 49, ll.2–3.
71. *ŚBh* II.2.3, p. 652, l. 9–p. 653, l. 13.
72. Rāmānuja denies the existence of *apūrva* 'which is not taught in the scriptures' in *ŚBh* III.2.37–40, since it is possible for him to explain the reason of the lapse of time between performing activities (*karman*) and starting the operation of their effects (*karman*) on the ground of the pleasure and displeasure of God without the concept of *apūrva*.
73. *GBh* X.2, p. 87, l. 23.
74. *VAS* §. 144, p. 173, ll. 11.
75. See *GBh* VII.18, VIII.14.
76. *GBh* III.9, p. 26, ll. 5–6.

77. *GBh* XVIII.54, p. 166, ll. 9–14.
78. *ŚBh* III.4.26, p. 953, ll. 10–11.
79. *ŚBh* IV.1.13, p. 989, ll. 3–4. My interpretation of *pāpman* is based on the explanation in *ŚBh* IV.1.14.
80. *ŚBh* IV.1.13, p. 989, ll. 10-12. My interpretation of *agha* is based on the explanation in *ŚBh* IV.1.14
81. According to Rāmānuja, even *parabhakti* cannot destroy the *karman* whose effects have already begun to operate (*ārabdhakarman*). It can destroy only the *karman* whose effects have not yet begun to operate (*anārabdhakarman*). One cannot, accordingly, attain *mokṣa* while living with some bodies to enjoy the fruits of the former *karman*.
82. *ŚBh* III.3.13, p. 857, l. 2. I have replaced *ādayaḥ* used in the original text edited by Karmankar with *anantatva* in accordance with the text: *Brahmasūtra-Śrībhāṣya with Śrutaprakāśikā*, ed. T. Viraraghavacharya, Madras: Ubhaya Vedanta Granthamala, 1967 (rpt. Madras: Visishtadvaita Pracharini Sabha, 1989), vol. 2, p. 474, l. 1.
83. *VAS* §.84, p. 122, ll. 3–4. On the point that Rāmānuja regards Knowledge and Bliss, natures of God, as one and the same, see Carman, op. cit., p. 112.
84. There are, strictly speaking, some differences in the essential natures of *Brahman* and an *ātman*. On this point, see *ŚBh* I.1.2.
85. *ŚBh* I.1.1, p. 97, ll. 9–10. Although Rāmānuja states this about *Brahman*, it is also applicable to the case of an *ātman* because the natures of both are the same in principle.
86. Rāmānuja never mentions *BhP*. Madhva, on the other hand, regards *BhP* as one of the authorities as a means of knowledge (*pramāṇa*), although 'the Gopāla-Kṛṣṇa element', points out in Bhandarkar, 'seems to be entirely absent from his system, and Rādhā and the cowherdesses are not mentioned.' (R.G. Bhandarkar, *Vaiṣṇavism, Śaivism and Minor Religious Systems*, Poona: Bhandarkar Oriental Research Institute, 1982 (rpt.), p. 87.) Vallabha regards *BhP* as an equal authority with the Veda, *Brahmasūtra*s and *BhG*, and 'the doctrine of Vallabhacharya', says von Glasenapp, 'can be characterized as a systematizing of the Doctrines of *BhP* in light of certain theoretical and sectarian observations.' (H. von Glasenapp, *Doctrines of Shri Vallabhacharya*, tr. B.S. Amin, Baroda: Shri Vallabha Publication, 1984, p. 87.) About Caitanya, Dasgupta states: 'The type of bhakti which is preached in BhP is well illustrated in the life of Chaitanya. . . . He had so thoroughly identified himself as a partner in BhP.' (S.N. Dasgupta, *Hindu Mysticism*, 1927, (rpt.) Delhi: Motilal Banarsidass, 1987, pp. 132–6.)

4

Theories of Salvation in the Teṅgalai and Vaḍagalai Schools

SADANORI ISHITOBI

Teṅgalai (the southern school) and Vaḍagalai (the northern school) are the two sub-sects of Śrīvaiṣṇavism.[1] The Teṅgalai school, with its centre in Śrīraṅgam, regards Tamil traditions as important. On the other hand, the Vaḍagalai school, based in Kañcī, gives importance to the Sanskrit traditions.[2]

At present, a great divide exists between the two in terms of doctrine and social system. In fact, intermarriages between the two sub-sects are extremely rare.[3] A sectarian consciousness arose in the minds of their practitioners during the seventeenth century.[4] Subsequently, in the nineteenth century, doctrinal tensions and social divisions too became apparent.[5] Although sectarian consciousness was not present among them *ācārya* like Piḷḷai Lokācārya (*c.*1213–1323),[6] and Maṇavāḷāmāmuni (*c.*1370–1443),[7] and Vedānta Deśika (*c.*1268–1369),[8] signs of antagonism were evident in their doctrines.

ĀCĀRYAS IN THE EARLY PERIOD

In the early period of Śrīvaiṣṇavism,[9] ācāryas like Yāmuna and Rāmānuja were confronted with the problem of how to create harmony between the Śrīvaiṣṇava doctrine of bhakti and the Vedāntic tradition. Two questions remained unanswered:

(A) How can *karman*, *jñāna*, and bhakti be related to each other?

(B) What is the appropriate position of Pāñcarātric *prapatti* in the Śrī-vaiṣṇava theory of salvation?

(A) In his *Gītārthasaṅgraha*, Yāmuna states that *karma-yoga* is service to God through austerity (*tapas*), pilgrimage (*tīrtha*), charity (*dāna*), sacrifice (*yajña*) and so on (*GAS* 23ab). He uses the notion of *sevana* or service to explain *karma-yoga*, while the *Bhagavadgītā* uses it to explain *bhakti-yoga* (*BhG* 14.26ab). Further, Yāmuna newly adopts the notions of easiness (*saukarya*) and swiftness (*śaighrya*) to explain *karma-yoga* (*GAS* 9a). *Jñāna-yoga* is fixation in the purified self by those who have overcome their mind; *bhakti-yoga* is fixation in meditation and similar practices, with a one-point love for the Supreme One (*GAS* 23cd–24ab). *Karma-yoga* and *jñāna-yoga* were regarded as auxiliary means of *bhakti-yoga*. In his *Ātmasiddhi*, Yāmuna states that the one-pointed (*aikāntika*) and absolute (*ātyantika*) *bhakti-yoga* of a person whose mind has been purified by *karma-yoga* and *jñāna-yoga*, is the means to attain *mokṣa* (*AS,* p. 14). Moreover, in his *Gītārthasaṅgraha*, he states that *bhakti-yoga* is brought about by *jñāna* and *karman* (*GAS* 3cd) and that *bhakti-yoga* is most excellent (*śraiṣṭya*)(*GAS* 16a). However, the relationship between the three *yoga*s remains implicit. They are described as connected to one another (*GAS* 24cd). In his *Gītārthasaṅgraharakṣā*, a commentary on Yāmuna's *Gītārthasaṅgraha*, Vedānta Deśika relates the three *yogas* as follows:

> In *karma-yoga*, the knowledge of *ātman* and the love for God must be present. In *jñāna-yoga*, *karman* which purifies the mind and bhakti towards God are imperative. Further, *bhakti-yoga* is followed by the other two (*yoga*s). Nevertheless, the three *yoga*s can be distinguished according to their principal element (*pradhāna*).[10]

Rāmānuja gives bhakti considerable importance because it is the essential purport of *Gītāśāstra* (*GBh* intr.18.1), or the most secret of all (*guhyatama*, *GBh* 9.1, 18.64). With regard to the other two *yogas*, he lays special emphasis on *karma-yoga*[11] because it is easy to practice (*suśaka, sukara*), free from failure (*apramāda*),[12] quick (*śaighrya*)[13] and independent (*nirapekṣa*).[14] Thus, *karma-yoga* is superior to *jñāna-yoga* which is not only difficult to practice (*duṣkara*) but also prone to failure (*sapramāda*). Therefore, even if a person has the qualifications necessary for *jñāna-yoga*, he should practice *karma-yoga*.[15] Adopting the theory of *jñāna-karma-samuccaya-vāda*,[16] Rāmānuja identifies bhakti with the knowledge (*vedana*) prescribed in the Upaniṣads, and he considers *karman* as the means to the knowledge.[17] He believes that mere *karman* yields only insufficient and unstable fruits,[18] but he does not deny that knowledge is considered equivalent to the abandonment of attachment to the fruits (*phala*), the action (*karman*) and the doer (*kartṛ*).[19] He explains that *karma-yoga* becomes a form of knowledge, and that knowledge becomes immanent in *karma-yoga*.[20] Bearing in mind the gap that exists between the Vedāntic tradition (which regards knowledge as essential) and the Pāñcarātric tradition (which considers practise as being extremely important), Rāmānuja's advocacy of the relationship between *karman* and *jñāna* is complicated and not entirely clear.[21]

(B) Although Yāmuna does not address *prapatti* in a definite manner, there are some references to it in *Stotraratna*. Influenced by the ideas of the *Ahirbudhnyasaṃhitā*, these references are in the form of expressions such as 'worthless' (*ākiñcana*), 'devoid of any other Saviour' (*ananya-gati*) and 'a vessel of thousands of sins' (*aparādha-sahasra-bhajana*) (*SR* 22cd, 48). The following passage of the *Ahirbudhnyasaṃhitā* forms the basis of these expressions:

> I am a vessel of sins. I have no worth. I have no one to depend on. Be my means (*upāya*) for me. (*ABS* 37.30–1)

Confessing that he does not perform any religious duties (*na dharma-niṣṭho 'smi*) and that he lacks the knowledge of self (*na cātma-vedi*) and bhakti (*na bhaktimām*), Yāmuna surrenders at the feet of God (*SR* 22ab). Therefore, I believe that even though Yāmuna does give importance to *prapatti*, he does not consider *prapatti* to be a means that is different from bhakti. Rāmānuja too regards *prapatti* as being important, and even in *Śaraṇāgatigadya*,[22] in which his sectarian consciousness is evident, he does not consider *prapatti* to be different from bhakti.

Given the above, it can be stated that the ācāryas of the early period, such as Yāmuna and Rāmānuja, laid emphasis on *karma-yoga*. Moreover, although they referred to *prapatti*, they did not ascertain its superiority over or equality to bhakti.[23]

PIḶḶAI LOKĀCĀRYA

After the thirteenth and fourteenth centuries, at a time when Piḷḷai Lokācārya and Vedānta Deśika were active, the problem pertaining to the relationship between *karman*, *jñāna* and bhakti had already been resolved, and hence, these ācāryas were not deeply concerned with it.

In his *Arthapañcakam*, Piḷḷai Lokācārya mentions the following five means to attain salvation: (1) *karman*, (2) *jñāna*, (3) bhakti, (4) *prapatti* and (5) *ācāryāpimāṉam* (trust in the Mediator) (*AP* Intr. 4).

Karma-yoga is to purge oneself of all sins by purifying the body by performing religious duties such as sacrifice (*yajña*), charity (*tāna*) etc.;[24] further, it is an auxiliary to *jñāna-yoga* (*AP* 4.1). The duties described by Piḷḷai Lokācārya are similar to those explained by Rāmānuja in *Gītābhāṣya* (4.28–9) and those mentioned in the *Yatīndramatadīpikā* (7.18)—a manual of the Vaḍagalai school. In his *Gītābhāṣya*, Rāmānuja states that *karma-yoga* helps a person attain the true knowledge of *ātman* (*GBh* 4.32, 5.1) and the experiences of *ātman* (*GBh* 5.3, 5.5). Furthermore, he states that *karma-yoga* destroy the past sin (*GBh* 3.5), cleanse the *manas* through purified actions (*GBh* 5.7), and becomes the means to salvation (*GBh* Intr. 2.39). Although Piḷḷai Lokācārya's concept of *karma-yoga* is nearly identical to this, his evaluation of *karma-yoga* differs from the *ācāryas* of the early period. As mentioned earlier, Yāmuna and Rāmānuja lay emphasis on the easiness and successfulness of *karma-yoga* and insist that *karma-yoga* is superior to *jñāna-yoga*. On the other hand, Piḷḷai Lokācārya does not give much importance to *karma-yoga* and regards it as a means to acquire control over greed and desire.[25]

In the *Arthapañcakam*, *jñāna-yoga* is the contemplation of God who abides in the heart lotus or the orb of the Sun. God is the embodied One, who bears a conch shell and disk, wears golden robes and a crown, and is accompanied by Goddess Śrī. Initially, the intuition (*anupava*) of God does not last for long. However, with time and adequate learning of the *yoga*, the duration of intuition increases. Finally, one can reach a stage where the intuition of God persists (*AP* 4.2). Rāmānuja and Piḷḷai Lokācārya differ in their concept of *jñāna-yoga*. Rāmānuja believes that a person who acquires the intuition of *ātman* by means of *jñāna-yoga* can also acquire it through *karma-yoga* (*GBh* 5.5). Further, a person who practises *jñāna-yoga* acquires the intuition of *ātman* with great difficulty, whereas a person who practises *karma-yoga* realizes *ātman* without delay (*GBh* 5.6). On the other hand, Piḷḷai Lokācārya regards *jñāna-yoga* as the auxiliary means to practice *bhakti-yoga* and the primary means of attaining isolation (*kaivalya*) or the emancipation (*mokṣa*) (*AP* 4.1).

With regard to bhakti, Piḷḷai Lokācārya and Rāmānuja, to an extent, share the same opinion. Bhakti is the intuition of the nature of uninterrupted and continuous contemplation of God, which resembles the flow of oil, and has the form of love.[26] Further, similar to Rāmānuja's concept of bhakti, bhakti is facilitated through practise and the acquisition of knowledge (*AP* 4.3). Piḷḷai Lokācārya, however, does not refer to *sādhana-bhakti* and *phala-bhakti*, taught in the *Yatīndramatadīpikā* 7.25.

In sum, with regard to the relationship between the means of salvation, *karman* is the auxiliary means of *jñāna* and *jñāna* is the auxiliary means of *bhakti*. Although theories pertaining to the relationship between these means in the thoughts of Yāmuna and Rāmānuja are intricate, Piḷḷai Lokācārya's belief is extremely simple and can be illustrated, as shown in Figure 1.

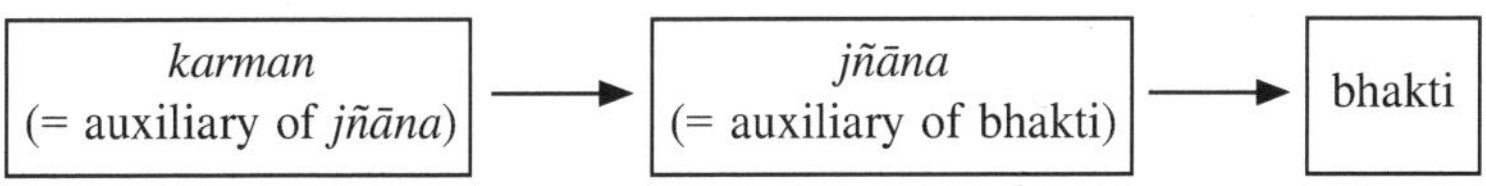

FIGURE 1

In *Arthapañcakam*, Piḷḷai Lokācārya refers to *prapatti* as one of the means to salvation, and explains it in detail (*AP* 4.4). He states that *prapatti* is easy to practice (*sukaram*) for those who do not have the adequate qualifications for bhakti (*aśaktar*) or cannot attain bhakti (*aprāptar*). He believes that *prapatti* yields results promptly (*śīkram*).[27] However, according to Rāmānuja, easiness and swiftness are the attributes of *karma-yoga*. Piḷḷai Lokācārya's thought that these attributes belong to *prapatti*, and not to *karma-yoga*, is remarkable and noteworthy. In *Śrīvacanabhūṣaṇa*, he states that *prapatti* is easy to practise because it implies 'to do nothing' as opposed to 'to do something' (*ŚVB* 101), it is accomplished by cessation (*nivṛtti*) which results from knowledge of the true self (*ŚVB* 135). Since the true nature of the self is to be subordinate to and serve God (*ŚVB* 73),[28] a person who is aware of his or her true nature will absorb himself or herself in God (*ŚVB* 108). Subsequently, one who is aware of God's beatitude will become ignorant of things other than God; a person who is aware of God's mercy will become indifferent to all things other than God. Moreover, one who wishes to conduct himself or herself rightly fears failure. Thus, these tendencies of ignorance, indifference, and fear cause a person 'to do nothing' (*ŚVB* 102, 103).

In contrast to the rituals prescribed by scripture, *prapatti* possesses no limitation in place, time, method, or qualification[29] (*ŚVB* 23, 25); moreover, *prapatti* can be performed by śūdras as well as women. According to the *Bhagavadgītā*, śūdras and women can attain salvation (*BhG* 9.32–3). However, Rāmānuja does not provide a definite comment on this in his *Gītābhāṣya.*[30] In *Śrībhāṣya*, Rāmānuja emphasizes that śūdras do not possess the necessary qualifications for acquiring the knowledge of *Brahman.*[31] On the other hand, in his *Vedārthasaṅgraha*, he supports the śūdras. He believes that they have an obligation to serve the people of the upper three *varṇa*s. In the *Manusmṛti*, the life of a śūdra has been compared to that of a dog, but Rāmānuja states that the life of a śūdra is not the same as a dog's because having 'a dog's life' means serving those who are not to be served (*VAS* 144). The *Yatīndramatadīpikā* asserts that only the upper three varṇas possess the necessary qualifications for practising bhakti (*YID* 8.18), not the śūdras. Further, giving śūdras such qualifications is inconsistent with the accounts stated under the topic of *apaśūdra* in the *Brahmasūtra* 1.3.33–9 (*YID* 8.19). Although the Teṅgalai school is innovative, the Vaḍagalai school is in accordance with the Vedāntic tradition. Perhaps the difference between the two results from Rāmāṇuja's ambiguous attitude towards the śūdras.

In *Śrīvacanabhūṣaṇa*, Piḷḷai Lokācārya states that an essential objective of *prapatti* is that it must be full of virtue (*kuṇa-pūrtti*) and that it is God's images that satisfy this requirement (*ŚVB* 34). Moreover, the object of *prapatti* must be accessible (*saulapya*) and God's images (*arcā*) possess accessibility (*ŚVB* 37). Thus, it is God's images that lead people to *prapatti* (*ŚVB* 40). In addition, he states that the people who are suitable for *arcā-prapatti* include the ignorant, the sage and the devotee (*ŚVB* 42). Further, ordinary people become devotees because of their ignorance. The *ācāryas* of the early period such as Nāthamuni, Yāmuna, and Rāmānuja became devotees because they realized that mere knowledge is insufficient and that God is the sole means to salvation. The Ālvārs became devotees because they had fervent religious beliefs (*ŚVB* 43).

Subsequently, Piḷḷai Lokācārya addresses the problem of whether or not *prapatti* is an *upāya*. He states that *prapatti* is neither an *upāya* nor does it have any auxiliaries (*aṅga*) (*ŚVB* 55, 56, 59). Further, he provides the reason why *prapatti* is not an *upāya* by explaining that even if a person performs *prapatti*, he cannot acquire God every time (*ŚVB* 142). In addition, *prapatti* is a means and also a fruit. Consider an instance where someone beckons a cow by showing it some grass, and then gives the grass to the cow; the grass becomes the means as well as the fruit. Similarly, *prapatti* is a means as well as a fruit (*ŚVB* 140, 141). Moreover, while bhakti can be practised by people themselves, *prapatti* can only be received through God's mercy; so *prapatti* is not considered as a mere *upāya*.

Although Piḷḷai Lokācārya grants importance to *prapatti* he suggests that love for an *ācārya* (*ācāryāpimāṉam*) is also a means. The *Yatīndramatadīpikā* also emphasizes the role of a teacher (*guru*) as follows:

> Such kind of *prapatti* is learnt through the mouth of the *guru*, in the secret scriptures, by the traditional method. (*YID* 7.28)
>
> A person who is intent on attaining salvation ..., relying on a teacher who possesses the necessary requirements of an *ācārya*, takes refuge in the mediatorial Śrī with the teacher's help. Then he is unable to practice other means such as bhakti. (*YID* 8.21)

However, the *Yatīndramatadīpikā* denies means other than bhakti and *prapatti* (*YID* 7.29). The inclusion of the love for an *ācārya* in the list of means is one of the characteristics of Piḷḷai Lokācārya's theory of salvation.[32]

Love for an *ācārya* aids both God and the subordinates (*śeṣa-vastu*) (*ŚVB* 429); this function of love corresponds to the mediatorial function (*puruṣakāra*) of Goddess Śrī. For instance, as a mother takes medicine herself to cure her sick baby, attributing the baby's sickness to herself, the mediator executes *upāya*s for those who lack the ability to practise the other four *upāya*s (*AP* 4.5). *Ācāryāpimāṉam*, identical to *prapatti*, is an independent *upāya* and an auxiliary to the other four *upāyas* (*ŚVB* 461). In addition, it is one of the easiest means. A person who cannot practise bhakti can perform *prapatti*, and a person who cannot perform *prapatti* can perform *ācāryāpimāṉam* (*ŚVB* 462). The fact that *ācāryāpimāṉam* is an independent means is not in conflict with the absoluteness of God, because people can attain their *ācāryas* through the grace of God (*ŚVB* 435), and because God is a greater benefactor than their *ācāryas* (*ŚVB* 436).

Rāmānuja insists on the importance of practice but Śaṅkara places knowledge on the highest pedestal. Further, Rāmānuja perhaps advocates the easiness of *karman* under the influence of the Pāñcarātra school. He emphasizes human being's love for God; on the other hand, Piḷḷai Lokācārya stresses God's love for human beings. As people become more clearly aware of the absoluteness of God, they also become more acutely aware of their own helplessness. Piḷḷai Lokācārya thus shifts the primary means to salvation from practices that are difficult to perform to practices, such as *prapatti* or *ācāryāpimāṉam*, that easier to perform. This shift corresponds to a social change when beliefs were popularized and salvation was extended to women and śūdras.[33]

VEDĀNTA DEŚIKA

Kañcī, the centre of Vaḍagalai school, prospered as a city of commerce and culture. This city was home to many temples of other schools as well as many *brāhmaṇas*. The ruler of Kañcī was interested in the Vedic culture and science.[34] Vedānta Deśika's teachings correspond to the Vedāntic tradition of the time.

Vedānta Deśika addresses the problems regarding salvation in his *Nyāyasiddhāñjana*.[35] In the second chapter *jīva-pariccheda*, he discusses the following four topics (*NSA*, pp. 297–328):

(A) the cause (*hetu*) of salvation (*mokṣa*)
(B) bhakti
(C) the qualifications (*adhikaraṇa*) of women and śūdras
(D) *nyāsa-vidyā*

(A) The cause of salvation is a particular form of knowledge (*jñāna-viśeṣa*) which is known as *upāsanā*, *vedana*, *dhyāna*, etc. It attains the form of bhakti (*bhakti-rūpāpanna*) and is consistently repeated till death (*NSA*, p. 297).[36] These explanations provided by Vedānta Deśika are similar to those presented by Rāmānuja.

It is not 'the mere knowledge of the truth' that can be the cause of salvation (*NSA*, p. 298). This is because the mere knowledge acquired through the sheer hearing of the Upaniṣads is not enjoined; moreover, salvation cannot be achieved even if mere knowledge is acquired, as is evident from the Āpastamba's sayings (*NSA*, pp. 298–9). Rāmānuja also believes that mere knowledge is not a means to attain salvation.[37] Therefore, these assertions made by Vedānta Deśika have been made before.

Subsequently, discussing *karman* (religious duties), Vedānta Deśika raised the question whether *karman* would be the cause of salvation. He proposes that *karman*, whether it functions as an independent means or collaborates with knowledge,[38] cannot be the cause of salvation.[39] This is because the scriptures prescribe knowledge (*vedana*) and prohibit any other means.[40] However, it is not inconsistent with the rules of the scripture to perform *karman* as an auxiliary to knowledge; this is because *karman*, when performed as an auxiliary, is no longer an independent means. Further, *karman* erases a person's past deeds which are obstacles in the path of obtaining the intuition of the supreme *ātman*; it also purifies the mind. Thus, *karman* functions as an auxiliary to knowledge (*NSA*, p. 302).

Karma-yoga and *jñāna-yoga* indirectly (*paramparayā*) function as the causes of salvation (*NSA*, pp. 302–3). Vedānta Deśika states that everything requiring an explanation has already been explained in the *Gītābhāṣya*;[41] he summarizes this as follows:

Karma-yoga is easy to perform, involves the *jñāna* and is independent.
Karma-yoga is quicker than *jñāna-yoga*.
It is difficult to obtain *jñāna-yoga* without *karma-yoga*.
Both *karma-yoga* and *jñāna-yoga* are the auxiliaries of *bhakti-yoga*.

Subsequently, he quotes a passage from Yāmuna's *Ātmasiddhi*,[42] and states the following. *Bhakti-yoga* is the means to attain the supreme *ātman*. However, if a person lacks the ability to perform *bhakti-yoga*, he or she must obtain the intuition of *ātman* to accomplish *bhakti-yoga*. *Jñāna-yoga* and *karma-yoga* are regarded as independent (*pṛthak*) means to attain the intuition of *ātman* (*NSA*, p. 307). *Jñāna-yoga*, which is related to the intuition of *ātman* as its subsidiary (*antaraṅga*), is initially difficult to practise (*duṣkara*). Therefore, a person who lacks the qualifications for performing *jñāna-yoga* must perform *karma-yoga* which yields the same fruit as does *jñāna-yoga*. Moreover, even if a person has the necessary qualifications for *jñāna-yoga*, he or she must perform *karma-yoga* for the benefit of the public if he or she has attained fame. Performing *karma-yoga* helps people who lack the ability to perform *jñāna-yoga* in that it provides them with that ability. These two bring to the people who practice them isolation (*kaivalya*) or the ability to perform willingly (*aiśvalya*) according to their own desires (*NSA*, pp. 307–8). Thus, it is only *bhakti-yoga* that can be the direct means to salvation (*NSA*, p. 308).

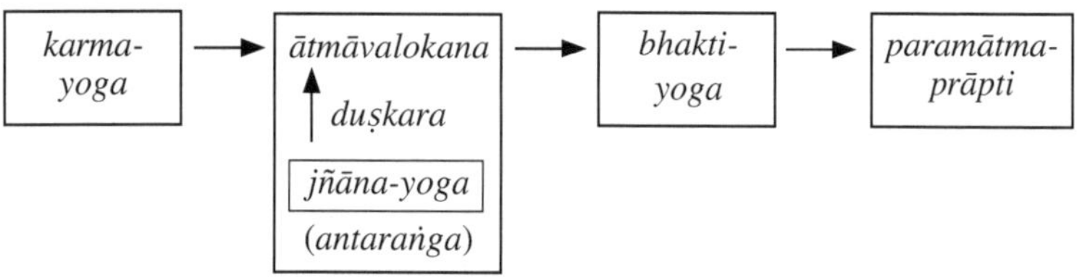

FIGURE 2

(B) With regard to bhakti, Vedānta Deśika believes that bhakti is love (*prīti*) for the Great One (*mahanīya*). Further, he classifies bhakti into (1) *para-bhakti*, (2) *para-jñāna* and (3) *parama-bhakti*, depending on the difference of the conditions (*avasthā-bheda*). The word bhakti is figuratively (*upacārataḥ*) used in the sense of admiration (*stuti*) or homage (*namaskāra*). The essential nature of *bhakti-yoga* is the *upāsanā* of the fourfold *ātman* (*cāturātmyopāsana-rūpa*), namely, Vāsudeva, Saṃkarṣaṇa, Pradyumna and Aniruddha.[43] Further, *bhakti-yoga* is diverse because of the differences of *ṣaḍ-vidyā*, *akṣara-vidyā* and so on (*NSA*, pp. 308–9). In Vedānta Deśika's *Nyāyasiddhāñjana*, it is not bhakti as love but bhakti as *upāsanā*—which has more intellectual character than the former—that is emphasized.

(C) Bhakti is achieved by those who belong to the upper three *varṇa*s and perform the duties prescribed in the scriptures according to their *varṇa*s and life stages (*NSA*, p. 309). However, Vedānta

Deśika argues that even women, and people who are left out of the life stages (*vidhura*) are capable of practising it. They can practice *brahma-vidyā* if they are qualified for chanting prayers (*japa*) and fasting (*upavāsa*) (*NSA*, p. 309). With regard to the śūdra, some of them are also capable of attaining salvation because they have already acquired the means to salvation in a former life, albeit not this one. In other words, in a former life, some of śūdras were born in one of the upper three *varṇa*s and have therefore already achieved the means to salvation; in this life, they have been born as śūdras as a result of past deeds. When the past deeds of a person are over, he or she can attain salvation. The *Chāndogyopaniṣad* states that Jānaśruti, who had been referred to as a 'śūdra' by Raikva, obtained wisdom.[44] This incident does not contradict the norms for the attainment of salvation (*NSA*, p. 310), because, as stated under the topic of *apaśūdra* in the *Brahmasūtra*, the word *śūdra* does not literally mean śūdra; it is believed that the word *śūdra* implies 'to go to grief'.[45]

It appears that Vedānta Deśika intends to harmonize the traditional viewpoint of the Vedānta, which restricts the qualifications within the upper three *varṇas*, with the innovative viewpoint of the Śrī-vaiṣṇava, which extends the qualifications to women and śūdras.

(D) Vedānta Deśika refers to *prapatti* as *nyāsa-vidyā*, which differs from the other *vidyā*s because it bears its original name (*NSA*, p. 312). Further, *prapatti* as an independent means is different from *prapatti* as subordinate to [*sādhana-*]*bhakti*. This is similar to the analogy that constant *jyotiṣṭoma* is different from temporary *jyotiṣṭoma* (*NSA*, p. 312). *Nyāsa-vidyā*, also known as *sādhya-bhakti*, is distinguished based on firm conviction.[46] *Sādhya-bhakti* is the conviction that God himself is the means to attain God (*NSA*, p. 311). Moreover, *sādhya-bhakti* is superior to *upāya-bhakti* (*sādhana-bhakti*), which is the conviction that bhakti itself is the means to attain God. This is because the former destroys even activated *karman* (*prārabdha*) whereas the latter only destroys inactivated *karman* (*NSA*, p. 311). Since *nyāsa-vidyā* is regarded as a special kind of knowledge (*buddhi-viśeṣa*), it does not contradict the following passage in the scripture:

There is no other path (*nānyāḥ panthā vidyate*). (*Śvet.Up.* 3.8)

Moreover, since *nyāsa-vidyā* is a special kind of bhakti (*bhakti-*

viśeṣa), it does not contradict the following passage (*NSA*, p. 311):

> But it is only through bhakti (*bhaktyā tv ananyayā*). (*Bhagavadgītā* 11.54)

Despite the fact that *nyāsa-vidyā* is a special kind of bhakti, it is a separate means because the two are different. *Nyāsa-vidyā* is practised once but bhakti repeatedly; moreover, *nyāsa-vidyā* is independent whereas bhakti is dependent.

In *Rahasyatrayasāra*, Vedānta Deśika explains the qualifications of bhakti and *prapatti* as follows:

> *Bhakti-yoga* is not attainable by those who do not belong to the upper three *varṇa*s, those who lack either the knowledge or the capability necessary for bhakti or both, even if they belong to the upper three *varṇa*s, and by those who experience extreme anguish with the unbearable delay of the fruit. (*RTS*, vol. 1, p. 331)

In other words, only those people who satisfy all the following three conditions are considered to possess the qualifications necessary for *bhakti-yoga*:

(1) Belong to the upper three varṇas
(2) Have the necessary knowledge and capacity
(3) Are capable of bearing the delay of the fruit

Thus, people can choose *prapatti* or bhakti according to their qualifications (*RTS*, vol. 1, p. 332).[47] Further, both *prapatti* and bhakti yield the same result. Subsequently, the question of why a person would choose a more difficult means when the result is the same arises. Vedānta Deśika answers this question as follows: *Prapatti* is not an easier means because it needs resolutions. In addition, the *Lakṣmītantra* states the following:

> That (*prapatti*) [appears] easy to perform, but, I think, it is [actually] difficult to execute.[48]

In sum, while Piḷḷai Lokācārya regards *prapatti* as easy to practise and yielding quick results, Vedānta Deśika regards it as hard to accomplish. He believes that *prapatti* is as difficult as bhakti. Moreover, he does not value *prapatti* more than bhakti. Thus, we are able to identify a conservative tendency in his thought.

CONCLUSION

The *ācārya*s of the early period, such as Yāmuna and Rāmānuja, endeavoured to create a synergy among the following schools. (1) the Āḻvārs who accentuated the passionate *prapatti*, (2) the Pāñcarātra school that emphasized rituals, and (3) the Vedāntic philosophy that stressed knowledge. Moreover, it was imperative for Yāmuna and Rāmānuja to address the three *mārga*s of the *Bhagavadgītā*, namely, *karma-yoga*, *jñāna-yoga* and *bhakti-yoga*. They attempted to relate the Pāñcarātric rituals to *karma-yoga*, and regarded them highly. Subsequently, they related the Vedāntic *jñāna* with *bhakti-yoga* (it was regarded as *jñāna-viśeṣa*). Further, they did not deny a person's ability to attain salvation and lay emphasis on God's transcendence. (Thus, people came to be regarded as worthless and incompetent.)

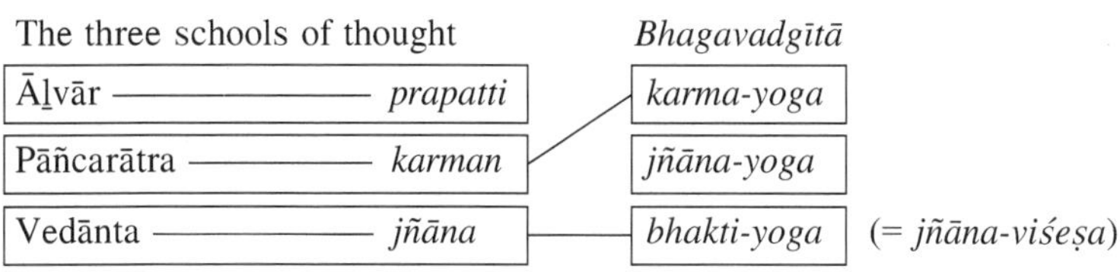

FIGURE 3

As a result, the positions of *prapatti* and *jñāna-yoga* remained ambiguous. Inheriting the traditional teachings expounded by Yāmuna and Rāmānuja, Vedānta Deśika attempted to adapt Śrīvaiṣṇavism and its thoughts to changes in its surroundings. The following are an indication of Vedānta Deśika's innovative thinking towards this purpose:

(1) Vedānta Deśika regards *jñāna* as an element of the intuition of *ātman*. Consequently, he eliminated the ambiguities regarding the position of *jñāna* that were present in the thoughts of the *ācārya*s of the early period.
(2) He regards *prapatti* (*nyāsa-vidyā*) as an independent means (*pṛthag-upāya*) of salvation and identifies it with *sādhya-bhakti* which is a special kind of bhakti (see Figure 4). Consequently, he clarified the appropriate position of *prapatti*.

bhakti (in a broad sense)
- *sādhya-bhakti* = *prapatti* (= *bhakti-viśeṣa*, *pṛthag-upāya*)
- *upāya-bhakti* = bhakti (in a narrow sense)

FIGURE 4

(3) He extends the qualifications necessary for *prapatti* to women and śūdras, albeit with some restriction.

However, it can also be stated that Vedānta Deśika displayed a traditional inclination in his thoughts based on the following facts. First, he regards *karman* as being important to a certain extent; second, he considers bhakti to be superior to *prapatti* and third, he extends the qualifications necessary for *prapatti* only to those who cannot practice bhakti.

On the other hand, Piḷḷai Lokācārya realizes that it is very difficult for most people to obtain a goal through their own efforts. Although he does not intend to deny the importance of bhakti, he does not consider bhakti to be an easy means for everyone; this is because bhakti has already been identified with the Upaniṣadic *upāsanā* by the *ācārya*s of the early period. Therefore, Piḷḷai Lokācārya includes *prapatti* and *ācāryāpimāṉam* as independently functioning *upāya*s, which, unlike the three *yoga*s, are easy to perform since they do not need any human effort. Thus, *prapatti* becomes a means and a goal. It is considered that women and śūdras can perform it. In other words, even if people cannot practise it, God does not abandon them; God provides them with *ācāryāpimāṉam*, which is comparatively an easier means because in this case the mediator, acting for the people, executes the *upāya*.

Thus, the signs of antagonism between the two sub-sects are evident in the thoughts of Piḷḷai Lokācārya and Vedānta Deśika, that is to say, Teṅgalai's populism and Vaḍagalai's traditionalism or the 'cat theory' and the 'monkey theory' of Śrīvaiṣṇavism in the later years.

ABBREVIATIONS

ABhN : *Aṣṭādaśabhedanirṇaya of Śrī Vātsya Raṅganātha*, Suzanne Siauve (ed. & tr.), Publications de l'Institut Francais d'Indologie, no. 58, Pondichéry, 1978.

ABS	:	*Ahirbudhnyasaṃhitā of the Pāñcarātrāgama*, 2 vols., M.D. Ramanujacharya (ed.), 2nd edn., Adyar Library and Research Centre, Madras, 1966.
AP	:	*Arthapañcakam of Piḷḷai Lokācārya* (E-text, http://www.srivaishnava.org/sva.htm).
ĀS	:	*Ātmasiddhi in Śrī-bhagavad-yāmunamuni-praṇītaṃ siddhitrayam*, P.B. Annangaracharya, 1954.
BhG	:	*Bhagavadgītā*.
GAS	:	Gītārthasaṅgraha Sri Abhinava Desika (Uttamur) J. Viraraghavacharya, eds., *Sri Bhagavad Gita with Sri Bhagavad Ramanujas Bhashya and Srimad Vedanta Desika's Commentary named Tatparya Chandrika*, Ubhayavedantagranthamālā, 1972.
GASR	:	*Gītārthasaṅgraharakṣā* in Śrīveṅkaṭanātha-Vedāntadeśika-viracitāḥ Rakṣāgranthāḥ, Ubhaya-vedāntagranthamālā, 1969.
GBh	:	*Sri Bhagavad Gita with Sri Ramanuja's Bhasya*, Sri Abhinava Desika J. Viraraghavacharya (eds.), Ubhayavedāntagranthamālā, Madras, 1972.
LT	:	*Lakṣmītantra*, Pandit V. Krishnamacharya (ed.), 2nd edn., The Adyar Library and Research Centre, Madras, 1975.
NSA	:	*Nyāya-siddhāñjana of Vedāntadeśika along with Hindi Translation*, Gaṅgānātha-Jhā-Granthamālā, Varanasi, 1966.
RTS	:	Sri Uttamur T. Viraraghavacharya (ed. & publ.), *Srimad Vedanta Desika's Srimad Rahasya Trayasara with Sara Vistara* (Commentary), 2 vols., Madras, 1980.
ŚBh	:	*Śrībhāṣyam* (Critical Edition), The Academy of Sanskrit Research Series, 4 vols., Melkote, 1985–91.
SR	:	*Stotraratna or the Hymn-Jewel of Śrī Yāmunācārya*, Swāmī Ādidevānanda (ed.), 3rd edn., Sri Ramakrishna Math, Madras, 1967.
ŚVB	:	*Śrīvacana Bhūṣaṇa of Piḷḷai Lokācārya*, Robert C. Lester (ed. and tr.), Kuppusvamy Sastri Research Institute, Madras, 1979.
VAS	:	*Rāmānuja's Vedārthasaṃgraha*, by J.A.B. van Buitenen, Deccan College Monograph Series 16, Poona, 1956.
YID	:	*Yatīndramatadīpikā of Śrīnivāsadāsa*, Swami Adidevananda (ed.), 2nd edn., Sri Ramakrishna Math, Madras, 1967.

NOTES

1. *Aṣṭādaśabhedanirṇaya* (attributed to Śrī Vātsya Raṅganātha, who flourished in the nineteenth century) compares the theories of Teṅgalai and Vaḍagalai. Teṅgalai is termed *dramiḍācārya* or *dramiḍa-prabandha-vyākhyātṛ* and Vaḍagalai is termed *saṃskṛtācārya* or *śrībhāṣya-mukhyayati-bhūmipati-prabandha-vyākhyātṛ*. In *ABhN*, references have often been made to Piḷḷai Lokācārya and his works, such as Arthapañcakam, Mumukṣuppaṭi and Śrīvacanabhūṣaṇa, have been quoted.

2. P.Y. Mumme in *The Śrīvaiṣṇava Theological Dispute, Maṇavāḷamāmuni and Vedānta Deśika*, Madras: New Era Publications, 1988, investigates the historical background and development of the two sub-sects of Śrīvaiṣṇavism.
3. G. Oddie, 'Sectarian Conflicts within Śrīvaiṣṇavism: Tengalais and Vadagalais in the Kāverī Delta, C.1800-1900', in *Bhakti Studies*, ed. G.M. Bailey and I. Kesarcodi-Watson, Delhi: Sterling, 1992, p. 85.
4. Mumme, *Śrīvaiṣṇava Theological Dispute*, p. 2.
5. Oddie, 'Sectarian Conflicts', p. 85.
6. Robert C. Lester, *Rāmānuja on the Yoga*, Madras: The Adyar Library and Research Centre, 1976, p. 1.
7. P.Y. Mumme, *The Mumukṣuppaṭi of Piḷḷai Lokācārya with Maṇavāḷamāmuni's Commentary*, Bombay: Ananthacharya Indological Research Institute, 1987, p. 16.
8. V.K.S.N. Raghavan, *History of Viśiṣṭādvaita Literature*, Delhi: Ajanta 1979, p. 27.
9. In this study, I would like to divide the history of Śrīvaiṣṇavism into the following two periods:
(1) The early and formative period (from the ninth to the twelfth century).
(2) The sectarian oriented period (from the thirteenth century onwards).
Nāthamuni, Yāmuna, and Rāmānuja belong to the early period, while Piḷḷai Lokācārya and Vedānta Deśika belong to the latter.
10. *nanu karma-yoge 'py ātma-jñānam ārādhya-prītis cānuvartate, jñāna-yoge 'py antaḥvaraṇa-śuddhy-arthaṃ niyataṃ karma na tyājyam, tad-ārādhyeśvara-bhaktiś ca / evaṃ bhakti-yoge 'pi tad-itarānuvṛttiḥ siddhā / ato vibhāgānupapattir ity atrāha trayāṇām apīti / pradhāna-bhūte kaśmiṃścit kśīra-śarkarādi-nyāyena guṇatayā itarānupraveśo na vibhāga-bhañjaka iti bhāvaḥ* (*GASR*, p. 487).
11. Cf. S. Ishitobi, 'Piḷḷai Lokācārya's Theory of *upāyas*' (in Japanese), *Hokkaido Journal of Indological and Buddhist Studies*, no. 15, 2000, pp. 157–69.
12. *suśakatvād asaṃbhāvita-pramādatvāc ca karmaṇaḥ* (*GBh* 3.8), *karma-yogasya suśakatvād apramāda-tvād* (*GBh* intr. 3.33), *karma-yogasya ... apramādatvāt sukaratvāt nirapekṣatvāc ca* (*GBh* intr. 5.1), *sukaram apramādam ca karma* (*GBh*, 18.48).
13. *karma-yogasya ... jñāna-niṣṭhāyāś śaighryaṃ* (*GBh* intr. 5.1), *yataḥ saukāryāc chaighryāc ca karma-yoga eva śreyān* (*GBh* intr. 5.8).
14. *karma-yogasya ... antargatātma-jñānatayā nirapekṣatvāt* (*GBh* intr. 3.33), *karma-yogasya ... nirapekṣatvāc ca* (*GBh* intr. 5.1), *tatra karma-yogasya nirapekṣa-yoga-sādhanatvam draḍhayituṃ* (*GBh* 6.1).
15. *jñāna-niṣṭhādhikāriṇo'py anabhyasta-pūrvatayā hy aniyatatvena duḥśakatvāt sapramādatvāc ca jñāna-niṣṭhāyāḥ, karma-niṣṭhaiva jyāyasī* (*GBh* 3.8).

16. S. Matsumoto, *A Study of Rāmānuja* (in Japanese), Tokyo: Shunjyusha, 1991, p. 112.
17. *evaṃ-rūpāyāḥ dhruvānusmṛtir eva bhakti-śabdena abhidhīyate; upāsana-paryāyatvāt bhakti-śabdasya* (*ŚBh* 1.1.1, vol. 1, p. 19), *evaṃ-rūpāyāḥ dhruvānusmṛteḥ sādhanāni yajñādīni karmāṇānīti yajñādi-śruter aśvavat ity-abhidhāsyate* (*ŚBh* 1.1.1, vol. 1, p. 20).
18. *kevala-karmaṇam alpāthira-phalatva-jñānam ca karma-mīmāṃsāvaseyam* (*ŚBh*, 1.1.1, vol. 1, p. 24).
19. *jñāna-yogaśaṃnyāsa* (*GBh*, 5.1, 5.2, 5.6, 6.2, and so on), *saṃnyāsa-tyāga* (*GBh* 18.2), *tyāgaḥ ... karmasu phala-viṣayatayā, karma-viṣayatayā, kartṛ-viṣayatayā ca ... saṃprakīrtitaḥ* (*GBh* 18.4).
20. It is said in *GBh* intr. 4.1, intr. 4.12, 4.24, 4.38, intr. 5.1, 6.1 and so on that *karma-yoga* becomes the form of knowledge. Moreover the inherence of knowledge in *karma-yoga* is mentioned in *GBh* intr. 4.1, 13.24 and so on.
21. B. Kimura tried to elucidate these tangled relations of the three *yoga*s in his thesis. Cf. B. Kimura, 'Rāmānuja on *jñāna-yoga*(1), (2)' (in Japanese), Tokai Bukkyo, No. 38, 39, 1993, 1994.
22. The authenticity of Śaraṇāgatigadya is challenged by R.C. Lester, *Rāmānuja on the Yoga*, Madras: Adyar Library and Research Centre, 1976, p. 151. However, Carman and Narayanan regard it as authentic (cf. J.C. Carman and V. Narayanan, *The Tamil Veda Piḷḷān's Interpretation of the Tiruvāymoḷi*, Chicago: University of Chicago Press, 1989, p. 42.) I have discussed this problem in my paper 'Rāmānuja's Concept of *Prapatti*: A Study on his Salvation Theory' (in Japanese), *Saṃbhāṣā* (Association of Indian and Buddhist Studies at Nagoya University), vol. 6, 1985, pp. 10–21). I find the authenticity of this work convincing.
23. Cf. S. Ishitobi, 'Yāmuna's Theory of Mokṣa and Sādhana'(in Japanese), *Journal of Indian and Buddhist Studies*, vol. XXXII, no. 1, 1983, 'Rāmānuja's Concept of *Prapatti*'. Th. A. Forsthoefel and P.Y. Mumme, 'The Monkey-Cat Debate in Śrīvaiṣṇavism: Conceptualizing Grace in Medieval India', *Journal of Vaisnava Studies*, vol. 8, no. 1, 1999, p. 4, point out that the works of Piḷḷai Lokācārya and Vedānta Deśika unravel the ambiguities of Yāmuna and Rāmānuja.
24. *karma-yōkam āvatu yajña, tāna, tapo, tyāna, santyā-vantana, pañca-mahā-yajña, aknihōtra, tīrtta-yātrā, puṇya-kṣētra-vāsa, kruccra, cāntrāyaṇa, puṇya-natī-snāna, vrata, cāturmāsya, palam-ūlāśana, śāstrāpyāsa, samārātana, japa, tarppaṇātitarmānuṣṭānattāl vanta kāya-śōṣaṇattālē pāpa-nāśam piṛantu, attālē intriya-tvārā prasarikkiṛa tarma-pūta-jñānattukku śaptātikaḷ viṣayamallamaiyālē viṣaya-sāpēkṣai piṟantu, yama niyama āsana prāṇāyāma pratyāhāra tyāna-tāraṇa samāti rūpamāṉa aṣṭāṅka-yōka kramattālē yokāpyāsa kālattaḷavum jñānattukku ātmavai viṣayam ākkukai* (*AP* 4.1).
25. *itutāṉ jñāna-yōkattukku sahakāriyumāy, aiśvaryattukku pratāna-sātanamum āyirukkum* (*AP* 4.1).

26. *pakti-yōkam āvatu ippaṭi tailatārāvat-aviccinna-smruti-santāna-rūpamāṉa anupavam prīti-rūpāpannam ākaiyum* (*AP* 4.3).
27. *prapatty-upāyam āvatu ippaṭi karma-jñāna-sahakrutaiyāṉa paktiyōkattil aśaktarkkum aprāptarkkum sukaramum āy śīkra-pala-pratamum āy* (*AP* 4.4).
28. Although Rāmānuja believes that knowledge and joy are the nature of the individual self (cf. *VAS*, p. 5), Piḷḷai Lokācārya says in *ŚVB* 73 they are accidental nature (*tamastam*) to the individual and only dependence on God (*dāsyam*) is the true nature of the self.
29. When people want to do *prapatti*, it makes no difference whether they are pure or impure (*ŚVB* 30).
30. H. Ikebe points out that Madhva accepts the qualifications of women and śūdras for salvation. See, H. Ikebe, 'Madhva's Way of the Interpretation of the Bhagavad Gītā' (in Japanese), *Hokkaido Journal of Indological and Buddhist Studies*, no.13, 1998, pp. 89–91.
31. *Śrībhāṣya* on *Brahmasūtra* 1.3.33–9 (*apaśūdrādhikaraṇa*). Cf. S. Matsumoto, 'Rāmānuja's View of the Śūdra' (in Japanese), *Hokkaido Journal of Indological and Buddhist Studies*, no. 14, 1999, pp. 177–96.
32. Nancy Ann Nayar says, 'the particular doctrine of *ācāryāpimāṉa* is not explicitly mentioned in the literature of the 12th century' (N.A. Nayar, *Poetry as Theology, The Śrīvaiṣṇava Stotra in the Age of Rāmānuja*, Studies in Oriental Religions, Wiesbaden: Otto Harrassowitz, 1992, p. 93).
33. Cf. S. Ishitobi, 'ācāryāpimāṉam' (in Japanese), *Hokkaido Journal of Indological and Buddhist Studies*, no.12, 1997, pp. 103–15.
34. Mumme, *Śrīvaiṣṇava Theological Dispute*, p. 8.
35. Cf. T. Mikami, *Nyāyasiddhāñjana of Vedānta Deśika, An Annotated Translation*, Sendai, 1999 (PDF document is available in 'Kyushu Indology' [http://homepage3.nifty.com/indology/]).
36. Vedānta Deśika cites *Brahmasūtra* 4.1.1 (*āvṛttir asakṛd upadeśāt*) and 4.1.12 (*āprayāṇāt tatrāpi hi dṛṣṭam*) for its sources.
37. Rāmānuja rejects the *jīvanmukti* theory, quoting Āpastamba Dharma Sūtra, in *Śrībhāṣya* 1.1.4 (*anena jñāna-mātrān mokṣaś ca nirastaḥ*, *ŚBh* 1.1.4. Cf. Mikami, Nyāyasiddhāñjana, p. 134).
38. It is the Mīmāṃsakas who maintain that *karman* works alone, and it is *Yādavaprakāśa* who insist that both knowledge and *karman* constitute the cause of the emancipation. Cf. S.M. Srinivasa Chari, *Fundamentals of Viśiṣṭādvaita Vedānta, A Study based on Vedānta Deśika's Tattva-muktā-kalāpa*, Delhi: Motilal Banarsidass 1988, p. 298.
39. Vedānta Deśika discusses the same problem in his *Tattvamuktākalāpa* 2.33.
40. *tam eva viditvā'timṛtyum eti nānyāḥ panthā vidyate'yanāya* (*Śvetāśvataropaniṣad* 3.8). Cf. Mikami, *Nyāyasiddhāñjana*, p. 135.
41. Cf. *GBh* 4.21, 4.24, 12.11, 12.12, intr. 13.1 and so on.

42. *AS*, p. 14.
43. Cf. *Śrībhāṣya* 2.2.41 (Mikami, *Nyāyasiddhāñjana*, p. 139).
44. *Chāndogyopaniṣad* 4.2.3–4.
45. The *Brahmasūtra* analyses the word 'śūdra' into two elements; that is to say, 'śug+ādravaṇa' (H. Nakamura, *The Philosophy of Brahmasūtra, History of Early Vedānta Philosophy*, vol. II, Tokyo: Iwanami Shoten, 1981, pp. 160–1).
46. T. Mikami points out that the firm conviction means the six components of *śaraṇāgati* in Pāñcarātrasaṃhitās. That is to say, *ānukulya-saṃkalpa*, *pratikūlya-varjana*, *mahāviśvāsa*, *kārpaṇya*, *goptṛtva-varaṇa* and *ātma-nikṣepa*. They are listed in *Ahirbudhnyasaṃhitā* 37.28–9 and *Lakṣmītantra* 17.60–1 (T. Mikami, *Nyāyasiddhāñjana*, p. 140).
47. *ABhN* reports the qualifications of bhakti in the Vaḍagalai-school as (1) knowledge, (2) ability, (3) attachment to the scriptures, and (4) tolerance for delay. One who lacks any of these must be qualified to *prapatti* (*ABhN*, p. 71).
48. *LT* 17.105cd.

5

Some Sources of Madhva's Bhakti Theory

HIROAKI IKEBE

R. Mesquita[1] says that the texts quoted by Madhva but unidentified their sources are made by himself. I agree with his opinion, but I think that Madhva must had his source of thought, if not of text. In order to clarify the source of Madhva's Bhakti theory from the point of thought, we focus on the means of emancipation, i.e. on bhakti and the state of *mokṣa* which is achieved by bhakti. First, we will review an outline of Madhva's salvation theory. Second, we will examine the concepts of bhakti and *mokṣa*, mentioned in the Nārāyaṇīya section of the *Mahābhārata* (*MBh*), the *Ahirbudhnya-saṃhitā* (*AS*), the *Lakṣmītantra* (*LT*) and the *Bhāgavata-purāṇa* (*BhP*); These texts are supposed as the sources of Madhva's salvation theory. Then we will compare the concept of Madhva with that of these texts.

AN OUTLINE OF MADHVA'S SALVATION THEORY[2]

In his *Gītābhāṣya* (*GB*), Madhva describes bhakti in the following way.

mokṣo hi mahā-puruṣa-arthaḥ / ... sa ca viṣṇu-prasādād eva siddhyati / ... sa cottkarṣa-jñānād eva bhavati /(*GB*, p. 18)

We achieve emancipation (*mokṣa*) only through the grace (*prasāda*) of Viṣṇu. That is to say, the grace of the God is the only means of emancipation. And we can get this grace of the God only through the knowledge of His greatness (*utkarṣa*). In his *Gītātātparya* (*GT*), Madhva says also that we can get this knowledge through our bhakti:

bhaktyā prasannaḥ paramo dadyāj jñānam anākulam /
bhaktiṃ ca bhūyasīṃ tābhyāṃ prasanno darśanaṃ vrajet /
tato'pi bhūyasīṃ bhaktiṃ dadyāt tābhyāṃ vimocayet / (*GT*, p. 4)

Here is a figure of the ladder to emancipation according to Madhva's description.

STEP 1

God = pleased

bhakti 1 ↑ ↓ *jñānam anākulam* (*parokṣa-jñāna*)

bhakta

STEP 2

God = pleased

bhakti 2 ↑ ↓ *darśana* (*aparokṣa-jñāna*)

STEP 3

God = pleased

bhakti 3 ↑ ↓ *mokṣa*

bhakta

When God is pleased with bhakti, He gives his bhakta two types of *jñāna*, i.e. knowledge and *mokṣa*, i.e. emancipation as His grace. Moreover we can understand that bhakti has three levels.

Next Madhva describes bhakti as follows:

brahma-rudra-ramā-ādibhyo'py uttamatvaṃ svatantratām /
sarvasya tad-adhīnatvaṃ sarva-sad-guṇa-pūrṇatām /
nirdoṣatvaṃ ca vijñāya viṣṇos tatrākhila-adhikaḥ /
sneho bhaktir iti proktaḥ sarva-upāya-uttamottamaḥ /
tenaiva mokṣo nānyena dṛṣṭmy-ādīs tasya sādhanam /(*GT*, p. 4)

māhātmya-jñāna-pūrvas tu sudṛḍhaḥ sarvato'dhikaḥ /
sneho bhaktir iti proktas tayā muktir na cānyathā / (*MBhTPN* 1.85, p. 8)

bhakty-arthāny akhilāny eva bhaktir mokṣāya kevalā /
muktānām api bhaktir hi nitya-ānanda-svarūpiṇī /
jñāna-pūrvaḥ paraḥ sneho nityo bhaktir itīryate / (*MBhTPN* 1.104–5, p. 9)

Thus for Madhva bhakti is *sneha* (affection) not mere emotional affection, but an intellectual affection based on the knowledge of the greatness of the God. We can clearly find this relationship between bhakti and knowledge in the ladder to emancipation.

Next we examine emancipation (*mokṣa*) in the salvation theory of Madhva. He agrees that there are four levels in emancipation: *sālokya*, *sārūpya*, *sāmīpya* and *sāyujya*.[3]

yesāṃ tv īṣad dṛśyate te na sāyujyaṃ prāptāḥ / sāmīpya-ādy eva teṣām / ataḥ prārabdha-karma-śeṣa-bhāvāt tad bhuktvā sāyujyāṃ gacchanti / (GB ad *BG* 2.50, p. 29)

And the level each individual soul can achieve is determined by *yogyatā* (fitness), i.e. *jñāna-ādhikya* (superiority of knowledge).

tatrāpi kramya-yogena jñāna-ādhikyāt samīpagāḥ /
sālokyaṃ ca sarūpatvaṃ sāmīpyaṃ yogam eva ca / (*BSBh* ad *BS* 4.4.19)

Here Madhva thinks that someone who should properly come to *sāyujya* might come temporarily to the lower level of emancipation on the way to doing *loka-saṅgraha*, which is mentioned in *BG*, and enjoying his *karman*. However he has not exhausted his *karman* yet, so he may feel displeasure and therefore still does not gain complete emancipation. We consider him as having achieved emancipation in the sense that he has emancipation for the lower souls.

Moreover Madhva maintains that there is a hierarchy in emancipated souls according to their bhakti.

yathā bhakti-viśeṣo'pi dṛśyate puruṣottame /
tathā mukti-viśeṣo'pi jñānināṃ liṅga-bhedane /
yogināṃ bhinna-liṅgānām āvirbhūta-svarūpiṇām /
prāptānāṃ paramānandaṃ tāratamyaṃ sadaiva hi /(*GB* ad *BG* 2.52, p. 30)

But Madhva does not think that the lower emancipation (i.e. *sālokya* and so on) are final emancipation.

na ca na ha vai saśarīrasya (*Chāndogya Upaniṣad* 8.12.1) *ityādi-virodhaḥ/ vailakṣaṇyāt tac-śarīrāṇām / abhautikāni hi tāni nitya-upādhi-vinirmitānīśvara-śaktyā /* (*GB* ad *BG* 2.50, p. 29)

Madhva maintains that an emancipated soul has a body, but this body is different from our ordinary body which is composed of elements. When Nārada visited *śvetadvīpa* (white island), he saw souls with bodies there. This story is told in the *MBh* and *BhP*.

prayogāc ca /
anindriyā anāhārā aniṣpandāḥ sugandhinaḥ (*MBh* 12.825*.1)[4]
deha-indriya-asu-hīnānāṃ vaikuṇṭha-pura-vāsinām (*BhP* 7.1.34)
ityādi dṛṣṭa-deheṣv eva /(*GB* ad *BG* 2.50, p. 29)

Madhva probably thinks that Vaikuṇṭha, described in the *BhP*, is the white island (*śvetadvīpa*) described in *MBh*, because there

Nārada visits a white island. And Madhva maintains that it is with emancipation that souls go to the white island.

na caiṣānyā gauṇī muktiḥ /
bahunātra kim uktena yāvac śvetaṃ na gacchati /
yogī tāvan na muktaḥ syād eṣa śāstrasya nirṇayaḥ
ity ādityapurāṇe tad-anya-mukti-niṣedhāt / ye tv atraiva bhagavantaṃ praviśanti te'pi paścāt tatraiva yānti /(*GB* ad *BG* 2.50, p. 29)

Thus, for Madhva emancipation is nothing but going to the white island. That is the basic principle of Madhva's salvation theory.

THE SALVATION THEORY OF THE PĀÑCARĀTRA

Next we examine the salvation theory of the Pāñcarātra. Because Madhva considers texts of the Pāñcarātra as the scripture (*sad-āgama*).

ṛg-ādayaś ca catvāraḥ pañcarātraṃ ca bhāratam /
mūlarāmāyaṇaṃ brahmasūtraṃ mānaṃ svataḥ smṛtam /
aviruddhaṃ ca yat tv asya pramāṇaṃ tac ca nānyathā /
etad-viruddhaṃ yat tu syān na tan mānaṃ kathañcana /
vaiṣṇavāni purāṇāni pāñcarātra-ātmakatvataḥ /
pramāṇāny eva manv-ādayāḥ smṛtayo'py anukūlataḥ /(*MBhTN* 1.30–3, p. 3)

Besides this, Madhva says in his other works[5] that the Pāñcarātra is scripture, like the four Vedas. Therefore we can say that Madhva's salvation theory is influenced by the salvation theory of the Pāñcarātra.

In his works Madhva often quotes texts called *saṃhitā*. But he does not name these. The *Sātvatasaṃhitā*, *Pauṣkarasaṃhitā*, *Jayākhyasaṃhitā* are regarded as the three treasures in the Pāñcarātra tradition, and *AS* and *LT* describe the theological theory of the tradition. These texts should have already existed at his time. Unfortunately, we cannot conclude whether the texts quoted by Madhva with the name saṃhitā as the scripture are the same as the existing texts of the saṃhitā of the Pāñcarātra or not.

In this article, we shall take up three texts, the Nārāyaṇīya section of the *MBh* (12.321–39), the *AS*, and the *LT*, as the comparative texts with the texts of Madhva. The Nārāyanīya is not properly a text of the Pāñcarātra, but this section is regarded as the oldest one to describe Pāñcarātra doctrine,[6] i.e. the theory of world creation based on the *vyūha* theory,[7] or the story of the white island. As in the above quotation, Madhva ranks the *MBh* as the fifth Veda and considers it scripture. Moreover, he quotes verses from this Nārāyaṇīya section.

THE STORY OF THE WHITE ISLAND IN THE NĀRĀYAṆĪYA SECTION

As mentioned above, Madhva thinks that there are four levels in the emancipated state, and he maintains that whichever levels of emancipation can be attained by emancipated souls, to come to the white island is emancipation. In other words, at the white island the emancipated souls enjoy the emancipated states, i.e. *sālokya* and so on. In the Nārāyaṇīya section, we can find a few descriptions of the white island[8] which are very important in the salvation theory of Madhva.

(1) *MBh* 12.322.8–12: the description of the white island and the white people which Nārada saw.
(2) *MBh* 12.323.22–45: the story of the visit to the white island by Ekata, Dvita, and Trita.
(3) *MBh* 12.323.24–6: the people of the white island are the *ekāntin* which are devoted to the God Nārāyaṇa.
(4) *MBh* 12.323.48: *abhakta* (i.e. those who aren't devoted to the God) cannot see the God.
(5) *MBh* 12.331.14: the direct sight of the God can be given by the grace of the God.

These descriptions are in accord with the salvation theory of Madhva, but they don't say that emancipation is coming to the white island. In the Nārāyaṇīya section, emancipation is to enter into (*pra√viś*) the God (*MBh* 12.326.19;41, 12.337.67). As mentioned above, Madhva agrees that it is one of the emancipated states to enter into the God, but for Madhva, definite emancipation is nothing but to come to the white island.

THE SALVATION THEORY OF THE *AHIRBUDHNYASAṂHITĀ*

Next, we will examine descriptions of the *AS*. In *AS* we do not find that emancipation means to come to the white island. But *AS* links emancipation closely with reaching the highest heaven (*parama-vyoman*) of the Nārāyaṇa.

śuddhā pūrva-uditā sṛṣṭir yā sā vyūha-ādi-bhedinī /
sudarśana-ākhyāt saṃkalpāt tasyā eva prabhā-ujjvalā //
jñāna-ānanda-mayī styānā deśa-bhāvaṃ vrajaty uta /
sa deśaḥ paramaṃ vyoma nirmalaṃ puruṣāt param //
niḥsīma-sukha-saṃtānam anavadyam anākulam /
tatrānanda-mayā bhogā lokāś cānanda-lakṣaṇāḥ // (*AS* 6.21–3)

That is to say, the highest heaven of Nārāyaṇa consists of the knowledge and the delight (*jñāna-ānanda-maya*), and the enjoyment consists of delight (*ānanda-maya bhoga*) there.

tad etat parama-vyoma leśatas te pradarśitam /
naiva varṣāyutenāpi vaktuṃ śakyo'sya vistaraḥ / (*AS* 6.31cd–32ab)

We cannot describe completely the highest heaven in detail, though we may spend a thousand years attempting to do so.

tat-padaṃ prāpya tattvajñā mucyante vīta-kalmaṣāḥ /
trasareṇu-pramāṇās te raśmi-koṭi-vibhūṣitāḥ //
āvirbhāva-tirobhāva-dharma-bheda-vivrajitāḥ /
paramaṃ te'dhvanaḥ pāraṃ vaiṣṇavaṃ padam āśritāḥ //
viśanti nāmam adhvānaṃ kāla-kalloka-saṃkulam / (*AS* 6.27–9ab)

It is emancipation to come to the highest heaven, and one who gets there will never return to this transmigrating world. And AS says that in the highest heaven we can see the God.

bhaktās te yādṛśe rūpe saṃsāra-padam āśritāḥ /
tādṛśaṃ te samīkṣante parama-vyoma-vāsinaḥ / (*AS* 6.29cd–30ab)

According to this description, we can understand that there are differences in the appearance of the God which the dweller in the highest heaven can see. This difference is determined by the one's faith during transmigration.

The highest heaven is Vaikuṇṭha according to Schrader and Gonda.[9] We confirmed that for Madhva the white island is Vaikuṇṭha. We can also say that in the Pāñcarātra, the highest heaven, Vaikuṇṭha, and the white island are the same[10] because the dweller in the highest heaven described in *AS* accords with the dweller in the white island described in Nārāyaṇīya section of *MBh*, though in *AS* we cannot find clear evidence. If we assume that the highest heaven (Vaikuṇṭha) of the Pāñcarātra and the white island of the Nārāyaṇīya are the same, we can conclude that *AS* says that emancipation is coming to the white island, which the Nārāyaṇīya doesn't say. And the position which says that emancipation is coming to the white island coincides with the position of Madhva.

But *AS* doesn't say that it is the ultimate emancipation to come to the highest heaven.

vihṛtya suciraṃ kālaṃ koty-ogha-pratisaṃcaram /
tato viśanti te divyaṃ sāḍguṇyaṃ vaiṣṇavaṃ yaśaḥ /(*AS* 6.30cd–31ab)

For *AS* the ultimate emancipation is the unification with God. To reach the highest heaven is a step to ultimate emancipation. This description is in accord with the description of the Nārāyaṇīya, but conflicts with the theory of Madhva.

Next, we examine the means of emancipation described in *AS*.

svarūpa-bhūtaṃ yat puṃso hitaṃ sukham udīritam /
bhagavan-mayatā sāsya bhagavattā-para-āhvayā /
atyanta-sādhanaṃ tasya yat tad dvedhā vyavasthitam /
vidhā jñānam iti tv ekā dharma ity aparā vidhā /
hetumad-dhetu-bhāvas tu vidhayor anayoḥ smṛtaḥ /
jñānaṃ tu hetumat tatra tac ca dvedhā vyavasthitam /
sākṣātkāramayaṃ caikaṃ parokṣaṃ param īryate /
hetumad-dhetu-bhāvo'yaṃ dvayor api nirūpyate /
hetumat tv aparokṣaṃ yat parokṣaṃ hetur ucyate /
anayor jñānayor dharmaḥ sa hetur iti gīyate /
sākṣāt parokṣe tat-sādhye hetus tan-mukhato hy asau /
asyāpi dve vidhe dṛṣṭe tattva-śāstra-abdhipāragaiḥ /
sākṣād ārādhana-ātmaikaḥ paras tu vyavadhānataḥ /(*AS* 13.11–17ab)

The benefit of human beings is emancipation,[11] and the means of human beings is both knowledge and *dharma*. Furthermore, both knowledge and *dharma* have direct and indirect ways, and there is a cause and effect relationship among these means. This description can be summarized as follows:

dharma (= worship of God)[12]

indirect worship (= worship mediated by the manifestation (*vibhūti*) of God)[13]

↓

direct worship (= worship of God who shows all of Himself)[14]

↓

jñāna (= knowledge)[15]

indirect knowledge (= knowledge of the Sāṅkhya)[16]

↓

direct knowledge (= knowledge of the Vedānta)[17]

This *dharma* is the worship of the God, and it is not *karmayoga*. But the idea that the means of emancipation are arranged along a ladder and that knowledge is classified into two categories, direct and indirect, accords with the salvation theory of Madhva.

THE SALVATION THEORY OF *LAKṢMĪTANTRA*

We can now examine the description of the *LT*. Like *AS*, *LT* does not say that emancipation is coming to the white island, but we can find a description about the highest heaven of Nārāyaṇa and a description that it is emancipation to come there.

tayor nau paramaṃ vyoma nirduḥkhaṃ padam uttamam /
ṣāḍguṇya-prasaro divyaḥ svācchandyād deśatāṃ gataḥ /
svakarma-nirataiḥ siddhair veda-vedānta-pāragaiḥ /
aneka-janma-saṃtāna-niḥśecita-kaṣāyakaiḥ /
kleśena mahatā siddhair antarāya-atigaiḥ kramāt /
saṃkhyā-vidhi-vidhānajñaiḥ sāṃkhyaiḥ saṃkhyānapāragaiḥ /
ratyāhṛta-indriya-gramair dhāraṇā-dhyāna-śālibhiḥ /
yaugaiḥ samāhitaiḥ śeśvat kleśena yad avāpyate /
acchidrāḥ pañcakālajñāḥ pañca-yajña-vicakṣaṇāḥ /
ūrṇe varṣaśate dhīrāḥ prāpnuvanti yad añjasā /
yat tat-purāṇam ākāśaṃ sarvasmāt paramaṃ dhruvam /
yat-padaṃ prāpya tattvajñā mucyante sarva-bandhanaiḥ /
sūrya-koṭi-pratīkāśāḥ pūrṇa-indv-ayuta-saṃnibhāḥ /
yasmin pade virājante muktāḥ saṃsāra-bandhanaiḥ /(*LT* 17.9–15)

That is to say, according to *LT* the highest heaven is the place that (1) where there is no sorrow and the God's six *guṇa*s itselves become the space, (2) where the person who arrives is the *siddha*, knower of the *pañcakāla*, (3) where emancipation is coming there and on arriving, being brightened there.

Here, the description that one who can come to the highest heaven is *siddha* accords with the description of the Nārāyaṇīya about the dweller on the white island. Therefore, we can conclude that the highest heaven described in *LT* is the white island described in the Nārāyaṇīya. Next, we examine the means of emancipation described in *LT*.

paramaḥ puruṣa-artho yas tvat-prītir tasya sādhanam /(*LT* 15.6)

LT says that the benefit of people is the favour (*priyā*) of the Goddess Lakṣmī. In *LT*, the *śakti* of Lakṣmī is divided into five parts and the fifth is grace (*anugraha*)—that is to say, we can achieve emancipation through this grace. But *LT* says that if we want the favour of Lakṣmī and Her grace, we require knowledge.

brahma nārāyaṇaṃ māṃ yaj-jñānenaivāpnuyād yatiḥ /
anthā nānyo'sti vijñānād ayanāya vipaścitām /
ñānaṃ tac ca viveka-utthaṃ sarvataḥ śuddham avraṇam /
vāsudeva-eka-viṣayam apunarbhava-kāraṇam /
ñāne tasmin samutpanne viśate mām anantaram /
tais tair upāyaiḥ prītāhaṃ jīvānām amala-ātmanām /
udbhāvayāmi taj-jñānam ātma-jyotiḥ-pradarśakam /
upāyās te ca catvāro mama prīti-vivardhanāḥ / (*LT* 15.11–14)

For entering into Lakṣmī = Nārāyaṇa, we need knowledge, and this can be attained through the favour of Lakṣmī. In this meaning, *LT* says the favour of Lakṣmī is the means of emancipation. *LT* says there are four ways to get her favour:

upāyāṃś caturaḥ śakra śṛṇu mat-prīti-vardhanān /
yair ahaṃ paramāṃ prītiṃ yāsyāmy anapagāminīm /
sva-jāti-vihitaṃ karma sāṃkhyaṃ yogas tathaiva ca /
sarva-tyāgaś ca vidvadbhir upāyāḥ kathitā ime /(*LT* 15.16–17)

That is to say, the four means are: (1) action (*karman*), (2) knowledge (*jñāna*), (3) *yoga*, and (4) renunciation (*tyāga*). Here, action means the *karmayoga* of the *Bhagavadgītā*, which is action without desire for fruits.[18] Moreover, LT says, for this action we need to reject action (*saṃnyāsa*).[19]

Knowledge means the knowledge of Sāṃkhya.[20] *LT* says there are three kinds of numbers in the Sāṃkhya.

saṃkhyās tisro hi mantavyāḥ sāṃkhya-śāstra-nidarśitāḥ /
rathamā laukikī saṃkhyā dvitīyā carcana-ātmikā /

samīcīnā tu yā dhīḥ sā tṛtīyā paripaṭhyate /
saṃkhyā-traya-samūho yaḥ sāṃkhyaṃ tat paripaṭhyate /(*LT* 15.24–5)

Among these three, the third is knowledge of Nārāyaṇa and Lakṣmī.

LT says the following about *yoga*:

upāyo yas tṛtīyas te vakṣyate yoga-saṃjñakaḥ /
yogas tu dvividho jñeyaḥ samādhiḥ saṃyamas tathā /
yama-ādy-aṅga-samudbhūtā samādhiḥ saṃsthitiḥ pare /
brahmaṇi śrīnivāsa-ākhye hy utthāna-parivrajitā /
sākṣātkāramayī sā hi sthitiḥ sad-brahma-vedinām /
dhyātṛ-dhyeya-avibhāgasthā mat-prasāda-samudbhavā /
saṃyamo nāma sat-karma paramātma-eka-gocaram /
tat punar dvividhaṃ proktaṃ śārīraṃ mānasaṃ tathā /(*LT* 16.30–3)

Gupta[21] explains *saṃyama* as follows : 'the Pāñcarātra's ritual worship of God and His Śakti. This involves visualizing the rituals as well as actually performing them.' From this, we can understand *saṃyama* as *dharma*, which *AS* labels as one of the means of emancipation. On the other hand, *samādhi* is meditation,[22] and in this we can see Brahman directly. Therefore, *samādhi* corresponds with *nididhyāsana*, which is the third of *jñānayoga* in Madhva's salvation theory.[23]

LT does not say that *karman*, *jñāna*, and *yoga*, are separately the means of emancipation. It says that they are organized along one ladder to emancipation.

prathamo ya upāyas te karma-ātmā kathitaḥ purā /
saṃjñānaṃ janayec śuddham antaḥkaraṇa-śodhanāt /
tena hi prīṇitā sāhaṃ sad-ācāra-niṣevaṇāt /
dadāmi buddhi-yogaṃ tam antaḥkaraṇa-śodhanam /
sāṃkhyaṃ nāma dvitīyo ya upāyaḥ kathitas tava /
parokṣaḥ śāstra-janyo'sau nirṇayo dṛḍhatāṃ gataḥ /
pratyakṣatām ivāpanno mat-prītiṃ janayet paramām /
ahaṃ saṃkhyāyamānā hi svarūpa-guṇa-vaibhavaiḥ /
udbhāvayāmi taj-jñānaṃ pratyakṣaṃ yad-vivekajam /
tṛtīyas tu samādhy-ātmā pratyakṣo'viplavo dṛḍhaḥ /
pratyakṣa-sattva-saṃbhūtaḥ prasāda-atiśayo hi saḥ /
tṛtīyasya vidhā yo'sau saṃyamo nāma varṇitaḥ /
bhogaiḥ śuddhais tridhodbhūtair atyanta-prītaye mama /
ahaṃ hi tatra viśvātmā viṣṇu-śaktiḥ parāvarā /
sākṣād eva samārādhyā devo vā puruṣottamaḥ /(*LT* 16.34cd–41)

Karman, *jñāna* and *yoga*, consist of one ladder to attain the direct vision of Lakṣmī or the God. Here is the figure of the ladder to emancipation according to the description of *LT*.

1. first means whose essence is *karman* (this makes the internal organs pure)
↓
2. occurrence of pure knowledge
↓
3. favour of Lakṣmī
↓
4. *buddhi-yoga* which is indirect affirmation (*nirṇaya*) (this makes the internal organs more pure)
↓
5. firmness (this is almost direct vision)
↓
6. the highest favour of Lakṣmī
↓
7. direct knowledge produced from discrimination (*vivekaja-pratyakṣa-jñāna*)
↓
8. *samādhi* and *saṃyama*
↓
9. the ultimate favour of Lakṣmī
↓
10. direct vision of Lakṣmī or *puruṣottama*

The accordance of this ladder of *LT* and the ladder of Madhva, is the scheme that the God is pleased with people's *karman* and gives knowledge as His grace. On the other hand, one difference between the ladder of *LT* and the ladder of Madhva is that *LT* does not bring bhakti into this ladder. As Tokunaga[24] pointed out, the idea of grace belongs to a different genealogy from the idea of bhakti in India. Consequently, Madhva created a new theory of salvation which incorporates the idea of grace and the idea of bhakti into one system.

The *LT* says *śaraṇāgati* is the fourth means of emancipation.[25]

upāyaś cāpy apyāyāś ca śāstrīyā nirmitā mayā /
vihitā ya upāyās te niṣiddhāś cetare matāḥ /
adho nayanty apāyās taṃ ya enān anuvartate /

ūrdhvaṃ nayanty upāyās taṃ ya enān anuvartate /
upāya-apāya-saṃtyāgī madhyamāṃ vṛttim āśritaḥ /
mām ekaṃ śaraṇaṃ prāpya mām evānte samaśnute /
ṣaḍaṅgaṃ tam upāyaṃ ca śṛṇu me padma-saṃbhave /
ānukūlyasya saṃkalpaḥ prātikūlyasya varjanam /
lakṣiṣyatīti viśvāso gopṛtva-varaṇaṃ tathā /
ātma-nikṣepa-kārpaṇye ṣaḍvidhā śaraṇāgatiḥ /
evaṃ māṃ śaraṇaṃ prāpya vīta-śoka-bhaya-klamaḥ / (*LT* 17.56cd–61)

This *śaraṇāgati* is mentioned as 'the ultimate secret among all of secrets' in the last part of the *BG* (18.64–6). And it becomes the teaching of *prapatti* of the Teṅgalai sect of the Śrīvaiṣṇava.[26] But Madhva does not emphasize either the *śaraṇāgati* or the *prapatti*. For him, there is only one way to emancipation.

THREE WAYS OF THE *BHĀGAVATA-PURĀṆA*

The *Bhāgavata-purāṇa* (*BhP*), as well as the Pāñcarātra, probably influenced the salvation theory of Madhva. Because (Madhva wrote a commentary on the *BhP*). So let us now examine the salvation theory of *BhP*. This too describes three ways to emancipation, i.e. *karmayoga*, *jñānayoga* and *bhaktiyoga*. Particularly in the twentieth chapter of the eleventh book, *BhP* says:[27]

yogās trayo mayā proktā nṛṇāṃ śreyo-vidhitsayā /
jñānaṃ karma ca bhaktiś ca nopāyo'sti kutracit /
nirviṇṇānāṃ jñāna-yogo nyāsinām iha karmasu /
teṣv anirviṇṇa-cittānāṃ karma-yogas kāminām /
yadṛcchayā mat-kathā-ādau jāta-śraddhas tu yaḥ pumān /
na nirviṇṇo nātisakto bhakti-yogo'sya siddhidaḥ /
tāvat karmāṇi kurvīta na nirvidyeta yāvatā /
mat-kathā-śravaṇa-ādau vā śraddhā yāvan na jāyate /(*BhP* 11.20.6–9)

The three ways are *karman*, *jñāna* and bhakti, and each is for the person who has that ability. And it is not necessary for the way of bhakti both to be disgusted with *karman* (*na nirviṇṇa*) and to remove the attachment (*na atisakta*). Moreover,

tasmān mad-bhakti-yutasya yogino vai mad-ātmanaḥ /
na jñānaṃ na ca vairāgyaṃ prāyaḥ śreyo bhaved iha /
yat-karmabhir yat-tapasā jñāna-vairāgyataś ca yat /
yogena dāna-dharmeṇa śreyobhir itarair api /

sarvaṃ mad-bhakti-yogena mad-bhakto labhate'ñjasā /
svarga-apavargaṃ mad-dhāma kathaṃcid yadi vāñchati /(*BhP* 11.20.31–3)

That is to say, those who go by the way of bhakti can get all things which those who go by the way of *karman* or go by the way of *jñāna* can get. And the things which can be got by *karman* or by *jñāna* will differ from, and are inferior to, things obtained by way of bhakti.

And *BhP* says that we can get emancipation without the *jñāna*.

mat-kāmā ramaṇaṃ jāram asvarūpavido'balāḥ /
brahma māṃ paramaṃ prāpuḥ saṅgācśata-sahasraśaḥ /
tasmāt tvam uddhavotsṛjya codanāṃ praticodanām /
pravṛttaṃ ca nivṛttaṃ ca śrotavyaṃ śrutam eva ca /
mām ekam eva śaraṇam ātmānaṃ sarva-dehinām /
yāhi sarva-ātma-bhāvena mayā syā hy akutobhayaḥ /(*BhP* 11.12.13–15)

Cowherdesses were able to reach Kṛṣṇa with faithful devotion without knowing His true form. Therefore, knowledge is not necessary for emancipation. It is sufficient to love Kṛṣṇa and to go to him for protection. Here *BhP* says that people should leave all things to love Kṛṣṇa. This corresponds with the *śaraṇāgati* described in *LT*. On the other hand, the knowledge is necessary for emancipation in the salvation theory of Madhva discussed above.

BhP says that the ultimate emancipation is the unification with the God.

mad-guṇa-śruti-mātreṇa mayi sarva-guhāśaye /
manogatir avicchinnā tathā gaṅgāmbhaso'mbudhau /
lakṣaṇaṃ bhakti-yogasya nirguṇasya hy udāhṛtam /
ahaitukya-vyavahitā yā bhaktiḥ puruṣottame /
sālokya-sārṣṭi-sāmīpya-sārūpya-ekatvam apy uta /
dīyamānaṃ na gṛhṇanti vinā mat-sevanaṃ janāḥ /
sa eva bhakti-yoga-ākhya ātyantika udāhṛtaḥ /
yenātivrajya triguṇaṃ mad-bhāvāyopapadyate /(*BhP* 3.29.11–14)

The devotees who serve *nirguṇa-bhakti*, which is the ultimate stage of bhakti, don't obtain emancipation of *sālokya*, etc., even though Kṛṣṇa says that He gives it to them. But they choose to serve Kṛṣṇa, and they get to unify with Kṛṣṇa; that is to say, they get *ekatva* (oneness). However, Madhva, whose fundamental principle is the difference from God, cannot agree with unifying with God.

CONCLUSION

We have examined the views of emancipation and the means of emancipation described in the Nārāyaṇīya section of *MBh*, the *AS* and the *LT*, and we have compared these with Madhva's theory. As a result of the examination, we have made clear the following points:

(1) As far as the story of the white island (*śvetadvīpa*) is concerned, the basic frame of the salvation theory of Madhva accords with the description of the Nārāyaṇīya section.
(2) In the Nārāyaṇīya section, emancipation is to enter into (*pra√viś*) the God. On the other hand, for Madhva, the definite emancipation is to come to the white island.
(3) Both *AS* and *LT* say that it is emancipation to come to the highest heaven which is the white island.
(4) But *AS* and *LT* say that it is not the ultimate emancipation to come to the white island, but it is the ultimate emancipation to unify with Nārāyaṇa or Lakṣmī.
(5) As far as the fundamental view of emancipation is concerned, there are big differences between Madhva's theory and the theory of the Pāñcarātra. However as far as the means of emancipation is concerned, there are many similarities between them.
(6) The theory on the means of emancipation, which maintains that some means of emancipation are integrated into one way and these means are organized into many steps that must be climbed step by step, is in accord with Madhva's theory. Furthermore, the idea that knowledge is divided into direct and indirect knowledge and that indirect knowledge is the knowledge of Sāṃkhya and the direct knowledge is the direct vision of the God (*sākṣātkāra*), agrees with Madhva's theory.
(7) Madhva's theory on the means is more similar to the theory of *LT* than that of *AS*.[28] The only difference between Madhva's theory and *LT* is whether bhakti is a part of the means of emancipation or not.

(8) *BhP* says the three ways are for different people with different abilities. This position is different from that of *BG* and of Madhva. Furthermore, for *BhP* bhakti is only a necessity for emancipation, while knowledge and action are not. But for Madhva, bhakti requires knowledge. Bhakti of *BhP* is like the feeling of blind love of cowherd girls for Kṛṣṇa, but the bhakti of Madhva is a rational one.

ABBREVIATIONS

AS : *Ahirbudhnya-saṃhitā of the Pāñcarātrāgama*, ed. M.D. Ramanujacharya and revised by V. Krishnamacharya, 2 vols., Madras: Adyar Library and Research Centre, 1916 (1st rpt. 1986).

BhP : *The Bhāgavatamahāpurāṇam*, Delhi: Nag Publishers, 1987.

BhPTPN : *Bhāgavatapurāṇatātparyanirṇaya*, SMG, vol. 4, pp. 1–844.

GB : *Bhagavadgītābhāṣya*, SMG, vol. 1, pp. 1–164.

GT : *Bhagavadgītātātparya*, SMG, vol. 1, pp. 1–164.

JT : Jayatīrtha, Prameyadīpikā, *The Bhagavad-gītā with Eleven Commentaries*, Critically edited by Shastri Gajanana Shambhu Sadhale, Delhi, Parimal Publications (Parimal Sanskrit Series No. 17).

LT : *Lakṣmī-tantra. A Pāñcarātra Āgama*, ed. V. Krishnamacharya, Madras: The Adyar Library and Research Centre, 1959.

MBh : *The Mahābhārata*, ed. V.S. Sukhtankar and S.K. Belvalkar, Poona: Bhandarkar Oriental Research Institute, 1925–66.

MBhTPN : *Mahābhāratatātparyanirṇaya*, SMG, vol. 2, pp. 1–491.

SMG : *Sarvamūlagranthāḥ*, 5 vols., ed. Bannaje Govindacharya, Bangalore: Akhila Bhārata Mādhva Mahā Maṇḍala Publication, 1969–74.

NOTES

1. R. Mesquita, *Madhva und seine unbekannten literarischen Quellen*, Wien: Institut Für Indologie der Universität Wien, 1997.
2. See Ikebe 2000.
3. See M. Monier-Williams, *Brāhmanism and Hinduism*, London: Murray, 1891, pp. 71; 118.
4. According to the footnote of the Poona edition, this verse is inserted after 12.325.1 in the manuscript T1, G3 and G6. *MBh* 12.325 is the story of the visit of Nārada to the white island.
5. See *GB* Introduction and *Viṣṇutattvanirṇaya*. And in the chapter of Madhva of the *Sarvadarśana-saṃgraha*, Madhva says he recognized Pāñcarātra as

the authority. By the way, Śaṅkara interprets *Brahmasūtra* 2.2.42–5 as a rejection of Pāñcarātra doctrine. And Rāmānuja interprets it as the first part of the argument (*pūrvapakṣa*) and the conclusion (*siddhānta*) of Pāñcarātra. On the other hand, in his *Brahmasūtrabhāṣya* Madhva interprets it as having no connection with Pāñcarātra, but, in his *Brahmasūtrānuvyākhyāna*, he rejects the interpretation of Śaṅkara and protects the Pāñcarātra doctrine.

6. See Matsubara 1990, p. 108.
7. The *vyūha* theory is told in the Bhīṣma-parvan of *MBh* (6.61.65–6). See Matsubara 1990, p. 108.
8. See Matsubara 1990, p. 108.
9. See Schrader 1973, p. 57, Gonda 1977, p. 62.
10. Matsubara (1994, p. 224, note 30) connects the highest heaven described in *AS* with the white island described in Nārāyaṇīya section.
11. And this benefit, emancipation, aims to being the Bhagavat. That is to say, here also it is said that emancipation is to unify with the Bhagavat.
12. See Schrader 1973, p. 130.
13. *AS* 13.18–21, Moreover *AS* (13.23–4) says that the teachings of the Veda and the Pāśupata tell the indirect worship.
14. *AS* 13.21–2, Moreover *AS* (13.22) says the that the teachings of the Sāttvata (Pāñcarātra) tell the direct worship.
15. See Schrader 1973, p. 130.
16. *AS* 13.25.
17. *AS* 13.26, Moreover *AS* (13.27–8) says that the *yoga* gives the self-control (*yama*) that direct knowledge requires.
18. See Gupta 1972, p. xxxi.
19. *LT* 15.19–23.
20. See Gupta 1972, p. xxxvi, *dvitīyaṃ sāṃkhya-vijñānam upāyaṃ śṛṇu sāṃpratam* / (*LT* 15.23).
21. See Gupta 1972, p. xxxii.
22. Ibid.
23. See Ikebe 2000, p. 225.
24. See M. Tokunaga, 'Bhakti : Kami heno sin'ai to kie' *Indo Shiso*, no. 2, Tokyo, 1989, p. 194.
25. See Gupta 1972, p. xxxii.
26. See Tokunaga, op.cit., pp. 185; 196.
27. See Koyama 1987.
28. Madhva agrees that the meditation (*upāsanā*) of the Goddess Śrī (=Lakṣmī) is also a means of emancipation. But he says that it is inferior and more troublesome than, meditation of Nārāyaṇa. Therefore we can say that the Goddess does not play a major role in the salvation theory of Madhva. Yet Madhva does not prohibit or exclude meditation of the Goddess. He only expands the object of the worship from the God to the Goddess. So we can imagine that a lot of elements of the Pāñcarātra which

emphasize worship of the Goddess being involved in the philosophical system of Madhva. In this article I found similarities between his theory and the theory of the Pāñcarātra, particularly the Lakṣmī-tantra, and conclude that because he used the *LT* (or similar texts), he had to import the elements of the worship of the Goddess which are described in that text for his salvation theory.

REFERENCES

Gonda, J., *Medieval Religious Literature in Sanskrit: A History of Indian Literature*, vol. 2, rasc. 1, Wiesbaden: Otto Harrassowitz, 1977.

Ikebe, H., 'Madhva's Salvation Theory', *The Way to Liberation*, New Delhi: 2000.

Koyama, T., 'Three Practical Ways in the Bhāgavata-Purāṇa', *Memoirs of Taisho University*, 1987.

Matsubara, M., 'Vyūha Theory in the Early Pāñcarātra: The Nārāyaṇīya Section of the Mahābhārata 12th Book', *The Mikkyo Bunka*, Koyasan, no. 172, 1990.

Pandurangi, K.T., *Essentials of Gitabhashya and Gitatatparya of Sri Madhwacharya*, Bangalore, 1987

Sanjukta Gupta, *Lakṣmī Tantra, A Pāñcarātra Text*, Leiden: E.J. Brill, 1972.

Schrader, F.O., *Introduction to the Pāñcarātra and the Ahirbudhnya Saṃhitā*. Madras: Adyar Library, 1973.

6

The Concept of Bhakti in the Tantric Tradition

KATSUYUKI IDA

The purpose of this paper is to observe how the concept of bhakti or 'devotion' has been accepted in the Hindu Tantric tradition. We will see that Tantric scriptures changed the idea of bhakti towards the divinity after the early medieval period in India, as per their own needs.

As L. Dumont pointed out, Bhaktism, or devotionalism is one of the major means to attain, through 'participating'[1] directly with God, final liberation (*mukti*). The devotee (*bhakta*), with the favour of God conferred him in return for enthusiastic devotion, attains the identity with his God. In this case, the immediate relationship between the devotee and the divinity is established. This is explained by Dumont as follows: 'As distinct from Tantrism, this, in my opinion, is a sanyasic development, an invention of the renouncer. This religion of love supposes two perfectly individualized terms; in order to conceive of a personal Lord there must also be a believer who sees himself as an individual' (Dumont 1980: 282).

On the other hand, Dumont argued that in Tantrism the aim is to attain final liberation through worldly enjoyment (*bhoga*), as a rejection of Vedic asceticism.

> There is also a large branch of Hinduism where I believe we can see the rejection of ascetic renunciation and also, in its place, that reversal of values we looked for earlier. This is Tantrism. An essential rite in the tantric cult, the *pañcatattva*, consists of the sacramental enjoyment of all that is forbidden or despised in ordinary life: meat and fish, alcohol, sexual intercourse. (Dumont 1980: 279)

Although individuals in both Tantrism and Bhaktism eagerly seek final liberation—which means becoming one with the supreme deity—the former is held as a complement or transcendent to Vedic asceticism, while the latter is a religion of individuals, and a product of the renouncer's thoughts and mysticism (ibid.: 285–6). In that case, how could it be possible for the concept of bhakti to be accepted by Hindu Tantrism, which is, as Dumont pointed out, a religion of the 'man-in-the-world'?

Presenting my conclusion in advance, I suggest that Hindu Tantrism is little influenced by the concept of bhakti—the enthusiastic devotion to God seen in Bhaktism, through which individuals attain final liberation. Instead, Tantrism, especially what Dumont called the 'conformist right-hand Tantrism', emphasizes devotion to the preceptor (*gurubhakti*), not to God.

Let us begin with the general concept of bhakti. While focusing on the usage of this word in classical Sanskrit literature, M. Hara offered suggestions that are valuable to our discussion. According to his analysis, 'bhakti has a personal connotation and implies a human relation'; furthermore, it implies 'one of a reverential or religious character'. He adds,

> We find construed with bhakti words which denote a reverential bow (*nam-*, *namra* etc.), courtesy (*upacāra*) or the granting of honour (*pūj-*). When we speak of a religious character, we are referring to a theistic, or more precisely, monotheistic religion. (Hara 1964: 132)

In addition, Hara claims that there is a connection between *śraddhā* (faith, belief, or trust) and bhakti, pointing out that the former is a fundamental principle, and the latter is a developed mode of it (ibid.: 145).

If we look into the Hindu epics, we will find good examples of this bhakti in the *Mahābhārata*. Devotion to Śiva (*śivabhakti*) appears in the seventh chapter of the Sauptikaparvan.[2] Furthermore, the famous *Bhagavadgītā*, inserted in the sixth book of the *Mahābhārata,* is popularly known as the first work focusing on bhakti as a means to attain final liberation (*mokṣa*).[3] In this scripture, it is repeatedly taught that it is by God's grace that individuals attain final liberation to become one with the highest God, Bhagavat (*BhG* 18.54–6).

In the wake of the above examples, the idea of a mutual

relationship between individuals and their gods was widespread in South Asia. After the seventh century, particularly in the Vaiṣṇava tradition, this tendency became widely popular even among the lower classes,[4] and influenced the Sanskritic culture of the brahmins as well. We may notice the resonance of such popular Bhaktism in, for instance, the *Bhāgavata-purāṇa*. Furthermore, the concept of devotion was also adapted, among others, within the Vedānta salvationism—as typically shown by Rāmānuja—as a primary/supplementary means of final liberation.

In addition, Tantrism was influenced by Bhaktism as well. We will examine the concept of bhakti in the Śaiva and Śākta scriptures in the following sections. In this paper, I use the word 'Tantrism' in a broad manner, to refer to the Śaiva and Śākta traditions; however, I will not use it with reference to the Tantric Vaiṣṇavas such as the Pāñcarātras.[5]

Prior to investigation of the concept of bhakti within Hindu Tantrism, I should point out that some of the materials utilized in this discussion are comparatively new scriptures, sometimes dated after the fourteenth century. Since the main purpose of this paper is to abstract the typical reaction pattern of Tantric scriptures towards the concept of bhakti, rather than follow the development of this concept within the Tantric tradition, I will refer to my sources without minute chronological details. Furthermore, I will roughly classify the usage of the word bhakti in Tantric scriptures, and try to understand how the concept changed within these texts. In this way, we will see how the transition from *devatābhakti* to *gurubhakti* took place.

It is only for the sake of convenience that Śaiva and Śākta are treated as separate traditions in this paper. We should suppose that there is no distinctive gap between the two, as A. Padoux stresses.[6] However, it must be noticed that the characteristics of Tantrism are often expressed more radically—and typically—in the Śākta tradition, which can be considered as a derivative of the Śaiva tradition.

DEVOTIONAL SONG FOR ŚIVA: *STAVACINTĀMAṆI*

To begin with, we will examine the *Stavacintāmaṇi* (*StC*), a Śaivasiddhānta scripture written by Bhaṭṭanārāyaṇa, who was a disciple of Vasugupta, presumably in the ninth century. This short composition seems to be 'possibly conceived immediately after the poet's return from the state of complete absorption' (Gonda 1977: 32). The author of *StC* enthusiastically expresses his feelings of bhakti to the many aspects of Śiva as follows:

In order to make unspotted the divine eyes of intelligence blinded by the impurity consisting of illusion (*māyā*), Oh Lord! devotion to you is a supreme ointment. Give [me] the state which is free from fear, which consists of happiness and is unique and imperishable. Come to me, quickly[7]. Oh God! What are you waiting for? (*StC* 88–9).

This text is infused with the sentiment of bhakti, resembling the devotional literature of the Vaiṣṇava cult. Extremely eager for an epiphany of Śiva, the devotee imagines him as a personified entity and the object of unstinting dedication, which differs greatly from the idea of *brahman* in the Advaita Vedānta teachings. According to *StC*, it is with the grace (*prasāda*) of Śiva that the devotee will attain final liberation (*StC* 30). This notion of bhakti is distinctly expressed in the following verses:

The one who has you as a foundation should contemplate intently as follows: 'I am fortunate. I am the one who has accomplished what is to be accomplished. I am great.' Your Honour is the One who makes every auspicious and inauspicious thing by Himself. Then, devotion to Your Honour is only the mother of auspicious things, Oh Lord! 'Do you fully enter the purified (*prasanna*) mind? Oh Master! Or, would [that mind] be made fully purified because of your entrance?' Thus, people are oscillating. But it is certain that only your standing here (inside of one's self) purifies the mind, Oh Master! It is a fulfilment, it is the highest position. (*StC* 115–18)

It is evident that the deepest feeling of love for a personified god and a firm belief in his grace are expressed eloquently in these devotional verses. The grace of Śiva takes the form of his entry (*praveśa*) into the devotee's mind. This is explained by Bhaṭṭa as purifying one's own mind or fulfilment (*siddhi*). Individuals are now involved in an intimate relationship with God, no longer requiring the help of intermediaries such as knowledge (*jñāna*) and ritual (*karman*).

With a few exceptions, strong feelings for and direct relationships with the divinity do not feature in most Śaivāgamas written in Sanskrit, regardless of whether they are theological treatises or ritual manuals. On the other hand, such a concept of bhakti became remarkably popular in the Tamil Śaivasiddhāntas.[8] However, that would take us far beyond the scope of our discussion.

BHAKTI IN THE ŚAIVA RITUAL

ŚAIVA SCRIPTURES: FROM *DEVATĀBHAKTI* TO *GURUBHAKTI*

Let us now turn to other Śaiva scriptures, primarily those concerning rituals and religious practices. The *Ajitāgama* (*AĀ*), a ritualistic manual probably written between tenth and twelfth centuries,[9] illustrates the well-organized ritual system of the Śaivasiddhānta school. Here, we will observe a typical example of bhakti to Śiva, expressed as ritual procedures. Chapter 76 of *AĀ* provides an explanation of both the rules for walking in clockwise direction (*pradakṣiṇa*) around the object of worship (images, *liṅga*s, sanctuaries, etc.) and for saluting (*namaskāra*). In this chapter, the word bhakti appears several times.

> If a man performs a salutation in front of Śiva once and with devotion, he obtains fruits much better than [the fruits] of the Horse Sacrifice (*aśvamedha*). If [he performs it] in five parts of [his] limbs, [he will obtain] three times [of the fruits] as said before. If [he performs it] in eight parts of [his] limbs, [the fruits] will be eight times. All of which is offered to Śiva, and the rituals performed [to Him], if [done] with devotion, are said to [give] unlimited times [the fruits]. Salutation performed to Śiva, even by wicked men, or with no devotion, or even once, will become the remover of all sins. Therefore, if a man regularly salutes the *liṅga* once and with devotion, he will have all his desires gratified, and rejoice with Śiva. (*AĀ* 76.23cd–27)

It is said that even a man who lacks devotion will attain his goal merely by saluting Śiva. Since the efficacy of the salutation is emphasized in this context, it seems to be evident that personal devotion to God is basically considered to be indispensable to the act of worshipping or any other religious practice. Without devotion the practitioner will never be able to gain the fruits of his practice.

The following is a quotation from the *Svacchandatantra* (*SvT*),[10] which is classified in the Bhairavāgama group and is mentioned by Abhinavagupta (tenth century). This portion, from the first chapter of *SvT*, is part of the description of the disciple whom the guru must avoid:

> Even if initiated (*dīkṣita*), one who is connected with deception, [who is] fraudulent, cruel, untrue, fond of contention, lustful, filled with impatience, devoid of devotion to Śiva .(*Śivabhakti*), and disgraces the *guru*'s instructions, does not partake of the final liberation (*muktibhaj*). (*SvT* 1.20–1)

Such references to the devotion to Śiva are too many to enumerate, and appear not only in the Siddhāntas, but also in the Trikas, Śāktas, and other Tantric traditions.[11] This requirement of devotion for religious practices reminds us of Hara's analysis. In this sense, the word bhakti is frequently used in the instrumental case, and carries a more general meaning of faith or belief.[12]

In Chapter 4 of the Caryāpāda (CP) in the *Mataṅgaparameśvarāgama* (*MPA*)—a important text among the secondary scriptures (*upāgama*)—there are five types of devotion:

> Five kinds of devotion are spoken about. They are defined as follows: by speech, mind, body, ritual (*karman*), and mental effort in the heart. For the sake of the man who is filled by this perpetually unhindered energy, and whose affection has vanished, the nature of Śiva appears manifested. (*MPA* CP 4.12–13)

Such enumeration of the types of devotion, which occurs widely seen in the Hindu tradition,[13] may denote all the practicable means showing their devotion. Then, such expressions suggest us that bhakti to the divinity should be understood as not only a mental attitude—some kind of trust, faith, or love, regardless of its intensity or immediacy—but also as a concrete action.

Devotion to the *Guru* in the Śaiva Scriptures

Disciples offer their devotion not only on Śiva, but also on fire (*agni*), their *guru*, scriptures (*śāstra*), and so forth. Once again, a good example of this can be taken from *SvT*:

> The disciple endowed with compassion; who is firm; devoid of deceit and deception; devoted to the divinity, fire, and [to his] *guru* (*devatāgnigurubhakta*); devoted to the scriptures (*śāstrabhakta*); who maintains firm observance [of the precepts]; who maintains willing obedience to [his] *guru*; and who

is joined with thoroughly extinguished senses, such a disciple should become a recipient of favour (*anugrahabhajana*). (*SvT* 1.18cd–20ab)

This statement explains what is required of disciples. As mentioned above, devotion to the god in question is indispensable to ordinary religious practice. In addition, devotion to fire, the *guru*, and scriptures are also mentioned. Similar examples are found in other texts as well: *TA* 8.334 (*guru, deva, agni, śāstra*); 17.73 (*guru, deva, śāstra*); 17.96 (*deva, agni, guru*); *NT* 22.71cd–72ab (*guru, deva, agni*); and *ĪŚGP* 35.9 (*guru, deva, mantra*).[14] We find in these statements also the word bhakti is utilized in the more general sense of 'faith' or 'belief'. It is a basic mental attitude towards the necessaries of religious activity, which can be contrasted with love or the strong devotional sentiment seen in the *StC*.

I will now propose two points. First, devotional service offered to *agni* is often described within these scriptures. This is most significant because it implies that there is a kind of continuity between the Vedic (or the 'orthodox' Brahmanical) lifestyle and customs and the Tantric traditions. In the orthodox Brahmanical convention, when twice-born students reside with their *guru* in order to study the Vedas, their duties include the kindling of the sacrificial fire (*agnikārya*) everyday. This is one of the most important duties for ascetic students (*brahmacārin*). We can observe such customary rules mainly in the Dharmaśāstras: *YS* 1.25, 35, 96; *MS* 2.69; *Arthaśāstra* 1.3.10, etc.[15]

Second, devotion to the preceptor (*gurubhakti*) is mentioned throughout the Śaiva Āgamas. As a basis for such devotion, the *guru*'s prominence is frequently discussed. The following passage is from Chapter 78 of *AĀ*, and mentions the characteristics of the teacher (*ācāryalakṣaṇavidhi*):

People call the teacher Śiva, and Śiva is said to be the teacher. If one knows indivisibility, he is said to be conversant with the Veda (*vedavid*). Then *śiva*[16] is said to be twofold, motionless (*sthāvara*) and moving (*jaṅgama*). Then, Śiva is said to be motionless, the teacher is said to be moving [Śiva]. Thus, one should perform that which is from the consecration ceremony (*pratiṣṭhā*) to the praising (*arcana*), with the help of the moving [Śiva] only.[17] (*AĀ* 78.29cd–31)

When a disciple performs a Śaiva ritual with the help of his *guru*, the latter is understood to be a 'moving Śiva' (*jaṅgama*).[18] Such statements are frequently found in the context of the initiatory ritual (*dīkṣā*). This passage appears right beside the rule of *dīkṣā* in Chapter 77. Generally speaking, *dīkṣā* is understood as ritual performed for the purpose of removing impurity in initiates and bestowing them with divine power derived from Śiva.[19] Throughout the initiatory ritual, the *guru* who conducts the initiates is considered to be a representative of Śiva, or Śiva himself. In other words, only Śiva is allowed to perform an initiatory ritual, so as to transfer his power to the initiates. Accordingly, it is quite natural that these Śaiva scriptures should repeatedly emphasize bhakti to the *guru*, who represents Śiva. There are several examples of the identification of *guru* and divinity, especially in the Śākta literature.

DEVOTION TO THE *GURU* IN THE ŚĀKTA SCRIPTURES

Guru as Divinity

The idea of *gurubhakti* becomes more acute within the Śākta tradition, which is recognized as a branch (or still as a development) of the Śaiva tradition, mainly of the Kaula group.

First, we shall examine the *Kulārṇavatantra* (*KA*), one of the most important Śākta-Kaula scriptures, which appeared no later than the fifteenth century.[20] Interestingly enough, devotion to the *guru*'s sandals (*pādukā*) and the relationship between *guru* and disciple are dealt with between the Chapters 12 and 14 of this text.[21] Similar to the Śaiva scriptures, *KA* also insists that the *guru* is none other than Śiva himself (*KA* 13.60). It is also mentioned that the *guru*'s compassion (*kṛpā*) is the basis for final liberation (12.13); he is neither mortal (*martya*) nor an ordinary man (12.45–6); he is father, mother, god Maheśvara (12.49). Moreover, *KA* states:

> 'I, Śiva, have no form, and [I am] not perceptible to humans, Oh Goddess.' Thus by the form of reverend *guru*, he (Śiva) protects virtuous disciples. The Supreme Śiva himself, constrained by the human skin before the eyes of men, secretly wanders on the earth for the sake of [giving] the grace to the good disciple. For the sake of protection for good devotees, although formless, Śiva who is the warehouse of compassion, having form, makes an effort in the world as if a mundane being (*saṃsārin*). Concealing the eye on the forehead, the digit of the moon and the two arms, I would stay on the ground in the form of a *guru*. (*KA* 13.53–6)

Further examples can be seen not only in the *KA* (7.68; 10.59–60) but also in other Śākta scriptures (*YH* 2.50–1ab; *TR* 1.29cd–30, 1.38; etc.). It seems clear that by such identification with Śiva, the *guru*'s importance was guaranteed and the disciple's devotion to his *guru* was justified.

Next, we shall examine the Nāthastotra, which comprises the last part of the first chapter of the *Tantrarājatantra* (*TR*)—scripture of the Śrīvidyā sect and probably written during the fifteenth century:[22]

> Oh Lord (Nātha)! Venerable one! I salute you, Śiva, the one having the form of Śiva, who perfected the descent of knowledge. Oh One who possesses many forms as his own! [I salute you] young, having nine forms, having one form as highest reality, splendour splitting all darkness of ignorance, filled with thought, you. [I salute you] self-dependent, having the shape which is prepared with compassion, having the Śiva as own nature, obedient to the devotees, having the pleasant form among the pleasant. [I salute you] the discriminative among the discriminating, reflective (*vimarśa*) among the reflecting, illuminated (*prakāśa*) among the illuminating, embodiment of intelligence of the intelligent. He (the disciple) should salute [the *guru*] from the front, both sides, back, above, below. Always grant me Your Honour's seat with the form of the heart.[23] (*TR* 1.96–100)

It is interesting that the words *prakāśa* and *vimarśa* are used for describing the *guru*. In Śaiva theology, Śiva as a Supreme Reality (or Śakti in the case of the Śākta tradition) consists of two main principles, *prakāśa* and *vimarśa*. The entire material world and all individuals evolve from the integration of these two principles. We should realize that the above expression is based on the concept of the essential identity of *guru*, Śiva, and Supreme Reality.

However, it should be recalled that the highest reality in the Śākta theory is Śakti, and not Śiva. Śiva has a mere subordinate position within the Śākta tradition, thereby giving Devī the central position as the primary principle of the world. Thus, it is likely that when the Śākta scriptures emphasize the *guru*'s importance and the necessity of the disciple's devotional services to him, they consider the *guru* a manifestation of the goddess, unique and of the highest divinity. In reality, however, the *guru* is mostly identified with Śiva, who has only secondary importance as Devī's spouse in Śākta theory. This inconsistency can be seen more explicitly in the second chapter of *TR*, which explains the two types of consecratory rituals (*pratiṣṭhā*):

He (disciple) should pay a fee to the *guru* who has the nature of Śiva. [He should offer] all of one's own, half of it, yet half of it, or by his order. If not, how will his (*guru*'s) power (*śakti*) would be transferred to him ? (*TR* 2.48cd–49)

Having invoked *vidyā* from his own innermost part (heart), having confirmed and worshipped [*vidyā*], [the guru] with the nature of Devī and with a perfect mind should utter in the [disciple's] ear [the *vidyā*] accompanied by the depositing (*nyāsa*) thirty times. He (disciple) should meditate with the mind on the unity of the divinity, the *guru*, *mantra*, self, and reality (*tattva*). He (disciple) should mutter [the *vidyā*] a hundred times. One who is in front of him (*guru*) should stay next to [the *guru*] for three days. (*TR* 2.54–5)

We find that here the *guru* is identified with Śiva as well as Devī, in a series of consecratory ritual procedures. One explanation for this inconsistency may be that the *guru*'s identity that is elaborated in the former Śaiva sects is still retained in the Śākta scriptures.

WORSHIP OF THE *GURU*

The following question arises: What is the actual content of such devotion to the *guru*? In other words, how do disciples express their devotion to their *guru* ? *KA* explains how a disciple should serve his *guru* in his daily life. The disciple must show respect for the *guru* through his mind, speech, and behaviour (*KA* 12.50).[24] More specifically, the disciple must keep his body for the *guru*, procure wealth for the *guru*, and even sacrifice his own life for the *guru* (12.53); he must offer the *guru* all his possessions and food (12.55). On the other hand, disciples must not desire the *guru*'s belongings or wife (12.74). Such statements are scattered in several Śākta scriptures (*TR* 2.82–3; *JA* 24.57–9ab; *KJN* 12.8–9; etc.) besides *KA*.

A detailed explanation is provided in *TR* regarding the ways to celebrate and perform services for the *guru*:

Then on the birthday of the *guru*, one should carry out a celebration respectfully. [He should offer] a special worship, a meal for the *yogins*, and homage to his (*guru*'s) feet. If [the *guru*] to be worshiped has died, or is far away, he (disciple) should worship the eldest son [of *guru*] or such. If he is staying in the same area, at the distance of one *yojana*, [disciple should perform] daily services. With a distance of six *yojana*s, [disciple should perform services] once as each season ripens, every year. If [the *guru*] is near, [disciple should perform] services following his order. He [should offer to the *guru*] a seat (*āsana*), a couch, cloth, ornaments, sandals (*pādukā*), shade, wife, and anything else the *guru* wants, and then he should worship. (*TR* 1.31–4)

Noting the demands for service to the *guru*, as mentioned above, we can recall the relationship between the *guru* and his disciples described in the post-Vedic scriptures. After performing the initiatory ceremony (*upanayana*), a disciple must reside with his *guru*, and offer him many kinds of service until his graduation ceremony (*samāvartana*). For example, the Dharmaśāstras mention the following: 'The disciple must give whatever he has got to his *guru*, and serve him through mind, speech, and behaviour' (*YS* 1.27);[25] the disciple must hold his *guru*'s feet (*pāda*) reverently with both hands (*MS* 2.71–72). Furthermore, the *MS* plainly praises the preceptor as well as his parents, regarding them as divinities:

The preceptor is an embodiment of Brahmā; the father is an embodiment of Prajāpati; the mother is an embodiment of the Earth (Pṛthivī); one's own brother is an embodiment of oneself. Healing the pain that [one's] mother and father endured at one's birth can not be possible even in a hundred years. He should do both of them favours constantly, and to his preceptor, always. When these three are satisfied, all penance (*tapas*) is completed. (*MS* 2.226–8)

We can easily recognize that these examples of praise of the *guru* in the Dharmaśāstras are very similar to those of the Tantric tradition. Then, it might be possible to say that devotion to the *guru* has its roots in the post-Vedic era.

Let us now return to the Tantric text. In addition to these services to the *guru*, a more stylized manner of adoration, or the worship of the *guru*'s sandals (*pādukā*) or feet (*pāda*), is described in many Tantric scriptures. It is widely known that there is, in Indian tradition, a custom of saluting by prostrating oneself before the sandals of a respectable person, in a physical expression of homage.[26]

The worship of the sandals became an abstraction in the Tantric tradition. *KA* and other Tantras refer to the *mantra* of sandals (*pādukāmantra*), which is composed of seven letters: *pādukāṃ pūjayāmi* (I worship [the *guru*'s] sandals).[27] It is quite plausible that disciples originally prostrated themselves before their *guru*'s sandals while reciting this *mantra*. On the other hand, we come across an interesting statement in *KA* showing us that the recitation of this *mantra* is often considered to be a means to fulfilment (*siddhi*) as well as a way to express adoration for the *guru*:

> One who recites the *pādukā* [*mantra*] with devotion even once, Oh Goddess! He is separated from all sins and obtains the highest stage. Whether pure or impure, if he bears *pādukā* in mind with devotion, he easily achieves religious merit, wealth, desires, and final liberation. (*KA* 12.9–10)

Contrary to the act of prostration before a person's feet, which can be seen in the daily life of the Hindus, this *mantra* gives us another image of the same act. The efficacy of this *mantra* for the purpose of obtaining fulfilment is frequently emphasized in most of the Tantras and also in the Purāṇas.[28] It is commonly said that the disciple will attain either final liberation (*mukti*) or mundane benefits (*bhukti*) by simply reciting this *pādukāmantra*.

Rendering service to the *guru*, reciting the *pādukāmantra*, and performing other kinds of worship,[29] the disciple attains the favour of his *guru*. It is often stated in the Śākta scriptures that the *guru*'s glance, filled with compassion, liberates his disciples.[30] Here, we can recognize the important characteristic of Tantrism, that is, the tendency to reinterpret a ritual performance as a means of final liberation.

CONCLUSION

We have outlined the concept of bhakti in the Tantric tradition. The major points are as follows.

First, enthusiastic devotion to the divinity, as demonstrated in Devotionalism, was not commonly accepted in Tantric tradition. Some of the Śaivasiddhānta verses, evidently influenced by the devotional movement, shared a strong devotional sentiment towards the Śiva. *StC* is a good example of this, as we have seen. However, this type of devotion did not become mainstream in Tantrism. With the exception of some *stotras* individually composed by devout authors as an expression of their religious passion, most of the Tantric scriptures written in Sanskrit scarcely show such enthusiastic devotion to the highest divinity.

While ritualism and philosophical reflection developed in such Sanskritic Śaiva Āgamas, the idea of an emotional and sometimes orgiastic devotion was carried over into the Tamil Śaiva-siddhāntas.

Second, instead of bhakti to the divinity, bhakti to the *guru* is remarkably emphasized in the Tantric scriptures, particularly in the Śāktas. In Tantric literature, roughly speaking, the word bhakti can be used in two different ways. First, as faith or belief in the divinity, which is clearly different from enthusiastic devotion. As Hara observes, it may be possible to say that such bhakti is developed from the *śraddhā*. Secondly, there is bhakti towards one's own *guru*. This usage can be derived from the former. Nevertheless, adding emphasis on its practical aspects, that is, contrary to the Devotionalism—which emphasizes mental devotion—Tantrism consistently insists on practical activity such as offerings, services, and so on. This emphasis on service of the *guru* may reveal the occupational aspect of the Tantric sects, which were widely popularized among the many social classes. It is quite evident, if we recall that the Śākta scriptures, without adequate consideration of theological consistency, speak of the *guru* not as Śakti but as Śiva. It seems that the importance and exalted status of the preceptor in Vedism, in which the same Brahmanical values are shared by all members, was obvious. On the other hand, in the medieval era, the *guru*'s authority was much needed to be assured in Tantrism, which had become more accessible to many social groups. While Devotionalism is grounded in the personal experience of mystic unity with the highest God, Tantrism regards the *guru*, who manages the ritual procedure and teaches the truth, as necessary for an individual's pursuit of final liberation. Hence the great importance of identifying the *guru* with the divinity is increased to the maximum.

Third, we may trace such *gurubhakti* back to the Brahmanical tradition, as typically found in the Dharmaśāstras. An emphasis on the *guru*'s importance can be observed not only in Tantrism but also in the 'orthodoxy' of Hinduism, where they consider themselves as 'Vedic'. We have seen that devoted service to the *guru* and maintenance of the sacrificial fire were among the duties of the Tantric disciples as well as of the *brahmacārin*s. This corresponds to Dumont's schema in which devotionalism is a religion of individuals, whereas Tantrism is an extension of the Vedic religion as group religion, or 'a religion in the world'.

Since Dumont ignores the fact that Bhaktism and Tantrism are theoretical frameworks reconstructed from the sources written in different religious situations, we are tempted to consider that there are two different religions. However, Bhaktism and Tantrism should be recognized as two aspects of the same religion, frequently coexisting in individuals. Returning to our discussion, it is likely that the functional importance of the *guru* has more to do with ritualism. From the theoretical aspect, the *guru*—identified with the highest divinity—can be regarded as abstract rather than personified. In unification with the highest reality, attained through service to one's *guru* and obtaining his grace, we can find a logic similar to that of Tantric ritualism. In other words, since all matter in the world is derived from the highest reality (the Goddess, in this case), individuals can attain unity with that Goddess with the help of devices such as *mantra*s and *yantra*s, frequently held to be representations of the highest reality. It seems quite natural that, within Tantrism, the concept of bhakti as devotion to the divinity has changed to devotion to the preceptor. We may consider Tantric ritualism as having developed from Vedic ritualism. In other words, such ritualism bears the aspect of religion in the world, and it never prevents devout individuals from building personal relationships with their God.

ABBREVIATIONS

AĀ (*Ajitāgama*)	:	*The Great Tantra of Ajita*, ed. N.R. Bhatt, J. Filliozat and P. Filliozat, 5 vols., Delhi: Motilal Banarsidass, 2005; *Ajitāgama*, ed. N.R. Bhatt, 2 vols., Pondichery: Institut Français d'Indologie, 1964–7.
ĪŚGP	:	*Īśānaśivagurudevapaddhati by Īśānaśivagurudeva*, ed. T. Ganapati Sastri, 4 vols., Delhi: Bharatiya Vidya Prakashan, 1988.

KA : *Kulārṇavatantra*, ed. T. Vidyāratna, Delhi: Motilal Banarsidass, 1965.
KC : *Kulacūḍāmaṇi Nigama*, ed. A. Avalon, Madras: Ganesh & Co., 1956.
KJN : *Kaulajñānanirṇaya of The School of Matsyendranātha*, ed. P.C. Bagchi, Varanasi: Prācya Prakāśan, 1986.
JA : *Jñānārṇavatantram*, et. G. Gokhale, Pune: Ānandāshram, 1952.
TR : *Tantrarājatantra*, ed. J.L. Shastri, Delhi: Motilal Banarsidass, 1981.
TA : *Tantrāloka of Mahāmaheśvara Śri Abhinavaguptapadācārya with Two Commentaries Viveka by Ācārya Śrī Jayaratha Nīrakṣīraviveka by Dr. Paramhans Mishra Hans*, ed. P. Mishra, 8 vols., Varanasi: Sampurnanand Sanskrit University, 1992–9.
NT : *Netratantram with the Commentary Udyota of Kṣemarāja*, ed. V. Dvivedi, Delhi: Parimal Publishers, 2000.
NP : *Nāradīyamahāpurāṇa*, Delhi: Nag Publishers, 1985.
BhG : *Bhagavatgītā in the Mahābhātata*, ed. and tr. J.A.B. van Buitenen, Chicago: The University of Chicago Press, 1981.
Mṛgendrāgama (Kriyāpāda et Caryāpāda) avec le commentaire de Bhaṭṭa-Nārāyaṇakaṇṭha, ed. N.R. Bhatt, Pondichery: Institut Français d'Intologie, 1962.
MPA : *Mataṅgapārameśvarāgama avec le commentaire de Bhaṭṭa Rāma-kaṇṭha*, ed. N.R. Bhatt, 2 vols., Pondichery: Institut Français d'Intologie, 1977–82.
MS : *Manusmṛti with the Sanskrit Commentary Manvarthamuktāvali of Kulluka Bhaṭṭa*, ed. J.L. Shastri, Delhi: Motilal Banarsidass, 1983.
YS : *Yājñavalkyasmṛti*, ed. N.R. Acharya, Nag Publishers, 1985.
YH : *Yoginīhṛdayam*, ed. V. Dviveda, Delhi: Motilal Banarsidass, 1988.
StC : *The Stavacintāmaṇi of Bhaṭṭa Nārāyaṇa with Commentary by Kṣemarāja*, ed. Mukunda Rama Shasrti, KSTS 10, Srinagar, 1918.
SP : *Somaśambhupaddhati*, ed. H. Brunner-Lachaux. 4 vols., Pondicherry: Institut Français d'Intologie, 1963–98.
Saundaryalaharī of Śrī Śaṅkara Bhagavatpadācārya, ed. A. Kuppuswami, Delhi: Nag Publishers.
SvT : *Śrī Svacchandatantra with Commentary Uddyota by Mahāmaheśvara Śrī Kṣemarāja*, ed. V. Dvivedi, 5 vols., Delhi: Motilal Banarsidass, 1992–3.

NOTES

1. Dumont 1980: 282.
2. In the story, Mahādeva (Śiva) made his appearance before Droṇa's son Aśvatthāman, who showed his devotion to Mahādeva, and granted him

protection. According to Dhavamony 1971: 75, however, 'the sacrificial connotation and reciprocal participation are still prevalent, and the pure notion of love of God is only implicitly, if at all, contained in these manifestations of bhakti'.

3. Zaehner 1969: 26–36.
4. Cf. Fuller 2004: 157; Brockington 1997: 133.
5. For a discussion on the definition of the term 'Tantrism', see Gupta 1979 and Padoux 2002.
6. Padoux 1990: 52.
7. In his commentary, *Vivṛtti*, Kṣemarāja explains this as 'enter (*ā*-√*viś*) into my own nature, rapidly'.
8. For the development of bhakti in the Tamil Śaivasiddhānta movement, see Dhavamony 1971: 126ff.; Zvelebil 1974: 54–8.
9. Cf. *AĀ* I, p. 38; Gonda 1977: 195ff.
10. Cf. Gonda 1977: 205–6.
11. 'After investigating by an examination of what is said by elders, the *guru* should give the grace to those who are impelled by the power of the great god (Maheśa)' (*Mṛgendrāgama* CP 1.23).
12. Here, for example, is a verse quoted from *SP*: 'He should offer food to the one having the *liṅga*, the twice born (*dvija*), the blind, and the poor, with devotion' (*SP* II, p. 179, 120ab).
13. See *YS* 1.156.
14. In Śākta-Kaula scriptures: *KJN* 12.9, 14.68, 20.18 (*guru*, *kaulāgama*), 14.8 (*deva*, *agni*, *yati*, *yoginī*); *KC* 2.17 (*guru*, *deva*).
15. Furthermore, we can find many examples of the *agnikārya* as a duty of the *brahmacārin* in the Gṛhyasūtras as well. See Einoo 1992.
16. In this portion, the word *śiva* is used in the neuter.
17. While Bhatt's old edition omitted this portion, his new edition adopted it from only one manuscript.
18. Dumont mentions that there is a social group called Jaṅgama in the northern districts of Mysore whose members are employed as religious functionaries by the Liṅgāyat sect (Dumont 1980: 189). Cf. Brockington 1997: 147. On the other hand, the contrast between the moving and the motionless is often expressed pertaining to the image of divinity. See Jansen 1995: 45.
19. 'It is true, only certain forms of *dīkṣā* can provide one with a divine state of existence or divine knowledge, but every *dīkṣā* does provide introduction into a new *sādhanā* with a new set of rules for rites and conduct (*samaya*)'. Gupta et al. 1979: 72.
20. Following Carlstedt's estimate, Bühnemann dated this text to between the eleventh and fourteenth centuries (Bühneman 1992: 61). However, there is no cogent evidence to prove this.
21. See Padoux 2000; Sakaki 2006.
22. Padoux estimates that this text dates back to the seventeenth century

(Padoux 2000: 43); However, the commentary on the *Śāradātilaka*—named *Parārthadarsa*—written at the end of fifteenth century, refers to *TR*. Thus it is reasonable to estimate that *TR* dates to the fifteenth century.

23. This is paralleled in *Nāradapurāṇa* 1.89.4cd–9ab.
24. Similar expressions can be found in *KJN* 12.8. On this point, refer to section 2.1 of this paper.
25. Cf. *MS* 2.192.
26. Cf. Jain-Neubauer 2000: 56ff. ; Fuller 2004: 3–4.
27. See *TR* 2.13–14; *YH* 2.78cd, *SU* 59. Then, other type of *pādukāmantra* can be seen in *JA* 16.63–4.
28. *NP* 3.65.50.
29. Cf. *TR* 2.23–33.
30. *YH* 2.84 and *Dīpikā*. Moreover, the idea of final liberation being acquired from a glance of compassion by the divinity can be seen in many places, cf. *Saundaryalaharī* 6 and 22.

REFERENCES

Bühnemann, G., 1992, 'On Puraścarana: Kulārṇavatantra, Chapter 15', *Ritual and Speculation in Early Tantrism*, Albany: SUNY Press, pp. 61–106.

Brockington, J.L., 1997, *The Sacred Thread: A Short History of Hinduism*, 2nd edn., Oxford: Oxford University Press.

Dhavamony, M., 1971, *Love of God: According to Śaivasiddhānta*, Oxford: Oxford University Press.

Dumont, L., 1980, *Homo Hierarchicus: The Caste System and Its Implications*, rev. English edn., Chicago: University of Chicago Press.

Einoo, S., 1992, 'Some Aspects of the Ritual Development in the Gṛhyasūtras', in Japanese, *The Memoirs of the Institute of Oriental Culture*, no. 118, pp. 43–86.

Fuller, C.J., 2004, *The Camphor Flame: Popular Hinduism and Society in India*, rev. edn., Princeton: Princeton University Press.

Gonda, J., 1977, *Medieval Religious Literature in Sanskrit*, A History of Indian Literature, vol. II, Fasc. 1, Wiesbaden: Otto Harrassowitz.

Gupta S., D. Hones and T. Goudriaan, 1979, *Hindutantrism*, Handbuch der Orientalistik, 2. Abt. 4, Band 2, Leiden: E.J. Brill.

Hara, M., 1963, 'Note on Two Sanskrit Religious Terms: Bhakti and *Śraddhā*', *IIJ* 7, pp. 124–45.

Jansen, R., 1995, *Die Bhavani von Tuljapur: Religionsgeschichtliche Studie des Kultes einer Gottin der indischen Volksreligion*, Stuttgart: Franz Steiner Verlag.

Jain-Neubauer, J., 2000, *Feet & Footwear in Indian Culture*, Toronto: Bata Shoe Museum.

Takashima, J., 1992, '*Dīkṣā* in the *Tantrāloka*', *Memoirs of the Institute of Oriental Culture,* no. 119, pp. 45–82.

Padoux A., 1998, 'Concerning Tantric Traditions', *Studies in Hinduism II: Miscellanea to the Phenomenon of Tantras*, pp. 9–20, VÖAW.

Padoux, A., 2000, 'The Tantric Guru', *Tantra in Practice*, Princeton: Princeton University Press, pp. 41–51.

Sakaki, K., 2006, 'Guru Worship in Natha Yoga and Sufism in Medieval India', in Japanese, *Hokkaido Journal of Indological and Buddhist studies*, no. 21, pp. 1–18.

Zaehner, R.C., 1969, *The Bhagavad Gītā: With a Commentary Based on the Original Sources*, Oxford: Oxford University Press.

Zvelebil, K.V., 1974, *Tamil Literature*, A History of Indian Literature, vol. X, Fasc. 1, Wiesbaden: Otto Harrassowitz.

7

Realization of Inner Divinity: Nātha Yogins in the Medieval Bhakti Movement

KAZUYO SAKAKI

THE PERSPECTIVE OF THIS STUDY

Is yoga an interiorized form of bhakti?[1] With regard to the concept of *sahaja*, Bhattacharyya (1989: xxvi) stated the following: 'The realization of God as identical with one's own self is the basis of most medieval bhakti movements'. Based on Bhattacharyya's observation, Nātha yogins can also be considered part of the bhakti movement.

The period during which the Nātha Sampradāya prevailed over almost all of India may have originated not later than the thirteenth century (Gonda 1977: 222; McGregor, 1984: 21). The Nātha Sampradāya was founded by Gorakṣanātha, a semi-legendary yogin said to have been a disciple of Matsyendranātha; it not only laid the foundation on which the active religious movement in medieval India developed, but also influenced other religious cults. It is believed that both Gorakṣanātha and Matsyendranātha amalgamated the ideas and practices of the Nātha Sampradāya with those of Tantrism and Śāktism (Gonda 1977: 221). They aimed at the realization of inner divinity through techniques based on the concept of the identity of the macrocosm and microcosm. Here the question of how they interiorized this experience—the realization of inner divinity—arose.

Most *bhakta*s achieved this realization by being in a state of ecstasy through deep piety. On the other hand, Tantrics, Siddhas, Sants, and Nātha yogins achieved it through the practical process of awakening the consciousness and transforming themselves into a divine entity in contemplation through purification, which is facilitated by *prāṇāyāma* and other yogic disciplines. This contemplation of the Oneness leads to salvation and liberation from worldly life (*jīvanmukti*), which is the ultimate objective of yoga. Tantrics, Siddhas, Sants, and Nātha yogins refer to it as a state of ultimate joy which signifies the union of the individual soul (*jīva*) with the transcendent reality that all this could be achieved through the process of purification.

Purity and impurity form the core of Hindu spiritual disciplines. Since the Vedic period, securing purity and destroying impurity have been the cardinal virtues, particularly in ritual performance and personal religious observance. Ritual purity ensures ascent to heaven and the attainment of salvation. In order to achieve it, certain vows should be observed and penances should be performed. On the other hand, the power of impurity can be channelled effectively through the equality of *karma* (*karmasāmya*); moreover, its benefits are the same as those of purity.

The purification of the body is obligatory for any Vedic ritual. In Pātañjala yoga, there are two kinds of purification: external and internal. The purification of the body, referred to as the purification of the elements (*bhūtaśuddhi* or *dehaśuddhi*), is a ritual common to both the Hindu Tantras (Pāñcarātra Vaiṣṇavism and Śaivism) and Mahāyāna Buddhism.

In Tantrism, the purification of the body is achieved by transforming the impure physical body into an individual who is qualified and suitable for the ritual. With the help of the Sāṃkhya doctrine of the evolution of the entire universe, the dissolution of the principles of the world (*tattva*) is interiorized. The ultimate objective of this ritual is to achieve a power that enables one to acquire true knowledge. With the manifestation of true knowledge through purification, impurities of the mind are removed; consequently, the individual transcends the subject–object dichotomy and is ready to realize the transcendent reality. Finally, such individuals are able to share the absolute blissful state with the *bhakta*s.

In Pātañjala yoga purification is the primary focus. Further, the result of purification is considered to extend to the entire process of yoga. Having inherited this tradition, Śaiva Nāthas also developed ways to realize purification. They developed physiological techniques through which they could transform their own body into a divine body with the force of imagination. Further, they intuitively experience the blissful emotion of a *bhakta* through meditation. So it is possible for us to refer to this state of mind as 'interiorized bhakti'.

This paper is about the religious practice of *prāṇāyāma* as a means of purification in the context of contemplation. Focusing on the purification of the *nāḍī*s and the elements, the manner in which *prāṇāyāma* functions in these processes will be investigated. By limiting the study to the Nātha tradition and relying particularly on the *Gorakṣaśataka* (*GŚ*) and related works, we address the question of how Nātha yogins realized inner divinity.

SOURCES

A number of Sanskrit works are attributed to Gorakṣanātha. Those in the form of manuscripts are: forty-five in the *New Catalogus Catalogorum* (vol. 6: 175–6), eighteen in the *Descriptive Catalogue of Yoga Manuscripts*,[2] twenty-eight according to Hazārīprasād Dvivedī (1996: 98–9), twenty-eight according to Pāṇḍeya (*GS*, 1976: ña) and over twenty-one according to Das Gupta (1995: 373).

The widespread Nātha movement resulted in the production of several legendary songs and oral traditions concerning the Nāthas. A number of vernacular literatures have also been attributed to Gorakṣanātha. Among them the compiler of the *Gorakhbānī* presented forty titles (Baṛthvāl 1994: 14–15). In addition, Singh considers that the *chanda*s or *pada*s of Gorakṣanātha and the *Gorakhbodh* (dialogue between Matsyendranātha and Gorakṣanātha) are more important than any other works (Singh 1938: 12).

Despite the difficulty of determining the authorship of these works, Dvivedī (1996: 99) considered that five Sanskrit works contain the authentic Nātha doctrine: *Amanaskayoga* (*AMN*), *Amaraughaśāsana* (*AMR*), *Siddhasiddhāntapaddhati* (*SSP*), *Gorakṣa Paddhati* (*GP*) and *Gorakṣa Saṃhitā* (*GS*).[3] Here, I restrict my focus to the *GŚ*,[4] and regard it as an authoritative Sanskrit work that is credited with the systemization of the doctrines and practices of Nātha yoga based on the opinion of Gopī Nātha Kavirāja and Briggs (1998: 256-7). Despite the fact that the title includes the word *śataka* (comprising a hundred verses), the variety of titles as well as the inconsistent number of verses resulted in problems related to the identification of the text (ibid.: 255–6; Bouy 1994: 16–18).

The number of the verses of the *GŚ* varies from 157 to 201. Some of these are published[5] in the *Gorakṣaśatakam* (*KGŚ*), *GP*, *Yogamārtaṇḍa* (*YM*) or *GS*.[6] However, their primary theme is nearly identical. When investigating the original manuscripts, Swāmī Kuvalayānanda and Shuklā located one manuscript that was preserved in the India Office Library; this manuscript contained 101 verses and addressed all six topics of yoga. It was published as the *KGŚ*. All the verses of this *śataka* can be found in the published text of the *GŚ* (*KGŚ* Introduction: 4-9).

The *GŚ* was also translated into Persian.[7] It is regarded as the translation of the conversation between Matsyendranātha and Gorakṣanātha. The translated version contains selected verses from the version that contained 201 verses; moreover, several similes which are not found in the *KGŚ* have been sequentially included in this translation. Certain ideas and practical techniques disseminated in Eurasia, the Middle East and North Africa through the Arabic and Persian translation of the Yogico-Tantric work entitled *Amṛtakuṇḍa* which conveys the name of Gorakṣanātha (Sakaki 2005: 136–8). Textual examination proves that the Nātha yogins and Islamic Sufis shared certain viewpoints; they appear to have influenced each other's practices and viewpoints (McGregor 1984: 21).

The *Haṭhayogapradīpikā* (*HYP*) of Svātmārāma, probably dated between the middle of the fourteenth and the middle of the sixteenth century, can be regarded as the most popular Haṭha-yogic digest. It is claimed to be a well-known authoritative treatise on yoga, but is an anthology of earlier or contemporary works (Briggs 1998: 253; Bouy 1994: 13). In addition, more than twenty verses of the *GŚ* have been quoted in the *HYP*. Making meticulous and tedious comparison, Bouy chose the *KGŚ* as the authoritative edition, despite some textual problems (Bouy 1994: 26).[8] Further, the sixth chapter of a comprehensive yogic work, *Vivekamārtāṇḍa* (*VM*), which is attributed to Viśvarūpa, contains most of the verses from the *GŚ*.

Further research to investigate whether a complete or differently arranged version exists will help resolve the problems pertaining to the original version of the *GŚ*. In this study, we will use the critical editions of Nowotny (*NGŚ*) as the source text and other related works as subsidiary tools.

THE CONCEPT OF PURIFICATION

Although there are various kinds of yoga, it can be stated that almost all yogic processes are means of purification. With regard to the eight limbs of yoga, the *Yogasūtra* (*YS*) begins by indicating the fact that the destruction of impurity (*aśuddhi*) results in the light of knowledge (*jñānadīpti*) and culminates in discriminating discernment (*vivekakhyāti*) (*YS* 2.28). Although the *YS* itself merely indicates the concept of purification and leaves the detailed means to the *guru*, it emphasizes the effects of purification.

Purification in Pātañjala Yoga

Patañjali, inheriting the principle from Vedic ritualistic tradition, first refers to cleanliness as the essential condition for realization of the ultimate goal of a qualified individual (*sādhaka*). Cleanliness is included in the following observances (*niyama*): cleanliness (*śauca*), contentment (*saṃtoṣa*), austerity (*tapas*), study of the sacred texts and repetition of *mantra*s (*svādhyāya*) and devotion to God (*īśvarapraṇidhāna*) (*YS* 2.32).[9]

In the first step of yoga practice (*abhyāsa*) is the consumption of pure food, referred to as moderate diet (*mitāhāra*). It is a way to externally purify the body. Although there is no reference to this in the *YS*, it is an important aspect in Haṭha-yoga. Cleanliness is external and internal. External cleanliness implies washing away the dirt on one's body with water, mud, ash, cow's urine or the gruel of barley (*TV* ad *YS* 2.32). As a result of external cleanliness, a feeling of disgust for one's own body and that of dissociation from others arise (*YS* 2.40).

Internal cleanliness implies destroying the impurities of the mind, such as desire, anger, and discontent, and preserving purity through good deeds and spiritual knowledge (*YS* 2.33).[10] The observance of internal purity results in the purity of the mind (*sattvaśuddhi*), gladness of the mind (*saumanasya*), one-pointedness (*ekāgrya*), control of the senses (*indriyajaya*), and readiness for realization of the Self (*ātmadarśanayogyatva*) (*YS* 2.41).

What brings purification of the mind? The practice of *prāṇāyāma* leads to affliction, which overshadows the cognitive faculty (*buddhi*); subsequently, *buddhi*'s own nature of illuminating (*prakāśatva*) arises (*YSBh* 2.52). It is in this state that the mind becomes suitable for concentration (*dhāraṇā*) (*YS* 2.53).

The following are the objects of *dhāraṇā*: a process of knowing (*grahaṇa*), essential nature (*svarūpa*), egotism (*asmitā*), inherence (*anvaya*) and purposefulness of sensation (*arthavattva*) (*YS* 3.47). All this can be achieved only after overcoming elements (*YS* 3.44) that include coarse form (*sthūla*), essential nature, subtle form (*sūkṣma*), inherence and purposefulness of the elements. The practice of purification of elements (*bhūtaśuddhi*) will be discussed in detail below. According to Patañjali, the synonymous usage of clarity is *vaiśāradya*. In other words, once the body is cleansed of the dirt, the illuminating nature of the intellect (*buddhisattva*) gains predominance; and this is referred to as clarity (*YSBh* 1.47).

Gladness of the mind is regarded as righteous thinking. *Saumanasya* leads to the bliss (*sahajānanda*) attained in the state of *samādhi*. *Ekāgrya* is one of the five states of mind (*cittabhūmi*) (*YSBh* 1.1).[11] In other words, concentrating the mind on one object eliminates distractions that are obstacles in the perception of the inner Self (*YS* 1.32). Control of the senses is achieved through the practice of withdrawal from the objects of sense and desire (*pratyāhāra*) (*YS* 2.54–5). Qualification for the realization of the Self includes clarity of the intellect, which is a means (*upāya*) to discriminate between *sattva* (*buddhi, prakṛti*) and *puruṣa* (*YS* 2.26).

Clarity of the intellect (*sattvabuddhi*) can be achieved by cleansing the impurity of *rajas* and *tamas*. Deeper knowledge then arises from discriminative discernment (*YS* 3.53). This deeper knowledge is referred to as a deliverer (*tārakam*),[12] and it encompasses all objects and all times within its sphere of action (*YS* 3.54). *Tāraka* literally implies that which takes one across the ocean of life and death. In the context of yoga practice, it implies a deliverer who makes an individual successful in his or her efforts. Moreover, it is said that this knowledge is born of one's own intuition (*svapratibhottham*) and cannot be learned from others (*an-aupadeśikam*) (*YSBh* 3.54). When the purity of intellect equals that of *puruṣa,* liberation (*kaivalya*) manifests itself; this is the ultimate goal of a qualified individual (*YSBh* 3.55).

In Pātañjala yoga, purification is a mediator that aids in the acquisition of the knowledge leading to liberation.[13] However, an in-depth explanation of the practical methods of the purifying process has not been provided.

Purification in Nātha Yoga

Pātañjala yoga is referred to as the eight-limbed yoga (*aṣṭāṅgayoga*). The commentator of the *YS* presents a counter argument suggesting that restraints (*yama*) and observances are not always included in the limbs of yoga (*YSBhV* 2.29).[14] Although the *GŚ* propounds six limbs and eliminates restraints and observances (*NGŚ* 7; *KGŚ* 4),[15] it refers to chastity, minimal eating, moderate diet, and abstention from worldly pleasures (*NGŚ* 54–5). In addition, the destruction of impurities is a primary subject in the practice of Nātha yoga.

With regard to external purification, Haṭha-yoga later developed six kinds of preliminary cleansing practices (*ṣaṭkarmāṇi*),[16] but there is no reference to this in the *GŚ*. However, in the *GŚ*, *śuddhi* and *śodhana* appear frequently in the context of the purification of *nāḍī*s (channels); the technical aspects of this practice will be discussed below. The concept of *nāḍī*s has been prevalent since the period of the classical Upaniṣads;[17] moreover, envisioned *nāḍī*s are portrayed as differently coloured minute channels passing out from the heart to the sun or extending in the body.

In a modern physiological context, *nāḍī*s are typically identified with nerve channels or vessels.[18] As carriers of *prāṇa*, they are moreover related to the subtle sphere. In Nātha yoga, *nāḍī*s have an important function. The concept of a subtle body is expressed in the following fundamental principles that should be known to the Nātha yogins: six energy centres (*cakra*) connected by the central *suṣumnā nāḍī*, sixteen centres of contemplation (*ādhāra*), three objects to be attained (*lakṣya*), five kinds of spaces in the physical body (*NGŚ* 13), one column with nine doors, and five tutelary deities (*devatā*) (*NGŚ* 14).[19]

It is believed that there are 72,000 *nāḍī*s in the subtle body and that they originate from a bulb (*kanda*) which is shaped like the egg of a bird and located below the navel and above the male organ (*NGŚ* 25; *KGŚ* 16). Among these, ten *nāḍī*s[20] are considered to be the carriers of the *prāṇa* and function accordingly (*NGŚ* 26–31; *KGŚ* 17–22). The most important *nāḍī*s are *iḍā*, *piṅgalā* and *suṣumnā*. Among these three, *iḍā* is situated on the left of the spinal column, *piṅgalā* on the right and *suṣumnā* in the middle (*NGŚ* 29); their tutelary deities are the Moon, the Sun and the Fire (*NGŚ* 32; *KGŚ* 23). In an anatomical context, *iḍā* and *piṅgalā* correspond to the laterovertebral sympathetic nerve chains and the *suṣumnā* corresponds to the spinal column.

Prāṇa passes through these *nāḍī*s in the form of breaths. In Nātha yoga, *prāṇa* has several meanings. Patañjali suggests that *prāṇa* means breath in general (*YS* 1.34; *NGŚ* 94, 96, 98; *KGŚ* 40, 43, 45). Similarly, *prāṇa* refers to the breath that is inhaled, while *apāna* refers to that which is exhaled (*HYP* 1.48). Further, it is referred to differently depending on its respective function (*NGŚ* 33–6; *KGŚ* 24–5). In addition, *prāṇa* is said to be located at the heart and *apāna* in the region of the rectum (*NGŚ* 34). Since reflection on the heart preserves life, *prāṇa* refers to all nervous signals or impulses (*NGŚ* 15, 28; *KGŚ* 23, 40). *Prāṇa* is also kind of sensation in the context of the awakening of *kuṇḍalinī* (*NGŚ* 137, 155–9, 184; *KGŚ* 61, 69–73, 94).

The regulation of *prāṇa* and *apāna* is a requisite for yogins. *Jīva* is under the control of *prāṇa* and *apāna*. It is like a wooden ball struck by a club, which moves up and down as a result of *prāṇa* and *apāna* passing through the left and right nostrils and does not rest (*NGŚ* 38–9; *KGŚ* 26–7). *Jīva* is also metaphorically described as a hawk tied to a string. Bound by the *guṇa*s, *jīva* (*citta*) is controlled by *prāṇa* and *apāna* (*NGŚ* 40; *KGŚ* 28). For this reason, the yogin should control *prāṇa* and obtain the immovability of the mind (*NGŚ* 90; *KGŚ* 39; *HYP* 2.2).

There is another reason to regulate breathing. As long as *prāṇa* is in the body, there is life; when *prāṇa* ceases to be, there is death (*NGŚ* 91; *HYP* 2.3). Thus, the cessation of breathing implies the union of *prāṇa* and *apāna*. In other words, when the *prāṇa* is merged with *apāna* and they are both led into the *suṣumnā nāḍī*, the union of *prāṇa* and *apāna* is accomplished. Thus, when all the *nāḍī*s that are filled with impurities are purified, the yogins become capable of restraining *prāṇa* (*NGŚ* 95; *HYP* 2.5). Therefore, yogins with a purified mind (*sāttvika dhī*) regularly practise *prāṇāyāma* in order to destroy the impurities in the *suṣumnā nāḍī* (*HYP* 2.6ab).

In Pātañjala yoga, one of the benefits of the observance of internal purity is the purification of the mind (*sattva śuddhi*) in the practice of *prāṇāyāma* (*YS* 2.52). What leads to this occurrence of the purification of the mind?

PROCESS OF PURIFICATION

'Yogins destroy disease by *āsana*, remove sin by *prāṇāyāma* (*NGŚ* 112ab; *KGŚ* 54ab), and attain steadiness of the mind by *dhāraṇā*, astonishing consciousness by *dhyāna*, and liberation by *samādhi*' (*NGŚ* 113ab). As Pātañjala yoga inherited the tradition of Vedic rituals, in Nātha texts the importance of *prāṇāyāma*[21] as purifier is repeatedly mentioned.[22] *Prāṇāyāma* is regarded as a form of great *tapas* (austerity), which creates the heat necessary to burn impurities. In other words, *prāṇāyāma* burns out the things that are born of external and internal impurities and of corporeal beings (*NGŚ* 103); moreover, it creates the fire (*pāvaka*) which feeds on the fuel of sin (*NGŚ* 111; *KGŚ* 53). This brings us to the question of how *prāṇāyāma* functions in the process of the purification of the *nāḍī*s.

Purification of the *Nāḍī*s

The first reference of the purification of the *nāḍī*s is in relation to *mahāmudrā*: 'Purification of the network of *nāḍī*s, the union of the moon and the sun and the drying up of the *rasa* (essence taken from food) are known as *mahāmudrā*' (*NGŚ* 77). This is regarded as one of the five *mudrā*s (*NGŚ* 57; *KGŚ* 32), and its practice is as follows: Having placed the chin on the chest, press the *yoni-sthāna* (region of perineum) with the left ankle and grasp the stretched right leg with both hands; practice *prāṇāyāma* in this position. This is a combination of *jālandharabandha*, half *paścimatāna-āsana*, and *prāṇāyāma* (*NGŚ* 78; *KGŚ* 33; *HYP* 3.9–12; *AMN* 29, 31). This should be practised equally with both the left and right nostrils (*NGŚ* 79; *HYP* 3.15).

The description provided in *NGŚ* 77 is based on this *mudrā*. Its benefits are mentioned in other texts as well: the removal of afflictions, the cessation of the activities of two *nāḍī*s (*HYP* 3.11–12; *AMR* 30–1), and digestive ability (*NGŚ* 80; *HYP* 3.16). Apart from these benefits, the practice of this *mudrā* leads to the destruction of all diseases (*NGŚ* 81; *HYP* 3.17). For this reason, it is known as a great *mudrā*.

The second reference to purification of the *nāḍī*s is found in *NGŚ* 95. Only when the entire network of *nāḍī*s that is filled with impurities is purified does the yogin become capable of restraining *prāṇa*. This implies that the purification of the *nāḍī*s is a prerequisite for the practice of *prāṇāyāma*. The ordinary process of *prāṇāyāma* is described in the following manner: Assuming a lotus posture, the yogin should inhale *prāṇa* through his left nostril, and having held it as long as he can, exhale it through the right nostril.

During this process, the visualization is required. The mode of *prāṇāyāma* through the left nostril is described as follows. Having inhaled *prāṇa* through the left nostril, hold the breath and contemplate on the image of the moon with nectar as white as curd, or cow's milk, or the colour of the purest silver, and exhale through the right nostril (*NGŚ* 96–7; *KGŚ* 43–4).

The following is the mode of *prāṇāyāma* through the right nostril. Having inhaled *prāṇa* through the right nostril, hold the breath while contemplating on the image of the disc of the sun with a mass of burning flames, and exhale through the left nostril (*NGŚ* 98–9; *KGŚ* 46). After a period of three months, as a result of this visualization while practising, a series of *nāḍī*s will be purified (*NGŚ* 100).

As a result of this practice, *prāṇa* is restrained at will, the digestive fire is kindled, and an internal sound (*nāda*) is heard (*NGŚ* 118);[23] subsequently, the individual is free of diseases (*NGŚ* 101).[24] The results of this kind of *prāṇāyāma* are nearly identical to those of *mahāmudrā*. The ability to hear the internal sound implies the absorption of the inner sound (*nādānusandhāna*); this is considered as the best way to lead *laya*.[25]

It should be noted that this sound is heard in the *suṣumnā nāḍī* when it is clean (*HYP* 4.68). In the preliminary stage (*ārambha*) of yoga, the knot of Brahmā (*brahmagranthi*) is pierced and unstruck sound is heard. In the second stage (*ghaṭa*), the knot of Viṣṇu (*viṣṇugranthi*) is pierced and as a result of the union of *prāṇa* and *apāna*, the sound like a kettle-drum (*bherī*) is heard. In the third stage (*paricaya*), *prāṇa* reaches the point between the eyebrows (*mahāśūnyam*) and the sound of a drum (*mardala*) is heard. In the fourth culminating stage (*niṣpatti*), the knot of Rudra (*rudragranthi*) is pierced and *anila* (*apāna*) reaches at the highest part of the head (*śarvapīṭha*); subsequently, the well-tuned sound of *vīṇā* is heard (*HYP* 4.70–6).[26]

The prescription of the second type of *nāḍī-śodhana-prāṇāyāma* is practised by restraining *apāna* in the following manner (*NGŚ* 102). Having restrained *apāna,* the *prāṇa* that remains in the body is raised to the sky through a passage in one *mātrā*. This might indicate the union of *apāna* with *prāṇa* in the *suṣumnā*. Further, this practice destroys the network of defects (*NGŚ* 104).

As mentioned, the union of *apāna* and *prāṇa* is repeatedly mentioned in the *GŚ*. 'Drawn up by way of *prāṇāyāma*, when *apāna* is united with *prāṇa*, one is released from all sins' (*NGŚ* 109; *KGŚ* 52). 'Having closed the nine gates and accompanied with fire, *apāna* is sucked up and held firmly, and led to the space' (*NGŚ* 110). This practise is regarded as an effective and powerful means of purification.

Purification of the Elements

There is another kind of purification related to *prāṇāyāma*—the purification of the elements (*bhūtaśuddhi*). This practice is very common in Tantrism[27] and Nātha yoga. This is one of the preliminary rituals preceding actual worship. The principle of this ritual is based on the notion that God is manifested in the body in the form of five elements. The complete system entails dissolving all five elements into their subtle origins and burning them to ashes, and then, giving birth to them by bathing them in nectar and creating a pure body owing to the course of evolution. This process can be referred to as physical and psychological purification.

In this process, in the first phase, the entire body is imagined as comprising five elements with symbolical attributes and seed syllables in each specified part, a qualified individual dissolves the five elements into their subtle origins during meditation with the practice of *prāṇāyāma*. At the end of this meditation, the individual imagines he has the nature of God. In the second phase, he burns up his elemental body with the fire that emanates from each seed syllable. Subsequently, he inundates himself or herself with the nectar that originates from *sahasrāra* (the topmost place of contemplation imagined as the thousand-petalled lotus). Finally, the individual accomplishes the deification of himself or herself in contemplation.

Pātañjala yoga considers this in the context of *dhāraṇā*. As mentioned previously, the subjugation of the elements can be achieved through concentration on the following forms: substances and characteristic, generic form, subtle element, inherent qualities, and purpose (*YS* 3.44). By practising this *dhāraṇā*, a qualified individual acquires supernatural powers such as being able to become as small as an atom, the perfection of the body and the capacity to be unobstructed by the properties of the elements (*YS* 3.45).

In Nātha yoga, *dhāraṇā* of the five elements (*pañcabhūtānām dhāraṇā*)[28] involves the practice of concentrating on each element in the specified part of the body. It is practised by holding the breath and visualizing each element in its symbolic form and colour, seed syllable, and tutelary deity in the specified part of the body[29] within the duration of five *ghaṭikā* (two hours) (*NGŚ* 154–60; *KGŚ* 68–75; *YTU* 84cd–102ab).

The region where each element is located in the body, its symbolic form, colour, seed syllable and tutelary deity in that order are as follows. Earth: heart, square, golden yellow, syllable *la* and Brahmā. Water: throat, a half-moon, white as jasmine, syllable *va* and Viṣṇu. Fire: palate, triangle, the colour of coral, syllable *ra* and Rudra. Air: the region between the eyebrows, circle, the colour of a mass of collyrium, syllable *ya* and Īśvara. Sky (*ākāśa*): *Brahmarandhra*, dot, the colour of pure water, syllable *ha* and Sadāśiva.

The Nātha yogins realized the relationship between the elements and *prāṇa*. According to the *Śivasvarodaya* (*ŚSV*), the basic text of the science of *svara*,[30] the five elements reside in the body in subtle forms (*ŚSV* 9). In a period of two and a half *ghaṭikā*s, each element successively rules in each *nāḍī* (*ŚSV* 72) and manifests itself (*ŚSV* 64). The elements prevail over the *nāḍī*s in the following order: Air, Fire, Earth, Water and Sky (*ŚSV* 71). Thus, in order to subjugate each element, a duration of five *ghaṭikā*s is required for this practice.

By practising this *dhāraṇā*, the body of a qualified individual possesses the nature of each element; subsequently, the power of each element can to some extent be acquired (*NGŚ* 160; *KGŚ* 74; *YTU* 83cd–103cd). The different kinds of *dhāraṇā* on each of the five elements are to be practised in thought, word, and deed; by following this technique, a qualified individual will be purged of all sins (*NGŚ* 161; *KGŚ* 75).

In later Haṭha-yogic literatures, the knowledge of the science of *svara* is applied to *kumbhaka* (retention of the breath); in the *Kumbhaka Paddhati* (*KP*), this is known as *tattva-kumbhaka.* The process involves inhaling prior to the rise of a particular element and exhaling at the end of the element's predominance. Through this practice, a qualified individual acquires the nature of and control over the respective element. Finally, the individual attains the divine body and is liberated (*KP* 122–5).

At the beginning of the prescription of the five kinds of *dhāraṇā*, the Persian translation of the *GŚ* mentions the process of dissolution of the universe (*PGŚ* 3b–4b).[31] This implies that Nātha yogins also considered *dhāraṇā* of the five elements in the context of the evolution of the universe.

TWO ASPECTS OF *PRĀṆĀYĀMA*

In Vedic ritual, the purification of the sacrificer is accomplished through *tapas.*[32] Based on this principle, *prāṇāyāma* was regarded as the highest form of *tapas.*[33] By using the power of the internal fire accelerated through *prāṇāyāma,* yogins are able to purify themselves and destroy external and internal impurities. On examining the process of purification of the *nāḍī*s and elements in a textual context, we can find the significance of the two aspects of *prāṇāyāma*: the Haṭha-yogic technique and *mantrajapa*. Next, we will discuss the manner in which these aspects are reflected in actual practices.

PRĀṆĀYĀMA WITH *MUDRĀ* OR *BANDHA*

The physiological techniques highlight the fundamental contribution of Nātha yoga to the development of *prāṇāyāma*. Several kinds of *mudrā* or *bandha* and *kumbhaka*s have been developed to ensure the smooth practise of *prāṇāyāma*. The mode of practise varies depending on the manuals and the preceptors; however, since this study is restricted to the *GŚ,* we will only discuss the practices mentioned in the previous section.

Typically, *mūla bandha* is practised for *pūraka* (the act of inhaling); *jālandhara bandha*, for *kumbhaka* and *uḍḍiyāna bandha*, for the *kumbhaka* before *recaka*. With regard to the purification of the *nāḍī*s, *mahāmudrā* is practised (*NGŚ* 76); both *mahāmudrā* and *mūla bandha* (*NGŚ* 59) serve as effective means to achieve the union of *prāṇa* and *apāna* through the cessation of inhalation and exhalation. *Jālandhara bandha* is effective for the cessation of activity in all the *nāḍī*s (*NGŚ* 62). *Khecarīmudrā* (*NGŚ* 138), *kākīmudrā* (*NGŚ* 139–40), and *śakticālanīmudrā* (*NGŚ* 52) are practised for the cessation of inhalation and exhalation.

This suggests that the visualization of the sun and the moon is also practised during *kumbhaka*. The modes of *kumbhaka* have been developed in later Haṭha-yogic literatures. The *KP* mentions fifty-seven different modes of *kumbhaka* in forty-seven stages. For the purification of the *nāḍī*s, three modes have been introduced (*KP* 114–20). The first mode involves inhaling through one nostril, and after holding the breath for as long as possible, exhaling through the other nostril while contemplating on *haṃsa*. Subsequently, the process is repeated by inhaling through the opposite nostril; finally, the first process is repeated. The second and third modes are identical to the *nāḍī-śodhana-prāṇāyāma* accompanied with the visualization of the sun and the moon. This leads to the following two questions: why were different types of *prāṇāyāma* developed? Why is the cessation of respiration necessary?

As indicated, the effect of combining *prāṇa* and *apāna* through *nāḍī-śodhana-prāṇāyāma* is the same. When the two unite, *prāṇa* simultaneously flows in the solar and lunar *nāḍī*s and heat develops near the region of the *kanda* (*NGŚ* 110). At the same time, a sensation is also felt by the individual on the back. This is described as the awakening of the *kuṇḍalinī*; in other words, the *prāṇa*—combined with the *apāna*—rises to the *sahasrāra* along the *suṣumnā nāḍī* piercing through three *granthi*s (*NGŚ* 50–2). This results in acquiring a nectar-like liquid that seeps from the moon, situated at the *sahasrāra*. In the *GŚ*, several *mudrā*s such as *jālandhara bandha, khecarīmudrā* and *viparītakaraṇī* are practised for this purpose. This process is a metaphor of death and the means of rebirth.

Nātha yogins determine the time of the day through the process of respiration. As mentioned earlier, the *iḍā* and *piṅgalā nāḍī*s pass through the left and right nostrils respectively (*NGŚ* 29, 32). When *prāṇa* passes through *piṅgalā* (symbolized by the sun), it is day, and when *prāṇa* passes through *iḍā* (symbolized by the moon), it is night. When *prāṇa* passes through both the *nāḍī*s and unites in the *suṣumnā nāḍī,* it implies the cessation of breathing and leads to a minimum of activity and delays death. Thus, *kāla* (death) is swallowed up by *suṣumnā nāḍī* (*HYP* 4.17). Thus, a yogin transcends day and night and conquers death.

According to *ŚSV* 37, the *iḍā, piṅgalā,* and *suṣumnā nāḍī*s respectively signify the rivers Gaṅgā, Yamunā, and Sarasvatī. The confluence of these three rivers is considered as Prayāga, which the *tīrtha* where an individual can attain liberation. Thus, when *prāṇa* flows through the *suṣumnā nāḍī, manonmanī* is achieved (*YS* 4.20). In *HYP* 4.3–4, *Rāja yoga, samādhi, unmanī* and *manonmanī, amaratva, laya, tattva, śūnyā, śūnya, paraṁpada, amanaska, advaita, nirālamba, nirañjana, jīvanmukti, sahajā* and *turyā* are used synonymously. The *GŚ* describes this state of mind in the following manner: 'Just as water dissolved in the ocean becomes one with it, the Self (*ātman*) and mind (*manas*) become one' (*NGŚ* 186; *HYP* 4.5). This is 'the state of equilibrium (*samarasatvam),* in which *prāṇa* is without any movement and the mind is absorbed (in the Self)' (*NGŚ* 187; *KGŚ* 94; *HYP* 4.6).

For the Nātha yogins, death can be overcome literally or figuratively, through *prāṇāyāma*. In ritual, this implies the deification of the human body and the realization of the Self in itself.

Prāṇāyāma Accompanied with *Mantra*

Mantra has the power to acquire knowledge leading to *samādhi.* All the processes of purification result in the acquisition of knowledge. In the practices of purification of *nāḍī*s and elements, *mantra-japa* plays an integral role in visualization.

In the process of the purification of the *nāḍī*s through *prāṇāyāma*, the respiration process is first considered the practice of the *haṃsa* *mantra.*[34] Nātha yogins visualize the *jīva* during the process of inhaling and exhaling. This process is considered as the repetition of the *mantra*. 'While exhaling breath, *jīva* goes out with the sound *ha*, and while inhaling breath, the soul enters into the body with the sound *sa*'. In this way, the breathing process is described as being an unconscious recitation of the *haṃsa mantra* (*NGŚ* 42). People normally recite the *haṃsa mantra* 21,600 times in a one day-night cycle (*NGŚ* 43).

This unconscious recitation of the *mantra* (*ajapā-japa* or *ajapā-gāyatrī*) is regarded as means of liberation (*mokṣadāyinī*) (*NGŚ* 44). Nātha yogins consider this *gāyatrī* as comprising the *prāṇa* which arises in the *kuṇḍalinī* (*NGŚ* 46ab). In *GhS* 5.85–90, this is practised in the *kevala-kumbhaka.*[35] In the cessation of respiration, a qualified individual mentally repeats the *haṃsa mantra* to measure the duration of a *kumbhaka*. This sound is considered to arise when *prāṇa* enters the *suṣumnā nāḍī* and is known as *mantrajapa* (*YB* 155–6).

Another *mantra* revealed in the *prāṇāyāma* is the *praṇava* (the sacred syllable *oṃ*). The *GŚ* recommends the repetition of the *praṇava* (*NGŚ* 83). Further, it states that the *praṇava* should be visualized as a revelation of the Sun, the Moon and the Fire (*NGŚ* 84). The seed syllables of the *praṇava* symbolize Brahmā, Viṣṇu, Maheśvara and the respective Śaktis (*NGŚ* 85–6), and they should be repeated with the voice, the body, and the mind (*NGŚ* 88). A person who continuously repeats the *praṇava* will be free of sin (*NGŚ* 89). Although the elements have been comprehensively enumerated, the question of how this can be practised remains.

In later Haṭha-yogic literatures, this practice is formulated in combination with the contemplation of each syllable during the practice of each component of *prāṇāyāma*. This is clarified in the explanation of *sahita-kumbhaka* (joined retention). The practice comprises *sagarbha-kumbhaka* which is accompanied with seed syllables, and *nigarbha-kumbhaka* which is without seed syllables. The process of an ordinary *sagarbha-kumbhaka* involves the contemplation of a deity along with its nature (*guṇa*) and colour as well as the seed syllables of the *praṇava*, all within a specified course of time (*mātrā*) (*GhS* 5–47).

The process of the *sagarbha-kumbhaka* is described as follows.

First, while contemplating on Brahmā, who is associated with *rajas*, is red in colour, and has the syllable *a,* inhale through the left nostril and repeat the syllable sixteen times. Second, while contemplating on Hari, who is associated with *sattva*, is of a dark complexion, and has the syllable *u*, hold the breath and repeat the syllable sixty-four times. Third, while contemplating on Śiva, who is associated with *tamas*, is white and has the syllable *ma*, exhale through the right nostril and repeat the syllable thirty-two times; subsequently, inhale through the right nostril, hold the breath by performing the *kumbhaka* and exhale through the left nostril, repeating the seed syllables in the way prescribed. This *prāṇāyāma* is practised repeatedly alternating the nostrils (*GhS* 5.48–53) and simultaneously visualizing the three deities with their symbolical seed syllables.

We have already discussed the worship and application of the *praṇava* as a time unit. At this point, we will address a later style of *prāṇāyāma* as the combination of *mantrajapa, prāṇāyāma*, and *dhyāna*. This practice is similar to the process of *bhūtaśuddhi*, which involves the contemplation of the five presiding deities with their specified seed syllables. In *GhS* 5.38–44, the process of the purification of *nāḍī*s adopts either of the following two types of purification methods: *samanu* and *nirmanu*. *Samanu* is accompanied by a *mantra* that needs to be mentally repeated for a specified number of times. In each case, the seed syllable is used for symbolizing the element and measuring the length of each part of *prāṇāyāma*.

There is also the *samanu-nāḍī-śuddhi* method. Assuming the lotus posture, after performing imposition of *guru* or other dieties on different parts of the body of the practitioner, contemplating the seed syllable of Air, inhale through the left nostril repeating the seed syllable of Air sixteen times. Having held the breath for the period during which the syllable is repeated sixty-four times, exhale through the right nostril repeating the syllable thirty-two times. Then contemplating the fire at the root of the navel raised and combined with Earth, inhale through the right nostril, repeating the seed syllable of Fire (*ra*) sixteen times. Having held the breath for a period during which the syllable is repeated sixty-four times, exhale through the left nostril and repeat the syllable thirty-two times. Finally, contemplate the Water (moon) in a full bright light, inhale through the left nostril repeating the seed syllable (*ṭha*) (moon) sixteen times. Having held the breath for a period during which the syllable *va* (the seed syllable of Water) is repeated sixty-four times and visualizing oneself bathing in the nectar and imagining the purification of all the *nāḍī*s, exhale and repeat the syllable *la* (the seed syllable of Earth) thirty-two times.

This is considered to be a preliminary purification undertaken prior to the practice of *āsana* and *prāṇāyāma* (*GhS* 5.45). Although its name refers to the purification of the *nāḍī*s, it is clearly closer to the Tantric practice of *bhūtaśuddhi*. On the other hand, *nirmanu-nāḍī-śuddhi* is practised only through bodily cleansings (*dhauti*) and does not require the recitation of any *mantra*.

Thus, the power of *prāṇāyāma*, combined with the chanting of *mantra*s that symbolize a specific deity or element, is reinforced during contemplation. This implies the practice of the worship of God in the form of *prāṇāyāma*.

CONCLUSION

The Nāthas, as an outshoot of Śākta Kaulamata, worshipped Śiva as their transcendent deity, but aimed at eliminating the dichotomy and returning to unity with the transcendent reality. This can be regarded as the reason for their prevalence across India and abroad.

An examination of the processes of purification in Nātha literatures reveals that the elements of the practises of purification in the Nāthas and Tantric or Āgamic rituals share a common base. Based on the identification of the body and the macrocosm and the inherited traditions of Pātañjala yoga and the Sāṃkhya philosophy, the purification of the body is achieved through the dissolution of the constituent elements into the cause by the practice of *prāṇāyāma* and contemplation. The ingrained concepts of knowledge and power sustain the practice of *prāṇāyāma*.

As Vedic rituals are integrated into the contemplative worship developed by Tantrism, the spirit of Pātañjala yoga is integrated into the natural and blissful state of mind developed by Nātha yogins. Although the instructions are simple and considerably borrowed from Pātañjala yoga, the *GŚ* reveals the fundamental concepts in Nātha yoga. In addition, the practice of a combination of yogic techniques accelerates the yogic process both internally and externally. *Praṇava* and *haṃsa* display the potential power to operate as powerful *mantra*s supporting concentration.

Considering *prāṇa* as a manifestation of the cosmic consciousness that is granted, Nāthas developed physical techniques to gain complete control over *prāṇa* which culminated in a control over the mind. Moreover, by formulating spiritual practises for spiritual death and rebirth through the processes of purification, they conquer death and become God himself as the result of their interiorized bhakti.

ABBREVIATIONS

AMN : *Amanaskayoga*, ed. Brahmamitra Avasthī, tr. Bajaraṃga Siṃha, Delhi: Swāmī Keśavānanda Yoga Samsthān Prakāśan, 1987.

AMR : *Amaraughaprabodha of Gorakhshanātha*, ed. with note by Mukund Rām Shāstrī, Srinagar: Research Department, 1918.

GhS : *Gheraṇḍa Saṃhitā* (2nd edn.), ed. Swāmī Digambarjī, M.L. Gharote, Lonavla: Kaivalyadhama S.M.Y.M. Samiti, 1997.

GP : *Gorakṣa Paddhati*, ed. Khemarāja Śrīkṛṣṇadāsa, with Hindi note by Mahīdhara Śarman, Bombay 2024 vs (1967).

GS : *Gorakṣasaṃhitā*, ed. Janārdana Pāṇḍeya, Vārāṇasī: Saṃpūrṇānanda Sanskrit Viśvavidyālaya, vol. 1, 1976.

GŚC : *Muktisopāna*, Ms. (Sanskrit), Tantra, 6617, Asiatic Society of Bengal.

HP : *Haṭhapradīpikā (with 10 chapters) of Svātmārāma and Yogaprakāśikā*, ed. M.L. Gharote, Parimal Devnāth, Lonavla: The Lonavla Yoga Institute, 2001.

HYP : *The Haṭhayogapradīpikā of Svātmārāma with the Commentary by Jyotsnā of Brahmānanda and English Translation*, Madras: Adyar Library and Research Centre, 1994 (rept.).

KGŚ : *Gorakṣaśatakam with Introduction, Text, English translation, Notes etc.*, ed. Svāmī Kuvalayānanda and S.A. Shuklā, Lonavla: Kaivalyadhama S.M.Y.M. Samiti, 1958.

KP : *Kumbhaka Paddhati of Raghuvīra, Science of Prāṇāyāma,* ed. M.L. Gharote, Parimal Devnāth, Lonavla: The Lonavla Yoga Institute, 2000.

NGŚ : *Das Gorakṣaśataka*, ed. & tr. Fausta Nowotny, Dokumente der Geistesgeschichte 3, Köln: Karl A. Nowotny, 1976.

PGŚ : *Pās-i Anfās* (Breath control), Ms. (Persian), Habib Ganj Collection 21/346, Maulānā Azad Library (Aligarh Muslim University).

SSP : *Siddhasiddhāntapaddhati,* ed. Rāmlāl Śrīvāstava, Gorakhapur: Gorakhanātha Mandir, 2038 vs (1981).

ŚSV : *Śivasvarodaya*, ed. and tr. Rām Kumār Rāy, Vārāṇasī: Prāchya Prakāśan, 1997.

TV : See *YS*.

VM : *The Vivekamārtāṇḍa of Viśvarūpadeva*, ed. K. Sāmbaśiva Śāstrī, Trivandrum: Government Press, 1935.

VS : *Vasiṣṭha Saṃhitā (Yoga Kāṇḍa)*, ed. Swāmī Digambarjī, Pītambar Jhā, Gyān Shankar Sahay, Lonavla: Kaivalyadhama S.M.Y.M. Samiti, 1984.

YB : *Yogabīja*, ed. and tr. Brahma Mitra Avasthī, Delhi: Swāmī Keśavānanda Yoga Sansthān Prakāśan, 2042 vs (1985)

YCU : *Yogacūḍāmaṇi-upaniṣad*, in A. Mahādeva Śāstrī (ed.), *The Yoga Upaniṣads with commentary by Śrī Upaniṣad Brahmayogin*, Madras: Adyar Library and Research Centre, 1968 (rept).

YM : *Yogamārtaṇḍa* in Kalyāni Mallik (ed.), *Siddhasiddhāntapaddhati and Other Works of the Nātha Yogis*, Poona: Oriental Book House, 1953. (*Siddhasiddhāntapaddhati* of Gorakṣanātha, *Yogaviṣaya* of Mīnanātha, *Amaraughaprabodha* of Gorakṣanātha, *Yogamārtaṇḍagrantha* of Gorakṣanātha (*YM*), *Gorakh Upaniṣad, Matsyendranātha kā pad; Cirapaṭajī kā Sabadī; Gopīcandajī kā Sabadī*)

YS : *Yogasūtra, Pātañjalayogadarśanam: Pātañjalayogadarśanam, Vācaspatimiśra-viracita Tattvavaiśārad* (*TV*), *Vijñānabhikṣu-kṛta Yogavārttika bibhūṣita Vyāsabhāṣya* (*YSBh*) *sametam*, ed. Nārāyaṇa Miśra, Vārāṇasī: Bhāratiya Vidyā Prakāśan, 1981.

YSBh : See *YS*.

YSBhV : *Yogasūtrabhāṣyavivaraṇa of Śaṅkara, Vivaraṇa text with English Translation, and Critical Notes Along With Text and English Translation of Patanjali's Yogasūtras and Vyāsabhāṣya*, ed. and tr. T.S. Rukmani, 2 vols., Delhi: Munshiram Manoharlal, 2001.

YTU : *Yogatattva-upaniṣad*, in A. Mahādeva Śāstrī (ed.), The *Yoga Upaniṣads with Commentary by Śrī Upaniṣad Brahmayogin*, Madras: The Adyar Library and Research Centre, 1968 (rept).

YY : *Yoga-yājñavalkya*, ed. John J. Ely, tr. A.G. Mohan, Madras: Ganesh & Co., 1989.

NOTES

1. Vaudeville (1974: 144) used a modified form of this expression in relation to the tenets of Kabir as a bhakta speaking the language of Yoga.
2. The eighteen texts in the Descriptive Catalogue of Yoga Manuscripts are as follows: *Amaraughaprabodha, Amaraughaśāsanam, Gorakṣa Gītā, Gorakṣa Paddhati, Gorakṣa Saṃhitā, Gorakṣaśataka, Jñānaprakāśaśatakam, Navaśaktiśatakam, Muktisopāna, Yogapaṭala, Yogamārtaṇḍa* (*YM*),

Yogābhyāsa-yoga, Vivekamārtaṇḍa, Śābara-tantram, Sāṣṭāṅga-yoganirṇaya (saṅgraha) and *Siddhasiddhāntapaddhati.*

3. Bouy regarded the *Gorakṣaśatakam, Amaraughaprabodha, Siddha-siddhāntapaddhati* and *Gorakṣopaniṣad* as basic authorities on the Nātha doctrine (1994: 18).
4. The *GŚ* is regarded as having widely influenced the Yoga-upaniṣads, particularly the *Yogacūḍāmaṇi-up.* and *Yogakuṇḍalinī-up.* that are largely based on the *GŚ*. For the corresponding verses, see Bouy 1994: 100, 102.
5. For the corresponding verses in the printed texts (Bouy 1994: 22).
6. For details, see Mallinson 2007: 166–7. There seems to be a certain amount of confusion with regard to this work. As mentioned by Bouy (1994: 18), the *Gorakṣa Saṃhitā* was published in 1974 by Camanlāl Gautama in Bareilly. This is the same version of the *GP* that includes a hundred verses in the first part and a hundred and one verses in the second part. Further, the text including the expanded version of the *Kubjikāmatatantra*, which belongs to the Kubjikāmata of Yoginīkaulamata, shares the same title. This *Gorakṣa Saṃhitā* consists of the Kādiprakaraṇam and Bhūtiprakaraṇam and is edited by Janārdana Pāṇḍeya in 1976. The original text appears to have had a third part entitled Yogaprakaraṇam; however, it is not included in this edition. See Heilijgers-Seelen 1994: 8–11.
7. *Pās-i Anfās (PGŚ)*, see Sakaki 2003. Cf. *Tarjmah-i Gorakh*, Ms. (Persian), Add. 5651, ff. 40a-47b, British Museum.
8. The *KGŚ* omitted two verses (vv. 81, 95) for a supplement; this part of the supplement has not been published thus far.
9. This is described as the dedication of all actions (*sarvakarmārpaṇam*) to the highest *guru* (*YSBh* 2.32).
10. In the *Bhagavad Gītā* (18.5), sacrifice, charity and penance are said to be the mental purifiers. *Vasiṣṭha Saṃhitā* (*VS*) 1.51 includes spiritual knowledge (*adhyātma-vidyā*) to this list.
11. The other states of mind are restless (*kṣipta*), infatuated (*mūḍha*), distracted (*vikṣipta*) and restricted (*niruddha*).
12. In *AMN* 1.3, *Tāraka yoga* is regarded as superior to all systems; moreover, it is considered beyond the reach of the Vedas and is a secret for scriptures and reveals the manner in which the great ocean of *saṃsāra* (worldly life) can be crossed. '*Tāraka*' is referred to as *Tāraka yoga* when it is associated with the mind, and it is termed *Amanaska yoga* (transcendent yoga) when it is associated with the mind and the objective world. Although there is no reference to *Tāraka yoga* in the *GŚ*, *HP* 10.4 refers to '*tāraka*' as the ultimate goal of yoga practice.
13. For the relationship between the concepts of purification, knowledge and power in the connection of Pātañjala yoga, see Pensa 1969: 194–216. Sferra treats these concepts in Vajrayāna texts, see Sferra 1999: 83–103.

14. The contents of the *niyama*s vary, depending on the texts. The *YTU* and the *HYP* consider abstention from injury (*ahiṃsā*) as the principal *niyama* and do not mention any others. Some Yoga-upaniṣads, beginning with the *Varāha-upaniṣad*, enumerate the following ten *niyama*s: austerity (*tapas*), contentment (*saṃtoṣa)*, theism (*āstikya*), charity (*dāna*), worship of God (*īśvarapūjana)*, listening to the doctrines (*siddhānta-śravaṇa*), modesty (*hrī*), chanting of *mantra*s (*japa*), decision (*mati*), and observance of vows (*vrata*). *SSP* 2.33 mentions the following six *niyama*s: dwelling aloof (*ekāntavāsa*), detachment (*niḥsaṅgāta*), indifference (*audāsīnya*), contentment with what is acquired (*yathāprāptisaṃtuṣṭi*), absence of sentiment (*vairasya*), and devotion to the *guru*'s feet (*guru-caraṇāvarūḍhatva*). *VS* 1.38 includes purification to its list of ten *yama*s; the other nine are as follows: non-violence, truth, abstention from theft (*asteya*), chastity (*brahmacarya*), fortitude (*dhṛti*), forgiveness (*kṣamā)*, compassion (*dayā*), straightforwardness (*ārjava*) and moderate diet.
15. Although Nātha yoga is known as the six-limbed yoga (*ṣaḍaṅgayoga),* all the Nātha texts do not follow this style; the *SSP* has eight limbs. Among the Yoga-upaniṣads, the *Amṛtanāda-up.*, *Kṣurikā-up., Dhyānabindu-up.* and *Yogacūḍāmaṇi-up.* have six limbs and the *Darśana-up.* has nine limbs.
16. For further information on each practice, see *HYP* 2.22–35; (*GhS* 1.12–60).
17. See *Bṛhadāraṇyaka-upaniṣad* 4.3.20, *Chāndogya-up*. 8.6.1, 2, 6, *Kaṭha-up*. 6.16 and *Praśna-up*. 3.6–7. For details, see Kane 1962: 1430.
18. See Apte 1967: 17-25; *KGS* 61-78.
19. The *GŚ* identifies each of the six *cakra*s by names depending on the region in which they are located: in an intermediate region between the rectum and the genitals (*ādhāra, mūlādhāra, Brahma cakra*), close to the origin of the genitals (*svādhiṣṭhāna*), in the region of the navel (*nābhi, maṇi-pūraka*), in the region of the heart (*hṛdaya cakra, anāhata*), in the region of the throat (*kaṇṭha, viśuddha*) and at the spot between the eyebrows or at the root of the palate (*tālu*). However, *NGŚ* 177 enumerates the following nine places of meditation: the anus, the male organ, the navel, the heart, the throat, the tongue, between the eyebrows, and *brahmarandhra* (aperture in the crown of the skull). In *SSP* 2.1-9, nine *cakra*s have been mentioned; the additional three *cakra*s are *tālu-cakra*, located at the root of the palate, *nirvāṇa-cakra*, located in the *brahmarandhra* and *ākāśa-cakra*, located at the highest point of *sahasrāra*. Further, the sixteen centres of concentration are the big toes, *mūla*, rectum, soft palate, deeper region of the palate, root of the tongue, point between the eyebrows, nose, root of the nose, the centre of the forehead and *brahmarandhra* (*SSP* 2.10–25). With regard to the three objects to be attained, the *NGŚ* refers to it as *trailokyam*; however, in *GP* 1.12, Briggs 1998: 13 and *YCU* 3c, it has been referred to as *trilakṣyam*. In this study, we refer to it as *trilakṣyam*. *Trilakṣyam*

refers to the internal objects, outer objects and objects of special attention (*SSP* 2.26-29). Further, the five kinds of space have been identified as *ākāśa* as an *ātman*, *parākāśa* as the darkness of the night, *mahākāśa* as being effulgent at the dissolution of the world, *tattvākāśa* as *prajñā* and *sūryākāśa* (2.30). The one column is known as the *vajradaṇḍa* (backbone) through which the *suṣumnā nāḍī* (or *brahmanāḍī*) passes. The nine doors are the nostrils, mouth, the eyes, the ear holes, anus and penis. The five tutelary deities, who are related to the five elements, are Brahmā, Viṣṇu, Rudra, Īśvara, and Sadāśiva (*NGŚ* 155–9). For details see Briggs (1998: 310, 317, 319), Banerjea (1983: 169–94).

20. The location and exit of ten *nāḍī*s are as follows: *iḍā* (left side), *piṅgalā* (right side), *suṣumnā* (mid region), *gāndhārī* (left eye), *hastijihvā* (right eye), *pūṣā* (right ear), *yaśasvinī* (left ear), *alambuṣā* (mouth), *kuhū* (*liṅga*, penis), and *śaṅkhinī* (*mūlādhāra*, anus) (*NGŚ* 29–31; *KGŚ* 20–2).
21. For the historical development of *prāṇāyāma,* see Kane 1962: 1432–44; Gharote 2003: 47–9; Einoo, 2002: 25–39.
22. In the *Yoga Bīja* (*YB*) ascribed to Matsyendranātha, the importance of *prāṇāyāma* is propagated. 'The adept who follows the path of yoga without the knowledge of the practice of *prāṇāyāma* is led astray' (*YB* 76), and 'the adept who wants to achieve success in yoga without controlling *prāṇa* or without practising *prāṇāyāma* is like a person who wants to cross the ocean with the help of raw earthen pitcher to lose his life' (*YB* 77).
23. While the *GŚ* only refers to the sound of a bell, *HYP* 4.85–7 explains the various kinds of sound that result from the absorption of the internal sound. Lakṣmīnārāyaṇa enumerated thirty kinds of sound in the *Bālabodhinī* which is a commentary of the *GŚ*, *GŚC* 50–2.
24. In the *GP*, the former part of this description ends abruptly at this point.
25. Although there is no reference to the four kinds of yoga in the *GŚ*, *AMR* 3 propounds the following four kinds of yoga: *Rāja, Mantra, Laya* and *Haṭha*. It regards all the four yogas as necessary for the fulfilment of *Rāja yoga*, and it regards *Laya yoga* as the method for the middle state.
26. These *granthi*s are located in the heart, the throat and between the eyebrows respectively in the *suṣumnā*. *HYP* 2.67 (*SSP* 2.13) recommends *Bhastrikā kumbhaka* for destroying these three knots.
27. For detailed textual studies, see Flood, 2006: 108–13, 138–43; Dviveda 1992: 121–4; Gupta 1992: 175–208.
28. This *pañcadhāraṇā* is included in *mudrā* in *GhS* 3.2, and is described precisely with each benefit in *GhS* 3.57–63.
29. In *YTU* 85–98 and *VS* 4.6–7, the location of each element is different. Earth: the region from the feet to the knees. Water: the region from the knees to the anus. Fire: the region from the anus to the heart. Air: the region from the heart to the middle of the eyebrows. Sky: the region from the middle of the eyebrows to the crown of the head. Further, the symbolic form of air is a hexagon. *YY* 8.9–11 mentions a different opinion with

respect to the location of the elements. Water: the region from the knees to the navel. Air: the region from the navel to the forehead. Sky: the region from the forehead to the *brahmarandhra*.

30. The *Sarvadarśanasaṅgraha* introduces the science of *svara* (*svaravijñāna*) in the description of *prāṇāyāma* under yoga. This science is also introduced in the *Ā'īn-i Akbarī* by Abu'l Faḍl (d. 1602) and the *ŚSV* was translated into Persian in several forms. See Sakaki 2005: 140; 2004: 134–5.
31. The *PGŚ* begins with an explanation of the evolution process and the nature of each principle. Following this, a description of the mind and the heart is provided. The text then enumerates forty-six different forms of manifestation of the mind, beginning with ignorance; these are to be cleansed for the attainment of liberation. In *VM* 5.29–39, too, eighteen *doṣa*s (defects), eight *rasa*s (tastes) and thirty-two *bhāva*s (emotions) are enumerated after the nature of each element has been described. *SSP* 1.44–9 considers the internal organ (*antaḥkaraṇa*) to be the self-manifestation of the cosmic mind of Śiva and classifies these manifestations into twenty-five different forms.
32. For more information on this relationship in the context of Vedic rituals, see Kaelber 1989: 45–60.
33. This is evident from *Manusmṛti* 6.70: 'Even three *prāṇāyāma*s performed according to the rules prescribed and accompanied by the *vyāhṛti*s and *praṇava* should be regarded as the great *tapas* (*paramam tapas*) for a brāhmaṇa'. Furthermore, the limbs of the yoga are described as followed: 'Just as in the case with metals wherein impurities are burnt when they are melted in the kindled fire, blemishes of the sense organs are destroyed by the control of breath; one should extinguish the blemishes by *prāṇāyāma*s, sin by *dhāraṇā*, contact with the objects of sense by *pratyāhāra*' (71–2). This reference of each limb of yoga is also found in *NGŚ* 111–13 (*KGŚ* 53–4; *HP* 1.39–40).
34. *Haṃsa mantra* appears to have been predominant among the Islamic Sufis. Shaṭṭārī Sufi Shaykh Muḥammad Ghawth Gwāliyarī (d. 1562) referred to the *haṃsa mantra* in the *Baḥr al-Ḥayāt* (Ocean of Life). Further, the famous poet Faiḍī (d. 1595) referred to the *ajapā-japa* in his *Shāriq al-Ma'rifa* (Rising of the Gnosis) and the Pārsī author of the *Dabistān-i Maẕāhib* (School of Manners) (*c*. 1653) is aware of this practice. The most elaborate reference is in the *Risāla-i Ḥaqq Numā* (Compass of Truth) and in the *Majma 'al-Baḥrayn* (Mingling of the Two Oceans) by Dārā Shukoh (d. 1659). See Sakaki 1999: 223–7.
35. The *HYP* suggests that *sahita-kumbhaka* is the common name for all types of *prāṇāyāma* and differentiates it from *kevala kumbhaka* (holding the breath as long as possible). *HYP* 2.44 enumerates eight kinds of *kumbhaka*, namely, *sūryabhedana, ujjāyī, sītkārī, sītalī, bhastrikā, bhrāmarī, mūrcchā* and *plāvinī*. The three types of *bandha*s help in pulling the breath into the *suṣumnā nāḍī* (*HYP* 2.46).

REFERENCES

Apte, M.V. 1967, 'Nāḍīs in Yoga', *Yoga-Mīmāṃsā*, 10.2: 17–24.

Banerjea, Akshaya Kumar, 1983, *Philosophy of Gorakhnath with Goraksha-Vacana-Sangraha*, Delhi: Motilal Banarsidass.

Baṛthvāl, Pītāmbardatt, 1994, *Gorakh-Bānī*, Prayāg: Hindī Sāhitya Sammelan, (5th edn.).

Bhattacharyya, Narendra Nath (ed.), 1989, *Medieval* Bhakti *Movements in India: Śrī Caitanya Quincentenary Commemoration Volume*, Delhi: Munshiram Manoharlal.

Bouy, Christian, 1994, *Les Nātha-Yogin et les Upaniṣads*, Paris: Édition-Diffusion de Boccard.

Briggs, George Weston, 1998, *Gorakhnāth and the Kānphaṭa Yogīs*, Delhi: Motilal Banarsidass (rpt).

Das Gupta, Shashibhusan, 1995, *Obscure Religious Cults*, Calcutta: Firma KLM (rpt).

Dviveda, Vrajavallabha, 1992, 'Having Become a God, He Should Sacrifice to the Gods', in Teun Goudriaan (ed.), *Ritual and Speculation in Early Tantrism: Studies in Honor of André Padoux*, Albany: SUNY Press, pp. 121–38.

Dvivedī, Hazārīprasād 1996, *Nātha Saṃpradāya*, Illāhābād: Lokabhāratī Prakāśan.

Einoo, Shingo, 2002, 'Two Ritual Topics in the Yājñavalkya Smṛti: The Tīrthas in the Hand and the Prāṇāyāma', *Journal of the Japanese Association for South Asian Studies* (*JJASAS*), 14: 25–39.

Flood, Gavin 2006, *The Tantric Body: The Secret Tradition of Hindu Religion*, New York: J.B. Tauris.

Gharote, M.L. and V.A. Bedekar, 1989, *Descriptive Catalogue of Yoga Manuscripts*, Lonavla: Kaivalyadhama S.M.Y.M. Samiti.

Gharote, M.L., 2003, *Prāṇāyāma: The Science of Breath — Theory and Guidelines for Practice*, Lonavla: Lonavla Yoga Institute.

Gonda, Jan, 1977, *Medieval Religious Literature in Sanskrit*, Wiesbaden: Otto Harrassowitz.

Gupta, Sanjukta, 1992, 'Yoga and Antaryāga in Pāñcarātra', in Teun Goudriaan (ed.), *Ritual and Speculation in Early Tantrism: Studies in Honor of André Padoux*, Albany: SUNY Press, pp. 175–208.

Heilijgers-Seelen, Dory, 1994, *The System of Five Cakras in Kubjikāmata-tantra 14-16*, Groningen: Egbert Forsten.

Kaelber, Walter O., 1989, *Tapta Mārga: Asceticism and Initiation in Vedic India*, Albany: SUNY Press.

Kane, Pandurang Vaman, 1962, *History of Dharmaśāstra*, Poona: Bhandarkar Oriental Research Institute, vol. 5, pt. 2.

Kunjunni Raja, K. (ed.), 1971, *New Catalogus Catalogorum*, Madras: University of Madras, vol. 6.

Mallinson, James, 2007, *The Khecarīvidyā of Ādinātha: A Critical Edition and Annotated Translation of an Early Text of Haṭhayoga,* London: Routledge.

McGregor, Ronald Stuart, 1984, *Hindi Literature from its Beginnings to the Nineteenth Century*, Wiesbaden: Otto Harrassowitz.

Pensa, Corrado, 1969, 'On the Purification Concept in Indian Tradition, with Special Regard to Yoga', *East and West*, 19: 194–228.

Sakaki, Kazuyo 1999, 'Myoonkansoohoo: Nāda no Kansoo to Sufi no Ẕikr (Nāda-upāsanā and Sufi Ẕikr)', in Japanese, *Hokkaido Journal of Indological and Buddhist Studies* (*HJIBS*), 14: 217–30.

——, 2003, 'Nātha-ha Kenkyuu - Iki no Hoji (A Study of Nātha Sampradāya: Pās-i Anfās)', in Japanese, *HJIBS*, 18: 107–21.

——, 2004, 'Zentetsugakukooyoo ni arawareta Svara no gaku (Svaravijñāna in the *Sarvadarśanasaṅgraha*)', in Japanese, *HJIBS*, 19: 169–93.

——, 2005, 'Yogico-Tantric Traditions in the Ḥawḍ al-Ḥayāt', *JJASAS*, 17: 135–56.

Sferra, Francesco, 1999, 'The Concept of Purification in Some Texts of Late Indian Buddhism', *Journal of Indian Philosophy*, 27: pp. 83–103.

Singh, Mohan, 1938, *Gorakhnath and Medieval Hindu Mysticism*, Lahore.

Vaudeville, Charlotte, 1974, *Kabir*, vol. 1, Oxford: Clarendon Press.

PART II

THE PHILOSOPHICAL INFLUENCE OF BHAKTI AND ITS POPULAR ACCEPTANCE

8

The Atmosphere of Bhakti in Literature: A Buddhist *Stotra*, a *Kathā* and a Folk Tale

YOSHIFUMI MIZUNO

Literature pertaining to bhakti comprises texts such as the *Bhagavad-gītā*, the *Nārāyaṇīya* chapter of the *Mahābhārata*, the *Bhāgavata Purāṇa* [=*BhP*] and other Purāṇas, some of the Vedānta philosophical works and sectarian literary works in medieval vernacular languages. Besides these literatures, both in courts and in temples or towns, numerous poets have composed poems and singers have been singing songs that characterize the atmosphere of bhakti, most of which have been transmitted from person to person but have not been preserved in the form of written texts.[1] Storytellers related narratives characterizing the atmosphere of bhakti to common citizens and transmitted them from generation to generation.

Many Sanskrit *kāvya* works, for example, Bhāsa's *Rāmacarita*, Kālidāsa's *Raghuvaṃśa*, and Kṛṣṇamiśra's *Prabodha-Candrodaya*, also contain some elements of bhakti, even though they were composed with the aim of entertaining royal persons in court. Court poets attempted to please its elite patrons, because the more these persons appreciated their presentations, the more money or bread they could earn. Court poets sometimes may have woven their own beliefs and thoughts into their works, but sometimes would have been compelled to adapt religious motifs from the *Mahābhārata* and *Rāmāyaṇa* or the Purāṇas, according to their patrons' inclination, even though their own beliefs and thoughts were different.[2]

Nevertheless, any type of literary expression reflects the mood of its time. Audiences and readers, who belong to the same culture that has generated such an atmosphere may be able to enjoy them with a sensitivity to the atmosphere such that they do not find it necessary to mention the atmosphere at each point. In my opinion, bhakti seems to be one example of something that produces such an atmosphere in a society—something that pervades the culture and is preserved in literary works.

Therefore, through intensive reading texts, even though it is not bhakti literature, we will be able to obtain considerable information on the extent to which Indian people had accepted the concept of bhakti and the intensity of the bhaktic circumstance in which they lived . In this article, from non-bhakti literatures such as a Buddhist *stotra* work, *kathā* work in Sanskrit and a folk tale which has various versions in modern vernacular languages, I will attempt to determine the factors of bhakti.

NINEFOLD BHAKTI: A BUDDHIST STOTRA

From the present viewpoint, the *Śatapañcāśataka* (or *Prasāda-pratibhodbhava-stotra*) [= *SPS*] of Mātṛceta (*c.* AD 200, converted to Buddhism from Śaivism (Bailey 1951; Tsuji 1990) has interesting verses; however, this is not so surprising because the religious activity of praising God or chanting hymns or *stotras*, may be common to monotheism and pantheism. I once introduced these verses in my article in Japanese,[3] focusing on a comparison of the implications of *kīrtana-* (or *japa-*) and *smaraṇa*. Bailey states that a hymn may be expected to contain something of the spirit of bhakti associated with the Mahāyānists and their forerunners, but it is a far cry from Mātṛceta's sober, reflective, almost impersonal verses to the fantasies of the *Saddharmapuṇḍarīka* or devotional fervour of Śāntideva (Bailey 1951: 18). Just as Bailey states, in the *SPS* we find some verses that contain something of the spirit of bhakti, regardless of whether or not they are impersonal. The verses (given below) appear to be especially valuable because they contain not only something of the spirit of bhakti but also the same terms as bhakti texts such as the *BhP*.

śravaṇaṃ *tarpayati te prasādayati darśanam /*
vacanaṃ hlādayati te vimocayati śāsanam // 92 //
prasūtir harṣayati te vṛddhir nandayati prajāḥ /
pravṛttir anugṛhṇāti nivṛttir upahanti ca // 93 //

kīrtanaṃ *kilbiṣaharaṃ* ***smraṇaṃ*** *te pramodanam /*
anveṣaṇaṃ matikaraṃ parijñānaṃ viśodhanam // 94 //
śrīkaraṃ te 'bhigamanaṃ sevanaṃ dhīkaraṃ param /
bhajanam nirbhayakaraṃ śaṃkaraṃ paryupāsanam // 95 //
śīlopasaṃpadā śuddhaḥ prasanno dhyānasaṃpadā /
tvaṃ prajñāsaṃpadākṣobhayo hradaḥ puṇyamayo mahān // 96 //
rūpaṃ draṣṭavyaratnaṃ te śravyaratnaṃ subhāṣitam /
dharmo vicāraṇāratnaṃ guṇaratnākaro hy asi // 97 //
tvam oghair uhyamānānāṃ dvīpas trāṇaṃ kṣatātmanām /
śaraṇaṃ bhavabhīrūṇāṃ mumukṣūṇāṃ parāyaṇam // 98 //
satpātraṃ śuddhavṛttatvāt satkṣetraṃ phalasaṃpadā /
sanmitraṃ hitakāritvāt sarvaprāṇabhṛtām asi // 99 //
priyas tvam upakāritvāt suratatvān manoharaḥ /
ekāntakāntaḥ saumyatvāt sarvair bahumato guṇaiḥ // 100 //
hṛdayo si nirvadyatvād ramyo vāgrūpasauṣṭhavāt /
dhanyaḥ sarvārthasiddhatvān maṅgalyo guṇasaṃśrayāt // 101 // (Bailey 1951: 103–10, emphases mine).

92. To hear you brings satisfaction, to see you brings tranquility, your speech refreshes, your teaching liberates.
93. Your birth rejoices the people, your growth delights them, your activity benefits, your ceasing destroys.
94. The celebration of you takes sin away, the remembrance brings happiness, the seeking gives understanding, the full knowledge purifies.
95. In approaching you is fortune, in honouring you exceeding wisdom, in worshipping you freedom from fear, in serving you prosperity.
96. You are a great lake of merit, pure through perfect conduct, calm through perfect meditation, unshakable through perfect wisdom.
97. Your form is a jewel to see, your fair speech a jewel to hear, your law a jewel to ponder; for you are a mine bearing jewels of merits.
98. You are the island of those swept along by the waves, the defence of the stricken in spirit the refuge of them who fear existence, the resource of them who desire release.
99. To all living things you are a good vessel because of your pure conduct, a good field by reason of the excellence of your fruit, a good friend because of the benefits you confer.
100. You are dear for your beneficence, charming for your tenderness, altogether beloved for your gentleness, honoured for all virtues.
101. You are charming because blameless, lovely of excellence of speech and form, wealth-bringing from the accomplishment of every aim, propitious because the receptacle of virtues. (Bailey 1951: 170–1)

These verses constitute a section (*pariccheda*) named Praṇidhi-stavaḥ or His vow, i.e. the benefits he confers on the world (Bailey's translation).

Meanwhile, in the *BhP*, which is believed to have been composed in south India in the ninth or tenth century (cf. Rocher 1986:144-51), Prahlāda responded as follows, when asked by his father, Hiraṇyakaśipu, to emulate his excellent teacher:

śravaṇaṃ kīrtanaṃ viṣṇoḥ smaraṇaṃ pādasevanam /
arcanaṃ vandanaṃ dāsyaṃ sakhyam ātmanivedanam // 23 //
iti puṃsārpitā viṣṇau bhaktis cen navalakṣaṇā /
kriyate bhagavaty addhā tan manye'dhītam uttamam // 24 //(*BhP* VII.5)

(1) To hear the names, episodes, etc., of Viṣṇu, (2) to sing of his name and glories, (3) to remember him (his name), (4) to render service unto him, (5) to worship him, (6) to pay obeisance to him, (7) to dedicate all one's actions to him, (8) to confide in him as a friend, (9) to offer one's body and belongings to his service and care. I consider it as the highest type of learning if one offers himself completely to the Lord and performs this ninefold devotion (complete dedication is regarded as the condition that precedes real devotion). (Tagare 1976: III.912)

This constitutes the ninefold bhakti whose purpose is believed to be to help devotees maintain contact with God. However, in this portion of the text, there is no mention of the effects of each aspect.[4] The mention of ninefold bhakti in the *Adhyātma Rāmāyaṇa* and *Rāmcaritmānas* is also very similar (Lutgendorf 2001: 125, 135); however, the terms are different from those in the *BhP*.[5]

I will compare each term of the ninefold bhakti with the corresponding term in the *SPS*.

Śravaṇa

First, *śravaṇa* is described in the *SPS* as the satisfaction that a man feels when he has heard Buddha's words. In the *BhP* too *śravaṇa* is described as follows:

yatra bhāgavatā rājan sādhavo viśadāśayāḥ /
bhagavad-guṇānukathana-śravaṇa-vyagra-cetasaḥ // 39 //
tasmin mahan-mukharitā madhubhic-caritra-pīyūṣa-śeṣa-saritaḥ paritaḥ sravanti /
tā ye pibanty avitṛṣo nṛpa gāḍhakarṇais tān na spṛśanty aśana-tṛḍ-bhaya-śoka-mohaḥ // 40 //(*BhP* IV.29) (Prabhupada: 89–90)

Oh, King! [He can listen to those stories] in places where pious and pure-hearted votaries of God narrate and listen to the glorification of the attributes of the Lord with eager hearts. There [to the congregation of devotees] flow forth on all sides rivers [entirely] of pure nectar [in the form] of stories of Lord Viṣṇu [the destroyer of demon Madhu] sweetly sung by noble souls. Oh King! Those who drink those [nectar-like stories] with intent ears and without being surfeited, are never touched [affected] by hunger, thirst, fear, sorrow and delusion. (Tagare 1976: II, 614)

Hearing the words or stories of Buddha or of Viṣṇu results in the five senses being satisfied.[6]

Kīrtana

The *SPS* and the *BhP* ascribe the same meaning to *kīrtana*, i.e. atonement. Rukmani introduces a verse from the *BhP* as follows:

kaler doṣa-nidhe rājann asti hy eko mahān guṇaḥ /
kīrtanād eva kṛṣṇasya mukta-saṅgaḥ paraṃ vrajet // 51 // (*BhP* XII.3)
[Rukmani 1970: 147].

Kali is certainly the store-house of all evils. But O king, there is one very great virtue and a good point in that age, inasmuch as by singing the name and the glory of Śrī Kṛṣṇa, that person is freed from all attachments and attains to the highest region (Vaikuṇṭha). (Tagare 1976: V, 2142)

I was able to find other verses that use the term *kīrtana* in the sense of purging of sins as follows:

praṇamya sirasādhīśam uttama-ślokam avyayam /
agāyata yaśodhāma kīrtanya-guṇa-sat-katham // 4 //
so 'nukampita īśena parikramya praṇamya tam /
lokasya paśyato lokaṃ svam agān mukta-kilbiṣaḥ // 5 // (*BhP* VIII.4)

He bowed down his head to the eternal Supreme Lord of excellent renown and he chanted the praise of his worth, extolling (innumerable) virtues and sacred episodes of that abode of glory.

Being favoured by the Lord with his grace, he was purged of all sins. Going round the Lord (reverentially) and paying him obeisance, he repaired his own region (of Gandharvas) in the very presence of all the people. (Tagare 1976: III, 1014)

In the *Nārada Bhakti Sūtra* (=*NBS*) as well, it is asserted that for worldly people, *śravaṇa* and *kīrtana* are two bhakti activities that are easier than others such as the abandonment of all sensible objects.

loke 'pi bhagavad-guṇa-śravaṇa-kīrtanāt // 37 // (*NBS* 37)

Smaraṇa

Even though in the *SPS* it is ambiguously stated that *smaraṇa* brings happiness, it must be the means for attaining God as is mentioned in the *Bhagavad-gītā* (VIII, 13-14). In the *BhP*, it is evident that remembrance *smaraṇa* of the gods is effective for satisfaction with divine love as well as for the purpose of atonement, just as in the case of *kīrtana* (VIII, 4, 17-24: ... *smaranti* ... *mucyante hy enaso 'khilāt.*).

ya etat kīrtayen mahyaṃ tvayā gītam idam naraḥ /
tvāṃ ca māṃ ca smaran kāle karma-bandhāt pramucyate // 14 // (*BhP* VII.10)

A person who recites this song (prayer) sung by you to Me and remembers you and Me, becomes free from the bondage of *karman* in due course. (Tagare 1976: III, 956)

smarantaḥ smarayantaś ca mitho'ghaughaharaṃ harim /
bhaktyā saṃjātayā bhaktyā bibhraty utpulakāṃ tanum // 31 // (*BhP* XI.3)

Remembering themselves and reminding each other of Hari who annihilates the mass of sins instantly, their devotion is developed unto Love divine and out of the thrill of ecstasy of this divine Love, the hair all over their bodies stands on end (and this spiritual delight of the disciples, gives the spiritual preceptor the highest delight). (Tagare 1976: V, 1909)

In the *Śāṇḍilya Sūtra* (*SBS*) as well, it is stated that *smṛti* (the remembrance of God) is effective for *prāyaścitta* (expiation) as well as *kīrtana*.

smṛti-kīrttyoḥ kathādeś cārttau prāyaścitta-bhāvāt // (*SBS* 2,2,19)

Pāda-sevana

In the *SPS*, the description that approaching (*abhi-gamana*) and serving (*sevana*) Buddha are for fortune and exceeding wisdom, respectively, seems to be comparable to *pāda-sevana* in the *BhP*.

dharmārtha-kāma-mokṣākhyāṃ ya icchec chreya ātmanaḥ /
ekam eva hares tatra kāraṇaṃ pāda-sevanam // 41 // (*BhP* IV.8)

If one wishes to be blessed with good fortune, with *dharma*, *artha*, *kāma* and *mokṣa* (righteousness, wealth, sense-pleasure, and liberation from saṃsāra), the worship of Hari's feet is the only course for attaining it. (Tagare 1976: II, 473–4)

na kāmaye'nyaṃ tava pāda-sevanād akiṃcana-prārthyatamād varaṃ vibho /
ārādhya kastvāṃ hy apavargadaṃ hare vṛnīta āryo varam ātma-bandhanam // 56 // (*BhP* X.51)

Oh, Omnipresent Lord! I do not seek any other boon from you; I only want to render service to your feet, which is regarded as the most covetable blessing according to those who have renounced everything and possess nothing of their own). Having propitiated you, the bestower of *mokṣa* (liberation), Oh Hari, what wise man would solicit from you a boon which will create a bondage to one's soul. (Tagare 1976: IV, 1578)

Arcana

Bhajat, translated as 'worshipping' by Bailey and mentioned in the *SPS* as something that brings freedom from fear, is the present participle of the verb √*bhaj* (to share). This is the root of bhakti and of the Hindi *bhajan*. It is uncertain whether *bhajat* in the *SPS* means the same as *bhajan* in the *BhP*, because the latter at present means a devotional song, and may have multiple connotations. However, from the viewpoint of comparing the description of the *SPS* and the ninefold bhakti, *bhajat* seems to be the same concept as *arcana* (worship, or praise) of the ninefold bhakti in the *BhP*, corroborated by the order of the terms presented. This may be the reason why the *BhP* states that enemies such as love, greed, fear (*bhaya*), etc., should be destroyed by the sword of spiritual knowledge sharpened by worship (*arcana*) of the feet of the most exalted souls (VII, 15, 43-5).

Meanwhile, in the *NBS*, *a-vyavṛtta-bhajana* (unretarded worship of God) is said to overcome the temptation of worldly desires and develop the love of God (*NBS* 36, tr. Sinha 1998: 18). This phrase seems to share the same view as the *SPS*, in which *bhajana* (worship of a Buddha) has been said to bring *abhaya* of freedom from fear.

Vandana, Dāsya

The concept of *pary-upāsana*, translated by Bailey as serving and mentioned in the *SPS* as for prosperity, might pertain to both *vandana* (paying obeisance) and *dāsya* (to dedicate all one's actions). It goes without saying that the prosperity by *pary-upāsana* is not worldly but unworldly. In the *BhP* as well, we find that it is by paying obeisance to the feet (of *brāhmaṇa*s) that he (Hari) gets Lakṣmī, goddess of prosperity (*BhP* VI.21.38).

tasyaiva me sauhṛda-sakhya-maitrī dāsyaṃ punar-janmani janmani syāt /
mahānubhāvena guṇālayena viṣaj-jatas-tat-puruṣa-prasaṅgaḥ // 36 //
bhaktāya citrā bhagavān hi sampado rājyaṃ vibhūtīr na samarthayat yajaḥ /
adīrgha-bodhāya vicakṣaṇaḥ svayaṃ paśyan nipātaṃ dhaninām madodbhavam // 37 // (*BhP* X.81)

May I, in every future birth, be blessed with his good-will, friendship, love and service. May I have the fortune of associating myself with his devotees and may I cherish my [ever-increasing] devotion to that abode of excellences and glorious powers.

God, eternal, omniscient and glorious, himself notices the downfall of the rich, caused by the pride of their wealth, and does not wish to confer wonderful affluence, kingship and other spiritual powers or authorities on his devotee [even though he may solicit it] but grants them to the shortsighted ones (Tagare 1976: IV, 1762).

Sakhya, Ātma-nivedana

The description of Buddha as a good friend for the people who praise him [*SPS* V.99] seems to be similar to the concept of *sakhya*. With regard to *ātma-nivedana* we cannot find the corresponding term in the *SPS*, probably because the concept is peculiar to the later bhakti.

As has been observed above, it is notable that a Buddhist *stotra* composed about 700 long years before and in the north-west of India, has almost the same concepts as those of the ninefold bhakti of the *BhP*. This is thought to indicate that Indian people who wanted to embrace the grace of the divine had similar tendencies of thought and like approach to the object of worship. This would, in turn, have been caused by the atmosphere of bhakti.

SIṂHĀSANA-DVĀTRIṂŚIKĀ

In the Sanskrit *kathā Siṃhāsana-Dvātriṃśikā* (*SD*), otherwise called *Vikrama-Carita* composed not before the 1200 (Edgerton 1993: pt. 1, liii), particularly the southern and metrical recensions out of the five main recensions (the others being Jaina, Vararuci and a brief recensions), we find expressions of the religious atmosphere of both bhakti and tantrism. The bravery and generosity of King Vikrama has been recounted over and over in thirty-two tales. Some of this deeds seem to spring from bhakti and from bhaktic circumstances. Below is my attempt to compare these events with the activities of bhakti, such as gift (*dāna*) or charity (*tyāga*) and self-sacrifice (*ātma-nivedana*), particularly as described in the *BhP*.

The plot fairly common to almost all the tales of the *SD* is that Vikrama displays great courage in saving someone or in doing something out of curiosity and ends up getting something, which he immediately offers as a gift or as charity to that another person. Let us now explore to whom Vikrama made such offerings and what these were. The numbers in parenthesis indicate the order of the tales in the southern recension.

Offerings to *Brāhmaṇa*s

a crore's worth of gold (1); wish (*vara*) (2); four magic jewels (3); absolution from the crime of kidnapping (4); city, wealth, and many women (6); a woman (9); fruits for agelessness (10); a *liṅga* that grants all desires (14); a woman and a kingdom (15); gold (16); two rings that yield a load of gold everyday (18); a potion and an elixir, one of which turns base metals into gold, the other giving freedom from old age and death (19); eight jewels that give eight supernatural powers (21); magic quicksilver (22); a jar of nectar to revivify an army (24); the cow of wishes (26); and money (29).

Offerings to persons who are not *Brāhmaṇa*s:

five jewels to a messenger (5); revival and a kingdom to a dead couple (7); fulfilment of a merchant's desire to fill a pond with water (8); a promise from a *rākṣasa* to abstain from eating men (11); nine jars of treasure to a merchant (12); merit obtained by chanting the sacred name in a river for twelve years and the power to go to heaven to a *rākṣasa* (13); saved a rival king from the daily sacrifice by offering his own body (17); a magic piece of chalk with which an army could be depicted, a wand by which an army could be brought to life with the right hand or dismissed again with the left and a magic cloth to grant all desires to a king (20); everything in his treasury to all people to come (23); wish to a gambler (27); all the tributes sent by a king to a juggler (30).

Of these eight are immaterial: the wish (2 and 27), absolution from the crime of kidnapping (4), revival (7), fulfilment of a desire (8), obtaining a promise (11), merit obtained by chanting the sacred name in a river for twelve years[7] and the power to go to heaven (13), and saving a rival king from the daily sacrifice (17).

These cases are illustrations of the transfer of merit (*pariṇāma(na)*), in that they are all immaterial and have been given by King Vikrama after he received them as a merit. Although it is extremely hard to precisely compare the concepts of *dāna* and *pariṇāma*, we will now concentrate on *dāna* and treat everything in the context of *dāna*.

As we have seen above, in the *SD*, offering a gift or donation is emphasized as an activity that should be undertaken not only for *Brāhmaṇa*s (poor *Brāhmaṇa*s in many cases) but also for ordinary persons in difficulty. In particular, in seventh tale (southern recension), there is a mention of the chapter on the giving of gifts (*dāna-khanda*) in Hemādri's (1260–1309) *Caturvarga-Cintāmaṇi*, a text of Dharma-nibandha, and it is portrayed that a merchant offered a gift much after these prescriptions were given and visited Kṛṣṇa in Dvārkā to obtain a fortune as reward.

The earliest phase of *dāna* might be limited to an honorarium from the client of a ritual ceremony to the *Brāhmaṇa* as its conductor. A *Brāhmaṇa* conducted a ritual ceremony and was given something as a reward. A client gave *dāna* and received a mental fortune as the result. In the case of Buddhism, *dāna* from a client was important for a monk to maintain a decent livelihood because he could not earn a living independently through any other means. The monks who received a *dāna* from volunteers, preached the teachings of Buddha to them in return. Imparting the teaching was also called *dāna* or *dharma-dāna*, which is different from *āmiṣa-dāna* which refers to giving material things such as money, food, and clothes.

With regard to the concepts or theories of the gift in ancient India, the investigation by Maria Heim (2004) is deep and comprehensive, based on the Dharma-śāstra, *nibandha* (Hindu), Jaina non-canonical works, and Theravāda Buddhist texts on lay conduct.

Although Heim introduces the phrase of the Dharma-śāstra that one who gives with *śraddhā* (esteem) and bhakti (devotion) to a worthy recipient, even if it is just a handful of vegetables, enjoys every happiness (Heim 2004: 45), she emphasizes the moral and ethical element. In the *BhP* as well, *dāna* is one of four *dharmas* (the others being *satya*, *tapas* and *vidyā* or *dayā*) (*BhP* III.12.41; XII.3.18), or of many more *dharmas* (*BhP* X.47.24).

Further, Heim (2004: 95) mentions another aspect of *dāna* as something that purifies the donor. We find the same aspect of *dāna* in the *BhP* is one among some elements whereby one can get rid of sins (*BhP* VI.2.17), by which an impure mind is made pure (*BhP* XI.6.9; XI.19.4.29.37), or by which Viṣṇu is gratified, especially when it is given to Caṇḍālas, to the poor, and to the blind (*BhP* VIII.16.61) (Acharya 1993: 255). Such a meaning occurs also in Mahāyāna Buddhism, wherein *dāna* had been listed as one among the six *pāramitā* (austerities) that should be performed by a monk whose every action is for the benefit of others.

In the context of religious austerities, especially in that of Mahāyāna Buddhism, *dāna* means *tyāga* (renunciation), an action for which the donor does not expect reward but attains a state of self-denial. Even the *BhP* has mentions of *tyāga*. It is a way to attain atonement (VI.1.13) or a means to mind control (X.47.33) or a stepping-stone to bhakti (XI.19.23). On the contrary, in the context of Vedic ritual, it is sometimes described as an obstacle to God (XI.12.1; 14.20).

In the *NBS*, two kinds of *tyāga*, namely *viṣaya-tyāga* (abandonment of sensible objects) and *saṅga-tyāga* (abandonment of attachment), are said to make the love of God possible (*NBS* 35).

As in Mahāyāna Buddhism, the gift of security (*abhaya-dāna*) is said to be most important in the *Viṣṇu Smṛti* (Sh. 92) (Acharya 1993: 5; Jolly 1965: 270-1). This is so because this gift is easier to offer than material things (*āmiṣa dāna*), which can be offered only by the rich, and the gift of doctrinal lecture, which can only be given by the person who has doctrinal knowledge.

The following verses have been quoted from an unknown Purāṇa in the thirteenth tale of the *SD*.

abhayaṃ sarva-bhūtebhyo yo dadāti dayāparaḥ /
tasya deha-vimuktasya kṣaya eva na vidyate // 6 //

. . .

mahatām api yajñānāṃ kālena kṣīyate phalam /
dattvā'bhayaṃ pradānasya kṣaya eva na vidyate // 8 //
dattam iṣṭaṃ tapas taptaṃ tīrtha-yātrā śrutaṃ tathā /
sarvāṇy abhaya-dānasya kalāṃ nārhanti soḍaśīm // 9 //
catuḥ-sāgara-paryantāṃ yo dadyād vasudhām imām /
yaś cābhayaṃ ca bhūtebhyas tayor abhayado'dhikaḥ // 10 //

. . .

paropakāra-vyāpāra-paro yaḥ puruṣo bhuvi /
sa saṃpadaṃ samapnoti parād api ca yat param // 14 // (*SD* XIII. southern recension) (Edgerton 1993: 2.115).

Whosoever is full of compassion and gives security to all creatures, he will never perish, even when he loses his body. (6) ... Even the fruit of great sacrifices is exhausted in time; if one gives security, the fruit of the gift is never exhausted. (8) Alms, offerings, asceticism performed, journeys of pilgrimage, and sacred lore as well, all are not worth the sixteenth part of the gift of security. (9) As between one who gives this whole earth bounded by the four seas and one who gives security to creatures, the giver of security is greater. (10) ... A man who makes it his supreme occupation to help others in the world, shall obtain good fortune and a [station] higher than even the highest [or final beatitude]. (14) (Edgerton 1993: 1.126)

These phrases seem to have come from the same concepts of *dāna* as those of Mahāyāna Buddhism.

In bhakti as well, the practice of giving security (*abhaya-dāna*) to another (*paropakāra*) brings ecstatic bliss to a bhakta as a donor, because he or she feels a sense of intimacy with God, who exists in everyone and everything in this world. The thought of the omnipresence of God[8] is inevitable in the theory of universal charity. In this respect, Anand aptly states that the *BhP* provides two reasons for the insistence on universal charity: God's love for all and God's presence in all (Anand 1996: 160). Further, he introduces the story of Rantideva[9] as an example of the latter. The story of Rantideva is as follows,

rantidevasya hi yaśa ihāmutra ca gīyate //2//
viyad-vittasya dadato labdhaṃ labdhaṃ bubhukṣataḥ /
niṣkiṃcanasya dhīrasya sakuṭumbasya sīdataḥ //3//
vyatīyur aṣṭacatvāriṃśad-ahāny apibataḥ kila /
dhṛta-pāyasa-saṃyāvaṃ toyaṃ prātar upasthitam //4//
kṛcchra-prāpta-kuṭumbasya kṣuttṛḍbhyāṃ jāta-vepathoḥ /
atithir brāhmaṇaḥ kāle bhoktu-kāmasya cāgamat //5//
tasmai saṃvyabhajat so'nnam ādṛtya śraddhayānvitaḥ /
hariṃ sarvatra sampaśyan sa bhuktvā prayayau dvijaḥ //6//
athānyo bhokṣyamāṇasya vibhaktasya mahīpate /
vibhaktaṃ vyabhajat tasmai vṛṣalāya hariṃ smaran //7//
yāte śūdre tam anyo'gād atithiḥ śvabhir āvṛtaḥ /
rājan me dīyatām annaṃ sagaṇāya bubhukṣate //8//
sa ādṛtyāvaśiṣṭam yad bahumānapuraskṛtam /
tac ca dattvā namaś cakre śvabhyaḥ śvapataye vibhuḥ //9//
pānīya-mātram uccheṣaṃ tac caika-paritarpaṇaṃ /
pāsyataḥ pulkaso'bhyāgādapo dehyaśubhasya me //10//
tasya tāṃ karuṇāṃ vācaṃ niśamya vipulaśramāṃ /
kṛpayā bhṛśa-saṃtapta idam āhāmṛtaṃ vacaḥ //11//
na kāmaye'ham gatim īśvarāt parām aṣṭarddhi-yuktām apunarbhavaṃ vā /
ārti prapadye'khila-deha-bhājām antaḥ sthito yena bhavanty aduḥkhaḥ //12//
kṣuttṛṭśramo gātra-priśramaś ca dainyaṃ klamaḥ śoka-viṣāda-mohāḥ /
sarve nivṛttāḥ kṛpaṇasya jantor jijīviṣor jīva-jalārpaṇān me //13//
iti prabhāṣya pānīyaṃ mriyamāṇaḥ pipāsayā /
pulkasāyād adād dhīro nisarga-karuṇo nṛpaḥ //14//
tasya tribhuvanādhīśāḥ phaladāḥ phalam icchatām /
ātmanāṃ darśayāñ cakrur māyā viṣṇu-vinirmitāḥ //15//
sa vai tebhyo namas-kṛtya nissaṅgo vigata-spṛhaḥ /
vāsudeve bhagavati bhaktyā cakre manaḥ param //16//
īśvarālambanaṃ cittaṃ kurvato'nanyarādhasaḥ /
māyā guṇamayī rājan svapnavat pratyalīyata //17//
tat prasaṅgānubhāvena rantidevānuvartinaḥ /
abhavan yoginaḥ sarve nārāyaṇa-parāyaṇāḥ //18// (*BhP* IX.21)

The glory of Rantideva is eulogized in this world as well as in heaven. By giving away wealth that came his way without efforts (like the sky) thinking it to be momentary, he became hungry and destitute of everything (including provisions even for the evening). While the hero suffered hardships along with his family, and forty-eight days passed during which he could not get even water to drink. In the morning (of the forty-ninth day), he happened to get by chance ghee, rice cooked in milk, and *saṃyāva* (an article of food consisting of wheat-flour, raw-sugar, ghee and milk) along with water. He whose family was distressed and trembling due to utter starvation and parched with thirst, was about to partake of the food when a *Brāhmaṇa* guest arrived. As he visualized Hari everywhere (and in everybody), he received the *Brāhmaṇa* with reverence and faith, gave him his share of food. The *Brāhmaṇa* took his meal and went his way. While he was about to partake of the remaining food which was distributed among themselves, another stranger—now a śūdra—arrived. He gave him the portion of the food so distributed, contemplating all the while on Hari, king of the earth. When the śūdra departed, another stranger surrounded by a park of hounds approached him and requested, 'Oh king! May food be served to me along with my dogs, who are hungry'. The king received them kindly and gave to him respectfully whatever food that remained with him and vowed to the dogs and the master of those hounds. Now some water, just sufficient to quench the thirst of one person, remained. While he was about to drink it, a Caṇḍāla came up and requested, 'Give water to me who am a low caste person'. Hearing his pitiful request uttered with great pain and exhaustion, the king, deeply moved and tormented with compassion, uttered the following nectar-like speech. 'I do not seek from the Almighty Lord the highest position attended with eight spiritual powers (e.g. *aṇiman*, *laghiman*, etc., detailed in the *Yogasūtra*), nor emancipation from *saṃsāra*; I would rather prefer to dwell in all beings and undergo suffering for them, whereby they may be free from miseries. By offering water which was essential to save the life of an unfortunate creature who craved for life, my personal hunger, thirst, exhaustion of limbs, distress, languor, grief, despondency and delusion—all have disappeared.' Expressing such nobility of heart, the king who was compassionate by nature and full of fortitude, gave that water to the Caṇḍāla, though he himself was on the point of death through thirst. To him, the lord of the three worlds (e.g. God Brahmā and others) who bestows fruits on those who seek them and who visited him in those illusory forms (a short while ago) under instructions from Lord Viṣṇu, revealed themselves to him. The king being entirely free from attachments, cherished no desires. Bowing down to them all, he concentrated his mind on glorious Lord Vāsudeva with utmost devotion, and sought no boon from them.

Concentrating his mind on the Almighty Lord as the only support, and cherishing no desire for any fruit [in return] there-from, *Māyā* the deluding potency of the Lord constituted of three *guṇas* [automatically] dissolved (disappeared altogether) like a dream, in the case of Rantideva, Oh king. By virtue of close association with him, all yogins who follows closely Rantideva (i.e. his path of intense, selfless devotion) became absolutely devoted to Lord Nārāyaṇa. (Tagare 1976: III, 1232–4)

The act of Rantideva seems to have been based on the same psychological state as that of Vikrama. The latter's giving of gifts seems to have stemmed from the bhaktic mind. The reason why the king could not help giving gifts, even his own body, may be that he loved everyone like God, and not because he felt it was his duty.

THE TALE OF CANDRAHĀSA

Folk tales have been preserved in various literary genres such as *kathā*, the canonical and commentarial works of Buddhism and Jainism, and in the Purāṇas. The reason for parallel stories in different works may be that they originated from the same folk tale. (Parallel implies that they have the same details and are not similar just by accident.) A composer or an arranger of such works might more often adapt a popular folk tale or known narrative for his own work rather than invent an original story. At the time of re-telling the story, he or she may add some elements to the existing one because he or she wants the new work to be appreciated by the audience. In this way, a story gets transmitted, suffering little change from one to another, regardless of whether it is narrated verbally or written as a text. Thus, we can say that according to its environment, such a story is as changeable as organic matter.

As I have investigated in the past, a well-known folk tale of Candrahāsa, of which historical transformations have taken place from ancient to modern times and in as large an area as Eurasia,[10] is a good instance of a story being enlarged or transformed with new elements.

The brief outline common to almost all the versions is as follows. A person of noble parentage one day hears the awful prophecy that an orphan will become his son and successor and decides to kill the orphan. Alternatively, a person, who had begun raising a foundling boy, believing a hopeful prophecy, decides to kill him because his wife bears him a son and the presence of the foundling is now burdensome to him. After some attempts to murder the boy, the person makes him deliver a letter saying that the bearer of the letter must be killed. However, on the way, while the boy is sleeping, by chance, a girl finds the letter and reads it. Since she has fallen in love with him at first sight, she rewrites the operative portion of the letter stating that the bearer of the letter should be made to marry her. Her mission is successful. Finally (or during a murder attempt in some older versions) the person's own son is killed in place of the boy, by a hired murderer.

This tale with the letter of death and the rewriting of the letter motifs, and folk tale versions can be found in AT930 (Uther 2004) and K511, K978 and K1612 (Thompson 1955 and 1958).

Here is a list of various older Indian versions of this tale with a rough estimate of each date and focus only on the one point of bhakti, without presenting of the argument on the worldwide and complicated transmission of this tale.[11]

- Jātaka of a child in the *Six Perfection Sūtra* (a Chinese Avadāna) tr. Liuidu Jijing (in Chinese) <AD3c.>
- 'The Tale of Ghosaka' in the *Manorathapūraṇī* (a Commentary of the Aṅguttara-Nikāya) by Buddhaghoṣa (in Pāli) *c.* 400–50
- 'The Tale of Ghosaka' in the *Dammapada Aṭṭakathā* by Buddhaghoṣa (in Pāli) *c.* 400–50.
- 'The Tale of Chandrahāsa' in the *Jaimini-Bhārata* (in Sanskrit) *c.* 1100.
- 'A Tale in the *Prabandha-cintāmaṇi*' by Merutuṅga (Jaina, in Sanskrit), *c.* 1306.
- The *Champaka-śreṣṭhi Kathānaka* by Jinakīrti (Jaina, in Sanskrit), *c.* 1450.
- 'The Tale of Damannaka' in the *Kathākośa* (Jaina, in Sanskrit), date unknown.
- 'The Tale of Chandrahāsa' in the *Bhakti-rasa-bodhinī* (commentay on a hagiography, *Bhakta-mālā* of Nābhādāsa) by Priyādāsa (Hindi), 1712.
- 'The Tale of Chandrahāsa' in the Amar Chitra Kathā Series No. 97 Anant Pai, ed., Subha Rao script, Pratap Mulick, n.d. Bombay; India Book House (in English), twentieth century.
- Other folk tale versions in vernacular languages.

There is a large time gap between the Pāli versions and the *Jaimini-Bhārata* version. A clear difference can be found between the versions before the fifth century and those on and after the *Jaimini-Bhārata* in terms of the construction of the plot. The clearest difference is that only the older Chinese and Pāli versions have the motif that the orphan was dispatched with the letter of his death to a potter but that the natural son relieved him of the role and was killed in a burning kiln by the potter.

With regard to the entire *Jaimini-Bhārata*, Derret (1970) determines that the *Jaimini-Bhārata*, which contains the tale of Chandrahāsa, has come from Europe, and some scholars such as Koskikallio (1993: 111) state that the *Jaimini-Bhārata* has a close connection with the Purāṇas which promoted the ideas of bhakti in Sanskrit literature; thus, the *Jaimini-Bhārata* seems to have followed a long and complicated process for its completion. It is necessary for us to examine this process conscientiously; however, at present, we do not have enough text data to do so. I will indicate only one point concerning the atmosphere of bhakti in the tale of Chandrahāsa.

In almost all the versions during the time of and after the *Jaimini-Bhārata*, with the exception of the Jaina versions, what protected the orphan was the power of a sacred stone—the *śālagrāma*—that had been given by Nārada Ṛṣi. In older versions, there is no mention of the *śālagrāma*.

It goes without saying that the *śālagrāma* (or *śāligrāma*) represents Viṣṇu, just as the *liṅga* represents Śiva. As many scholars state,[12] stories about the *śālagrāma* and its power are told in various Purāṇas. Among them, one of the oldest mentions may be in the Vana Parvan of the *Mahābhārata*.[13] Śaṅkara Ācārya makes a mention of the *śālagrāma* in his *Vedāntasūtra*,[14] but this could be much later that the popular worship of the *śālagrāma*. However, the mention of the power of the *śālagrāma* in 22 verses (80–102, in chapter 58) at the end of the story of Candrahāsa seems to be on the same line with the Purāṇas, such as the *Padma Purāṇa*, the *Agni Purāṇa* and the *Garuḍa Purāṇa* (Kirfel 1935; Oppert 1986).[15]

This is a good instance of the rising atmosphere of bhakti among the people breaking into the stream of the literary transmission—in this case of a folk tale—and influencing the construction of the plot.

CONCLUSION

We have investigated the atmosphere of bhakti in three types of non-bhakti literary works. In the former two, we read texts focusing on the concept and the meanings of technical words, i.e. on an abstract idea; in the case of the latter, we focused on the embodied matter, which can be regarded as a symbol of advanced devotional activities in a society.

The intense atmosphere of bhakti was present in each work, and it has become clear that the tradition of bhakti devotion can be detected not only in bhakti literatures but elsewhere also. In other words, we are apt to slot all kinds of literature into frames or genres, according to a stereotype, and to search for a required answer only in the texts of one or other genre. Until such a stereotype has not been broken, we will be forced to view things from a narrow perspective.

Even when we research the cultural phase of bhakti and the doctrinal modification of bhakti in the complete history of Indian society, we need to examine all kinds of literature, especially literary works. The reason for this is that literature is testimony to the lives of persons.

ABBREVIATIONS

AdhR : Munilal, tr., *Adhyātmarāmāyaṇa* with Hindi Translation, Gorakhpur: Gita Press, n.d.

BhG : *Bhagavad-gītā.*

BhP : *Bhāgavata Purāṇa*, C. L. Goswami, tr., *Śrīmad Bhāgavata Mahāpurāṇa* (With Sanskrit Text and English Translation), Gorakhpur: Gita Press, 1971.

MBh : *Mahābhārata*, Poona Critical Edition.

NBS : Nandalal Sinha, tr., *Bhaktisūtra of Nārada*, New Delhi: Munshiram Manoharlal, 2nd edn., 1998 (1st edn. 1918).

RCM : Hanumanprasad Poddar, comm., *Śrī Rām-carit-mānas*, Gorakhpur; Gita Press, 11th edn., 1949.

SBS : Nandalal Sinha, tr., *Śāṇḍilyasūtram*, with the Commentary of Svapneśvara, New Delhi: Munshiram Manoharlal, 2nd edn., 1998 (1st edn. 1918).

NOTES

1. According to Callewaert (1992) article, when the repertories grew larger, some singers or musicians began to write the music down in something akin to a notebook in order to aid recall.

2. Rūpa Gosvāmi (1500–50?), the author of the *Bhakti-Rasāmṛta-Sindhu*, might have composed his poetry not for entertainment but for missions of bhakti. Wulff (1984: 5) introduces Sukumar Sen's view that Rūpa Gosvāmi's *Vidhagdhamādhava* and the other drama have indeed been read through the years by Vaiṣṇavas, not simply as works of literature, but as vehicles of religious truth.
3. Yoshifumi Mizuno, 2000, 'Chanting of Sacred Names in India (in Japanese)', *Śūnyatā and Reality, Volume in Memory of Professor EJIMA Yasunori*, Tokyo; Shumju-sha, 2000, pp. 481–500.
4. According to Tagare's note Jīva Gosvāmin's *Krama-sandarbha* provides an excellent exposition of bhakti and its nine forms, which deserve perusal in the original (Tagare 1976: III, 921); however, I was unable to obtain this reference.
5. In the *Adhyātmarāmāyaṇa*, the line-up of the ninefold bhakti is as follows:

   sat-saṅgati-, kathā-lāpa-, guṇeraṇa-, vyākhyā-, ācāryopāsana-, pūjana-, mantropāsaka-, bhakta-sarvabhūta-pūja-bāhyārtha-virāga-, and *tattva-vicāra-.* (*AdhR* III.10.21-7: p. 163)

   I would like to introduce two verses before the above-mentioned line-up of the ninefold bhakti.

   puṃstve strītve viśeṣo vā jāti-nāmāśramādayaḥ /
   na kāraṇaṃ mad-bhajane bhaktir eva hi kāraṇam //20 //
   yajña-dāna-tapobhir vā vedādhyayana-karmabhiḥ /
   naiva draṣṭum ahaṃ śakyo mad-bhakti-vimukhaiḥ sadā // 21// (*AdhR* III,10: p. 163)

   As Lutgendorf mentions (Lutgendorf 2001:125), in the *Rām-Carit-Mānas*, there is a mention of the ninefold bhakti, which is similar to that in the *AdhR*.

   navadhā bhagati kahaũ tohi pāhīṃ /
   sāvadhāna suni dharu mana māhīṃ //
   prathama bhagati saṃtanha kara saṃgā /
   dūsari rati mama kathā prasaṃgā //4//
   gura pada paṃkaja sevā tīsari bhagati amāna /
   cauthi bhagati mama guna gana kara-i kapama taji gāna //35//
   maṃtra jāpa mama dṛṛha bisvāsā /
   paṃcama bhajata so beda prakāsā //
   chaṭha dama sīla birati bahu karamā /
   nirati niraṃtara sajjana dharamā //1//
   sātavã sama mohi maya jaga dekhā /
   moteṃ saṃta adhika kari lekhā //
   āthavã jathālābha saṃtoṣa /
   sapanehūṁ nahiṃ dekha-i paradoṣā //2//
   navama sarala saba sana chalahīnā /
   mama bharosa hiyã haraṣa na dīnā //
   nava mahūṁ eka-u jinha keṃ hoī /
   nāri puruṣa sacarācara koī //3// (*RCM* III, dohā 35, 4–36,3)

6. Bailey (1951: 199–209) introduces some valuable parts of the commentary of Nandipriya in the appendix of his edited book. According to its mention of the related matter, Nandipriya has taken an example of householder Anāthapiṇḍada as proof of effective *śravaṇa*. In this case *śravaṇa* means to hear the word 'Buddha', that is, the name of Buddha and not his words.

   Even in the *Saddharmapuṇḍarīka* (XXIV, Samanta-mukha-parivarta, v. 4), although there did not exist the term 'name' in the phrase, it has been interpreted as 'hearing the name (of Avalokiteśvara)' and has been translated so.

   śravaṇo atha darśano pi ca anupūrvaṃ ca tathā anusmṛtiḥ /
   bhavatīha amogha prāṇināṃ sarva-duḥkha-bhava-śoka-nāśakaḥ // (Wogihara 1994: 368)

   The phrase *te śravaṇa* in the *SPS* which is translated 'to hear you' by Bailey might be able to be interpreted 'to hear your name'.
7. In this respect, this gift of merit is considered in the examples of transfer of merit (Hara: 1999).
8. In the *BhP*, there are some mentions of the omnipresence of God. Some examples are as follows:

   imaṃ lokaṃ tathaivāmum ātmanam ubhayāyinam /
   ātmānam anu ye ceha ye rāyaḥ paśavo gṛhāḥ // 39 //
   visṛjya sarvān anyāṃś ca mām evaṃ viśvato-mukham /
   bhajanty ananyayā bhaktyā tān mṛtyor atipāraye //40// (*BhP* III.25)

   I take them beyond Death (i.e. *samsāra*) those who abandon this world as well as the next and their Self which wanders in both these worlds along with their *liṅga śarīra* (subtle body) and who give up their wealth, cattle, houses and other such belongings and resort (Tagare 1976: I, 365)

   loke vitatam ātmānaṃ lokaṃ cātmani saṃtatam /
   ubhayaṃ ca mayā vyāptaṃ mayi caivobhayaṃ kṛtam //52// (*BhP*, VI, 16)

   One should understand that his own Self is pervading the whole of the universe [as the subject of experience] and that the universe is resting on the *Ātman* (i.e. is superimposed on the Soul) and that both [one's own Self and the universe] are pervaded by me [as the prime cause] (Tagare 1976: II, 864-5).

   satyaṃ vidhātuṃ nija-bhṛtya-bhāṣitaṃ vyāptiṃ ca bhūteṣv akhileṣu cātmanaḥ /
   adṛśyatātyadbhuta-rūpam udvahan stambhe sabhāyāṃ na mṛgaṃ na mānuṣam // 18 // (*BhP* VII.8)

   In order to prove true the utterance of his devotee and to vindicate His (omni-)presence in all creatures and things, He manifested himself in the pillar of the assembly hall assuming an extremely wonderful form which was neither human nor beastly (Tagare 1976: III, 934).

The *Śāṇḍilya Sūtra* also has a mention of the omnipresence of God (*SBS* 2,1,18).

9. The *MBh* also has mentions of Rantideva, one of which is as follows:
   sāṃkṛte rantidevasya sa śaktyā dānataḥ samaḥ /
   brahmaṇyaḥ satya vādī ca śibir auśinaro yathā // (*MBh* III.278.17)
   Here also, Rantideva is famous for his generosity.
10. Yoshifumi Mizuno, 'The Letter of Death Motif : To the East or to the West?' (in Japanese), *Trans-Cultural Studies* (Tokyo University of Foreign Studies), vol. 10, 2007, pp. 78-102.
11. Some of them are as follows:
    W. Crooke, 1989, 'On the Folklore in the Stories' (An introduction in) *Hatim's Tales: Kashmiri Stories and Songs* by Aurel Stein, New Delhi, pp. xxx-xlvii.
    George A. Grierson, 1910, 'Gleaning from the Bhakta-mālā', *Journal of the Royal Asiatic Society*, 1990–1, pp. 87-109, 269–306.
    A. Berriedale Keith, 1993 (1st Indian edn.), *A History of Sanskrit Literature*, Delhi: Motilal Banarsidas (1st edn.: 1928).
    J. Shick, ed., n.d., *Das indische Hamlet-Epos, Aus dem Jaiminibhārata, separatabdruck aus dem Corpus Hamleticum* (1912).
    W.L. Smith, 1997, 'The Jaiminibhārata and its Eastern Vernacular Versions', *Societe Orientalis Fennica* (*Studia Orientalia*, vol. 82), Helsinki, pp. 193-208.
    Aurel Stein, 1989 (rpt.), *Hatim's Tales: Kashmiri Stories and Songs*, New Delhi: Gyan Publ. House (1st edn.: 1917).
    A. Weber, 1869, 'Über eine Epistode im Jaimini-Bharata (entsprechend einer Sage von Kaiser Heinrich III und dem "Gang nach dem Eisenhammer")', *Monatsberichte der Preussischen Alademie der Wissenschaften*, Philosophisch-Historische Klasse, pp. 10–48, 377–87.
    J. Talboys Wheeler, 1867, *The History of India from the Earliest Ages*, vol. 1 *The Vedic Period and the Mahābhārata*, London; N. Trübner & Co., (ch. IV: Chandrahāsa and Bikya, pp. 522–34.)
12. Rocher 1986: 106. Margaret H. Case, *Seeing Krishna: The Religous World of a Brahman Family in Vrindaban,* Oxford: Oxford University Press, 2000, pp. 35 ,73, 75-6, 84. Diana L. Eck, *Darśan: Seeing the Divine Image in India,* New York: Columbia University Press, 1998, pp. 32–6. J. Gonda, *Aspects of Early Viṣṇuism*, Delhi: Motilal Banarsidass, 1969, rpt. (1st edn.: Leiden, 1954). Vettam Mani, 1975, *Purāṇic Encyclopaedia*, Delhi: Motilal Banarsidass (1st edn. in Malayalam: 1964), pp. 672–3. H. Krishna Sastri, *South India: Images of Gods and Goddesses*, New Delhi: Asian Educational Service, 1995, pp. 70–1. George Thibaut, tr., *Vedānta Sūtras with the Commentary by Śankarācarya*, Sacred Books of the East Series, vol. 34, Delhi: Motilal Banarsidass, 1962, rpt. (1st. edn.: Oxford, 1904), pp. 126, 178. Monier Williams, *Religious Thought and Life in India*, pt. 1, London: John Murray, 1883, pp. 69, 412.

13. *tato gaccheta rāja-indra-sthānaṃ nārāyaṇasya tu /*
sadā saṃnihito yatra harir vasati bhārata /
śālagrāmaḥ iti khyāto viṣṇor adbhuta-karmaṇaḥ // (*MBh* III,82,106)
14. P.V. Kane, *History of Dharmaśāstra*, Poona; Bhandarkar Oriental Research Institute, 1974, vol. 2, pt. 2, p. 715.
15. I found parallel verses regarding the meaning of the greatness of the *śālagrāma* in the Jaimini version and in the Purāṇas introduced by Kirfel (1935) as follows:

yadi yuktā mahāpāpair janma-koṭi-samudbhavaiḥ // 89 // (Ch.58)
mucyante nātra saṃdehaḥ śālagrāma-śilārcanāt /

(If the people who are debased by major sins because of ten million instances of births can attain moksha, there is no doubt about the fact that their worship of the śālagrāma will be beneficial.)

prasaṅgāt kathāyiśyāmi śālagrāmasya lakṣaṇam /
śālagrāma-śilā-sparśāt koṭi-janmāghanāśanam // 1 //

Garuḍa Purāṇa (45, 1), *Padma Purāṇa* (IV,78,16), *Agni Purāṇa* (48) [Kirfel 1935:167]
(By merely touching to the *śālagrāma*, the sins of ten million instances of births will be purged out.)

REFERENCES

Acharya, Kala, 1993, *Purāṇic Concept of Dāna*, Delhi: Nag Publisher.

Anand, Subhash, 1996, *The Way of Love, the Bhāgavata Doctrine of Bhakti*, New Delhi: Munshiram Manoharlal.

Bailey, Shackleton, ed., 1951, *The Śatapañcāśatka of Mātṛceta*, Sanskrit text, Tibetan translation & Commentary and Chinese translation, Cambridge.

Callewaert, Winand C., 'Singers' Repertories in Western India', in *Devotional Literature in South Asia: Current Research, 1985-1988*, ed. R.S. McGregor, Cambridge: Cambridge University Press, pp. 29–35.

Derrett, J. Duncan M., 1970, 'Greece and India Again: The Jaimini-āśvamedha, the Alexander-romance and the Gospels', *Zeitschrift für religiong- und geistesgeschichite*, Bd.22, pp. 19–44.

Edgerton, Franklin, ed. & tr., 1993, *Vikrama's Adventure or the Thirty-two Tales of the Throne*, 2 parts, rpt., Delhi: Motilal Banarsidass 1st edn.: in Harvard Oriental Series, Cambridge, 1926.

Gokhale, Balkrishna Govind, 1981, 'Bhakti in Early Buddhism', Jayant Lele, ed., *Tradition and Modernity in Bhakti Movements*, International Studies in Sociology and Social Anthoropology, vol. 31, Leiden: E.J. Brill, pp. 16–28.

Haksar, A.N.D., tr., 1998, *Siṃhāsana Dvātriṃśikā, Thirty-two Tales of the Throne of Vikramaditya*, Delhi: Penguin Books India.

Hara, Minoru, 1994, 'Transfer of Merit in Hindu Literature and Religion', *The Memoirs of the Toyo Bunko*, vol. 52, pp. 103–35.

Heim, Maria, 2004, 'Theories of the Gift in South Asia: Hindu, Buddhist and Jain Reflections on Dāna', *Religion in History, Society and Culture*, vol. 9, New York & London: Routledge.

Jolly, Julius, tr., 1965, *The Institute of Vishnu (Viṣṇu-smṛti)*, Sacred Books of the East Series, vol. 7, Delhi: Motilal Banarsidass, rpt.

Kato, Junichiro, 2002, 'Changes in the Interpretation of Dāna in the History of Ancient Indian Buddhism' (in Japanese), *Studies in Indian Philosophy and Buddhism* vol. 9, pp. 41–52.

Kirfel, Willibald, 1935, Vom Steinkult in Indien, *Studien zur Geschichte und Kultur des Nahen und Fernen Ostens*, Paul Ralhe zum 60 Geburstag, Leiden, pp. 163–72.

Koskikallio, Petteri, 1993, 'Jaiminibhārata and Aśvamedha', *Wiener Zeitschrift für die Kunde Südasiens, Supplement, Proceedings of the VIIIth World Sanskrit Conference*, Vienna: 1990, pp. 111-19.

Lutgendorf, Philip, 2001, 'Dining Out at Lake Pampa: The Shabari Episode in Multiple Rāmāyaṇas', Paula Richman, ed., *Questioning Ramayanas: A South Asian Tradition*, Berkeley: University of California Press, pp. 119–36.

Oppert, Gustav, 1986, *On the Original Inhabitants of Bhāratavarṣa or India*, New Delhi: Unity Book Service (1st edn., 1983), pp. 337–59.

Patki, Rajani S., 1996, *The Concept of the Upāsana: Worship in Sanskrit Literature*, Sri Garib Das Oriental Series, no. 198, Delhi: Sri Satguru Publ.

Prabhupada, Bhaktivedanta Swami, 1970, *The Nectar of Devotion, the Complete Science of Bhakti-yoga*, Mumbai: The Bhakivedanta Book Trust.

Rocher, Ludo, 1986, *The Purāṇas, A History of Indian Literature*, vol. II, fasc. 3, Wiesbaden: Otto Harrassowitz.

Rukmani, T.S., 1970, *A Critical Study of the Bhāgavata Purāṇa (with Special Reference to Bhakti*, The Chowkhamba Sanskrit Studies, vol. 77, Varanasi: Chowkhamba Sanskrit Series Office.

Singh, R. Raj, 2005, 'Eastern Concepts of Love: A Philosophical Reading of Nārada Bhakti Sūtra', *Asian Philosophy*, vol. 15, no. 3 pp. 221-9.

Tagare, Ganesh Vasudeo, tr., 1976, *The Bhāgavata Purāṇa*, Ancient Indian Tradition and Mythology Series, 4 vols, Delhi: Motilal Banarsidass.

Thompson, Stith, ed., 1955, *Motif Index of Folk-Literature*, 6 vols, Bloomington: Indiana University Press.

Thompson, Stith and Jonas Balys, 1958, *The Oral Tales of India*, Bloomington: Indiana University Press.

Tsuji, Naoshiro, 1970, 'On the New Publication of the *Śatapañcāśatka of Mātṛceta* (in Japanese)', *The Journal of the Research Department of The Toyo Bunko* vol. 33, pt. 3-4, pp. 155-72.

Uther, Hans-Jörg, 2004, *The Types of International Folktales: A Classification and Bibliography, based on the System of Antti Aarne and Stith Thompson* (FF Comunications, no. 286), 3 vols, Helsinki: Academia Scientiarum Fennica.

Wogihara, Unnrai and C. Tsuchida, tr., 1994, *Saddharmapuṇḍrīka-sūtra, Romanized and Revised Text of the Bibliotheca Buddhica Publ.*, Tokyo: Sankibo Buddhist Book Store.

Wuff, Donna M., 1984, *Drama as a Mode of Religious Realization: The Vidagdhamādhava of Rūpa Gosvami,* California: Scholar Press.

9

Jñāneśvar's Interpretation of the *Bhagavad-gītā* I–VI*

IWAO SHIMA

Bhakti and Tantrism are the major currents that constitute medieval Hinduism. Roughly speaking, it is considered that the bhakti movement, which has its origins in the *Bhagavad-gītā*, developed through the following forms. Initially, the bhakti movement showed a major rise in the activities of Tamil religious poets, such as Āḻvārs in south India from the middle of the seventh century to the middle of the ninth century. Then, this movement originated in the non-Aryan soil of Tamil Nadu and was adopted in the Brahmanical tradition. Brahmanism reinterpreted bhakti—which originally had the strong characteristic of being passionate—to celebrate its harmony with the principle of intellectual meditation, which in turn originated in the Upaniṣads (for example, Yāmuna, Rāmānuja and Madhva). In such a case, it can be stated that the *Bhagavad-gītā*, which has already established its legitimacy as the sacred scripture of the Brahmanical tradition, played an extremely important role in establishing the legitimacy of bhakti (for example, the interpretation of *Bhagavad-gītā* by Yāmuna, Rāmānuja and Madhva). Thus the bhakti movement which established its legitimacy within Sanskritic Brahmanism, spread to the west, north, east through the sacred Sanskrit language of the brahmins of that time (for example, Nimbārka and Vallabha). Simultaneously, from the tenth century onwards, the rapid and successive development of local languages

*This article was originally written in Japanese and published in *Indian Thought and Buddhist Culture: Essays in Honour of Professor Junkichi Imanishi on his Sixtieth Birthday*, Shunjusha, Tokyo, 1996. It is translated into English by Sudan Shakya (Research Fellow of Department of Indology and History of Indian Buddhism, Tohoku University).

facilitated the infiltration of bhakti into all the classes of society as a form of faith that accepted no caste distinctions. There was the Teṅgalai school of the south, the Vārkarīs in the west, the followers of Rāmānand, Kabīr, or Vallabha in the north and the Caitanya school of the east). In such movements, Jñāneśvar (1271–93), regarded as the founder of the Vārkarī movement, is important. He represents the earliest stage of the development of bhakti in Marāṭhī.

Jñāneśvar composed, the following four works all of which were written in the old Marāṭhī: The *Jñāneśvarī* (his commentary on the *Bhagavad-gītā*), *Amṛtānubhav* (an independent philosophical treatise), *Cāṃgadevpāsaṣṭī* (short poetry constituting 65 verses offered to the great *yogin* Cāṃgadev), and a *Gāthā* (collection of songs (*abhaṅg*) that expound bhakti to the highest God, Viṭhobā). Focusing on these four works, most Indian researchers have thus far researched Jñāneśvar as a saint poet of Mahārāshtra; various opinions have been expressed, depending on the point of view. These views can be roughly divided into two groups: a first group examining *Amṛtānubhav*, focusing on his philosophical thought and comparing Śaṅkara and Rāmānuja, and a second group that mainly focuses on his bhakti thought, examining the *Jñāneśvarī* and *Gāthā*, and relating it with the formation or deployment of the Vārkarīs or with the that of the Marāṭhī language and the culture. Although it is always stated that the philosophy of Jñāneśvar is highly influenced by the Bhaktism of the Bhāgavatas and Tantrism of the Nātha sect, research on the Tantric aspect has not yet been undertaken.

Thus, in this paper, I utilize my past research (on the history of the interpretation of the *Bhagavad-gītā* after Śaṅkara) and focus particularly on Chapters 5 and 6, where we can see a noticeable influence of the Nāthas, which is recognized as one of the characteristic features of the *Jñāneśvarī*. Following this, I will point out the fact that bhakti and Tantrism actually bear overlapping aspects.

A HISTORY OF THE INTERPRETATION OF THE *BHAGAVAD-GĪTĀ* FROM ŚAṄKARA TO MADHVA

Śaṅkara's (700–50) is the oldest existing commentary on the *Bhagavad-gītā* and is fairly unique because the bhakti wasn't assigned so much importance in this treatise in comparison with the later commentaries. In other words, Śaṅkara uses two fundamental frameworks—'*dharma* characterized by action' that directly brings about secular prosperity (i.e. *karmayoga*) and '*dharma* characterized by non-action' that directly leads to liberation (*jñānayoga*). Like *jñāna* or the thing that helps *jñāna* shine, bhakti is something understood from the intellectualistic perspective. That is to say, basically, *jñānayoga* by rejecting *karman* is considered the principal means to liberation. On the other hand, *karmayoga* (basically Vedic rituals) performed with pure devotion to God without thought of the result, is positioned as a secondary means to liberation, and consists of the following stages:

karmayoga → the purification of the mind → meditation → further purification of the mind → attainment of the knowledge of *ātman* (*jñānayoga*).

And the main topic of the *Bhagavad-gītā* is considered so as to criticise the theory of combination of *jñāna* and *karman* from the dual framework of *jñāna* and *karman*.

In contrast to Śaṅkara's dual framework of interpreting the *Bhagavad-gītā*, Yāmuna (tenth to eleventh century) introduced a triadic one. This comprises *karman, jñāna,* and bhakti, with *bhaktiyoga* foremost. In other words, in the *Gītārthasaṃgraha* (2.4), he outlined the composition of the *Bhagavad-gītā* as follows: in Chapters 1–6 *karmayoga* and *jñānayoga*; in Chapters 7–12, *bhaktiyoga* produced by *karmayoga* and *jñānayoga*; in Chapters 13–18 other miscellaneous topics. This was an attempt to establish a framework of interpretation that served as the starting point for other interpretations in the latter period which focused on bhakti.

Following this framework, it was Rāmānuja (1017–1137) interpreted the *Bhagavad-gītā* in a concrete manner rather than providing a supplementary explanation to it. First, he placed bhakti on the highest position by explaining the stages to salvation as follows:

knowledge of *ātman* → *karmayoga* or *jñānayoga* (Chapters 2–5) → the contemplation of *ātman* culminating in its realization (Chapter 6) → *bhaktiyoga* (Chapters 7–12) → the attainment of God or salvation.

Although he referred to *jñānayoga* in theory as well, he included *jñānayoga* in a category of *karmayoga*, and explained that premising the rejection of *karman*, *jñānayoga* is actually difficult to perform. In this manner, Rāmānuja re-evaluates *karmayoga* and acknowledges *jñānayoga*, to which Śaṅkara assigned only secondary importance. Moreover, he avoids Śaṅkara's opinion that *jñānayoga* is the only means to liberation. On the other hand, by identifying bhakti with sensation (*vedanā*) and meditation (*upāsanā*, *dhyāna*, *nididhyāsana*, *smṛti*), he attempts to establish harmony with the Upaniṣadic tradition of intellectualism and meditation.

Then, Madhva (1197–1276), following the triadic framework of interpretation (*karman* and *jñāna* (Chapters 1–6), bhakti (Chapters 7–12) and other miscellaneous issues (Chapters 13–18)) also understands the *Bhagavad-gītā* by placing *bhaktiyoga* over *karmayoga* and *jñānayoga*. As per my current observations, there exist some difference between Madhva and Rāmānuja. First, with regard to *karmayoga* and *jñānayoga*, Madhva considered that the former path implies the renunciation of *karman* based on desire (*kāmyakarmaparityāga saṃnyāsa*); conversely, it implies performing *karman* without desire, and it is such actions that purify the mind, produce *jñāna,* and lead to liberation (*akāmyakarmaṇām antaḥkaraṇaśuddhyā jñānān mokṣa bhavati*, Madhva ad *Bhagavad-gītā* III.4). Accordingly, the main issue is not the abandonment of social action—for example, whether one should attain *jñāna* by abandoning the duties of a householder like Sanaka (*gṛhasthādikarmatyāgena jñānaniṣṭhāḥ sanakādivat*, III.4), or by executing the duties of a householder, like King Janaka (*tatsthā eva jñānaniṣṭhāś ca janakādivat*, III.4). The main point of Madhva's view seems to revolve around the mind of an individual: whether an individual is based upon the law of God (*maddharmasthā*, III.4) without being driven by his own desire when performing actions. The renunciation of action cannot itself function as the means to liberation (*ata na karmatyāga eva mokṣasādhanam*, III.4).

Thus, on the one hand, Madhva shows the stages of liberation as being similar to those delineated by Śaṅkara rather than Rāmānuja:

karmayoga → purification of mind → *jñānayoga* → direct vision of *ātman* → salvation (*aparokṣajñānād eva mokṣaḥ*, III.20).

On the other hand, he does not assign importance to the path of knowledge with the renunciation of action (the renunciation of action in Madhva's interpretation),[1] which Śaṅkara explains as the principal means to liberation, that is, the path of knowledge exemplified by Sanaka's decision. In addition, it seems that unlike Rāmānuja, Madhva attempts to emphasize differences with Śaṅkara more distinctly, for example, a liberated person is not integrated into *brahman* (*na caikībhūta eva brahmaṇā saḥ* II.50) and one who gains direct perception also has the possibility of transmigration (*jñāninām api sati prārabdhakarmaṇi śarīrāntaraṃ yuktam,* II.72).

JÑĀNEŚVAR'S INTERPRETATION OF THE *BHAGAVAD-GĪTĀ*

Dividing the *Bhagavad-gītā* into three parts—*karmayoga* and *jñānayoga* (Chapters 1–6), *bhaktiyoga* (Chapters 7–12), and other miscellaneous topics—Jñāneśvar places *bhaktiyoga* at the highest position, over *karmayoga* and *jñānayoga*. However, if we examine his interpretation in detail, his views differ in some aspects from those of earlier commentators. For example, though the commentators believe in the same final goals of *karmayoga* and *jñānayoga* (*Jñāneśvarī* 3.18), *karmayoga* leads to gradual steps toward liberation (*mokṣa*), while *jñānayoga*—the direct vision of the identity of *brahman* and *ātman* through mediation—is the immediate means to liberation (3.42–3). In other words, it can be stated that Śaṅkara's thought, which is the object of criticism for Rāmānuja and Madhva, surfaces here again, focusing only on *karmayoga* and *jñānayoga* and excluding *bhaktiyoga* assumed after *jñānayoga*.

Within Chapters 1–6 where *karmayoga* and *jñānayoga* are mainly discussed—as some researchers regard Jñāneśvar as 'completely non-dualistic' (*pūrṇa-advaita*)[2] and as he himself discusses the identity of *brahman* and *ātman* (6.383; 398, etc.) and explains that the world is *māyā* (2.105; 166; 4.44, etc.)—his interpretation of the *Bhagavad-gītā* is characteristically under the strong influence of Śaṅkara's thought. Besides, he states the method of Tantric meditation developed in the Nāthas (the method of meditation by being trained in the Nāthas; he himself describes it in 6.291) as a time-consuming *karmayoga* that gradually leads to the direct vision of the identity of *brahman* and *ātman*, especially as stated in Chapters 5–6.

THE METHOD OF MEDITATION DESCRIBED IN *JÑĀNEŚVARĪ* (CHAPTERS 5–6)

In Chapter 5 of *Jñāneśvarī* (5.149–56), Jñāneśvar describes the method of meditation with the aim of attaining brahmanhood with the following bodily posture. First, a *yogin* regards detachment from desire as a support without being deeply attached to an object and concentrates his mind internally. Next, he raises the consciousness to the point between the eyebrows, where the three *nāḍī*s termed *idā*, *piṅgalā*, and *suṣumnā* meet. Then he interrupts his breath, through which *iḍā* and *piṅgalā* flow, and makes *prāṇa* and *apāna* flow equally into the space at the top of the head. By controlling breath in this manner, when the sense organ (*manas*) dissolves into the space at the top of head and self-consciousness loses out, he will awaken to the *ātman* and will become the space—*brahman* itself—while keeping his own body.

In Chapter 6, this method of meditation is described in detail using broader spaces (6.152–330), as well as the method of *aṣṭāṅgayoga* (6.54–60). It is stated that on the tip of a tree known as action, tens of millions of fruits, the cessation of the action will be ripen. Many yogins who follow this method will reach the space at the top of the head through *suṣumnā* and then attain final liberation. This method which was experienced and formulated by such yogins is explained as follows (6.163 onwards, commentary on the *Bhagavad-gītā* VI.11–15).

First, the practitioner should choose the place to sit for meditation. The following are the criteria for a suitable place: from where one does not will to stand up and where detachment from desire will increase; a place that provides satisfaction on sitting down and produces firmness in the mind; a place where practice is performed spontaneously and where the mind is filled with experiences; a place that urges even a heretic to practise asceticism; a place that if accidentally approached by a person filled with desire will make him unwilling to depart and will awaken him to detachment from desire; a place that is beautiful and pure; where only the yogins reside and ordinary people never visit; where trees bear abundant fruit; where the water in the rivers or fountains abound during all seasons; a place that is neither cold nor hot but where soft breeze blows continually; a silent place that animals do not visit, nor parrots nor bees; where swans float on the water and one can occasionally spot *cakravāk* birds and hear the call of the cuckoo; where the peacock appears ooccasionally; where there is a monastery or a Śaiva temple. One should set up the seat in such a favoured place.

Next, the method of making a seat is described. Soft *kuśa* grass shoots of the same length should be well twined and spread out on the ground. On this, one should place the fur of a deer, which is placed inside a folded cloth. The seat should be on a position that is neither too low nor too high.

Taking the seat, the yogin concentrates the internal organs (*antaḥ-karaṇa*) on one point and reminds the *guru*. After paying respects to the *guru*, the internal and external parts of the yogin are filled with purity. The firmness of the self-consciousness dissolves, and the object of the sensory organs becomes unaware, the impulse of the sensory organs disappears, and thinking organs become firm within the heart (*hṛdaya*). When the sensory organs, the thinking organ, and the heart gradually become one, he can concentrate his mind and control his breath, and his consciousness is concentrated inward. He finally approaches *samādhi*.

The yogic posture (*mudrā*) can be described as follows. The yogin brings his calves close together near the thigh and sits down carefully by placing the soles at the root of the body which is known as *ādhāracakra*. He turns the surface of the right foot towards the ground and presses the part between the penis and the anus with the right foot and then places the left foot on the right foot (3.42–3). In this case, there is a space of the breadth of four fingers between the penis and the anus. A space for one finger will remain in the centre when it leaves the space of one and half fingers each from the side of the penis and that of the anus. He then covers that space with the heel of the right foot and pushes his body upwards. The lower part of the back is pushed up so that the body may not feel it. Such a style of sitting, applying the whole weight of the body to the heel of a leg, is called *mūlabandha* or *vajrāsana*. When such a yogic posture (*mudrā*) is conducted on the *ādhāracakra*, the downward path of *apāna* will be closed and it begins to go back inwards. He puts the little rounded palms on the left foot naturally as a result, his shoulder seems slightly larger than before. The head stands firmly and the eyes begin to close and become half-opened.

His sight is now focused inward and does not reach outward, and it then turns to the tip of the nose. The posture with the throat compressed, chin held between the collarbones and strongly pushed on the chest, with the larynx hidden, is known as *jālandharabandha*. Next, he pushes the navel upwards, pulls his stomach in, after which the cavity in the heart expands. Now, the *uḍḍiyānabandha* is made below the navel and above the *svādiṣṭhānacakra*. Thus, when the mark of such practices appears in the external body, the inner organs lose their activities. In other words, the ability to think (*kalpanā*) is reduced and it loses its influence on objects, and finally, the thinking organs relax naturally.

The *apāna*, the lower flow of which is interrupted by the *mūlabandha*, is compressed once and then immediately begins to expand to the upper part. It then begins to struggle with the *maṇipūracakra*. The *apāna* moves around in the stomach and expels waste, overturns the sea of seven *dhātu*s, removes the mountain of fat and extracts marrow from the bones. It produces illness and will be eliminated immediately and stirs the elements of the earth and water inside the entire body.

The Śakti called Kuṇḍalinī is awakened by the heat of the *āsana*. The Kuṇḍalinī, that was shut in a narrow space and was sleeping wound in a three and a half coils, turning the head downward, awakens on being pressed by the *vajrāsana*. The Kuṇḍalinī unties the coil and appears standing on the navel. During the long sleep the Kuṇḍalinī has been hungry. She is irritated by hunger and opens her mouth upwards. She eats up the wind which fills the cavity in the heart and also eats the meat of the body. She seeks flesh from the sole to the palm, in every joint of all the limbs. After seizing all the vitality to the end of the nail and having washed out the skin, she then uses a skull without leaving the *ādhāracakra*. Furthermore, she rubs into the bone and scratches the blood vessels. The growth of the *yogin*'s hair stops in that case. The thirsty Kuṇḍalinī fills her mouth in the sea of seven *dhātu*s and heats up the body of the *yogin*. When the breath of the yogin escapes in a finger's breadth from a nasal cavity, the Kuṇḍalinī raises if sickle-shaped neck, pulls back the breath inside, and makes it flow inside the body. Then the *apāna*, originally flowing downwards contracts upwards, while the *prāṇa* originally flowing upwards contracts downwards.

However, the curtain of the six *cakra*s still remains midway where both cross. They will never be mixed together. The Kuṇḍalinī consumes all the matter which consists of the elements of the earth and water within the body. After satiating herself, she becomes quiet and rests near the *suṣumnā*. The poison voided from her mouth leads to refreshed vitality. When the poison cools the yogin's body, it regains its original state. In this manner, the *nāḍī*s are closed and the difference of the nine winds ceases to exist. The physical functions stop. The *iḍā* and the *piṅgalā* become one, the knot of the three *nāḍī*s unties, and the six *cakra*s open their curtain. The lake of lunar nectar that lies between the eyebrows inclines and the nectar then pours into the mouth of the Śakti called Kuṇḍalinī.

The taste of the nectar passes through the *cakra*s which open the curtain. Carried by *prāṇa*, it fills the body and then penetrates it. Though the body is infused with brightness, it is still covered by the veil of the skin. In the next step, after the skin has flaked off, the *yogin*'s body becomes as beautiful as white marbles or buds from jewels. The *yogin* steadily becomes younger, like a child. The teeth are replaced with new ones, the hair grows newly, the surface of his hands and feet becomes like a red lotus flower and the eyes shine beyond description. Even though the body of the *yogin* is made of gold, it is light like air because it no longer contains the elements of water and earth. The *yogin* can now look beyond the oceans, hear the sound of the heaven, read the minds of the ants, and even ride on the wind.

The Kuṇḍalinī, *prāṇa* in her hand, ascends the stairway of the sky and climbs the steps of *suṣumnā*. She then attains the space of the *yogin*'s heart, after which the sound of *anāhata* begins to emanate. A door to *brahman* opens spontaneously in the heart when this sound is heard in the sky. The Kuṇḍalinī situated in the heart feeds the consciousness that remains here in another great sky, bearing the shape of a lotus bud. In this manner, the Kuṇḍalinī abandons her glory as the lord staying in the cavity of the heart and becomes the *prāṇa*. The Kuṇḍalinī is absorbed into the earth in the cavity of the heart. In other words, the essence of the Śakti merges into the Śakti itself. The five elements have now completely vanished. This is the secret of the tradition of the Nāthas: that the *yogin*'s body is swallowed by the body itself (up to 6. 292); in other words, he attains final liberation with the help of physical performance.

Following this, with regard to the yogin's supernatural powers so gained, the process of becoming one of the Śakti and the highest *ātman*, or the Kuṇḍalinī and Śiva after the disappearance of the five elements (6.298–311), and the process of attaining the state of *brahman* (6.312–30) are also explained.

CONCLUSION

I have observed the relations among *karmayoga, jñānayoga, bhaktiyoga* in the commentaries on the *Bhagavad-gītā* written by Śaṅkara, Yāmuna, Rāmānuja, Madhva, and Jñāneśvar. I attempted to point out the characteristics of the interpretation offered by Jñāneśvar. It is considerably influenced by Śaṅkara's thought and accepts the style of meditation developed mainly in the Nāthas. In particular, when considering the fact that the Tantric meditation of the Nāthas is adopted in the *Jñāneśvarī*, which promotes *bhaktiyoga*, I would state that bhakti and Tantrism show overlapping aspects. However, even though *bhaktiyoga* is assumed after *jñānayoga*, the latter is considered—at least in Chapters 1–6—as meditation to attain the final liberation which is nothing but a direct vision of the identity of *brahman* and *ātman*, presented in the non-dualistic theory of Śaṅkara.

Accordingly, I could not conclude for certain as to whether this Tantric meditation of the Nāthas found in *Jñaneśvarī* indicates the overlapping of Tantrism with Śaṅkara's non-dualistic path of final liberation, or the overlapping of Tantrism with bhakti. It is essential to clarify the whole picture of Jñāneśvar's understanding of bhakti for solving that problem. In addition, I speculate that it is important to discuss the similarity and difference between the Tantric meditation of Jñāneśvar and that of Nāthas, and to consider how his Tantric philosophy and the philosophy of the Nāthas play a role in Hindu Tantrism.

NOTES

1. Śaṅkara does not differentiate between *saṃnyāsa* and *tyāga* (*yadi kāmyakarmaparityāgaḥ phalaparityāgaḥ vā arthaḥ vaktavyaḥ, sarvathā parityāgamātraṃ saṃnyāsatyāgaśabdayoḥ ekaḥ arthaḥ syāt, na ghaṭapaṭa-*

śabdau iva jātyāntarabhūtārthau, Śaṅkara ad *Bhagavad-gītā* XVVIII.2), while Madhva differentiates between them.

2. Cf. Dandekar 1969.

REFERENCES

Abbott, J.E. (tr.), *Stotramālā: A Garland of Hindu Prayers (From Dnyaneshvar to Mahipati)*, The Poet-Saints of Maharashtra Series 6, Poona: Scottish Mission Industries, 1929.

Abbott, J.E. and N.R. Godbole, *Bhaktavijaya: Stories of Indian Saints*, 2 vols., Delhi: Motilal Banarsidass, 1933.

Bahirat, B.P., *The Philosophy of Jñānadeva*, Bombay: Popular Book Depot, 1961.

Dandekar, S.V., *Dhyanadeo*, New Delhi: Maharashtra Information Centre, 1969.

——— (ed. & tr.), *Sārtha Jñāneśvarī*, Poona: Svānand Prakāśan, 1986.

Deleury, G.A., *The Cult of Viṭhobā*, Poona: Deccan College, 1960.

Deshpande, P.Y., *Anubhavāmṛtarasarahasya*, 3 vols., Nagpur, 1962–8.

———, *Jñānadeva*, New Delhi: Sahitya Akademi, 1973.

Eck, D.L. (ed.), *Devotion Divine*, Paris–Groningen: École Française d' Extrême Orient–Forsten, 1991.

Edwards, J.F., *Dhyāneshwar, the Out-caste Brahmin*, The Poet-Saints of Maharashtra Series 12, Poona: Scottish Mission Industries, 1941.

Eintwistle, A.W. and F. Mallison (eds.), *Studies in South Asian Devotional Literature: Research Papers, 1988–1991*, Paris: École Française d' Extreme Orient, 1994.

Feldhaus, A., *The Religious System of the Mahānubhāva Sect*, New Delhi: Manohar, 1983.

Gokhale. V.H. (ed.), *Amṛtanubhava*, Poona, 1967.

Karandikar, V.R. and M.R. Lederle, 'Philosophy in Marathi', *Philosophy in the Fifteen Modern Indian Languages*, ed. V.M. Bedekar, Poona: Continental for the Council for the Marathi Encyclopedia of Philosophy, 1979.

Kimura Bunki, 'Jñāna-yoga of Rāmānuja' 1–2, *Tokai Bukkyo* 38–9, 1993–4.

———, 'Rāmānuja's Philosophy of Tyāga and Karma-yoga', *The Study of Indology and Esoteric Buddhism*, Kyoto: Hozokan, 1993.

Lederle, M.R., *Philosophical Trends in Modern Maharashtra*, Bombay: Popular Prakashan, 1976.

Lele, J. (ed.), *Tradition and Modernity in Bhakti Movement*, Leiden: Brill 1981.

Macnicol, N. (ed.), *Śrī Jñāneśvara Darśana*, 2 vols., 1934.

Maṃgarūṛkar, A. (ed. & tr.), *Jñāneśvarī*, 3 vols., Bombay, 1994.

McGregor, R.S. (ed.), *Devotional Literature in South Asia: Current Research, 1985–1988*, Cambridge: Cambridge University Press, 1992.

Milton, I. and N.K. Wagle, *Religion and Society in Maharashtra*, South Asian Studies Papers 1, Toronto: University of Toronto, 1987.

Mokashi, D.B. and Philip. C. Engblom (tr.), *Palki, an Indian Pilgrimage*, Albany: SUNY Press, 1987.

Panse, M.G., 'Index Verborum of Jñāneśvarī', *Bulletin of the Deccan College Research Institute,* vol. X, no. 3 (1950); no. 4 (1952).

———, 'Linguistic Peculiarities of Jñāneśvarī', *Bulletin of the Deccan College Research Institute*, vol. X, no. 2, 1951.

Pednase, S.D., *Jñāneśvarance Tattvajñāna*, Bombay, 1941.

Pradhan V.G. (tr.), *Jñāneśvarī: A Song-Sermon on the Bhagavadgītā*, 2 vols., London: A George Allen & Unwin Publication, 1986.

Raghavan, V., *The Great Integrators: The Saint Singers of India*, Delhi: Publication Division of Ministry of Information and Broadcasting, 1966.

Rājavaḍe, V.K. (ed.), *Śrī Jñāneśvarī*, Bombay: Goverment Central Press, 1963.

Ranade, R.D., *Pathway to God in Marathi Literature*, Bombay: Bharatiya Vidya Bhavan, 1961.

Ranade, R.D., *Mysticism in Mahārāshtra*, Delhi: Motilal Banarsidass, 1982.

Ranade, M.G., *Rise of the Maratha Power and Other Essays*, Bombay: University of Bombay, 1960.

Sakhare, S. (ed.), *Śrīsakalasantagāthā*, Poona: Shri Santwangmay Prakashan Mandir, 1961.

Sardar, G.B., *The Saint-Poets of Maharashtra*, K.A. Mehta (tr.), New Delhi: Orient Longmans, 1969.

Schomer, K. and W.H. Mcleod (eds.), *The Sants: Studies in a Devotional Tradition of India*, Delhi: Motilal Banarsidass, 1987.

Shima, I., 'Śaṅkara's Interpretation on the *Gītā', Bukkyo Bunkashi Ronshu*, 1992.

Shima, I., 'Historical Development of Salvation Theories Found in Commentaries on the *Bhagavadgītā*: From Śaṅkara to Rāmānuja', *Journal of the Japanese Association for South Asian Studies,* vol. 4, 1992.

Sontheimer, G.D., 'Ursprung und Entwicklung der Bhakti-Bewegung in Maharashtra', *Indo-Asia*, 1981.

Thiel-Horstman, M. (ed.), *Bhakti in Current Research, 1979–1982*, Berlin: D. Reimer Verlag, 1983.

Tulpule, G.V., *Pañca Santakavī*, Poona: Suvicāra Prakāśan Mandal, 1984.

Tulpule, S.G., *Classical Marāṭhī Literature*, A History of Indian Literature, vol. IX, Fasc. 4, Wiesbaden: Otto Harrassowitz, 1979.

———, *Mysticism in Medieval India*, Wiesbaden: Otto Harrassowitz, 1984.

———, 'Spiritual Autobiography in Marathi: A Tradition Lost and Renewed', *South Asian Digest of Regional Writing* 5, 1976.

Vaudeville, Ch., 'Paṇḍharpūr, the City of Saints', *Structural Approaches in South Asian Studies*, ed. H.M. Buck and G.E. Yocum, Chambersburg: Wilson Books, 1973.

———, 'Cult of the Divine Name in the Haripāṭha of Dñānadev', *WZJSO*, XII–XIII, 1968.

———, 'The Sant Tradition in Medieval and Modern India', *The Sant Tradition in India*, Berkeley, 1980.

Yārdī, M.R. (tr.), *Surasa Jñāneśvarī*, Poona: Bharatiya Vidya Bhavan, 1991.

Zelliot, E., 'The Medieval Bhakti Movement in History', *Hinduism: New Essays in the History of Religions*, ed. B.L. Smith, Leiden: E.J. Brill, 1976.

Zelliot, E. and M. Berntsen, *The Experience of Hinduism: Essays on Religion in Maharashtra*, Albany: SUNY Press, 1988.

Zelliot, E. and A. Feldhaus, 'Marathi Religions', *Encyclopedia of Religion*, New York: Macmillan, 1986.

10

The Bhakti in Tukārām's *Abhaṅgas*

CHIHIRO KOISO

Bhakti is discussed as both a philosophical and a religious notion. However, it is mainly, understood as a religious practice. In the *Bhāgavata dharma* (i.e bhakti discussed in *Bhāgavata-purāṇa*) religion is understood as the elevation of man to God, and the descent of God to man. Religion incorporates three aspects, viz., subjective, social or objective, and transcendental. The concept of search for liberty or *mokṣa* is classified under the subjective aspect, and is considered to be the most important. The objective view of religion incites us to consider the individual in relation to other individuals and nature. Religion is often considered 'a social phenomenon', comprising of the members of the society.

BHAKTI IN THE *BHĀGAVATA DHARMA* AND TUKĀRĀM

Bhakti is rooted in a very humanistic feeling. The adoration of someone or something is inherent in human nature. *Bhakti-mārga* is universal in that it is open to all. The path of bhakti is the religion for all. One more important notion concerning bhakti is that of the 'grace of God'; God can be realized only by His grace. Merely practising *sādhanā* is insufficient; the bhakta should completely surrender. It is for this reason that, the practice of *bhakti-mārga* does not allow any room for arrogance. Bhaktas who understand true bhakti are totally humble. Humility is the most essential and elementary attribute of the bhakta.

The concept of bhakti according to the *Bhāgavata dharma* includes all necessary principles regarding social philosophy. If a true bhakta attains the state of *parā-bhakti*, he is able to see God everywhere, within himself as well as outside himself; this state is characterized by absolute *samatva* (equality). According to the advaitic approach, everything is filled with nothing but *brahman*. There is no room for discrimination. B.R. Kulkarni (1973: 15-16) says, '*samatva* is the behavioural aspect of the realization of the supreme moral law ... *samatva* is the fountainhead of all individual and social virtues and the highest ethical ideal'. *Samatva* can be considered the essence of morality and social philosophy. *Bhakti-mārga* is open to all human beings, without distinction of *varṇa* or creed. 'A person from any *varṇa* can develop moral strength and overcome the misfortunes of this earthly life. This was the type of confidence which the movement instilled even among the lowest strata of people' (Sardar 1969: 16). The *samatva* approach can be in the writing of the saint-poets of Maharashtra.

Serving the *sarvabhūta* (all being) as God is the approach of the *samatva* followed by *advaita-bhakti*. This concept of *sarvabhūta* is fundamental in understanding the *Bhāgavata dharma*. *Sarvabhūta* actually implies all beings and it indicates the pursuit of not only the *abhyudaya* but also *niḥśreyas*. The *Gītā* clearly mentions '*sarvabhūtahite ratah* (involved in doing good to all creatures)' (*BhG* 5.25). Commenting on this *śloka*, S. Radhakrishnan says,

> To do good to others is not to give them physical comforts or raise their standard of living. It is to help others to find their true nature, to attain true happiness. The contemplation of the Eternal Reality in whom we all dwell gives warmth and support to the sense of the service of the fellow-creature.[1]

The end of human life is absolute happiness. In order to attain it one should follow the true *dharma*. This is essential in understanding the Hindu way of life. *Dharma* refers to 'duties' in the subjective sense. According to Swami Yuktānanda, '*Dharma* means man's view of himself based on a self analysis of the uniqueness of human character. It is unique because it is *mānava-dharma* without which man loses his identity or humanness'. *Dharma* is the law of one's being. *Svadharma* is mentioned in the *Bhāgavata dharma* in relation to *dharma*.

Whenever bhakta serves *sarvabhūta* as God, his attitude towards *sarvabhūta* must unconditionally be that of *niṣkāmata*. *Niṣkāma-*

karma is understood as action without expectation of reward and is practised with a detached attitude. It may be described as the practice of offering actions to God. This does not imply that one must give up action altogether; one must only abandon the desire for its fruit. Thus there is total humility and dedication.

Tukārām revealed his concept of bhakti and his humility in the form of *abhaṅga*. *Abhaṅgas* are poetical composition peculiar to the saint-poets of Maharashtra such as like Jnāneśvar, Nāmdev, Tukārām, Eknāth, and Rāmdās and others.

In this article refer to the *abhaṅga*s of Tukārām in *Sārth Śrītukārām Mahārājancī Gāthā*, ed. Jog Maharaj, *Śrītukārāmaci Gāthā*, ed. S.K Neurgaonka.[2]

Tukārām saids,

avaghīn bhuten sāmyā ālīn / dekhilīn myā kaen hotīn /
viśvās to kharā mag / pānḍurangakṛpecā //
mazhī koṇī na dharo śankā / ho kān lokān nirdvandva /
tukā mhane jeje bhete / te te vāṭe mī aise // (1508)

When will I attain the state where I will be able to see God in every living being? I am sure that is the day when I will receive the boon of Lord Pāṇḍurang. I hope that I will not frighten any living being, and that all beings never experience sorrow, bliss, fear, hope and despair and all attain the state of non-duality, viz. uniting with me. Tukā says that I want to feel my presence in whomsoever I come across.

This *abhaṅga* reveals the gist of Tukārām's concept of bhakti and his humility. At the same time this *abhaṅga* reminds us of Jñāneśvar's approach to bhakti expressed in the following *obī*,

je je bhete bhūta / te te mānije bhagavanta //
hā bhaktiyogu niścit / jāna mājhā // (J 10.118)

You regard every person you come across as God. Know that this is the true *yoga* of the devotion.

According to these notions, bhakti is not merely worshipping God, but the service of all beings as if they were God. Additionally, bhakti can be a social force. Whatever works men undertake in society, if they are inspired by the love of God, they will experience no conflict with society. S. Radhakrishnan says:

When we see the One-self in all things, equal-mindedness, freedom from selfish desires, surrender of our whole nature to the Indwelling Spirit and

> love for all arise. When these qualities are manifested, our devotion is perfect and we become God's own men. Our life then is guided not by the forces of attraction and repulsion, friendship and enmity, and pleasure and pain, but by the single urge to give ourserlves to God and therefore to the service of the world which is one with God. (Radhakrishnan 1992: 229)

Bhakti encompasses all the virtues. The saint-poets of Maharashtra enumerate various moral virtues; they are individualistic and practical. 'An acute analysis and a detailed and vivid description of the various virtues, the attainment of which is regarded as an essential condition of mystic life, form a special feature of the works of Jñāneśvara, Tukārāma, Ekanātha and Rāmadāsa' (Gajendragadkar 1983: 365). Virtue, according to these saint-poets, is preparatory to mystic realization. 'The first necessity of a moral life was resistance to evil solicitations. Social justice and social harmony would demand forbearance from certain types of acts which were anti-social or subversive to social discipline. Hence, it was considered that prescriptions must be supplemented by prohibitions, and incentives by restraints' (Bhattacharrya 1983: 629). Thus, virtues are aspects of one central virtue bhakti. Bhakti is the central thread that ties all moral qualities. Sardar mentions, 'All the saints sought to make "the social order" a vehicle for the new spirits' (Sardar 1969: 32). The core of that social order was bhakti. Bhakti is the base that touches upon all the important virtues that the saints have propounded. We should concurrently bear in mind that according to the *Bhāgavata dharma*, bhakti is not merely a means to attain *mokṣa*, but the end in itself.

The saint-poets of Maharashtra contributed to the progress of society by teaching and practising bhakti. They were realistic and worked within the framework of society to reduce social inequality. The circumstances of their time did not allow them to pursue any radical social change. However, they made an enormous contribution, that is worth considerable deliberation. They provided spiritual support and guidance to the masses to lead them to an ideal way of life. *Bhakti-mārga* is, as we have already considered, liberal; to the common man, emotional and volitional approaches are more effective, easy and natural; further, these are also considered as being open to all.

Tukārām expresses his views in his *abhaṅga*s and *kīrtana*s. His compositions are widely sung even today, and many of them are also regarded as proverbs. N.H. Kulkarnee (1989: 208) states that the reason for Tukārām's popularity is that his spirituality and longing for Viṭṭhal are deeply rooted in humanism. He lived in an era when Marāṭhī literature was flourishing; this is reflected in his *abhaṅga*s. Although he was a householder, he was not interested in worldly life. His *abhaṅga*s are simple, straightforward and powerful. As Tukārām was always contemplating God, he reiterates the importance of worshipping Viṭṭhal. In one of her *abhaṅga*s, Bahinabai states that Jñāndev laid the foundations of the worship of Viṭṭhal, Nāmdeva built its walls, Eknāth gave it a central pillar, and Tukārām became its 'crown' or 'spire'[3] (Chitre 1991: intro.). In his *abhaṅga*s, Tukārām emphasizes seeing Viṭṭhal in everything in animate as well as inanimate entities. Tukārām believes that the Lord is present in the image of Viṭṭhal in the Pandharpur temple. He supports image worship. 'Though Tukārām continues the practice of image worship, he seeks to steer clear of idolatry. He believes that God whom he worships in the idol is transcendent in His intrinsic reality. He is not limited to the image' (Dabre 1987: 25). Tukārām says, 'He has neither form nor name. He has no place in which to seek shelter. Viṭṭhal our mother and sister, is present wherever we go. He has no form nor does He change. He fills the entire creation' (*TG* 2935).

Another notable point is that according to the *Gītā*, true bhakti is generated in man only after a vision of God. 'He who, undeluded, thus knows Me, the highest Person, is the knower of all and worships Me with all his being (with his whole spirit)' (*BhG* 15.19). Tukārām reiterates this point:

hoilā sadbhakati yāne panthe / sadbhakti ẓāliyā sahaja sākṣātkāra.

R.D. Ranade says 'It is only when a man has attained to the full knowledge of God that he is able to meditate on Him with full devotion. In fact, highest devotion and realization seem to be in reciprocal causation. Unless a man comes to possess the highest devotion, he will not have a vision of God, and unless he has the vision of God, true bhakti will not spring in him.' This implies that attaining *jñāna* is indispensable for becoming a true bhakta. Therefore, as mentioned earlier, a bhakta is a *jñānin* and a *yogin* at the same time. From this point of view, we can understand the synthesis of all the four *yoga*s.

We can thus state that the true bhakta is an ideal member of the society. An ideal bhakta is he who performs his own prescribed duty (*svadharma*), serves all beings equally without expecting anything in return, and pursues a way of realizing the Ultimate Reality with intense love towards God. Love is a core quality of a true bhakta. A bhakta is also a virtuous and morally perfect being. A true bhakta's way of life is that of harmony. The true bhakta is he who prays for the happiness and harmony of the entire universe.

PRACTICE OF *NĀMASMARAṆA*

Nāmasmaraṇa is included in the nine forms of bhakti (*navavidhā bhakti*)[4] in the *Bhāgavata-purāṇa* (*BhP*). *Nāmasmaraṇa*, is also known as *nāmajapa*, *nāmasaṅkīrtana*, and so on, means bearing in mind the name or names of God. *Nāmasmaraṇa* is not merely chanting or repeating the name of God, but constant remembrance, in times of prosperity as well as adversity. According to Gondhalekar (Godbole) Mahārāj, *nāma* itself is an *avatāra* (descent) of God. Many saints and thinkers emphasize the importance of *nāmasmaraṇa*. Although the *BhP* calls it one of the nine forms of bhakti, all the saints, especially the saints of Maharashtra, have given it supreme importance.

It is universally believed that there exists power in words and name. Almost all primitive religions have a belief that a person who knows the name of a divine entity can control it. They think that the name itself has strong magical powers. According to the Hindu tradition, *saguṇa sākāra īśvara* also has *nāma* (name) and *rūpa* (form) along with *asti, bhāti* and *priyā*. The entire Universe has both *nāma* and *rūpa* as the conditions of manifestation. The superiority of *nāma* and *rūpa* has been discussed at length. In fact, it is difficult to conclude as to which is superior, but saints show a preference for *nāma*, because *rūpa* is destructible but *nāma* is abiding. By *nāma* we can imagine a *nirākāra* God. *Nāma* can be considered the link between *nirākāra* (without form) God and *sākāra* (with form) God. The saints express their devotion that is beyond specific qualities to *nirguṇa* God who is beyond specific qualities; they demonstrate it through familiar symbols or attributes of a *saguṇa* God. *Nāma* touches the innermost essence of the bhaktas. S.G. Tulpule (1984: 143) refers to *nāmasmaraṇa* as follows, 'It keeps him ever awake in his spiritual endeavour and it unites him with God'. Through constant remembrance of God, bhaktas can constantly sense God's proximity. The very core of bhakti is the constant thought of God.

The practice of *nāmasmaraṇa* begins at the verbal level; gradually however, it leads the practitioner into an increasingly deeper state, finally leading to the *parā* state. All saints emphasize *nāmasmaraṇa* as a means to attain *parā-bhakti*. Consciousness of the name leads bhaktas to the consciousness of the Ultimate Reality that is God. This may be a slow process to attain God, but it is definite.

The practice of *nāmasmaraṇa* is open to all. It is simple and requires no skill to practise. Anyone can practise it any time and anywhere as there are no restrictions or prohibitions. Over the years, it is still considered as a very powerful means. Whether our mind is disturbed or at peace, *nāmasmaraṇa* should never cease.

According to Tukārām, the sole way to the realization of God is through constant repetition of the name of god. In his *abhaṅga*s, he repeats the importance of the *nāmasmaraṇa*. *Nāmasmaraṇa* is not a monopoly of the saint-poets. Its importance is referred to in many other religions and in many texts of Hinduism. The reason may be its simplicity and familiarity. By chanting the name of God we can connect. S.G. Tulpule (1991: 50) asserts that the practice of *nāmasmaraṇa* is instrumental in replacing the object of our thoughts; it is a phrase that triggers the process of changing the structure of our consciousness. It is commonly believed that *jīva* will become Śiva through the utterance of the name. This implies that once an individual soul begins to utter the name it is ultimately bound to become the cosmic soul. In other words, the name is a strong catalyst to change *jīva* into Śiva. Furthermore this can be practised by anybody, anywhere and at any time. There are no regulations for uttering the name. We can always feel God's presence and be united with Him by uttering His name. Thus, *nāmasmaraṇa* plays an important role in *sādhanā*: it constantly reminds us of God and His nature.

Tukārām is enthusiastic about the divine name. It is said that his *guru* Bābājī Caitanya imparted a *nāma-mantra*, Rāma-Kṛṣṇa-Hari to him in a dream, which fulfilled his heart's desire.

'If we only utter the name of God, God will stand before us' (*TG* 2021).

'Uttering the Name will lead us to God if no obstacle intervenes. A fruit becomes ripe on a tree only if it is not plucked' (*TG* 695). 'The ship of God's name will ultimately carry one across the ocean of life. It will save both the young and the old' (*TG* 2457). 'This is the only way to attain ultimate bliss. It is the easiest way to practise to follow. Wiseman will be satisfied with this' (*TG* 2458).

Tukārām clearly mentioned that his way of bhakti is *nāmasmaraṇa*.

muktivarīl bhakti *jān / akhaṅd muhīn nārāyaṇ /*
mag dev bhakt zālā / tukā tukīn utarlā // (4161)

The person who always has God name in his mouth will be solid devotee of God. Tukā says that he himself became the devotee of God in this manner.

Tukārām explains the concrete states when we practice *nāmasmaraṇa*, as follows,

nām ghetān kanth śītaḷ śarīr / indriyā vyāpār nāṭhavatī //
goḍ gomten hen amṛtāsī vāḍ / kelā kaivāḍ mājhyā citten //
premarsen zālī puṣt angkānti / trividh sānḍitī tāp ange //
tukā mhaṇe tethe vikārācī māt / bolon naye, hit sakḷāncen // (2260)

If we chant the name of God, our throat and body will become cool and the restless sense organs will forget their functions. If we concentrate on devotion to God, our voice as well as the restlessness of our sense organs will calm down. The name of God is sweeter than *amṛta*. My mind is eager to seek only the name of God. My body is nourished by the desire to seek the name of God. *Nāmasmaraṇa* keeps the three heats at bay. Tukā says that there is no room for feelings of lust or rage. Bodily suffering will also never occur.

govind govind / manā lāgliyā chand //
mag govind te kāyā / bhed nāhīn devā tayā //
ānandlen man / premen pājhartī locan // (2327)

Chant Govind, Govind, you will feel affection, and your body will unite with Govind, you will no longer feel any difference between you and God. In this state your mind will be filled with bliss; tears will automatically flow from your eyes.

Tukārām ironically mentions

nām ghetān vāyā gelā / aisā koṇen āikilā /
sāṅgā vinaviton tumhānsī / sant mahant siddh ṛṣī /
nāmen tarlā nāhīn koṇ / aisā dyāvā nivaḍūn // (2392)

I have never heard that practising *nāmasmaraṇa* leads to ruin. O saints, O liberated person, *ṛṣis*, please tell me if such things would have happened if one would not have raised oneself above the shackles of daily life.

PRACTICE OF *BHAJANA* AND *KĪRTANA*

Bhajana and *kīrtana*, included in the nine forms of bhakti, are important means to attain *parā-bhakti*. Here I shall consider *bhajana* and *kīrtana* from the perspective of their importance in attaining *parā-bhakti*, especially according to *Bhāgavata dharma* in Maharashtra.

Bhajana and *kīrtana* are very essential means to pursue *bhakti-mārga*. Etymologically, *bhajana* is derived from the root √*bhaj*, meaning 'to share, to enjoy, to adore, to worship'. *Bhajana*, therefore means 'sharing, service, adoration, worship'. Currently *bhajana* is used in a special context, 'a hymn, or verse to be sung to God'. *Bhajana* consists of singing the glory of the God while fully exerting one's general ability to sing. The specific meaning of *bhajana* in Maharashtra, especially for the Vārkarī *sampradāya*, is singing the devotional songs of the saints. In the Vārkarī *sampradāya*, *bhajana* and *kīrtana* play an important role in attaining *parā-bhakti*. This is because Vārkarīs are acquainted with the teaching of the saints through *bhajana* and *kīrtana* rather than through the written scriptures. We will now examine the role of *bhajana* and *kīrtana* and examine its effectiveness in pursuing *bhakti-mārga*.

In reality bhakti through *bhajana* is a dialogue between God and the bhakta. *Bhajana* can be regarded as mediator between the God and the bhakta. The bhakta can feel close to his God by singing and being engrossed in *bhajana*. One important merit of *bhajana* is that it is equally easy to practise for every bhakta. P.C. Engblom (1987: 25) says, 'What makes *bhajana* so attractive a *sādhanā* (spiritual means) is that it is comparatively accessible to the common man or woman and does not require esoteric disciplines. A *bhajana* is an act of the most complete self-abnegation and total self-surrender to Viṭṭhal'. Through *bhajana* the bhakta can have easy access to God. This *bhajana* is equally accessible to all bhaktas. Vārkarī refers to the sect that is also 'on the road' engrossed in dancing and singing *bhajanas*. G.A. Deleury (1960:

88) also mentions that 'The singing of the hymns is one of the most important functions of the pilgrimage. As most of the pilgrims are illiterate, the singing of religious hymns is for them what the reading of spiritual books is for other communities. It is through the medium of these hymns that the Vārkarī traditions and teachings are transmitted from generation to generation'. Singing *bhajana* is not only important to have access to God, but also to obtain proper knowledge about the teachings of their tradition. Thus, the Vārkarī tradition applies its methods of moral and spiritual teaching to the cultural level of simple people. Because the previous saint-poets have written a vast amount of poems which contain moral and philosophical teachings, singing and listening to *bhajanas* has obtained greater significance.

Kīrtana employs the same methods. In the *BhP*, it is said that in the *kaliyuga*, only *nāma-saṅkīrtana* can be given priority (*BhP* 12.3.51). *Kīrtana* is a type of religious exposition of the *abhaṅga*. During a *kīrtana* a *kīrtanakār* intermittently speaks to the audience, sporadically interrupting his preaching in order to sing some hymns. *Kīrtana* consists of *bhajana*s, *abhaṅga*s and narrations. It is mandatory for the *kīrtanakār* to study the scriptures and recite passages from memory. The primary object should be one's own happiness because *kīrtana* brings peace to the mind and simultaneously showing the path of bliss to others. 'The rhythmic accompaniment in a *kīrtana* makes the audience forget their physical existence completely; it leads to a kind of trance that makes the entire body airy, or weightless' (Nemade 1981: 121). There will be a possibility of mass ecstacy also one important aspect of *kīrtana*. Through music, people become spiritual, and therefore music can be used for promoting devotion. On the other hand, one can indulge in music for its own sake (Tulpule 1990: 151). The promoters of bhakti would consider the art of music from a religious perspective. *Bhajana* ceases if it is devoid of devotion to God.

The powerful instrument of *bhajana* was used for a long period to maintain the popularity of the Vārkarī tradition among the masses. Tukārām emphasizes the importance of *kīrtana*:

> *Kīrtana* is the mediation of God Himself... there is no merit on earth which is equal to that of the *kīrtana*. Believe me, says Tukā, God stands up where

kīrtana is being performed...a man who performs the *kīrtana* not only saves himself but also others. Without doubt, says Tukā, one can meet God by performing a *kīrtana*. (Ranade 1988: 322)

According to Damle (1960: 74), one of the purposes of *kīrtana* is 'social education of the people'. It is actually an effective medium of social education. He explains three types of *kīrtana*, viz., *nāradīya kīrtana*, *vārkarī kīrtana* and national *kīrtana* (which is a modern development). *Nāradīya kīrtana* is the narrative type of *kīrtana*, but *vārkarī kīrtana* is a panegyric type. It mainly comprises singing the glory of God and his name and is also known as *nāma-saṅkīrtana*. The common aim is social education. Ranade (1984: 109) speaks of the effectiveness of the *kīrtana* as follows:

Firstly, it appeals to the solo as well as to the communal or the collective elements simultaneously. Secondly, it is multifaceted in the sense that it has speech, song, dance, mime and narration; therefore, like a good dramatic piece, it has something for every stratum of Indian society. The bases for its hold over the people are therefore comprehensive.

In a *kīrtana*, it is necessary to explain what is God's love as well as what exactly is implied by the knowledge of the self and the nature of the Supreme Spirit in a simple and attractive way. The aim of *kīrtana* is to impress on the audience the identity of the *brahman* with *ātman*, or of God with His devotees. *Bhajana* and *kīrtana* provide mental preparation for getting to be one with God. While attending *bhajana* and *kīrtana* sessions, people share common experiences and emotions, thereby developing an intense awareness of themselves as bhaktas.

The art of performing *kīrtana* involves various skills. *Kīrtana* can be a synthetic art including deep knowledge of all kinds (philosophy, literature, drama, music, etc.) and performing talent. Damle refers to the qualities of the *kathākār* (*kīrtanakār*) as follows, 'the first and foremost quality desired of a *kathākār* was a deep sense of devotion to God. The *kathākār* should be steeped in the traditional literature of the Vārkarī sect. In fact, the *kathākār* should be a very faithful follower of the sect. Then, of course, he should have a fair amount of acquaintance with the Hindu *śāstra*s and lore' (Damle 1960: 74). If the *kīrtana* is performed with intense love of God, the audience will doubtless listen with interest. Furthermore attending a *kīrtana* session helps bhaktas to gain knowledge about the well-known saints of the past and their teachings. At the same time, those attending can participate by singing *bhajana*s and by sharing an intense love of God with the *kīrtanakār*.

nijlyāne gātān ubhā nārāyaṇ / baislyā kīrtan kritān ḍole //
ubhā rāhoniyān mukhīn nām vade / nāce nānā chanden gobind hā //
mārgīn cāltān mukhīn nām vāṇi / ubhā cakrapāṇi māgen puḍhen //
tukā mhaṇe yāsī kīrtanācī goḍi / premen ghālī uḍi nāmāsātīn // (1629)

God loves *kīrtana*. Wherever *kīrtana*, *nāmasmaraṇa* and *bhajana* are performed, he comes and sits to listen. To express the true meaning of *nāmasmaraṇa*, Tukā says that even when people murmur the name of God while lying down, Viṭṭhal will come and stand by them to listen. However if people sit and perform *kīrtana*, then God will rush forth to listen to them. If some devotees chant the name of God while standing, God will come dancing. If devotees practise *nāma-japa* while travelling, God will follow those travellers and listen. Tukā states that Viṭṭhal loves *kīrtana*. Whenever he listens to the chanting of his own name he becomes totally content and comes, and sits beside me.

dās zālon haridāsāncā / buddhikāyāmanen vācā //
tethen premācā sukāḷ / ṭaḷmṛdangakalloḷ //
nāse duṣṭabuddhi sakaḷ / samādhī harikīrtanīn //
aiktān harikathā / bhakti lāge tyā abhaktān //
dekhoni kīrtanācā rang / kaisā ubhā pānḍurang //
hen sukh brahmādikān / mhne nāhīn nānīn tukā // (1122)

I have become a devotee of Hari's devotee. I will utilize my brain, body and everything I have for them. What a bliss I receive! The rain is falling with affection. The sounds from the clappers and drums indicate the bliss of the devotees'. Bad notions and thoughts disappear and the devotees experience the bliss of *samādhi*. Listening to *Hari-kathā* is such a sweet and fascinating experience that even a faithless person will become a devotee. In *kīrtana*, there are dances and songs, and Lord Pāṇḍurang will be present to listen. Tukā says that such bliss is never found in *brāhman* and the others.

ubhyā bājārānt kathā / he ton nāvḍe panḍharināthā //
avghen potasaṭīn ḍhong / tethen kaincā pānḍuraṅg //
lāvī anusandhān / kānhīn deīl mhanaūn //
kāy kelen rānḍlenkā / tulā rāzī nāhīn tukā // (2488)

Some people go to the bazaar or the streets to perform *kīrtana* for the sake of fame. They have no affection for God, they only have the skills to pretend to be devotees of the Lord. Blaming those hypocrites, Tukā says that God despises such show of affection and devotion; it is only for filling the stomach. Tukā blames those who explain the religious teachings with the hope of receiving something from the onlookers.

murtimant dev nāndto panḍharīn / yer te digāntrīn pratimārūp //
zāuniyān vanā karāven kīrtan / mānunī pāṣāṇ viṭṭhalrūp //
tukā mhaṇe mukhya pāhize hā bhāv / bhāvāpāsīn dev śīghra ubhā // (4006)

God has assumed a form, the form of Viṭṭhal, and has made Pandharpur his abode. Similarly, He and his consort reside in many places. However, they are all symbolic of only one God. If you wish to go to the forest and do *kīrtana* then, God will definitely appear. Tukā says that it is very necessary to practise *kīrtana* with genuine affection. If there is affection, there will be faith, and God prefers places where there is faith.

Some say that Tukārām received his spiritual initiation from Caitanya in a dream. Others claim that it was during a period of intensive meditation that Tukārām's *guru*, Bābājī Raghavacaitanya, initiated him, whereupon he renounced his inheritance and gave himself completely to meditation and *nāma* and *kīrtana*. His unique way of practising bhakti involves becoming completely engrossed in *nāma* and *kīrtana*.

nāma sankīrtan sādhan pain sopen / jaḷtīl pāpen janamāntaricin /
na lage sāyās jāven vanāntrā / sukhen yeto gharā nārāyaṇ // (2458)

Chanting the name of Hari is one of the easiest ways of practising bhakti. Though this, the sins of life are burnt to ashes. If we practise this easy method there is no need to go the forest to follow ascetic practice and go on a pilgrimage. By chanting the name of Hari, God himself visits our home.

CONCLUSION

The *Bhāgavata dharma* in Maharashtra revolved around the central image of Viṭṭhal; the saints of Maharashtra knew how to synthesize the *saguṇa* and the *nirguṇa* aspects of God, and preached an easy means to the realization of God. Eknāth says, 'the *saguṇa* or the manifest of the Unmanifest is beyond the grasp of the intellect. Hence, with discrimination and love, the aspirants concentrate their minds on the Manifest and save themselves easily. A mind can easily think of the visible rather than the invisible. Thus, idol worship is meant for one who cannot realize His presence in all beings. Let a man begin somewhere, and by gradual steps he may be led to higher stage' (*EB* 27.351–2, 372).[5]

Tukārām's approach to bhakti can be summarized as follows. Make God the centre of your life. Walk the path of love. Serve mankind, and thus, see God in all. Cast away the clothes of traditions that you have inherited, for often those can bind you from growing in the Love of God. Tutārām did not favour elaborate rituals, displays of asceticism, or preoccupation with austerities. He would say that even dogs may have a saffron colour, bears a matted fur. If living in caves indicates spirituality, then rats who inhabit caves must be doing *sādhanā*. He was opposed to the acquisition of *siddhi*s as these were obstructions to authentic *sādhanā*. Faith in providence was crucial to *sādhanā*. He believed that He who facilitates the milk from the breast for the infant and the One who permits the bursting of foliage from the branches will certainly take care of me. The most important of all was the privilege of being a bhakta and to exercise in life, *nāma japa*. He would say that even God does not know the value of His name. Even God is not aware of the power of His name. How can He be? The lotus cannot smell its own fragrance, only the bee can. The cow knows not the sweetness of its milk, only the calf does. The oyster knows not the value of its pearl, only the jeweller does.[6]

Tukārām says in his *abhaṅgas*:

saguṇ nirguṇ tuj mhane ved/ tukā mhaṇe bhed nāhīn nānvān// (1455)

The Vedas tell you about *saguṇa* and *nirguṇa*, but they never affect your real self.

Tukārām believed the body to be the temple of the living lord, and idol worship and rituals had no meaning for him. However he never denied *saguṇa-sākāra* God.

Tukārām further says:

advay ci dvay zālen ci kāraṇ/ dharilen nārāyaṇen bhaktisukh//
aprokṣ ākār zālā caturbhuj/ ekatatv bīz bhinna nāhīn// (3749)

Basically I believe in non-dualism, but Nārāyaṇa assumed form and descended on the Earth to give bliss to the devotees. He has become the God Viṣṇu with four arms, but the essence never changed.

ABBREVIATIONS

BDCPRI	:	Bulletin of Deccan College Postgraduate Research Institute.
BhG	:	*The Bhagavad-gītā*, tr. S. Radhakrishnan, Delhi: Oxford University Press, 1992 (rpt.).
BhP	:	*The Bhāgavata-purāṇa*, tr. G.V. Tagare, Ancient Indian Tradition and Mythology, vols. 7-10, Delhi: Motilal Banarsidass, 1976–8.
J	:	*Jñāneśvarī*, ed. Jñāneśvarī Sanpādan Samiti, Bombay: Maharashtra Śasan, Śikṣaṇ Vibhāg, 1991.
TG	:	*Tukārām-Abhaṅgagāthā*, Hindi tr. & Comm. V. Vedalankar, vols. 1-3, Pune: Gurukul Pratiṣṭhān, 2003.
MM	:	R.D. Ranade, *Mysticism in Maharashtra*, Delhi: Motilal Banarsidass, 1988.

NOTES

1. Reference from Introduction of *The Bhagavad-gītā*, tr. S. Radhakrishnan. Here Radhakrishnan discusses the real meaning of bhakti.
2. However the order of *abhaṅga*s is different. I follow that of *Tukārām-Abhaṅggāthā,* which is edited on the basis of the Mumbai Sasan edition of *Tukārām Gāthā*, v 1950. Unfortunately, I could not refer to this book. The translation of the *Gāthās* was undertaken by me as a first attempt.
3. Reference from *Santa Bahinabāīnca Gāthā*, ed. S.A. Javadekar, Pune, 1979, p. 69, no. 143. The same *abhaṅga* has been translated by S.G. Tulpule (1979: 393) 'By the favour of the saints the edifice was erected. Jñānadeva laid the foundation and raised the temple. Nāmadeva, his servant, enlarged it to its present size. Eknāth, of Janardana, gave it the support of pillar in the form of the Bhāgavata and Tukā became the pinnacle over which flies the banner of Bahina'.
4. According to the *BhP*, bhakti is practised through a ninefold path, viz., *śravaṇa* (hearing the names of Viṣṇu), *kīrtana* (chanting praises and stories of Viṣṇu), *smaraṇa* (remembering God), *pādasevana* (worshipping Bhagavat's feet), *arcana* (offering worship), *vandana* (prostration), *dāsya* (servitude), *sakhya* (friendship), *ātmanivedana* (offering oneself as well as one's dependants and belongings to Him) (*BP* VII-5-23) *BP* tr. G.V. Tagare.
5. Tr. R.D. Ranade in *MM*, p. 247.
6. Quoted from www.ambahouse.org/tukaram.html. Tukārām's approach towards bhakti has been beautifully summarized.

REFERENCES

Abhyankar, S., *Sant Tukārāmanca Bhaktiyog*, Pune: Aditya Pratisthan, 2001.

Abbott, J.E., *Life of Tukārāma*, Delhi: Motilal Banarsidass, 1986.

Chitre, D.P., *Punha Tukārām*, Mumbai: Popular Prakashan, 1995.
———, *Tukārām Says Tukā*, New Delhi: Penguin Classics, 1991.
Damle, Y.B., 'Harikathā, A Study in Communication', *BDCPRI*, vol. 20, pp. 63–107.
Deshpande, K. and M.V. Rajadhyaksh, *A History of Marathi Literature*, New Delhi: Sahitya Akademi, 1988.
Dabre, T., *The God-Experience of Tukārām: A Study in Religious Symbolism*, Pune: Jnana-Deepa Vidyapeeth, 1987.
Dode, A., ed., *Śrī Tukārāmdarśan*, Mumbai: Sudarsan, 2005.
Engblom, P.C., Introduction in D.B. Mokashi *Palkhi*, tr. P.C. Engblom, Albany: State University of New York Press, 1987.
Fraser, F.N. and K.B. Marathe, *The Poems of Tukārāma*, Delhi: Motilal Banarsidass, 1991.
Gajendragadkar, K.V., 'The Maharashtra Saints and Their Teachings', in H. Bhattacharyya (ed.), *The Cultural Heritage of India*, vol. IV, Calcutta: The Ramakrishna Mission Insttitute of Culture, 1983, pp. 356–76.
Kulkarni, N.H, 'Medieval Maharashtra Muslim Saint Poets', in N.N. Bhattacharyya, ed., *Medieval Bhakti Movements in India*, Delhi: Munshiram Manoharlal, 1989, pp. 198–231.
Kulkarni, B.R., *Lokmanya Tilak's Metaophysic of Morals*, Pune: Poona University, 1973.
Lele, J., 'Jñāneśvar and Tukārām: An Exercise in Critical Hermenutics', in N.K. Wagle and M. Israel, eds., *Religion and Society in Maharashtra*, Toronto: University of Toronto, 1987.
Nemade, B., 'The Revolt of the Underprivileged: Style in the Expression of the Warkari Movement in Maharashtra' in J. Lele, ed., *Tradition and Modernity in Bhakti Movements*, Leiden: E.J. Brill, 1981.
Pendse, S.D., *Sākṣātkārī Sant Tukārām*, Pune: Continental Prakashan, 1982.
Ranade, A., 'Keertana: An Effective Communication', *On Music and Musicians of Hindustan*, New Delhi: Promilla and Co., 1984, pp.109–37.
Ranade, R.D., *Mysticism in Maharashtra*, Delhi: Motilal Banarsidass, 1988.
Sardar, G.B., *The Saint Poets of Maharashtra* tr. K. Metha, Bombay: Orient Longmans, 1969.
Sārth Śrītukārāmaci Gāthā, ed. & tr. Visnubuva Jog Maharaj, Mumbai: Kesav Bhikaji Dhavle, 2003.
Śrītukārām Mahārājancī Sārth Gāthā ed. S.K. Neurgaonkar, Pracary Dandekar Dharmik, Pune: Śikṣanik va Sanskritik Vaṅgmay Prakaśan Mandal, 2003.
Tukārām-Abhaṅgagāthā, Hindi tr. & Comm. V. Vedalankar, 3 vols., Pune: Gurukul Puratisthan, 2003.
Tulpule, S.G., *Classical Marathi Literature from the Beginning to A.D.1818*, A History of Indian Literature, vol. IX, fasc. 4, Wiesbaden: Otto Harrassowitz, 1979.
———, *Mysticism in Medieval India*, Wiesbaden: Otto Harassowitz, 1984.
———, *The Divine Name in the Indian Tradition*, Shimla: Indian Institute of Advanced Study, 1991.

11

A Study of an Aspect of Kabīr's Bhakti with the Text and Translation of the *Gyāna Caumtīsā* in the *Bījak*

TAIGEN HASHIMOTO

This brief article aims to unveil one aspect of Kabīr's multivalent thoughts by presenting the full text and translation of the *Gyāna Caumtīsā*, the second part of the Sabada (Skt. *śabda*) section in the *Bījak*—the collection of Kabīr's utterances.

The Bījak is believed to have been compiled towards the end of the seventeenth century in the region surrounding Banāras (Vārāṇasī). This region is considered to be Kabīr's birthplace, and it is here that he is said to have lived as a *Julāhā* (Muslim weaver), using current language (*bhāṣā*), i.e. old Hindī, to instruct the residents on bhakti to the Ultimate Existence that is found in the depth of one's own heart.

Kabīr explained the concepts of the Ultimate Existence and bhakti in the following words:

sunna sahaja mana sunrate pragaṭa bhaī eka joti /
tāhi purkha kī hauṁ balihārī nirālamba jo hoti // (ramainī, 6 sākhī)

Upon contemplating the empty (*śūnya*), the innate (*sahaja*) in my heart, there shone forth a light.
To that Being (*puruṣa*), based on nothing, I devote myself.

Emptiness (*śūnya*) is the kernel of Mahāyāna Buddhism; it refers to the non-existence of an individual substance because of the relationship between or relativity of many phenomena. Over time, however, with the conceptual change in the notion of enlightenment, there evolved a school of thought that recognized the innate existence of enlightenment in a person. The term 'innate' (*sahaja*) is a reference to this concept, and 'empty' implies perfect freedom without constraint. This philosophical belief is called 'tantric thought'; it emphasizes *sahaja* and preaches that one can achieve deliverance from *saṃsāra* in this life. The yogic ascetics of the Nāth group that propagated *Haṭhayoga*—a practical system of *yoga*—promulgated tantric thought among people of the generation that preceded Kabīr's. Kabīr, considered to be a successor to this school of thought, expressed existence as *puruṣa*. In the *Ṛgveda*, this existence is understood as a Space God, and in classical Indian philosophy, it is the Pure Spirit. Moreover, it is 'a thing with no substratum' (based on nothing). Kabīr declares his resolution to devote himself to this existence that is beyond all attributes. In bhakti thought, the phrase 'devote myself' extols ardent love for and faith in a personified god with perfect attributes. Kabīr, as such, preached devotion to the one true existence, that can be found in the innermost recesses of the individual heart. Holding firm to this standpoint, Kabīr condemned the ritualism and obstinate doctrinarism of both Hinduism and Islam, and impugned discrimination based on religious faith and the caste system.

Thus far, the second part of the *Sabada* has not been sufficiently discussed by scholars. This part of the *Bījak* is regarded to be composed in the style of the folk songs of the region surrounding Banāras. This appears to be one of the reasons why scholars have paid less attention to it although it deserves to be studied in detail. To correct for this deficiency, I drafted a Japanese translation of the entire ***Bījak*** and published it under the title *Indo Chūsei Minshū Shiso no Kenkyū*' (*Research on the Popular Thought in Medieval India*, Tokyo, 2006). In this book, I have also presented the full text of the *Bījak* in the Roman script with diacritical marks. For this Japanese translation, I used the Kabīr Caurā edition of the *Bījak* as the original text. This version was published in 1982 in the form of a *guṭakā* (a pocket book used for daily prayers) by the Kabīr Caurā Maṭh, Banāras. This is the first version which has been edited using the scientific method of philology, invented by Dr. Śukdev Siṃh, collaboration with the Ācārya Gaṅgāśaraṇ Śastrī of the Kabīr Caurā Maṭh. Siṃh is a well-known specialist in the field of philological research on Kabīr's *Bījak*, and had been a Reader at the Hindī department of the Banāras Hindū University.

I referred to some commentaries on the *Bījak* to aid me in translation, but found that these did not provide the exact or literal translation of the verses. Moreover, they did not offer adequate explanations for some words or phrases that were difficult to understand. These commentaries include: Gaṅgāśaraṇ Śāstrī, *Bījak Ṭīkā Manoramā* (*BTM*), Vārāṇasī: Kabīrvāṇī Prakāśan Kendra, 1989. Abhilāṣdās, *Bījak Pārakh-prabodhnī-vyākhyā* (*BPP*), Illāhābād: Pārakh Prakāśak Saṃsthān, 1969.

I also found many useful suggestions in the work of outstanding scholars who have discussed this subject. These include Charlotte, Vaudeville's, *Kabīr* (Oxford: Clarendon Press, 1974) and *A Weaver Named Kabir* (Delhi: Oxford University Press, 1993) and Linda Hess and Shukdev Singh's, *The Bījak of Kabīr* (Delhi: Motilal Banarsidass, 1986).

For a critical analysis of the text, I consulted Callewaert's edition: Winand M. Callewaert and Bart Op de Beeck (eds.), *Nirgun-bhakti-sagar: Devotional Hindi Literature*, 2 vols. (Delhi: Manohar, 1991).

TEXT AND TRANSLATION OF THE *GYĀNA CAUṀTĪSĀ*

Gyāna Cauṁtīsā
Thirty-four wise sayings

oṃkāra ādi jānai likhikai meṭai tāhi so mānai /
oṃkāra kahai saba koī jina yaha lakhā so biralā hoī //

He who knows the root of the Sacred Sound OM can recognize the one who writes and erases the world.
Everyone utters 'OM', but very rarely would you find a person who is certain of its meaning.

kakā kaṁvala kirana mau pāvai sasi bigasita sampuṭa nahiṁ āvai /
vāṁha kusuma raṅga jo pāvai augahi gahike gagana rahāvai // 1 //

The letter 'ka': If you spot a lotus flower in the moonbeam,
the moon will not be able to enter the casket.
You will sight a red-yellow colour there, and perceive something strange and live in that space.[1]

khakhā cāhai khori manāvai khasamahiṁ chāṁṛi dojaga ko dhāvai /
khasamahiṁ chāṁṛi chimā ho rajiye hoya na khīna achai pada lahiye // 2 //

The letter 'kha': If you expect [it], you should correct your falseness.
If not, you would be discarding the Lord and choosing Hell.
Do release your enemies and forgive them.
[Then] there will be no sorrow, and you can be inviolate.

gagā gura ke bacanahiṁ māna dūsara sabda karo nahiṁ kāna /
tahāṁ bihaṅgama kabahuṁ na jāi augha gahike gagana rahāi // 3 //

The letter 'ga': Reflect on the teachings of your Guru and do not pay attention to the words of any other person.
Where birds cannot go, you will perceive something strange and live in that space.

ghaghā ghaṭa binase ghaṭa hoī ghaṭahiṁ meṁ ghaṭa rākhu samoī /
jo ghaṭa ghaṭe ghaṭahiṁ phiri āvai ghaṭahiṁ mā phira ghaṭahi samāvai // 4 //

The letter 'gha': Since one body is created only when another is broken, one body must merge with another.
When a body produces an embryo and another being is created, one body merges with another again.

ṅaṅā nirakhata nisi dina jāī nirakhata naina rahe ratanāī /
nimikha eka jo nirakhai pāvai tāhi nimikha meṁ naina chipāvai // 5 //

The letter 'ṅa': When you stare at something day and night, your eyes turn red.
For an instant, while staring, you close your eyes.

cacā citra raco baṛa bhārī citra choṛi taiṁ cetu citrakārī /
jinha yaha citra vicitra hoya khelā citra choṛi taiṁ cetu citelā // 6 //

The letter 'ca': A huge painting was created.
Do throw away the picture and pay attention, oh painter.
What a strange picture it was. Give up your painting and wake up, painter.

chachā āhi chatrapati pāsā chaki kina rahahu meṭi saba āsā /
maiṁ tohīṁ china samujhāvā khasama chāṛi kasa āpu bandhāvā // 7 //

The letter 'cha': The Emperor drew near.
Why have you given up all desires and why are you content?
I will convince you of one thing. Why disregard your Lord and bind yourself?

jajā ī tana jiyata jāro jauvana jāri jukti tana pāro /
jo kachu jukti jāni tana jarai ī ghaṭa joti ujiyārī karai // 8 //

The letter 'ja': Do not reduce this body to ashes while living.
Burn away your youth and train your body to live according to manners.
If you understand manners and burn your body, it will glow like fire.

jhajhā arujhi sarujhi kita jāna arujhina hīṇḍata jāya parāna /
koṭi sumera ḍhūṁṛhi phiri āvai jo gaṛha gaṛhe gaṛhaiyā so pāvai // 9 //

The letter 'jha': Where do you go, all confused and lost?
While searching, you will find yourself befuddled and will lose your life.
After searching through millions of high mountains, the person who built the fort will be able to find it.

ñañā nigraha saṁnehu karu niruvāru chāṁṛa sandehu /
nahiṁ dekhe nahiṁ bhājiyā paramạ sayānapa yehū // 10 //

The letter 'ña': Exercise control and abandon your doubt with discretion.
Do not look, and do not run away. This is the wisest choice.

jahāṁ na dekhi tahaṁ āpu bhajāū jahāṁ nahiṁ tahāṁ mana lāū /
jahāṁ nahiṁ tahāṁ saba kachu jānī jahāṁ hai tahāṁ le paicānī // 11 //

Run by yourself to an invisible place and focus your mind on the place that houses nothingness.
Discover all in nothingness, and gain understanding in the place that has something.

ṭaṭā vikaṭā bāṭa mana māhīṁ kholi kpāṭa mahala moṁ jāhīṁ /
rahā laṭāpaṭi juṭi tehi māhiṁ hohiṁ aṭala taba katahuṁ na jāhī // 12 //

The letter 'ṭa': Although your heart is in turmoil, throw open the door, and proceed to the palace.
If you control the unrest in that palace, you will become unshakable and will not need to go anywhere.

ṭhaṭhā ṭhaura dūri ṭhaga niyare nita ke niṭhura kīnha mana ghere /
je ṭhaga ṭhage saba loga sayānā so ṭhaga cīnha ṭhaura pahicānā // 13 //

The letter 'ṭha': Although the final destination is far away, deceit is near and savagely envelopes your heart at all times.
Recognize the fraud who deceives the wise and discover your destination.

ḍaḍā ḍara upaje ḍara hoi ḍarahī meṁ ḍara rākhu samoī /
jo ḍara ḍare ḍarahiṁ phiri āvai ḍarahī meṁ phira ḍarahu samāvai // 14 //

The letter 'ḍa': Because fear dwells in your heart, you feel threatened; instil fear into fear.

When fear itself is afraid and you experience fright, fear will be embedded in fear.

ḍhaḍhā hīṁḍata hī kita jāna hīṁḍata ḍhūṛhata jāī prāna/
koṭi sumera ḍhūṛhi ḍhūṛi phiri āvai jehi ḍhūṛhā so katahūṁ na pāvai // 15 //

The letter 'ḍha': Where will you search?
While you are engrossed in your search, you will lose your life.
Even after searching millions of high mountains, that which you seek is nowhere to be found.

ṇaṇā dui basāye gāūṁ reṇā ḍhūṛhe terī nāūṁ /
muye eka jāya taji dhanā mare ityādika kete ganā // 16 //

The letter 'ṇa': The one who created two villages looked for your name in the sand.
He died, leaving behind his wealth. Why should the dead be counted?

tatā ati triyo nahiṁ jāī tana tribhuvana meṁ rākhu chipāī /
jo tana tribhuvana māhi chipāvai tatvahi mili tatva so pāvai // 17 //

The letter 'ta': Nothing is more important than the three *guṇas*.
Let your body lie hidden in the threefold world.
He who hides his body in the threefold world will discover the truth in truth.

thathā ati athāha thāho nahiṁ jāī ī thira ū thira nāhiṁ rahāī /
thore thore thira hou bhāī bina thambhe jasa mandila thambhāī // 18 //

The letter 'tha': It is very deep, and it is not possible to reach the bottom.
This is unshakable while that is not.
Make it unshakable gradually, oh brothers, like building a temple without pillars.

dada dekhahu binasana hārā jasa dekhahu tasa karahu bicārā /
dasahuṁ duāre tārī lāvai taba dayāla ke darasana pāvai // 19 //

The letter 'da': Look, everything breaks. Think as you look.
When you lock ten gates, you can worship the merciful.[2]

dhadhā aradha māṁhi andhiyārī aradha choṛi uradha mana tārī /
aradha choṛi uradha mana lāvai āpā meṭi ke prema baṛhāvai // 20 //

The letter 'dha': In the lower path, there is darkness.
Leave this way and set your heart on the upper path.

Abandon the lower path and follow the upper path;
give up self-indulgence and let your heart be filled with love.

nanā vo cauthe maharh jāī rāma kā gadahā hoya khara khāī /
āpā choṛo naraka baserā ajahuṁ mūṛha cita cetu saberā // 21 //

The letter 'na': He will reach the fourth state,[3]
[the others will] become the donkey of Rāma and graze grasses.
Abandon self-indulgence, [otherwise] you shall fall into Hell.
Stupid heart, awake now; it is morning.

papā pāpa kareṁ saba koī pāpa kare dharama nahiṁ hoī /
papā kahe sunuhu re bhāī hamare se ina kichuvo na pāī // 22 //

The letter 'pa': Everyone commits sin, and there is no justice.
The letter 'pa'[4] says, 'Listen, oh brothers, you will not benefit from serving me'.

phaphā phala lāge baṛa dūrī cākhai satagura dei na tūrī /
phaphā kahai sunuhu re bhāī sarada patāla kī khabari na pāī // 23 //

The letter 'pha': Fruits grow [on a tree] very far away.
Even if Sadguru tastes them, he does not offer them to you.
The letter 'pha' says, 'Listen, oh brothers, nobody knows what Heaven and Hell are like'.

babā barabara lare saba koī barabara kare kāja nahiṁ hoī /
babā bāta kahai arathāi phala kā marama na jānahu bhāī // 24 //

The letter 'ba': Everyone makes idle talk and does not work.
[Pandits] preach about true meaning,
[but people] do not know the essence of fruits (*nirvāṇa*), oh brothers.

bhabhā bhabhari rahā bharapūrī bhabhare te hai niyare dūrī /
bhabhā kahai sunuhu re bhāī bhabhare āvai bhabhare jāī // 25 //

The letter 'bha': As fear and wrongdoing increase, he who is near grows distant.
The letter 'bha' says, 'Listen, oh brothers, fear and wrongdoing will come and will fade away'.

mama ke seye marama nahiṁ pāī hamare se ina mūla gamāī /
māyā moha rahā jaga pūrī māyā mohahiṁ lakhau vicārī // 26 //

A person enjoys 'ma',[5] does not grasp the essence of life,
and loses the kernel of the self through self-indulgence.

The attachment to *māyā* (false illusion) pervades the world.
Understand the fascination that māyā holds and reflect on it.

yāyā jagata rahā bharapūrī jagatahuṁ te hai jānā dūrī /
yayā kahai sunuhu re bhāī hamahiṁ te ina jai jai pāī // 27 //

The letter 'ya': The world is filled with *māyā*. Distance yourself from the world.
The letter 'ya' says, 'Listen, oh, brothers,
the world rejoices in victory gained through self-indulgence'.

rarā rāri rahā arujhāī rāma kahai dukha dārida jāī /
rarā kahai sunuhu re bhāī satagura pūñchi ke sevahu āī // 28 //

The letter 'ra': You got entangled in disputes;
if you take the name of Rām (the Innate Absolute), there will be neither pain nor poverty.
The letter 'ra' says, 'Listen, oh, brothers, ask Sadguru, then come and serve.'

lalā tuture jānāī tuture āya tuture paracāī /
āpa tuture aura ko kahai ekai kheta dūnoṁ nirabahaī // 29 //

The letter 'la': A lisping [teacher] instructs [a student].
The lisping [student] approaches and the lisping [teacher] preaches about enlightenment.
When one lisping person instructs another, they both plough one field.

vavā vaha kahai saba koī vaha vaha kahe kāja nahiṁ hoī /
vaha to kahai sunai jo koī saraga patāla na dekhai joī // 30 //

The letter 'va': Everyone says, 'That, that', and no work is done.
Whoever listens to another saying 'That'.
can not distinguish [the boundary between] Heaven and Hell.

śaśā sara nahiṁ dekhai koī sara sītalatā ekai hoī /
śaśā kahai sunuhu re bhāī sūnya samāna cala jaga jāī // 31 //

The letter 'śa': Nobody looks at water
[and makes the mistake of believing that] water and coldness are the same.
The letter 'śa' says, 'Listen, oh, brothers, the world collapses like an empty space.'

ṣaṣā khara khara kareṁ saba koī khara khara kare kāja nahiṁ hoī /
ṣaṣā kahai sunuhu re bhāī rāma nāma le jāpu parāī // 32//

The letter 'ṣa': Everyone says, 'True, True', and in doing so, no work is done.
The letter 'ṣa' says, 'Listen, oh brothers,
devote yourself to meditate on and repeat the name of Rām'.

sasā sarā raco bariyāī sara bedhe saba loga tavāī /
sasā ke ghara suna guna hoī itanā bāta na jānai koī // 33 //

The letter 'sa': Everyone is forcibly cremated on firewood,
pierced by an arrow, and broiled in the heat of the fire.
In the house of the letter 'sa',[6] there is nothing other than emptiness.
Nobody knows of such a thing.

hahā hāya hāya meṁ saba jaga jāī harakha soga saba māṁhiṁ samāī /
haṃkari haṃkari saba baṛa baṛa gayaū hārā marama na kāhū payaū // 34 //

The letter 'ha': Everyone lets out a sigh and dies. But there is joy and sorrow in everyone.
Great people died with the word 'alas' [on their lips]
but no one has understood the essence of their sorrow.

kṣakṣā china meṁ paralaya sama miṭi jāī cheva pare taba ko samujhāī /
cheva pare kāhu anta na pāyā kahai kabīra agamana goharāya // 35 //

The letter 'kṣa': The moment the universe is dissolved,
everything will pass away. Who will make this known at the time of a person's death?
'No one has understood the Ultimate at the time of their death',
Kabīr cautions us in advance, declaring loudly.

The *Gyāna Cauṁtīsā* can be considered to have been influenced by the previous Tantric mystic thought on the syllables of Devanāgarī letters. On the other hand, it can be also considered that Kabīr was trying to teach the common people the existence of Ultimate Being in the innermost mind, by using this poetic type so as to enable the common people to memorize the Devanāgarī letters.

NOTES

1. *BTM* compared this pada with the *Chāndogya-upaniṣad* 8.1.1.
hariḥ auṃ. atha idam asmin brahmapure daharaṃ puṇḍarīkaṃ ve daharo'sminn antrākāśaḥ tasmin yad antaḥ tad anveṣṭavyam tad vā va vijijñāsitavyam.
hariḥ auṃ, in this *Brahman* town is the abode of a small lotus flower, in

which there is a space / The essence should be searched for and understood.

2. Both *BTM* and *BPP* interpret 'ten gates' as 'ten types of organs'.
3. *BTM* explains 'the fourth state' as the fourth state of consciousness (*turīya*), according to the Advaita Vedānta, which is beyond the states of waking, dreaming, and deep sleep, and which pervades and transcends all these states.
4. This 'pa' seems to symbolize '*pāpa* (sin)'.
5. *BPP* explains that 'the letter "ma" refers to "*māyā*".' I have adopted this interpretation.
6. *BPP* interprets 'the house of the letter "sa" to mean ignorance'.

12

Analytical Study of *Bhaktirasa* as a Religious Sentiment Established by the Gauḍīya Vaiṣṇava School

MASARU TONGUU

The teachings of Caitanya, the founder of the Bengali Vaiṣṇava School (Gauḍīya Vaiṣṇava, hereafter G.Vai.), were theoretically constructed by his followers. The essential points of this school's theory were the worship of Kṛṣṇa and bhakti as the important means, and the school elaborates its unique opinions on the latter point. In this paper, based primarily on the *Dakṣiṇavibhāga* of *Bhaktirasāmṛtasindhu* written by Rūpa Gosvāmī—one of the direct and important disciples of Caitanya, I will try to analyse this bhakti as *rasa*.

BHAKTI

It is difficult to determine the origin of the word 'bhakti'[1] itself, even though we encounter it here and there in several Upaniṣads.[2] It is evident, however, that the word has a religious meaning with regard to the worship of Kṛṣṇa or Vāsudeva which appears in the *Bhāgavata-purāṇa* (*BhP*) and the *Bhagavad-gītā*.[3] With these books as the background, religious movements based on the concept of bhakti were active in the eighth century. In the *Śāṇḍilya-sūtra*,[4] bhakti implies yearning for and becoming absorbed in God and surrendering each and every action to God,[5] or the supreme love dedicated God in *Nāradabhaktisūtra*.[6] However, as the Advaitavāda school founded by Śaṅkara, who insisted on monism, became more influential, this dualism adhering to the concept of bhakti began to decline. In the twelfth century, the Vaiṣṇava movement was, on the other hand, in the process of becoming classified into branches known as the four *sampradāya*s as a reaction to Śaṅkara's philosophy.

Meanwhile, the *BhP*, which mysteriously describes the romantic relationship between Kṛṣṇa and the Gopīs[7] in Vṛndāvana, had a profound influence on the concept of bhakti in medieval times: it emphasizes bhakti as the best means to attain God everywhere in the work.

This paper will analyse the concept of bhakti propounded by the G.Vai. based primarily on The *Bhaktirasāmṛtasindhu* and the *Bhaktisandarbha.* G.Vai. made an epoch-making contribution to the Vaiṣṇava movement in India by adding new ideas to the concept of bhakti. As stated above, established its philosophical core with their own interpretation of *BhP*, which can be seen in their detailed investigation of bhakti. The representative scholarly works are *Bhaktirasāmṛtasindhu* (*BRAS*) by Rūpa Gosvāmī and *Bhaktisandarbha* by Jīva Gosvāmī. Thus, in this paper, I am going to analyse the bhakti propounded by G.Vai. based primarily on these two works below.

G.Vai. does not completely negate important and orthodox philosophical concepts such as *jñāna* or *karman* and place them under bhakti or regard them as dependent on bhakti; that is, they insist on the supremacy of bhakti.[8] They emphasize its superiority in comparison to *jñāna* by stating, 'The joy of (attaining the knowledge of) *brahman* after several million years' efforts is not comparable to a drop of the joyful ocean attained by bhakti.'[9] 'The only bhakti (of this type) makes Kṛṣṇa, who is surrounded by those dear to him, enjoy love itself and fascinates him.'[10] Additionally, bhakti is said to be the fifth *puruṣārtha*; the other four are insignificant, like weeds, in front of the bhakti.[11]

G.Vai. explains that this bhakti exists both in Kṛṣṇa and *nityaparikara* (eternal followers of Kṛṣṇa in Vṛndāvana),[12] and that the relationship between them is that of *śakti* and *śaktimat*, because bhakti is a special function of *hlādinīśakti*, which is one of Kṛṣṇa's *svarūpaśakti*. Kṛṣṇa gladdens not only others but also himself as the light breaks through the darkness to illuminates other and the light itself.[13]

Bhakti is said to stem from God's mercy (*kṛpā* or *anugraha*), but God does not directly show his mercy to his believers (Jīva). Instead, God exhibits mercy through the righteous Vaiṣṇava.[14] There are two types of righteous Vaiṣṇava, who are different from *jīva* and *nityaparikara*. The first is a person who experiences *brahman* through the way of *jñāna*; the other, a person who attains divine love through the way of bhakti.[15] This indicates that *jīva* cannot directly contact with Kṛṣṇa or with *nityaparikara* like Rādhā, but that *jīva* can approach sages or other types of believers. Additionally, the experiences of these righteous Vaiṣṇavas will determine the kinds of experiences of each *jīva*.

A *jīva* will have an inclination (*ruci*) towards what is worshipped when he/she visits a righteous Vaiṣṇava; faith (*śraddhā*) will be born in the *jīva*'s mind.[16] Therefore, a *jīva* has to listen to the truth by accepting one or several of such Vaiṣṇava as their initiators (*śravaṇaguru* or *śikṣāguru*).[17] In contrast with this *śikṣāguru*, the teacher will teach the *jīva* a deep *mantra* that is required for meditation. There should be only one *mantraguru*, and the teacher should be regarded as the same as God.[18] From this state of *ruci*, a *jīva* moves to the next stage of worship (*upāsanā*) with the guidance of the *mantraguru*;[19] the object of worship will depend on whether the *guru* is *jñānasiddha* or *bhaktisiddha*. The former guides the *jīva* to the worship of attributeless *brahman*, and the latter guides him or her to the worship of Bhagavat-Kṛṣṇa with attributes. The second type of *jīva* is also classified into *ahaṃgraha-upāsanā* and *bhaktirūpa-upāsanā*.[20] Worship acquired with the assistance of *jñānasiddha* is called *jñānarūpa-upāsanā*. *Ahaṃgraha-upāsanā* is also said to worship God by presuming oneself to be God with śaktis.[21]

Bhaktirūpa-upāsanā has the primary characteristic of perfect service (*sevā*) to God as well as a secondary characteristic which enables the *jīva* to obtain everything.[22] The *sevā* mentioned here refers to physical, verbal and mental obedience to God.[23] Bhakti defined in this way is the usual sense of the term and is divided into the following three types:[24]

Āropasiddha: the bhakti that does not naturally grow in *jīva* but is matured in it through repeated behaviour related to God.

Saṅgasiddha: the bhakti that does not naturally grow in *jīva* but which arises in it through repeated meetings with sages.

Svarūpasiddha: the bhakti that grows naturally in *jīva* by listening to or singing poems from sacred books like *BhP.*

Bhakti classified in this manner is once again categorized as follows (the number indicates the page in the *BhS*).

āropasiddha	*bhagavatprīṇanarūpa*	(pp. 378–81)
	tasmiṃs tattyāgarūpa	
saṅgasiddha	*sakāma*	
	kaivalyakāma	*sakaitava* (pp. 381–6)
	bhaktimātrakāma	
svarūpasiddha	*sakāma*	
	kaivalyakāma	(pp. 386–9)
	niṣkāma	*akaitava* (pp. 391–6)

As a result of the above-mentioned analysis, the *niṣkāma-svarūpasiddha-bhakti* is defined in *BRAS* 1.1.11 as follows:

anyābhilāṣitāśūnyam jñānakarmādyanāvṛtam /
anukūlyena kṛṣṇānuśīlanam bhaktir uttamā //

The supreme bhakti is the pursuit of Kṛṣṇa which is realized by pleasing Kṛṣṇa (*ānukūlyena*),[25] and is not covered by knowledge or any behaviour and that requires no other aspiration (than bhakti).

Further, this bhakti indicates the best bhakti, which is differentiated from general bhakti (*sāmānyabhakti*). This supreme bhakti is again categorized into three types, namely, *sādhana-*, *bhāva-*, and *premabhakti.*

sā bhaktiḥ sādhanam bhāvaḥ prema ceti tridhoditā // BRAS 1.2.1

Among the three, *sādhana-bhakti*[26] is explained as follows:

kṛtisādhyā bhavet sādhyabhāvā sā sādhanābhidhā / BRAS 1.2.2a

The realization of *bhāva* which is to be accomplished is called *sādhana-bhakti.*

This *sādhanabhakti* is of two types, i.e. *vaidhī* and *rāgānugā*,[27] and the former arises according to the regulations prescribed in *śāstra*.

śāsanenaiva śāstrasya sā vaidhī bhaktir ucyate / *BRAS* 1.2.6b

Jīva Gosvāmī (JG) states that this regulation (*vidhi*) is also of two types; the first becomes the basis for being invited to follow the way of bhakti; and the second, basis for what to do and what not to do when intended.[28] The varieties (*bheda*) or elements (*aṅga*) of this *vaidhibhakti* are variously enumerated, and JG grades them into the following eleven types.[29]

1. *śaraṇāpatti*: reliance on God as the only one shelter.
2. *gurusevā*: services to a religious leader.
3. *śravaṇa*: listening to the name, the appearance and sports (*līlā*) of Kṛṣṇa that appears in sacred books, especially in the *BhP*.
4. *kīrtaṇa*: singing aloud the phrases in sacred books, especially *nāmasaṅkīrtana* is the best in Kali period.
5. *smaraṇa*: five kinds of remembrances of the name of God by concentrating one's mind.
6. *padasevā*: services offered to the feet of images of God in temples by way of pilgrimages.
7. *arcana*: religious rites of worship taught by the *mantraguru* or prescribed in the Āgama.
8. *vadana*: behaviour's expressing respects such as a salute.
9. *dāsya*: doing one's best towards God in a slave-like manner.
10. *sakhya*: feeling like a friend to God.
11. *ātmanivedana*: surrendering everything that is private to God.

In all, RG enumerates sixty-four types of *vaidhibhakti* by adding fifty-three to the eleven given above. He refers to the first three types as primary ones,[30] that is, reliance on a religious teacher (*gurupadāśraya*), initiation and education by the teacher (*dīkṣā-śikṣādi*), and services to the teacher with perfect trust (*viśrambhena gurusevā*). *Vaidhibhakti* is attained by way of one or many of them (*ekāṅga or anekāṅga*).

Rāgānugabhakti, on the other hand, is explained by RG as follows:

virājantīm abhivyaktam vrajavāsijanādiṣu /
rāgātmikām anusṛtā yā sā rāgānugocyate // *BRAS* 1.2.270[31]

Rāgānuga-bhakti is that which follows the bhakti whose essence is the brightly shining *rāga* possessed by the people in Vraja (which is one of Kṛṣṇa's residences).

According to this explanation, the *jīva* who live in this phenomenal world cannot directly serve Kṛṣṇa with bhakti; instead, they approach Kṛṣṇa only by imitating the *rāgātmikabhakti* possessed by the Vraja people. RG continues to explain *rāgātmikabhakti* by stating, 'rāga is the natural occurrence of the rapt condition of one's mind towards the dearest one (Kṛṣṇa), and the bhakti that embodies this condition is called *rāgātmika*'.

iṣṭe svārasikī rāgaḥ paramāviṣṭatā bhavet /
tanmayī yā bhaved bhaktiḥ sātra rāgātmikoditā // *BRAS* 1.2.272[32]

The *rāgātmikā* has two varieties. One consists of the love possessed by cowgirls (Gopī) in Vraja and is shown for the cowgirl's enjoyment and to delight Kṛṣṇa (*kāma-rūpa*). The other is the love possessed by Kṛṣṇa's parents, Nanda and Yośodā, or by the cowboys (Gopa), who are Kṛṣṇa's friends; this love is based on the relationship between Kṛṣṇa and his friends. Thus, the two types of *rāgātmikā* are *kāmānugā* and *sambandhānugā*. Although *kīrtana* and others can be acknowledged in this *rāgātmikābhakti*, they are not essential. Therefore, the *rāgātmikā* is not *sādhanabhakti*,[33] even though it exists. This very *rāgātmikā* is the *premabhakti* to which I refer later, and it is accorded the highest status among all the bhakti.

Next, RG explains *bhāvabhakti* as follows: *bhāvabhakti* is the one which is clean and consists of special *sattva*[34] (the mixture of *hlādinīśakti* and *saṃvitśakti* among the divine *svarūpaśakti*), and which is equal to the solar ray of love and smoothes one's heart with the relish (*ruci*) of hopes that one can possess for oneself.[35]

śuddhasattvaviśeṣātmā premasūryaṃśusāmyabhāk /
ruchibiś cittamāsṛṇyakṛd asau bhāva ucyate // BRAS 1.31

In other words, *bhāvabhakti* is the dawn of *premabhakti*,[36] the emergence of Kṛṣṇa's *premabhakti*.

This *bhāvabhakti*, *vaidhī* or *rāgānugā*, is classified into three types: what will arise as a result of *sādhanabhakti*'s development by adhering to it (*sādhanābhiniveśaja*), what will arise from Kṛṣṇa's grace (*Kṛṣṇaprasādaja*), and what will arise from believers' grace of Kṛṣṇa's *nityaparikara* such as Rādhā. The important point here is that *kṛṣṇabhakta*'s grace or mercy which does not directly operate on *jīva* can function at the stage of *bhāvabhakti*. I think that this will be possible in the case of the *jīva* such as *śikṣāguru*, *mantraguru*, or ancient sages. More specifically, the general *jīva* has to ascend to the upper stages a step at a time; however, a special *jīva* (Caitanya perhaps)[37] will be thought to directly arrive at this stage or the next one. This is clear because the bhakta is divided into several types in the chapter named *vibhāva* of *BRAS* to which I refer later.

This *bhāva* is also called *rati* (love), and can be observed in those people who seek emancipation through *jñāna* or *yoga*; however, the word is modified by the word *ābhāsa* (pretended). RG argues that, in order to avoid confrontations with philosophical schools (especially Advaita Vedāntin), this *Ratyābhāsa* may sometimes develop into the true *rati*. This kind of attitude can clearly be observed in the argument of *acintyabhedābheda*—there were people among the Vedāntin who tried to appease bhakti schools though they maintained their own positions.[38]

When this *bhāvabhakti* becomes dense, smoothes one's mind perfectly, and intensifies the feeling that Kṛṣṇa should be possessed as a child, friend or lover, the bhakti is called *premabhakti*.

samyaṅmasṛṇitasvānto mamatvātiśayāṅkitaḥ /
bhāvaḥ sa eva sāndrātmā buddhaiḥ premā nigadyate // BRAS 1.4.1

Additionally, just as *bhāvabhakti* can arise from *sādhanabhakti*, *premabhakti* also has two types; the first arises from *vaidhī* or *rāgānugā*; the second, from Kṛṣṇa's grace.

bhavottā 'tiprasādotthaḥ śrīharer iti sa dvidhā / BRAS 1.4.4

Once again, the type that arises due to God's grace is of two types; the type that is based on the knowledge that God is great (*māhātmyajñāna*) and the type is pure (*kevala*) [based on the knowledge that God is sweet and elegant (*mādhurya*)].[39] The *bhāvabhakti* that arises from God's grace is primarily experienced by *nityaparikara*, and the former may appear in those who rely on *vaidhī*, and the latter in those who rely on *rāgānugā*.[40]

RG ends the Pūrvavibhāga of *BRAS* after explaining the general process by which *preman* gradually grows in the mind of *jīva* as follows:

1. belief in it is born by listening to *śāstra* through the mouth of a sage (*śraddhā*)
2. to have continuous association with the sage to learn religious rules (*sādhusaṅga*)
3. various behaviours related to worship (*bhajanakriyā*)
4. withdrawal from the worthless (*anarthanivṛtti*)
5. confidence (*niṣṭhā*)
6. to take immense pleasure in worship itself (*ruci*)
7. the birth of affection (*āsakti*) [*sādhanabhakti*]
8. the sprouting of passion (*bhāva*) [*bhāvabhakti*]
9. the arrival at love (*preman*) [*premabhakti*].

ādau śraddhā tataḥ sādhusaṅgo 'tha bhajanakriya/
tato 'narthanivṛttiḥ syāt tato niṣṭhā rucis tatas //
athāsaktis tato bhāvas tataḥ premābhyudañcati /
sādhakānām ayaṃ premṇaḥ prādurbhāve bhavet kramaḥ // BRAS 1.4.15–16

RG deliberates *preman* in the *Ujjvalanīlamaṇi*, which is an auxiliary work to *BRAS* by subdividing *prema* into *rati*, *preman*, *sneha*, *māna*, *praṇaya*, *rāga*, *anurāga* and *mahābhāva*,[41] however, I do not discuss the details here.

Thus far, I have been discussing the bhakti propounded by the G.Vai. primarily based on the previously mentioned works by RG and JG above. This discussion leads me to the following conclusion.

When the school tried to establish its philosophical position, they defined the relationship between Kṛṣṇa and Rādhā as *acintya-bhedābheda* from a new point of view. They avoided confrontations with other philosophical schools at the time by adapting the relationship to that between Kṛṣṇa and *Brahman* as well as that between Kṛṣṇa and *Paramātman*. They assumed the same attitude in the investigation of bhakti, as well. Though G.Vai. regards the bhakti towards Kṛṣṇa as the sole bhakti, it does not deny the bhakti towards other deities. The proof for this is the differentiation of bhakti into *uttamā* and *sāmānya* by RG. Although RG himself does not examine *sāmānya bhakti*, JG's analysis indicates it. That is why the *svarūpaśakti* is referred to for the first time when *bhāvabhakti* is mentioned. There must be an appearance of *svarūpaśakti* in *sāmānya bhakti*, in as far as it is called bhakti, but it seems to appear imperfectly because G.Vai. does not mention it. As other deities are, so to speak, only *avatāra* of Kṛṣṇa, according to G.Vai., the perfect pastime (*vilāsa*) of *svarūpaśakti* is possible only for Kṛṣṇa. The bhakti founded by G.Vai. is illustrated on the next page from the viewpoint of its relationship with Kṛṣṇa. This bhakti generally develops from *sādhanā* into *preman* with *bhāva* in between, and is naturally possessed by *jīva*, who tastes (*rasa*) the joy of love when it is stimulated (by teachings or rarely by *prasāda*) and manifests itself (*abhivyakta*). G.Vai. uses the *rasa* theory in order to prove this concretely.

RASA

The word *rasa*, which derives from the verb √*ras* (to taste) means 'taste' or 'flavour'. This word is used in the *Taittirīya Upaniṣad* when *Brahman*, which consists of existence, knowledge and joy (*saccidānanda*), is explained.

raso 'vai saḥ /
rasaṃ hy evāyaṃ labdhānandī bhavati / 2.7

Apart from this abstract meaning of taste, there were scholars in India—such as Caraka—who analysed this *rasa* from the viewpoint of natural science.

On the other hand, *rasa* was also researched in the field of dramaturgy; Bharata (*c.* the fourth or fifth century) is said to have been the first person who systematized this research. It is also said that Abhinavagupta, approximately in the tenth century, established the Indian rhetoric through active discussions about rhetorical issues proposed after the *Nāṭyaśāstra* written by Abhinavagupta. G.Vai. skillfully employed the *rasa* theory, which was expanded by the schools of rhetoric as one of its fields, and tried to explain the foundation of their own theological philosophy. Thus, we require a contrasting comprehension of G.Vai.'s *rasa* with that of rhetorical schools in order to clearly understand G.Vai.'s *bhaktirasa*. From this perspective, in the next section of this paper, I am going to examine the historical movements of the rhetorical schools after Bharata and analyse G.Vai.'s *bhaktirasa* in relation to the second chapter of *BRAS*.

Bharata defines *rasa* as follows: 'The *niṣpatti* (birth) of *rasa* comes from the *saṃyoga* (union) of *vibhāva* (stimulative elements), *anubhāva* (the appearance of internal feelings such as singing), and *vyabhicāribhāva* (emotions acknowledged temporally)'.[42] Further, he states that '*Rasa* is to be tasted, and an educated person will taste the eternal feeling (*sthāyībhāva*) represented (on the stage) by the various psychological expressions that accompany the words, gestures and *sattva* (which give birth to tears as an exhibition of internal feelings), and acquire joy and satisfaction.'[43] Bharata indicates the superiority of *sthāyībhāva* over other *bhāva*, and concludes that the *sthāyībhāva* that accompany *vibhāva*, *anubhāva* and *vyabhicāribhāva* will be named *rasa*.[44]

Scholars after the period of Bharata raised many different questions regarding the meaning of this definition of *rasa*, because Bharata himself explained neither the *saṃyoga* nor the *niṣpatti* that he used in his definition. As a result, the following four opinions about the interpretation of both words emerged among those scholars.

(a) *Utpattivāda:* In approximately the ninth century, Bhaṭṭa Lollaṭa interpreted the words in Bharata's definition as 'the *saṃyoga* of *vibhāva*, etc., is their union with *sthāyin*: the *niṣpatti* of *rasa* arises from that union. In such a case, *vibhāva* is the cause of the production of mental functions (*cittavṛtti* or feeling) whose essence is *sthāyin*'.[45] Additionally, he states, '*rasa* is the very *sthāyin* that is intensified by *vibhāva*, etc., and that exists in both a character (*anukārya*, or the role that is to be played) and an actor (*anukartṛ* or a person who plays the role)'.[46] His idea is characterized by two points. He does not take an audience (*sāmājika* or *sahṛdaya*) into consideration, and regards the relationship between *sthāyin* and *vibhāva* as a simple one between *utpādaka* and *utpādya* (*kārya* and *kāraṇa*, or cause and effect). In other words, *rasa* is intensified *sthāyin* and is simply produced by its union with *vibhāva*.

(b) *Anumitivāda:* Śaṅkuka, who is said to have appeared immediately after Bhaṭṭa Lollaṭa, states that *rasa* is an imitation of the mental conditions of a character to be played. His definition is as follows:

> An actor first acquires *vibhāva* as a cause, and then *anubhāva* as a result, as well as *vyabhicāribhāva*, which accompanies it. Though it is an imitation, an audience does not realize that. (The audience) perceives *sthāyin* as existing in an actor by the *vibhāva* that is (*sthāyin's*) liṅga (just as the existence of a fire is inferred by observing a trail of smoke). Since it is an imitation of *sthāyin*, which essentially exists in a character such as rāma (the *sthāyin*) is called *rasa* in a different manner.[47]

Thus, Śaṅkuka understands the word *saṃyoga* as the relationship between that which makes awake (*gamaka*) and that which is made awake (*gamya*), which exists between three qualities such as *vibhāva* and *sthāyin*.[48] Additionally, he states that *sthāyin* exists in *anukārya*, and *vibhāva*, etc., in *anukartṛ*, and that *sthāyin* is tasted as *rasa* by inference. He emphasizes, of course, that this is not the object of the general inference, although it is inferred.[49]

(c) *Bhuktivāda:* Bhaṭṭa Nāyaka, who belonged to the earlier tenth century, insists that *rasa* is neither perceived, nor arises, nor is something resident that is expected to manifest itself[50] as Abhinavagupta's opinion to be referred later. He defines *rasa* as

> [A word that] has potential except for its indicative function, for realizing [*sthāyin* which is different from our daily feelings] with the nature of generalization *vibhāva* etc. (*sādhāraṇīkarana*), and *sthāyin* is realized as *rasa* by them. [An audience] purely enjoys it as a joy similar to what is brought when *Brahman* is attained.[51]

His opinion is summarized as follows: Poetical compositions (*kāvya*) or dramas (*nāṭaka*) are understood through the *abhidhā* function of words, and the *vibhāva* or *sthāyin* described in them are simultaneously generalized through another function called the *bhāvaka* of those words. The (*ālambana*) *vibhāva* of Rāma or Sītā, who are described or played, transcends being Rāma (*rāmatva*) or being Sītā (*sītātva*) and becomes a generalized couple (*naranārī*) by the *bhāvaka* function; evening (*sandhyā*) or dawn (*uṣā*) is also generalized. Nevertheless, the *sthāyin* like the love between Rāma and Sītā, is transformed into the universal *rasa* of love. The audience purely enjoys this universal love temporally and apart from daily feelings.

One of two notable points in this definition by Bhaṭṭa Nāyaka is that the enjoyment of *rasa* is similar to that of *brahman*, although it is not identical.[52] The second point is the introduction of the word 'generalization', which had been playing an important role in the history of Indian rhetoric since then. Bhaṭṭa Nāyaka, however, does not investigate it from the viewpoint of the pure function of words. He merely states that an audience enjoys the *rasa* that is generalized by words. Abhinavagupta criticizes this.

(d) *Abhivyaktavāda:* The three above-mentioned ideas are contained in *Abhinavabhāratī*, the commentary to the *NS* by Abhinavagupta (AG), who appeared in the latter half of the tenth century. After AG introduces these three prior opinions on *rasa*, he develops his own theory. First he cites Bharata's passage, and states that the purpose of *kāvya* is *rasa*;[53] then, he investigates *rasa*.

A person with a literary sensibility grasps the literal meaning of *kāvya*, and simultaneously generalizes it in his mind. Regarding the feeling of fear (*bhaya*), AG states that 'What is grasped with a [different] perception [from the daily one] without obstacles [like discomposure, the specific place or time] and is felt as if it directly entered one's mind and seems to be displayed in front of one's eyes, is the *rasa* of fears [in *kāvya*].'[54] This kind of fear generalized by perception does not exist in a specific person such as *nāyaka*. Just as we infer the existence of not a specific fire but a general one, when we see smoke, and not a specific smoke, an audience feels a generalized fear from 'trembling'. This fear accords with the *sthāyin* that exists in one's mind since the ancient times in the form of *vāsanā* (unconscious impression) and invokes *rasa*.[55] In other words, the love whose essence is relished, comes to appear in this pure perception.[56]

Based on the statement above, AG states that 'The *bhāva*, whose essence is relished, will grow into *rasa* [when] it is perceived with the perception of having no obstacles'. Therefore, *rasa* perceived in this way exists only when tasted, and it is different from the *sthāyin* that exists eternally.[57] Accordingly, AG's interpretation of *rasaniṣpatti* is 'what is the origination of flavour (*rasanā*) related to *rasa*, no less'.[58] He concludes that 'the combination of *vibhāva*, etc., gives birth to a flavour, and that *rasa* is the extraordinary truth related to this kind of flavour'.[59] Though he bases his theory on the concept of the generalization of Bhaṭṭa Nāyaka who seems to be influenced by Mīmāṃsaka, with this conclusion, AG declares that *rasa* is not what is not enjoyed by a person who perceives something that is externally expressed, but what is perceived and tasted when *sthāyin*, which internally exists as *vāsanā* is perceived as something universal and is manifested.

This theory of *rasa* established by AG was passed down to the next generation as a component of the mainstream of Indian rhetoric; from then on, the target of discussions about the *rasa* was the number of *rasa*s. Bharata enumerated eight *rasa*s,[60] while rhetoricians after him repeatedly engaged in discussions on whether *śānta* was the ninth *rasa*. Since V. Raghavan discussed the number of *rasa* in detail in 'The Number of *rasa*s', I avoid a detailed description. However, the investigation of whether the *śānta* is *rasa* is mainly related to the issue of *svarūpayogyatā*. Whether a certain *bhāva* is counted as *rasa* must be decided on the following three points; whether it is an independent *bhāva* (*svarūpayogyatā*), whether it has *vibhāva*, and whether it has the subject (*puruṣa-yogyatā*). When AG stated that *sneha*, *laulya* and *bhakti* were included among *rati* or *utsāha*,[61] or when *bhakti* was said to be only *vyabhicāribhāva* in *Kāvyaprakāśa*,[62] the nature of *svarūpayogyatā* as *rasa* was brought into question. In order to acknowledge bhakti as *rasa*, G.Vai. solved this question in its original manner.

BHAKTIRASA

After RG discussed *bhakti* in the first chapter (Pūrvavibhāga) of the *BRAS*, he attempted to prove that the *bhakti* is *rasa* in the second chapter (Dakṣiṇavibhāga). His definition of *bhaktirasa* is as follows: 'By listening [to stories about Kṛṣṇa], *kṛṣṇarati* which is the *sthāyībhāva* that becomes something to be tasted with *vibhāva*, *anubhāva*, *sāttvika* and *vyabhicāribhāva* in the mind of a believer, it is called *bhaktirasa*'.

vibhāvair anubhāvaiś ca sāttvikair vyabhicāribhiḥ /
svādyatvaṃ hṛdi bhaktānām ānītā śravaṇādibhiḥ // *BRAS* 2.1.5

The person who is qualified for tasting this *bhaktirasa* is the one who possesses the *vāsanā* of the correct bhakti in one's mind (2.1.6). When we read these two verses, RG's definition of *rasa* seems to be based on AG's *rasa* theory that I discussed above. However, I do not believe that the *bhakta* and *adhikārin* described here are equal to the *sāmājika* in AG's theory. In other words, we should not infer that the *bhakta* is not the same as the *adhikārin*, and that the word *kṛṣṇarati* simply means the love that is directed towards Kṛṣṇa.

RG refers to *vibhāva* first as 'the cause of love (*rati*) with two varieties—*ālambana* and *uddīpana*' (2.1.14),[63] and states that 'Kṛṣṇa and Kṛṣṇa's *bhakta* are *ālambana*, and the former is the target of love, while the latter is their (*bhāva*'s) foundation' (2.1.15). *Kṛṣṇabhakta*s are then subdivided as follows. *Sādhaka*, who must surmount some obstacle to change over to the *rasa* condition: *sādhanasiddha*, who attains the *rasa* condition with effort: *kṛpāsiddha*, who attains the *rasa* condition as a result of divine mercy (the latter two are called *samprāptasiddha*) and *nityasiddha* (*gopa-gopī*, etc.) who is always under the *rasa* condition.

The following four points are clarified when I summarize the relationship between Kṛṣṇa and *kṛṣṇabhakta* against the background of the bhakti that is analysed in the first section of this paper from the viewpoint of the *acintyabhedābheda* of G.Vai.

(1) *Svarūpaśakti* must be included within Kṛṣṇa, who is always satisfied with himself as the ultimate truth. (Abheda)
(2) Kṛṣṇa tries to obtain much more satisfaction and differentiate *hlādīniśakti* from among the *svarūpaśakti* by his *acintyaśakti* (inscrutable power). He then enjoys sports with the *gopa-gopī*, etc., by building up the relationship of the *rasa* called bhakti between them and himself. They are called *nityasiddha* at this stage. (*Bheda* 1)
(3) Although the highest truth of G.Vai. is completely described in the second stage, the school explains the *paramātman* aspect of Kṛṣṇa in order to elucidate the relationship between God and the phenomenal world, and also demonstrates the *brahman*

aspect of Kṛṣṇa to harmonize their theory with those of the traditional systems of Indian philosophy at the time. On that basis, Kṛṣṇa is supremely placed; he is the target who everybody aims to satisfy. *Sādhaka*, *sādhanasiddha* and *kṛpāsiddha* are believers in this stage. In addition, *śikṣāguru*, *dīkṣāguru* and the sages in ancient times are included here. (*Bheda* 2)

(4) Though the general *jīva* is originally the *aṃśa* of Kṛṣṇa and is endowed with bhakti, it is hidden as *vāsanā* by Kṛṣṇa's *māyāśakti*. The *bhakta* in this stage is *adhikārin*. (*Bheda* 3)

The relationship of *acintyabhedābheda* with (1), (2), (3) and (4) is acknowledged here.

We can understand the 2.1.5 of *BRAS* as the stage of transition from (1) to (2), and the word *kṛṣṇarati* as having a bilateral character, that is, it is not only the *rati* which exists in Kṛṣṇa (*kṛṣṇasya rati*), but the *rati* which is aimed at Kṛṣṇa (*kṛṣṇaviṣayā rati*). Thus, 2-1-5 indicates the second stage with the meaning that Kṛṣṇa is the target of love (*ratyader viṣayatvena*).

G.Vai. reveals this philosophy by skillfully using the traditional *rasa* theory and aim to establish their superiority of their idea.

Next, RG discusses *uddīpanavibhāva*. With the definition '[They are] Kṛṣṇa's attributes (*guṇa*) which stimulate *bhāva*, his achievements (*ceṣṭā*), ornaments (*prasādhana*), etc.', he conducts a detailed investigation on it by citing numerous examples. After ending discussions of this *vibhāva*, he proceeds to *anubhāva*.

Anubhāva is defined as follows: 'It is like an external change by which one can realize *bhāva* in one's mind, and it is also called *udbhāsvara*.'

anubhāvās tu cittasthabhāvānām avabodhakāḥ /
te bahirkriyāprāyāḥ proktā udbhāsvarākhyayā // 2.2.1

After RG enumerates the thirteen *anubhāva*, beginning with a dance (*nṛtya*), and discusses each of them in detail,[64] he explains *sāttvika*, which is defined by Bharata as 'the *sattva* formed in one's mind—it is explained by the fact that tears or horripilation which come from *sattva* must be indicated'.[65] His explanation is, however, based on his own viewpoint. He states that '*sattva* is the mind which is directly or indirectly[66] captured by the *bhāva* related to Kṛṣṇa, and *sāttvika* is produced from that mind.'

kṛṣṇasambandhibhiḥ sākṣāt kiñcid vā vyavadhānatah /
bhāvaiś cittam ihākrāntam sattvamity ucyate budhaih //
sattvād asmāt samutpannā ye ye bhāvas te tu sāttvikāḥ / 2.3.1–2a

Keeping in mind its differences from *anubhāva*, RG explains the process in which *sāttvika* is produced. According to his explanation, when one's mind (*citta*) attains the state of *sattva*, one entrusts himself to the vital air (*prāṇa*) in the body. Then, the *prāṇa* changes and shakes one's body. As a result, the state of *sāttvika* can be observed in the body (2.3.15).[67] This means that *anubhāva* indicates *bhāva* directly by external movements, while *sāttvika* indicates it indirectly. RG does not forget, however, that there is another explanation by which *sāttvika* is included in *anubhāva* or *vyabhicāribhāva*.

Bharata explains *vyabhicāribhāva* by stating that 'it works on every *rasa* from various directions' and by analysing the word as *vi* = *vividha*, *abhi* = *ābhimukhya*, and *cara* = *gatyartha*.[68] On the other hand, RG understands the word as *vi* = *viśeṣana* and *abhi* = *ābhimukhya*, and states that '*vyabhicāribhāva* is what is communicated by words, gestures and *sattva*, etc. by working on *sthāyin* from a special direction[69] [which corresponds to each sthāyin]' (2.4.1–2a).

As Bharata does not theoretically clarify the relationship between *rasa* and *sthāyin* in the manner in which AG does,[70] there is hardly any difference in both definitions. In this respect, RG follows the traditional *rasa* theory as stated above and moves on to the investigation of each of the thirty-three *vyabhicāri*. He argues there that these thirty-three *vyabhicāri* and eight *sthāyin* are main *bhāva*, which can be divided into two categories: native ones (*svābhāvika*) and acquired. Though the *rati* stated below is the former and only one, it will appear in a different way due to the variety of bhakti (2.4.250–2, 254). RG ends this section of the *vyabhicāribhāva* with an investigation of the different *bhakta*, which is stated once in the section of *vibhāva*, from the viewpoint of the condition of *bhakta*.

RG, who has indicated the *puruṣayogyatā* of *bhaktirasa* in the definition of *bhakta* and *parikarayogyatā* in the definition of *vibhāva*, states that the *bhaktirasa* supported by G.Vai. is the best among all the *rasa* by referring to *svarūpayogyatā* in the next section of *sthāyin*.

The *sthāyin* is defined as follows:

Being accompanied by harmonious feelings [such as *hāsa*], inharmonious feelings [such as *krodha*] and all other *bhāva*, the one who dominates like a good king is called *sthāyin*, and the *rati* aiming at Kṛṣṇa stated previously is *sthāyin* here in this *bhaktirasaśāstra*.

aviruddhān viruddhāṃś ca bhāvān yo vaśatām nayan /
surājeva virājeta sa sthāyī bhāva ucyate //
sthāyī bhāvo 'tra sa proktaḥ srīkṛṣṇaviṣayā ratiḥ / 2.5.1–2a

This *sthāyin* is further divided into *mukhya* and *gauṇa*; the former is discussed first. There are five varieties of *mukhya*; *śuddha*, *prīti*, *sakhya*, *vātsalya* and *priyatā*. These are only different names by which the same *rati* possesses as a function of itself (2.5.7). In other words, which *rasa* is tasted depends on the differences of *bhakta*'s *vāsanā*.

Gauṇa is defined as 'The special *bhāva*, which arises when [*ālambana*] *vibhāva* dominates, is felt [by bhakta] through the contraction of *rati* itself, and it becomes *gauṇarati* (2.5.39)'. In reference to the *hāsa*, as Kṛṣṇa's words, costume, etc., differ from ordinary ones, the essential *rati* towards Kṛṣṇa is weakened; consequently, the aspect of a laugh is emphasized as *hāsa* (2.5.43, 53). Accordingly, *gauṇa* does not always become *sthāyin* and *rasa*. In other words, this occurs only when it is related to the existence of the *rati* that is *mukhyasthāyin*. This is why RG places *rati* and the seven *sthāyin*—except *nirveda*, which is acknowledged by traditional rhetoricians—under this *gauṇasthāyin*.

RG counts up as many as forty-nine *bhāva*s that do not conflict with the traditional one. In other words, he classifies one *rati* as *mukhyasthāyin*, seven like *hāsa* as *gauṇasthāyin*, as well as thirty-three *vyabhicāribhāva* and eight *sāttvika* (73–4). Thereafter, RG arranges *vibhāva*, etc., once again based on the traditional definition (86–9); however, he emphasizes the excellence of G.Vai's theory by placing traditional theories under it without completely denying them, as is seen in the case of *acintyabhedābheda*.

eteṣām tu tathābhāve bhagavatkāvyanāṭayoh /
sevām āhuḥ param hetuṃ kecit tatpakṣarāgiṇah // 90 //
kim tu tatra sudustarkamādhuryyādbhutasaṃpadaḥ /
rater asyāḥ prabhāvo 'yam bhavet kāraṇam uttamam // 91 //

As is clearly understood from two verses above, the forty-nine *bhāva* stated previously can become *vibhāva*, etc., only by means of the effective power of [Kṛṣṇa] *rati* itself, and not when we enjoy *kāvya* or *nāṭaka*. This is because the *bhāva* known as *rati* is a kind of amorous sport played by *mahāśakti* [known as *hlādinī*] which Kṛṣṇa possesses as one of his countless powers. Then, RG concludes that its essence is *acintya* (inscrutable) and impossible to be theoretically proved.

mahāśaktivilāsātmā bhāvo 'cintyasvarūpabhāk /
ratyākhyā ity ayaṃ yukto na hi tarkeṇa vādhitum // 92 //

This kind of relationship between *rati* and *vibhāva*, etc., is explained in the verse numbers 94, 95, 98 and 99. The relationship can simply be illustrated as follows:

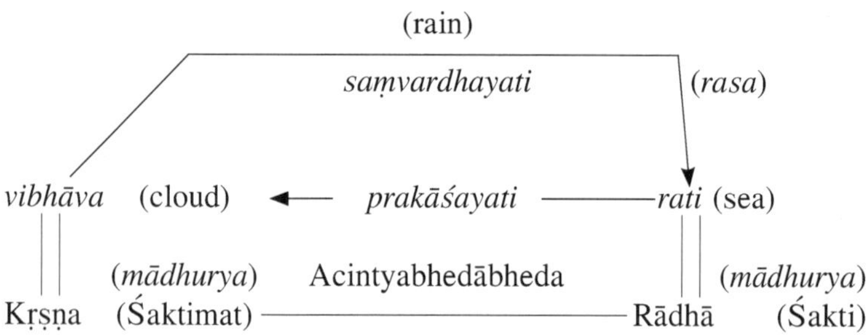

Even though RG does not completely negate *kāvya* or *nāṭya*, he states, instead, that the forty-nine *bhāva* may lead to *vibhāva*, etc., when a sprout of Rati begins to grow in Kṛṣṇa's *bhakta*, because the sprout is the very cause for that. A wise *bhakta*, however, can derive much greater enjoyment by listening to only a little about Kṛṣṇa, thus the effective force of the Rati is a much greater cause than *kāvya* or *nāṭya* (96–7). Then RG states (on grounds of the conventional idea of generalization) that 'The stable fixity of *rasa* is difficult to understand due to its supernatural essence (*alaukika*), and every *bhāva* shines [between the *bhāva* of the present and the past *bhakta*] and is generalized as one on the basis of the stable fixity of *rasa*.'

alaukikyā prakṛtyeyaṃ sudurūhā rasasthitiḥ /
yatra sādhāraṇataya bhāvāḥ sphuranty amī // 101 //

Moreover RG agrees with the views of other rhetoricians regarding the word *alaukika*. In order to be sure, he proceeds to explain the word from G.Vai.'s viewpoint. An important issue regarding the location of *rasa* now arises. Where is *rasa* placed among *anukārya*, *anukartṛ* and *sāmājika*? Traditional rhetoricians believe that *rasa* exists neither in *anukārya* nor in *anukartṛ* because the former feels love for oneself, and *anukārya* is only an imitator. All things considered, the love is *laukika* as it is practical; therefore, *rasa* does not exist in them. On the other hand, in the case of *sāmājika*, people enjoy generalized love itself—the love is *alaukika* because it is impractical. Therefore *rasa* exists in *sāmājika*.

RG agrees with this view and begins to introduce his opinion (107). In the case of *kṛṣṇarati*, the word *alaukika* is used because the Rati is not concerned with our phenomenal world, but with the divine world. As a result, this very *kṛṣṇarati* is *alaukika*, and it surpasses everything in every possible manner. This *rati* becomes special *rasa* in [the minds of] the *bhakta* [who are Kṛṣṇa's favourites such as Rādhā as *anukārya*] when the *rasa* is related to Kṛṣṇa. This means that the *rasa* also exists in *anukārya*.

alaukikī tv iyaṃ kṛṣṇaratiḥ sarvādbhutādbhutā /
yoge rasaviśeṣatvaṃ gacchanty eva haripriye // 108 //

The *rati* established in this manner becomes eight kinds of *bhaktirasa*, which correspond to the different types of *bhakta* (113–18).

Previously, while discussing *vibhāva*, I stated that there were two possibilities in understanding the compound *kṛṣṇarati* used in *BRAS*: *kṛṣṇasya rati* and *kṛṣṇavicayā rati*. I will classify the compound from a different angle, the verses of Dakṣiṇavibhāga in which Kṛṣṇa, *rati* and related words are used.

A: *keśavarater* (1.4), *kṛṣṇaratiḥ* (1.5), [*alaukikī*] *kṛṣṇaratiḥ* (5.108), *vallabhādhiśanālambanā ratiḥ* (5.110), *kṛṣṇaratyāḥ* (5.128), *kṛṣṇabhaktirasaḥ* (5.130), *bhagavadrasaḥ* (5.131)

B: *ratyader viṣayatvene* (1.16), *utpannaratyāḥ* (1.276), *kṛṣṇe premāṇāṃ paramaṃ gatāḥ* (1.290), *kṛṣṇasambandhibhiḥ—bhāvaiś* (3.1), *śrīkṛṣṇaviṣayā ratiḥ* (5.2), *kṛṣṇe—ratir* (5.9), *kṛṣṇe jātā śātiratir* (5.18), *tatrāsaktikṛd* (5.28), *rater kāraṃbhūtā*—(5.85)

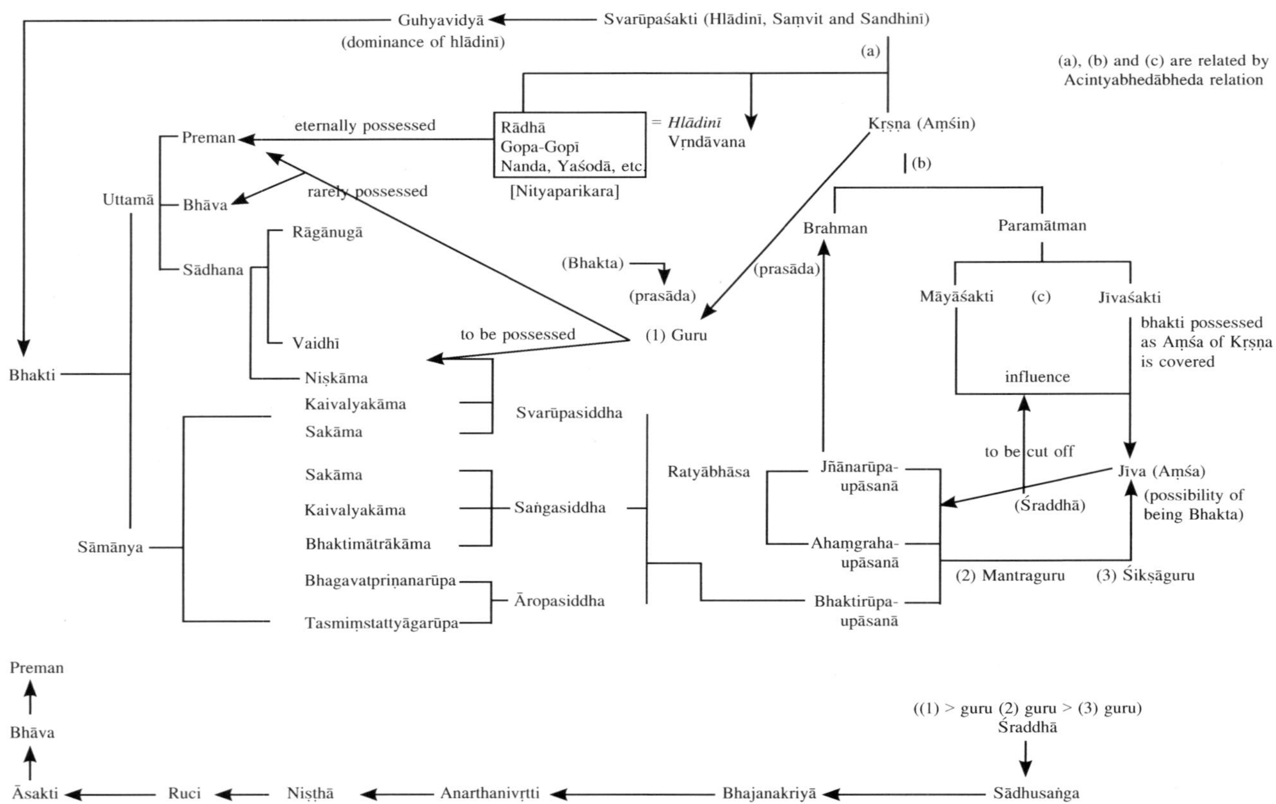

Bhaktirasa established by the Gauḍīya Vaiṣṇava School

The words classified in the A group are used in the situations where *rasa* and *rati* are discussed from the standpoint of G.Vai.'s. The words can be understood in both ways stated above, except (5.110).

The words classified in the B group are used in the situations where *rati* is discussed in contrast with the views of traditional rhetoricians. The interpretation of these words is that *kṛṣṇarati* is *kṛṣṇaviṣayā rati*.

Considering this fact, I believe that G.Vai. insists on the excellence of *bhaktirasa* with its own religious meaning, although it attempts to avoid confrontations with the traditional rhetorical schools. Accordingly, RG seems to create the impression that the *kṛṣṇarati* of 5–1 means *kṛṣṇaviṣayā rati* by using the word *purokta* in 1-2.

CONCLUSION

G.Vai. regards the Kṛṣṇa-Radhā relationship as *acintyabhedābheda*, and places the idea at the core of the school's philosophy. While they try to avoid confrontations with other philosophical sects, they regard their own philosophy as the highest. Bhakti towards Kṛṣṇa is thus placed above all others. However, they do not negate bhakti towards other deities. Neither does this school deny the traditional *rasa* theory when it discusses bhakti as *rasa*. Rather, the school subordinates it to G.Vai.'s theory in order to emphasize the excellence of *bhaktirasa* in the religious meaning of the school. They do not actively demonstrate this in order to avoid confrontations with the traditional *rasa* theory that the interpretation of the word *kṛṣṇarati* is clearly *kṛṣṇaviṣayā rati*.[71]

In contrast, the fact that RG does not present as many quotations in *sthāyīlaharī* as in the *laharī* of *BRAS* indicates that he emphasizes *sthāyin*, which is important in the discussion of *rasa* in order to show the *svarūpayogyatā* of *baktirasa* and to justify the school's theory.

In addition, the process of bhakti from *sādhanā* to *preman* via *bhāva* might be deliberated by bearing in mind the fact that *rasa* proceeds from *vibhāva*, etc., to *rasa* via *rati*.

ABBREVIATIONS

AbhiBh : The *Abhinavabhāratī* of Abhinavagupta → *Nāṭyaśāstra* (*NS*).
AE : *The Aesthetic Experience According to Abhinavagupta*, R. Gnoli, Varanasi: Chowkhamba Sanskrit Series Office, 1968.
BhS : *Bhaktisandarbha* ed. Radharanaman Gosvami, Calcutta, 1962.
BhaS : *Bhagavadsandarbha*, Jadavpur University Sanskrit Series, Calcutta: Jadavpur University, 1972.
BRAS : *Bhaktirasāmṛtashindhu*, ed. Haridas Das, Calcutta, 1960.
CCA : *Caitanyacaritāmṛta*, ed. R. Nath, Calcutta, 1963.
CCU : *Śrī Caitanyacariter Upādān*, V. Majumdar, Calcutta, 1959.
CTP : *Śrī Caitanya O Tāṃhār Pārṣadgaṇ*, G. Raychaudhuri, Calcutta, 1957.
NS : *Nāṭyaśāstra* with *AbhiBh*, Gaekward's Oriental Series 36, 2nd edn., Baroda: Oriental Institute, 1956.
PS : *Paramātmasandarbha*, Jadavpur University Sanskrit Series, Calcutta: Jadavpur University, 1972.
TS : *Tattvasandarbha*, Jadavpur University Sanskrit Series, Calcutta: Jadavpur University, 1967.
UN : *Ujjvalanīlamaṇi*, ed. Durgaprasad, Kavyamala Series 95, Bombay, 1932.
VChG : *Vṛndavaner Chay Gosvāmin*, N. Jana, Calcutta, 1970.
VFM : *The Early History of the Vaiṣṇava Faith and Movement in Bengal From Sanskrit and Bengal Sources*, Sushil Kumar De, Calcutta: Firma KLM Private Limited, 1961.

NOTES

1. The following papers examine the two religious terms, bhakti and *śraddhā*: 'Note on Two Sanskrit Religious Terms, *Bhakti* and *Śraddhā*', M. Hara, *IIJ*, vol. VII, 1964, no. 2/3 pp. 124–45; M. Dasgupta, 'Śraddhā and Bhakti in Vedic Literature', *IHQ*, vol VI.
2. *yasya deve parā bhaktir yathā deve tathā gurau /*
   tasyaite kathitā hy arthāḥ prakāśante mahātmanaḥ // (*Śvetāśvatra Up.* 6.23).
   In addition, C. Mukherjee points out *śloka* 2 of the *Kaivalya Up.*
3. S.K. De, *Aspects of Sanskrt Literature* pp. 91–100.
4. *sā paramānuraktir īśvare //* (1.1.2).
5. *tadarpitākhilācāratā* /(19).
6. *sā tv asmin paramapremarūpā* /(2).
7. Rādhā is not praised as the best woman yet in *BhP*.
8. JG cites 2.2.15 and 1.2.22 of *BhP*,
   ityādinā ca karmeṇa sadyomukti- kramamuktyupāyau jñānayogau uktvā tato

'pi śreṣṭhatvam bhaktiyogahetubhagavadaripitakarmaṇa evoktvā sakṣādbhaktiyogasya kaimutyam evānītam / (*BhS* p. 38)

9. *brahamānand bhaved eṣa cet parārddhaguṇīkṛtah naiti bhaktisukhāmbhodheḥ paramāṇutulām api* // (*BRAS* 1.1.21)
   Cf. (*ray kahe*) *jñān śūnya bhaktimātra sār* // (*CCA* 2.8.55b)
10. *kṛtvā harim premabhājam priyavargasamanvitam / bhaktir vaśī karotīti* (*BRAS* 1.1.22)
11. *kṛṣṇaviṣayakapremā param puruṣārtha /*
    yārāge tṛṇatulya cāri puruṣārtha //
    pañcam puruṣārtha premānandāmṛtasindhu /
    brahmānandādi ānanda yār nai ekbindu // (*CCA* 1.7.81–2)
12. *bhaktir bhagavati bhakteṣu ca nikṣiptanijo ubayakoṭiḥ sarvadā tiṣṭhati* / (*PS*, p. 68)
13. *tasya paramānandaikarūpasya svaparānandinī svarūpaśaktir yā hlādinī nāmnī vartate, prakāśavastunaḥ svaparaprakāśanaśaktivat paramavṛttirūpaivaiṣā / tāñ ca bhagavān svavṛnde nikṣiptam eva nityaṃ vartate* / (*BhS*, p. 226)
14. *yā kṛpā tasya satsu vartate sā satsaṅgavāhanaiva vā satkṛpāvāhanaiva satī jīvāntare saṃkramate na svatantrā* / (ibid., p. 301)
15. *atra jñānamārge brahmānubhavino mahānto bhaktimārge labdhabhavavatpremāṇo mahānto iti lakṣaṇasāmānyam iti jñeyam* / (ibid., p. 308)
16. *tathābhajanamārgaviśeṣe ca rucir jāyate* / — *tato bhagavataḥ sarvasminn evāvirbhāve tathāvidho 'sau sadā sarvadā virajāte ity evaṃ rūpā śraddhā āyate* / (ibid., p. 334)
17. *teṣv ekato 'nekato vā śrīgurutvenāśritāc chravaṇaṃ kriyate* / (ibid., p. 334)
18. *śrīmantragurus tv eka eva* / (ibid., p. 334)
    svagurau bhagavaddṛstih kartavyaḥ / (ibid., p. 336)
    In addition the difference between *mantraguru* and *śikṣāguru* is described in detail between pp. 351 and 356 of the *BhS*.
19. The teachings imparted from *ruci* to *mantraguru* are called *pūrvāṅga-upāsanā*.
    rucyādinā gurvāśrayānte upāsanāpūrvāṅgarūpaḥ / (ibid., p. 358)
20. *atra sāṃmukhyaṃ dvividhaṃ nirviśeṣamayaṃ saviśeṣamayañ ca / atra pūrvaṃ jñānam / uttaran tu dvividham——ahaṃgrahopāsanārūpaṃ bhaktirūpañ ca* / (ibid., p. 358)
21. *ahaṃgrahopāsanaṃ tacchaktiviśiṣta īśvara evāham iti cintanam* / (ibid., p. 361)
22. *atha bhaktiḥ / tasyās taṭasthalakṣaṇaṃ svarūpalakṣaṇañ ca yathā garuḍapurāṇe*—— / *'yayā sarvam avāpyate' iti taṭasthalakṣaṇam* / —— / *sevāśabdena sarūpalakṣaṣam* / (ibid., pp. 361–2)
23. *sā ca sevā kāyika-vācika-mānasātmikā trividhaivānugatir ucyate* / (ibid., p. 363)

24. *aropasiddhā svato bhaktitvābhāve 'pi bhagavadarpinādinā bhaktitvam prāptā karmādirūpā / saṃgasiddhā svato bhaktitvābhave 'pi tatparikaratayā saṃsthāpanena —— labdhatadantaḥpātā jñānakarmatadaṅgarūpā / svarūpasiddhā cājñānadināpi tatprādurbhāve bhaktitvāvyabhicārinī sākṣāt tadanugatyātmā tadīyaśravaṇakīrtānadirūpā /* (ibid., p. 364)
25. JG annotates on this word as follows:
ānukūlyañ cāsminn uddeśāya śrīkṛṣṇāya rocamānā pravṛttiḥ /
prātikūlyan tu tadviparītam jñeyam / (JG's commentary on the *BRAS*)
26. Because bhakti exists eternally as Kṛṣṇa's *Śakti*, what did not exist before will not appear when it is said to be realized (*sādhya*). This means that the bhakti that eternally exists will become visible from an invisible state.
27. *vaidhī rāgānugā ceti sā dvidhā sādhanābhidhā / (BRAS* 1.2.5)
tad evam bahudhā sādhitaiṣakiñcanātyantikīty ādisañjnā bhaktir dvidhā vaidhī rāgānugā ca iti / (BhS, p. 396)
28. *sa ca vidhir dvidhaḥ tatra prathamaḥ pravṛttihetuḥ, tadanukramakartavyā kartayānām jñānahetuś ca dvitīyah /* (ibid., p. 396)
29. Cf. *BhS*, pp. 397–538.
30. *trayam pradhānam evoktaṃ gurupādāśrayādikam // (BRAS* 1.2.83b)
Cf. the *CCA* 2.22.61–84.
31. After this definition, the *CCA* explains the following:
rāgātmikābhakti mukhyā vrajavāsijane /
tār anugata bhaktir rāgānugā nāme // (2.22.85)
32. *Rāga* is explained by JG and *CCA* as follows:
viṣayinaḥ svābhāviko viṣayasaṃsargecchātiśayaḥ premā rāgaḥ / (BhS, p. 338).
iṣṭe gāḍhtṛṣṇā rāg ei svarūplakṣaṇ /
iṣṭe āviṣṭatā ei taṭasthalakṣaṇ // (CCA 2.22.86).
33. *tad evam tattadabhimāṇalakṣanabhāvaviśeṣeṇa svābhāvikarāgasya vaiśiṣṭye sati tattadrāgaprayuktā śravaṇakīrtanasmaraṇapādasevanavand anātmanivedanaprāyā bhaktis teṣāṃ rāgātmikā bhaktir ucyate / tasyāś ca sādhyāyāṃ rāgalakṣanānāṃ bhaktigaṅgāyāṃ taraṅgarūpatvāt sādhyatvam eveti natu sādhanaprakāraṇe' smin praveśaḥ / (BhS*, p. 540)
34. JG's commentary on this is:
atra śuddhasattvaṃ nāma bhagavataḥ svaprakāśikā svarūpaśakteḥ saṃvidākhyā vṛttiḥ, natu māyāvṛttiviśeṣaḥ / —— / śuddhasattvaviśeṣatvaṃ nāma cātra yā svarūpaśaktivṛttyantaralakṣaṇā / —— / tayoḥ (saṃvit and hlādinī) samavetayoḥ sāṛatvam / (JG's commentary on the *BRAS*).
35. *rucibhiḥ prāptyabhilāṣasvakartṛkānukūlyābhilāṣasauhārdābhilāṣaiś cittārdratākṛd iti /* (ibid.)
36. *premṇaḥ prathamacchavirūpaḥ /* ibid.
37. Though the G.Vai split into several groups such as the Navadvīpa sect, which regarded Caitanya as Kṛṣṇa immediately after his death or even while he was alive, and the Vṛndāvana sect which regarded Caitanya as

bhakta equal to *nityaparikara*, etc., I do not deal with these details here.

38. Among them, the famous Vedāntin is Madhusūdana Sarasvatī, the author of *Bhaktirasāyana*. Cf. *Bhaktirasāyana*, Bhūmikā, p. 13.
39. *kevalo mādhuryamātrajñānayukta ity arthaḥ* / (JG's commentary on the *BRAS*).
40. *māhātmyajñānayuktaś ca kevalaś ceti sa dvidhā* / (*BRAS* 1.4.11)
harer atiprasādo' yam saṅgadānādir ātmanah // (ibid. 1.4.9)
mahimajñānayuktaḥ syād vidhimārgānusāriṇām /
rāgānugāśritānāṃ tu prāyaśaḥ kevalo bhavet // (ibid. 1.4.14).
41. *syād dṛḍheyam ratiḥ premā prodyan snehaḥ kramād ayam* /
syān mānaḥ praṇayo rāgo 'nurāgo bhāva ity api // 53 (*UN*, p. 416).
42. *vibhāvānubhāvavyabhicārisamyogād rasaniṣpattiḥ* / (*NS*, p. 272)
Though I give explanatory translations for *vibhāva*, etc., here, I cannot find English or Japanese words that suitably express the nuance of each Sanskrit term. For example, the word *bhāva* has some nuances such as state or condition, or psychological state or feeling. S.K. De gives the following translations, although he admits that each word is difficult to translate: *rasa* = sentiment, *bhāva* = (inward) Emotion, *vibhāva* = exitant, *anubhāva* = ensuant, *sāttvika* = external sign of internal emotion, *vyabhicāribhava* = auxiliary feelings, and *sthāyībhāva* = dominant feelings.
43. *rasa iti kaḥ padārthaḥ / ucyate āsvādyatvāt / katham āsvādyate rasaḥ / —— / nānābhāvābhinaya-vyañjitān vāgaṅgasattvopetān sthāyibhāvān āsvādayanti sumanasaḥ prekṣakāḥ harṣādīṃś cādhi- gacchanti* / (*NS*, p. 288)
44. *vibhāvanubhāvavyabhicāribhāvaparivṛtaḥ sthāyī bhāvo rasanāma labhate* / (ibid., p. 349)
45. *vibhāvādibhiḥ saṃyogo 'rthāt sthāyinaḥ, tato rasaniṣpattiḥ / tatra vibhāvaś cittavṛtteḥ sthāyyātmikāyā utpattau kāraṇam* / (*AbhiBh*, *NS*, p. 272).
46. *tena sthāyy eva vibhāvānubhāvādibhir upacito rasaḥ* / —— / *sa cobhayor apy anukārye' nutartary api* —— / (ibid).
47. *(tasmād) dhedubhir vibhāvākhyaiḥ kāryaiś cānubhāvātmabhiḥ sahācārirūpaiś ca vyabihicāribhiḥ prayatnārjitatayā kṛtrimair api tathānabhimānair anukartṛsthatvena liṅgabalatah pratīyamānaḥ sthāyī bhāva mukhyarāmādigata sthāyyanukaraṇarūpaḥ anukaraṇarūpatvād eva ca nāmāntareṇa vyapadiṣṭo rasaḥ* / (ibid., p. 275)
48. —— *samyogāt gamyagamakarūpāt* —— (*KPr*, ch. 4, p. 55)
49. *anumīyamāno 'pi vastusaundaryabalād rasanīyatvenānyānumīyamānavila kṣaṇaḥ* / (ibid).
50. *bhaṭṭanāyakas tv āha / raso na pratīyate, notpadyate, nābhivyajyate* / (*AbhiBh*, *NS*, p. 276)
51. —— *vibhāvādisādhāranīkaraṇātmanābhidhāto dvitīyenāṃśena bhāvakatvavyāpāreṇa bhāvyamāno raso'——parabrahmāsvādasavidhena bhogena paraṃ bhujyata iti* / (ibid.)
52. cf. *AE* Introduction, p. XXV, translation, p. 48, pp. 82–4.

53. *'kāvyārthām bhāvayantīti bhāvaḥ' tat kāvyārtho rasaḥ* / (*AbhiBh*, *NS*, p. 27)
54. *nirvighnapratītigrāhyaṃ sākṣad iva hṛdaye niviśamānaṃ cakṣor iva viparivartamānam bhayānako rasaḥ* / (ibid., p. 279).
55. *na parimitam eva sādhāraṇyam api tu vitatam, vyāptigrāha iva dhūmāgnayor bhayakampayor eva vā* / —— *sarvasāmājikānām ekaghanataiva sutarāṃ rasapripoṣāya sarveṣām anādivāsanācitrīkṛtacetāsām vāsanāṣaṃvādāt* / (ibid., p. 279).
56. *sarvathā tāvad eṣāsti pratītir, āsvādātmā yasyām ratir eva bhāti* / (ibid.)
57. *carvyamāṇataikasāro na tu siddasvabhāvas tātkālika eva na tu carva. nātiriktakālāvalambī sthāyivilakṣaṇa eva rasaḥ* / (ibid., p. 284)
   This AG's opinion is summarized in *KPr* as follows:
   kāvye nāṭye ca tair eva kāraṇātvādiprihāreṇa vibhāvanādivyāpāravattvāt alaukikavibhāvadiśabdavyavahāryair —— *sādhāraṇyena pratītair abhivyaktaḥ samājikānāṃ vāsanātmatayā sthitaḥ sthāyī ratyādiko* —— *sādhāraṇyena svākāra ivābhinno 'pi gocarīkṛtaś carvyamāṇataikaprāṇo vibhāvādijīvitāvadhiḥ* —— *carvyamāṇaḥ* —— *brahmāsvādam ivānubhāvayam alaukikacamatkārakārī sṛṇgārādiko rasaḥ* / (*KPr*, Ch. IV, pp. 57–9)
58. *tarhi sūtre niṣpattir iti katham* / *neyaṃ rasasya, api tu tadviṣayarasanāyāḥ* / (*NS*, p. 285)
59. *tena vibhāvādisamyogād rasanā niṣpadyante tatas tathāvidharasanāgocaro lokottaro 'rtha rasa iti tātparyam sūtrasya* / (ibid., p. 285)
60. *śṛṇgārahāsyakaruṇā raudravīrabhayānakāḥ* /
   vibhatsādbhutasañjau cety aṣṭau nāṭye rasāḥ smṛtāḥ // (6.15).
61. *ārdratāsthāyikaḥ sneho rasa iti tv asat* / *sneho hy abhisaṅgaḥ* / *sa ca sarvo ratyutsāhādav eva paryavastyati* / —— *evaṃ bhaktav api vācyam iti* / (*AbhiBh*, pp. 341–2).
62. *ratir devādiviṣayā vyabhicārī tathāñjitaḥ* / *bhāvaḥ proktaḥ* // (4.35).
63. *vibhāvaḥ kāranam nimittam hetur iti paryayaḥ* / (*NS*, p. 346).
64. *anubhāvyate 'nena vāgaṅgasattvakṛto 'bhinaya iti* /
   atra ślokaḥ vāgaṅgābhinayeneha yasmād artho 'nubhāvyate /
   śakhāṅgopāṅgasaṃyuktas tv anubhāvas tataḥ smṛtaḥ // (*NS*, p. 347)
65. —— *sattvam nāma manaḥprabhavam* / —— *etad evāsya sattvaṃ yat* —— *'śruromañcau darśayitavyau iti kṛtvā sāttvikā bhāvā ity abhivyākhyātāḥ* / (*NS*, pp.374–5)
66. Visvanatha Cakravartin states that the word *sākṣāt* is used when one is captivated by the five major *rati*s, and that the word *vyavadhānata*s is used when one is captivated by the seven minor *rati*s.
   atra mukhyaratyā ākrāntatvaṃ sākṣāttvaṃ guṇaratyākrantatvaṃ vyavadhānatvam iti jñeyam / (VC's commentary on *BRAS*).
67. RG classifies the eight *sāttvika* into water that can be equated with tears, etc., because the anchorage of *prāṇa* which runs through one's body is

divided into five elements, i.e. earth, water, etc. However, I am not sure whether this idea is RG's original one.

68. *vi abhi iti etau upasargau / cara iti gatyarthe dhātuḥ/ vividham ābhimukhyena rasesu carantīti vyabhicāriṇaḥ* / (*NS*, p. 355).
69. VC says that the word *ābhimukhya* is *sāhāyya* (assistance). *viśeṣanā-bhimukhyena viśeśasāhāyyena* / (VC's commentary on *BRAS*)
70. The word *sthāyībhāva* is not included among the definitions of *rasa* in the *NS*; the word became one of the objects of argument among rhetoricians after Bharata.
71. This seems to be suggested by the words used in 94, 95, 98 and 99 which I include in neither group A nor group B.

13

Rāma in the Eyes of his Consort, Sītā: A Study of Tulsīdās's *Rāmcaritmānas*

TEIJI SAKATA

Of the two ancient epics, the *Rāmāyaṇa* describes the deeds of its protagonist, Rāma, while the theme of the *Mahābhārata* is the titanic battle waged between two families of the Bharata dynasty. Both epics have been sung, narrated, and enacted since ancient times, through the middle ages, and up to the present in India.

The *Rāmāyaṇa* has achieved a wider geographic reach than the *Mahābhārata*. Indian culture has spread to South-East Asian countries like Thailand and Indonesia. In these countries, along with the countries of the Indian subcontinent like Nepal, Bangladesh, Sri Lanka and Pakistan local versions of the deeds of Rāma have also been narrated and enacted for centuries.

Among the many versions of Rāma's stories inherited to the present, we will choose as our source material one important version highly esteemed in the Hindi-speaking belt of north India, the *Rāmcaritmānas*, of the sixteenth century written by Tulsīdās, a Vaiṣṇava priest.

Our interest here will be focused on Rāma's acts observed by his wife, Sītā. With Sītā, we will follow Rāma and observe his acts in the story.

The main text upon which this paper is based is *Rāmcaritmānas*, edited and annotated by Hanumānprasād Poddār and published by Gītā Press. The English translation that this paper refers to is the one by R.C. Prasad, with occasional changes made by the present writer. R.C. Prasad's translation is based on the original version edited by Hanumānprasād Poddār.

Prior to examining the expressions adopted by Sītā towards Rāma, a brief history of the many stories on Rāma will be described, and the titles of the seven sections of the *Rāmcaritmānas* will be listed, followed by an overview of the ways in which Tulsīdās's version is appreciated and performed today in northern India.

Rāmāyaṇa, or the acts of Rāma, was known in India around 500 BC and the story has been reproduced and enjoyed ever since. The acts of Rāma are narrated and enjoyed in the form of stories, ballads, dramatic performances, TV programmes and comic books.

The first well-established and widely received version of Rāma's story is the ancient Indian epic, *Rāmāyaṇa*. This epic is accepted as a homogeneous work by a single author, Vālmīki; however, critical examination now suggests that it must have passed through many stages of development and it contains numerous interpolations (Stutley 1985: 246–7). Various stories of Rāma have been told and sung as oral traditions, and some of them were edited into literary forms. The so-called *Vālmīki Rāmāyaṇa* is a typical case of an oral tradition being channelled into a literary work.

This *Rāmāyaṇa* was followed by many stories on Rāma in both classical and modern Indian languages. *Adhyātma Rāmāyaṇa* was written in Sanskrit in the fifteenth century to offer a philosophical interpretation of Rāma's story of the days; among the many other stories about Rāma in modern Indian languages, Kamban̲'s version in the twelfth-century Tamil, Kṛttivāsa's version in the fifteenth-century Bengalī, and Tulsīdās's version in the sixteenth-century Hindī have been widely appreciated and their later editions or reproductions are enjoyed even today by the people of each region (Richman 2001: 1–21).

The *Rāmcaritmānas* is an important Hindī version of the epic. Its author, Tulsīdās, was a Vaiṣṇava priest, understood to have been born in a poor brahmin family in 1532 and died in 1623. He completed the manuscript around 1580. In addition to *Rāmcaritmānas*, Tulsīdās wrote the *Kavitāvalī*, *Gītāvalī*, and *Pārvatī Maṅgal*.

The title *Rāmcaritmānas* was rendered into English as *The Holy Lake of the Acts of Rama*, with which title W.D.P. Hill's English translation was published by Oxford University Press in 1952.

Rāmcaritmānas consists of seven sections: (1) The Boyhood of

Rāma; (2) The Incidents at Capital Ayodhyā; (3) Rāma's Life in the Forest; (4) Rāma's Stay at the Monkey King's Residence; (5) The Beautiful Passage of Rāma to Laṅkā; (6) The Battle in Laṅkā, the Demon's Island; and (7) The Conclusion with Rāma's Return to Ayodhyā and his Coronation.

The construction of these sections is very similar to that of *Vālmīki Rāmāyaṇa*, but there are some important differences between the two, as will be mentioned later.

Rāmcaritmānas of the sixteenth century is still enjoyed by the people of northern India. It is read and performed in the Hindī speaking belt on popular occasions. For instance, the full text of the *Rāmcaritmānas* is often read out in Hindu families on auspicious occasions such as the birth anniversary of a boy (Lutgendorf 1991: 73–83). The dramatized version, the *Rāmlīlā*, is performed in open-air theatres every autumn in the towns and villages (Avasthī 1979: 38–60); numerous copies are published and purchased, and it is often said that the Rāma's story by Tulsīdās is to Hindus what the Holy Bible is to Christians.

I now examine and draw the multiple personas and roles of Rāma observed by Sītā. In other words, we will attempt to see how Rāma is perceived in the eyes of Sītā on the basis of Tulsīdās's *Rāmcaritmānas*.

To do so, the expressions adopted by Sītā in addressing and imagining Rāma at various stages of the story will be quoted in English translation with the corresponding original Hindī words. Thus 'beloved husband' *piya* (II.64.1) means that the expression is found in Section II, *dohā* 64, *caupāī* 1.

Gods, goddesses and important characters including heroes and heroines in the Hindu world very often have many names according to their origins, roles, and appearances. For example, the god Viṣṇu has one thousand names—to be chanted by his devotees—including *keśava*, the one with beautiful hair; *pītāmbara*, the one dressed in yellow clothes; and *madhusūdana*, the destroyer of the demon Madhu.

Rāma, born the eldest son of King Daśaratha of the Raghu dynasty, also has many names in Sanskrit and Hindī. He is generally addressed and described as *rāma*, the charming one; *raghunātha*, lord of the Raghu dynasty; *raghusiṁha*, the lion of the

Raghu dynasty; *prabhu*, the ruler; and *svāmī*, the master. Observed in the eyes of his consort, Sītā, he is described as *piya*, beloved husband (II.64.1); and *sītāpati*, the husband of Sītā (II.243); he is also addressed by Sītā as *pati*, husband (II.247.3).

Rāma is also believed to be the incarnation of the God Viṣṇu who manifested himself as the prince in order to bring solace to all creation (I.191). Moreover, he is referred to as *hari*, one of many names for Viṣṇu (V.14.1).

RĀMA IN THE EYES OF SĪTĀ THROUGH THE DEVELOPMENT OF THE STORY

It is apparent that Rāma plays three roles: as a human being, he is the eldest son of Daśaratha who protects his subjects; to Sītā, he is the beloved husband; in addition, he is the incarnation of Viṣṇu, who manifested himself in order to bring solace to all creation.

Boyhood

The section covering life of Rāma from the birth to marriage, is so extensive that it occupies about one-third of the entire book. The development of the story will be described below in two subsections, from Rāma's Birth to Rāma and Sītā's Meeting and the wedding and after.

From the Birth of Rāma to his Meeting with Sītā

Rāma and his three brothers were born into the house of Raghu (*raghukula*) as incarnations of Viṣṇu (*avatāra*) in order to relieve the earth of its burden (I.187.3, 4).

Sage Viśvāmitra, on finding them grown up and well trained, assigned Rāma—the lord of the Raghus (*raghunātha*)—and his younger brother Lakṣmaṇa the task of exterminating the demons (*asura*) tormenting the sage (I.207.5).

Led by Viśvāmitra, Rāma and Lakṣmaṇa walked a long distance and eventually reached Mithilā, where a bride-winning tournament was being organized for Sītā. The brave who could bend a huge iron bow would win Sītā's hand in marriage. Rāma decided to participate in this tournament (I.214–61).

One of Sītā's companions observed the situation and was concerned that the bow was too stiff to be bent by a delicately built youth (*mṛdugata kisora*) (I.223.1). Meanwhile, Sītā visited the temple of the Gaurī and implored her for a handsome and worthy spouse (*anurūpa subhaga baru*) (I.228.3).

On her way back from the temple, Sītā wandered in her garden along with her companions (I.229.1). It was there that Rāma caught a glimpse of Sītā, and was enraptured by her beauty (*siyā sobhā*) [I.230.3]. Sītā also noticed the two comely princes (*kisora suhāe*) and her eyes were filled with longing and gladness. She was gazing at the Raghus' master (*raghupati*) and lion (*raghusiṃha*). She let Rāma (*rāma*) into her heart (I.232.1-3, 234.2-4). It was thus that Rāma and Sītā set eyes on each other. Their love story begins at this point.

As the tournament got underway, none of the participating kings or princes could even lift the bow, let alone bend it (I.253.2). Rāma then stepped forward (I.256). Sītā looked upon the Lord *prabhu* Rāma approaching the ground and resolved to love him even at the cost of her life (*prema tana*) (I.259.4).

As he entered the ground, the charming (*rāma*) Rāma first glanced around the crowd of spectators. The gracious (*kṛpāyatana*) Rāma then turned his eyes towards Sītā (I.260). He grasped the bow in his hands and drew it tight. The bow instantly snapped into two halves (I.261.4). Thus Rāma won the tournament and the hand of Sītā of Mithilā.

The Marriage and After

The wedding ceremony of Rāma and Sītā is the main focus of this subsection. It began with the bride casting the wreath of victory (*jayamālā*) on the breast of the bridegroom. Through this action, the bride thereby announced to the public that the bridegroom was the winner of the tournament. Drawing close to Rāma, Sītā beheld his beauty (*rāma chabi*) (I.264.2) as she cast the wreath of victory on his breast (I.264.4).

A Hindu wedding ceremony reaches its climax when the bridegroom and the bride (*kuaru kuarī*) take seven steps around a fire (*kāla bhavari*) (I.325.1). The couple did this, and Rāma then applied the vermilion onto Sītā's head (*rāma siyā sendūra dehī*) to signify that he acknowledged her as his wife (I.325.4). Rāma's brothers Lakṣmaṇa and Śatrughna also wed another daughter of Janaka and his niece, respectively, on the same day (I.325.3). The three couples returned to the Ayodhyā to a joyous reception by the sages and people there. Songs blessing the couples rang out all three spheres: on the earth, in the sky and in the heavens (I.361.2).

As we examine the appearances and acts of Rāma as perceived by Sītā, the following facts are highlighted.

At first sight, Rāma was captivated by Sītā's beauty (I.230.3). Sītā was also enraptured by the two comely princes (I.232.1). These observations are based solely on appearances.

Yet, both Rāma and Sītā had some information about each other. Rāma was aware that the girl in the garden was the princess of Videha (*bidehakumārī)* (I.230.4), and Sītā had been apprised by her companions that the charming prince was the master of Raghu dynasty (*raghupati*) (I.232.2). We can assume that the appearances supported by details of family lineage laid the foundation for their relationship.

Sītā watched Rāma eagerly when the Lord (*prabhu*) approached the venue of the tournament, and she resolved to love him even at the cost of her life (*prema tana*) (I.259.4). Rāma noticed this (I.260), and her love gave him the courage to lift and bend the heavy bow. Sītā and Rāma wished for each other's happiness. Their courageous actions and sincere wishes augured favourably.

During their wedding ceremony, Sītā closely observed Rāma and noticed his beauty (I.264.2). She then cast the wreath of victory on his breast (I.264.4).

It should be noticed that during the scene, Sītā often adopted the word Rāma among many other names for him. As stated in Sanskrit and Hindī *rāma*, means 'the charming'. Let us confirm that Rāma is the name of Daśaratha's eldest son, and its etymological connotation is 'charming'.

Thus, in this Section One of this story, Rāma is perceived by Sītā 'a charming prince', 'the lion of the Raghus' and 'Lord'. It seems that the term 'Rāma' for 'charming' is adopted by Sītā as she watches him intently.

The Incidents at Capital Ayodhyā

This second section focuses on the incidents at Daśaratha's capital Ayodhyā. The aged king received the three newly wedded couples with joy and decided to appoint, Rāma, the eldest, the crown prince. People received this news with gladness and preparations for the ceremony commenced (II.1–10).

It was at this point that Kaikeyī, one of Daśaratha's three wives, requested the king to appoint instead her son, Bharata, as the crown prince and to send Rāma to a forest on a fourteen-year exile. These requests were part of three wishes that Queen Kaikeyī had been granted by the king in return for having once saved his life when he was in a critical condition. The king was morally obligated to fulfil them (II.24–33).

On being informed of these requests, Rāma expressed to the king his willingness to dwell in the forest for fourteen yeas. His consort, Sītā, was eager to accompany him (II.58). Rāma and his mother tried to persuade her to remain in the capital, saying that the forest was too inhospitable an environment for a delicate young lady to live in (II.59–63). Sītā heard the soft and tender words of her beloved husband (*piya*) (II.64.1), but said, 'Oh lord of my soul (*prāṇanātha*), with my lord (*nātha*), a hut of leaves will be as comfortable as some divine abode' (II.65.3).

Sītā's earnest request moved Rāma. The gracious lord of the solar race (*bhānukulanātha*) said, 'Come with me to the forest' (II.68.2). Then Rāma's younger brother Lakṣmaṇa offered to join them as well (II.73–4).

The Lord (*prabhu*) set forth with his spouse and brother, leaving everyone bewildered (II.79). On their journey to the forest, they were offered food and shelter by local people.

Eventually, they found a proper place to dwell in the forest at Citrakūṭa, the wonderful peak. When the gods learnt that the site had found favour in Rāma's eyes, they all came, disguised as local tribes—Kols and Kirātas—and constructed a pair of huts of leaves and grass for the noble trio. In that lovely abode the Lord (*prabhu*), attended by Lakṣmaṇa and Sītā, shone glorious (II.132–3). Subsequently, Daśaratha passed away, overcome with agony at losing Rāma (II.152–3).

Throughout this period, Rāma's younger brother Bharata had been out of the capital and unaware of all that had transpired. When he knew what had happened, he went to Citrakūṭa Peak to ask Rāma to return to Ayodhyā. But Rāma was determined to fulfil his promise to his father. Bharata then asked for Rāma's sandals, so that he could set them on the throne and govern the people as the acting crown prince (II.156–326).

The most important incident of this section is the exile of Rāma, who was accompanied by Sītā and Lakṣmaṇa. Sītā expressed her eagerness to go with Rāma to the forest and Rāma tried to persuade her to remain in the capital. In these dialogues, Sītā had the opportunity to address Rāma directly, and Rāma responded to her personally. Thus, this scene presents the most intimate atmosphere between the royal couple.

In this context, Sītā addresses Rāma as 'beloved husband' (II.64.1), 'lord of my soul' and 'my lord' (II.65.3). When Rāma decided to let Sītā accompany him to the forest, he was described as 'the gracious lord of the solar race', which connotes that Rāma, in this context, had the authority (II.68.2).

Life in the Forest

Rāma, along with Sītā and Lakṣmaṇa, was leading a simple life in the forest. One day, Śūrpanakhā, sister of the demon Rāvaṇa, chanced upon Rāma and Lakṣmaṇa. She fell in love with Rāma and disguised as a beautiful maiden, she courted him. Rāma, of course, rejected her advances, and Lakṣmaṇa struck off her nose and ears (III.17.1–17). She returned to Laṅkā and entreated her brother Rāvaṇa to avenge this deed (III.23.4).

Rāma foresaw this. He who offers compassion and joy (*kṛpā sukha bṛnda*), with a smile said to Janaka's daughter (*janakasutā*) Sītā (III.23), 'Listen, beloved wife (*priyā*), I will put you in pure fire (*pāvaka*) to protect you from the demons' (III.24.1). Sītā entered into the fire, keeping the image of the feet of her husband and Viṣṇu (*prabhupada*) in her heart, leaving only an illusion behind (III.24.2).

When Rāma and Lakṣmaṇa were out hunting, Rāvaṇa, disguised as an ascetic, forced Sītā into his chariot, and drove away quickly

(III.28.4–29.12). Enroute to his island, Laṅkā, Sītā was able to leave behind a piece of cloth murmuring the name of Viṣṇu (*harināma*) who is incarnated as Rāma (III.29.13). However, as previously arranged by Rāma, the kidnapped Sītā was merely an illusion.

Ravana confined Sītā to a grove of fear-free trees (*asoka padapa*) (III.29a). There, Sītā constantly repeated the name of Hari (*harināma*) (III.29b).

In this rather short section, Rāma offers compassion and joy. His role here is to protect his wife—Janaka's dear daughter—from Rāvaṇa. For Sītā, Rāma here is Viṣṇu himself charged with protecting the entire universe.

Stay at the Monkey King's Residence

In this section of the story, Rāma resided with the monkey king and allied with monkeys and bears. Meanwhile, Sītā was confined by Rāvaṇa to his garden. Thus we find no significant reference by Sītā to Rāma here.

The Beautiful Passage of Rāma to Laṅkā

While looking for Sītā, Rāma found that Sītā had been confined by Rāvaṇa in Laṅkā. To rescue her, he proceeded to the shore opposite the island. Then Hanumān, the monkey commander, jumped into Laṅkā and found the palace of the Rāvaṇa, and the grove of fear-free trees (*asoka bana*) where Sītā had been confined (V.4.1–8.4). She was in the grove, contemplating Rāma's lotus feet (*kamala pada*) (V.8).

Hanumān tried to inform Sītā that he was Rāma's envoy and had come to find ways to rescue her. He dropped the signet ring that Rāma had given him. Sītā picked it up in her hand and looked at the lovely ring inscribed with Rāma's name (V.12.6–13.1). This convinced her that Hanumān was a servant of merciful Lord (*kṛpasindhu*) Rāma, a devotee of Hari (V.13.2–14.1).

Hanumān set fire to many places in Laṇkā, causing a great turmoil there. Then he went back to see Sītā and requested her to wait patiently until the brave prince of the Raghus (*raghubīra*) arrived with his troops to free her (V.16.2). She unfastened a jewel in her hair and gave it to Hanumān as her token. Receiving this precious token, he set forth for the camp of the lord of the Raghus (*Raghupati*), in order to apprise him of all he had witnessed in Laṅkā (V.27.1–27).

Rāvaṇa's younger brother Vibhīṣaṇa was concerned about the situation and he entreated Rāvaṇa to release Sītā. This infuriated Rāvaṇa and he expelled his younger brother. Vibhīṣaṇa headed for Rāma's camp and sought protection, swearing to serve Rāma. Rāma accepted him (V.38.1-43).

Thus, in this section, Rāma is for Sītā the one with lotus feet, the merciful God Hari or his incarnation. When the plan for Sītā's rescue was discussed, Rāma was described by Sītā as the lord of the Raghus. Here we can observe the transformation of Rāma—in Sītā's eyes—from a spiritual being into the mighty leader of the lineage.

Battle in Laṅkā

Rāma's troops of monkeys and bears carried heaps of tall trees and huge mountains, and constructed a bridge over the ocean between their camp and Laṅkā (VI.1.3-4). Rāma, Lakṣmaṇa and their army crossed this bridge and reached the opposite shore (VI.5.1-5). News of this reached the ten-headed Rāvaṇa. His consort, Mandodarī, tried to persuade him not to fight with Rāma, to submit to him and release Sītā. She advised him to retreat into woods and entrust the kingdom to their sons. But Rāvaṇa resolved to fight Rāma (VI.6.1–10).

Rāma approached Rāvaṇa's palace after slaying the demon's two sons (VI.37).

While Sītā was waiting for Rāma to come to her rescue, she imagined him as the lord of the Raghus (*raghupati*) or a storehouse of grace (*kṛpānidhāna*) (VI.99.5–6). Janaka's daughter (*Jānakī*), Sītā was in distress during her separation from the charming one (*rāma*) (VI.100.2).

At the culmination of a series of fierce battles waged around Rāvaṇa's palace, Rāma and Rāvaṇa confronted each other. Rāma shot a volley of arrows which cut-off Rāvaṇa's arms and ten heads to the ground (VI.101.2).

Hanumān visited Sītā. She blessed him, saying 'May Rāma, the

Lord of Kosala (*kosalapati*), be ever gracious to you!' (VI.107), and requested him to make it possible for her to see with her eyes the dark and delicate form of Rāma (*syāma mṛdu gata*) (VI.108.1). Rāma sent a beautiful palanquin for her. Sītā got into it, with her thoughts fixed on her loving Lord Rāma (*rāma sanehī*), the abode of bliss (*sukhadhāma*) (VI.108.4).

Thus she returned to Rāma. Rāma, the all-merciful uttered some reproachful words (concerning her chastity during her confinement in Rāvaṇa's fort) and suggested that she should be proven pure through an ordeal by fire. With her thoughts focused on the Lord (*prabhu*), the princess of Mithilā entered the flames and said, 'Glory to the lord of Kosala (*kosales*)'. The fire goddess brought the hand of the noble lady (*śrī*) to Rāma proving her chastity (VI.108–9.2).

The gods and saints as well as the monkeys and bears came to bless and thank Rāma for his deeds (VI.109–13). Impressed by their devotion, the king of the Raghus (*raghurāī*) was eager to take them all to his capital, Ayodhyā, and he seated them in a flying car that had been kept ready. The beautiful car took off from Laṅkā and headed northwards (VI.119.1–3).

In this section too, we come across different expressions relating to Rāma that have been imagined and articulated by Sītā.

She was in distress during her separation from the charming Rāma. When she yearned for him to rescue her, she imagined him as the lord of the Raghus or the storehouse of grace. After Rāma vanquished Rāvaṇa and it became clear that she would be reunited with him, Sītā imagined Rāma in a very intimate way as the loving lord and the dark and delicate form. At the scene of the ordeal by fire, Sītā entered the flames imaging Rāma as the king of Kosala. She was proven pure by the fire goddess and was understood by Rāma as the noble lady and Rāma was charming in Sītā's eyes.

Concluding Section

Rāma, Sītā and Lakṣmaṇa were welcomed with joy by gods, saints and the people of Ayodhyā, including his mother and brothers (VII.5.11). The people of the capital were glad to see Sītā, the perfection of beauty and virtue (*rāmarūpa guṇa khāni*) on the left of Rama (VII.11b).

As King Daśaratha had passed away during Rāma's exile, Rāma, the Lord of the three spheres (*tribhuana sāī*) ascended to the throne (VII.12.4). Having sung praises on the acts of Rāma, the gods, sages, monkeys and bears returned to their own spheres and homes (VII.12b).

Rāma then governed the country and led a peaceful life with Sītā. Sītā knew that her husband (*pati*) was an ocean of mercy (*kṛpāsindhu*), and she always strove for the comfort of her husband (*pati anukūla*). She worked according to the wishes of Rāmacandra who is as beautiful as the moon (*rāmacandra*) (VII.24.2–3). Enjoying this peaceful life, Sītā gave birth to two sons, Lava and Kuśa (VII.25.3).

In this concluding section, Sītā is the perfection of beauty and virtue. There was no longer any doubt about her chastity and as a result, she enjoyed a peaceful life with Rāma and bore him two sons in the palace.

The enthroned Rāma was respected by everyone in the capital as the Lord of the three spheres. When all his supporters left Ayodhyā, he was described as Sītā's beautiful husband with an ocean of mercy—a cherished companion for his wife.

CONCLUSION

I have outlined three phases or roles of Rāma: the incarnation of Viṣṇu, the eldest prince of King Daśaratha and heir to the throne, and the beloved husband of Sītā. I have examined these phases and roles as observed by Sītā.

In this story, Rāma is seen differently depending on the circumstances he encounters. For example, when Sītā was awaiting rescue by Rāma she imagined him as 'the Lord of Kosala' (VI.107). Just after her rescue, she remembered him as 'the dark and delicate form of Rāma' (VI.108.1). It should be noted that the crown prince was transformed into her husband within a moment. I am convinced that the author of *Rāmcaritmānas* consciously described Rāma in terms that suited the scenes in the story, and succeeded in presenting vivid images of Rāma to Sītā as well as to the readers.

At this point, it should be clarified that the present paper has two limitations. The first is caused by the fact that some important expressions adopted in addressing and imagining Rāma have multiple meanings with minutely different connotations. For example, the word *nātha* basically means a protector or owner, from which 'husband' or 'deity' could be derived. Similarly, the word *prabhu* could refer to a ruler, a master, a sage and a deity. These expressions appear very often in Rama's story by Tulsīdās. The same expression works differently depending on the situation in the story. It is also probable that an expression used in a given scene may contain two or three connotations: for example, husband, king and deity. In such a case, one phase of Rāma comes to the fore while the others are relegated. In this study, annotated editions and translations were consulted in an effort to understand the true connotations of the expressions in the context of the scenes of the story. However, it cannot be stated with certainty that my interpretation is always correct.

The second limitation is a natural consequence of observing Rāma through the eyes of Sītā. If Rāma is observed through the eyes of his ministers or his enemies, different pictures could be conjured.

This study concludes with a brief comparison between the *Vālmīki Rāmāyaṇa* (hereafter sometimes abbreviated as *VR*) and Tulsīdās's Hindī version, *Rāmcaritmānas* (hereafter sometimes abbreviated as *TM*). For *VR*, reference is made to Rāmanārāyaṇa Śāstrī's version published by Gītā Press.

In the first section of *TM*, Rāma had a glimpse of Sītā (I.230.3) and Sītā also saw the master of the Raghus (I.232.2) before the tournament. In this way Rāma and Sītā first set eyes on each other and fell in love. There is no mention to this effect in *VR*. *TM* appears to accord importance to the personal and intimate relations between Rāma and Sītā.

The concluding section of *TM* differs substantially from that of *VR*: in *VR*, Sītā was obliged to leave Rāma after her chastity was called into question by the people; however in *TM*, Sītā spent the rest of her life happily with Rama (VII.11b). She was proven to be chaste as the kidnapped Sītā in *TM* was an illusion conjured by Rāma while the real Sītā was under the protection of the fire goddess (III.24.1).

Observing this substantial difference between the two stories, we may presume that the *Vālmīki Rāmāyaṇa* adopted the traditional tragic ending of an ancient epic while Tulsīdās's sixteenth-century Hindī version tried to bring peace and happiness to the contemporary people through the mercy of Lord Viṣṇu.

Let us recall the opening scenes of Tulsīdās's Hindī version, *Rāmcaritmānas*: Rāma and his three brothers were born into the house of Raghu as the incarnations of Viṣṇu in order to relieve the earth of its burden (I.187.3–4). It follows that Rāma or his subjects can find no reason to expel Sītā from the palace. She is included among those to whom Viṣṇu is to bring relief. It is now apparent that the happy ending was planned at the very beginning of this story by Tulsīdās, a devotee of the supreme Viṣṇu.

REFERENCES

Avasthī, Indujā, *Rāmlīlā: Paramparā Aur Sāhitya*, Naī Dillī: Rādhākṛṣṇ Prakāśan, 1979.

Lutgendorf, Philip, *The Life of a Text: Performing the Ramcaritmanas by Tulsidas*, Berkeley: Unversity of California Press, 1991.

Poddār, Hanumānprasād (ed.), *Śrīrāmcaritmānas (saṭīk)* 12th edn, Gorakhapur: Gītā Press, 1961.

Prasad, R.C. (tr.), *Tulasidasa's Shriramacaritamanasa*, Delhi: Motilal Banarsidass, 1990.

Rāmanārāyaṇa Śāstrī (ed. & Hindi tr.), *Maharṣi Vālmīkipraṇīta Śrīmadvālmīkīya Rāmāyaṇa*, Gorakhapur: Gītā Press, 1960.

Richman, Paula, 'Questioning and Multiplicity of the Rāmāyaṇa Traditions', in P. Richman (ed.), *Questioning Rāmāyaṇas*, Berkeley: University of California Press, 2001.

Stutley, Margaret and James Stutley, 'Rāmāyaṇa', in *A Dictionary of Hinduism: Its Mythology, Folklore and Development, 1500 BC–AD 1500*, London: Routledge & Kegan Paul, 1985 (1st publ. 1977).

14

Saint Ramalingar and the Exemplification of God as Effulgence

HIROSHI YAMASHITA

This paper studies Saint Ramalingar (irāmaliṅkar,[1] 1823–74), otherwise known as Vaḷḷalār, who was a mystic and one of the exponents of the southern reform movement in nineteenth-century India.[2] It attempts to shed light on his devotion and practices from a new perspective. The focus is not the metaphysical aspects of his theology, but the imagery of God and the mode of worship in his rituals and versifications, based primarily on literary materials along with the first hand information gained at the headquarters founded by his organization.

SAINT RAMALINGAR'S LIFE AND HIS ENCOUNTER WITH THE DIVINE LIGHT

Before discussing in-depth, we shall briefly trace the major incidents which occurred in the devoted life of the saint by focusing mainly on the earlier phases of his biography.[3]

According to the widely accepted tradition, Ramalingar was born in 1823 in Marutūr, a village about 15 km north-west of Chidambaram[4] in the South Arcot (present Kaṭalūr) district of Madras Presidency (present Tamil Nadu). His father, Rāmaiyā Piḷḷai, was an accountant, according to another legend, school teacher in this village. He belonged to the community of Karuṇīkars[5] and was a faithful devotee of Śiva. Ramalingar was his fifth child (the third son).

Ramalingar's birth is embroidered by mythical episodes as often found in the case with pre-modern Hindu saints. A legend goes as follows. An unknown sage appeared unexpectedly in Rāmaiyā's household and foretold the birth of a divine child and the child's destiny. This sage vanished after leaving the house. In reality, it was Śiva incarnated as a sage. A biographer narrates that Ramalingar was already conscious in his mother's womb and prayed to God for His 'light' of protection. These anecdotes were obviously incorporated later, perhaps even after his death, in his biography. Such fanciful incidents reflect the fictional tradition of south Indian hagiographic literature as typically observed in the *Tiruttoṇṭar-purāṇam* (*Periya-purāṇam*), among others.

Rāmaiyā died when Ramalingar was only six months old. Ciṉṉammai (Ciṉṉammāḷ), Rāmaiyā's sixth wife and Ramalingar's mother, retreated with her family to Ciṉṉakkāvaṉam, her birthplace near Puṉṉēri in Chinglepet (present Tiruvārūr) district north of Madras. However, in a couple of years, they again shifted to Madras and finally settled there. The family lived under the tutelage of Capāpati Piḷḷai, Ramalingar's elder brother. Capāpati fostered his younger brother and, together with his wife, tutored him at home instead of giving him a formal school education. Legend states that Capāpati earned his living by delivering religious discourses at local temples.[6]

Saint Ramalingar's infancy was embellished with wonders. One legend states that, when he was five (or six) months of age, he was taken to have *darśana* at the Naṭarāja Temple in Chidambaram; there, he burst into laughter in ecstasies of delight on seeing the deity. Appaya Dīkṣita (Appayya Tīṭcatar), a renowned Advaitin hailing from Kāñcīpuram, happened to witness this and admired the divine infant. Appaya Dīkṣita, a historical figure who lived in the sixteenth or seventeenth century, was unmistakably not contemporaneous with Ramalingar. So, this anecdote is pure invention.

In his boyhood, Ramalingar did not exhibit any interest in learning and unsure of what to do with him, his family tentatively provided him with a separate room upstairs. Thereafter, he stopped wandering and, in turn, remained indoors day and night for some reason or the other. Finally, one day, he was found lost in deep contemplation of Murukaṉ in the room, the door shut, a mirror hung on the wall and a lamp lit in front of him. This constitutes the semi-legendary incident which directly connects Ramalingar with 'effulgence' for the first time in his known biography. At the age of nine, he impressed people with a flow of improvised verses during his pilgrimage to the Murukan̲ temple in Tiruttan̲ikai, northern Tamil Nadu, and when he was about twelve years of age, he began religious activity, including discourses on Śiva, annotating divine scriptures, and so forth.

During this period, he composed many devotional poems, paying homage to various temples in the vicinity of Madras including the celebrated shrine in Tiruvor̲r̲iyūr, as mentioned in the *Tēvāram*. These poems were later incorporated into his six cantos of *Tiruva-ruṭpā*, the vast collection of his poetry.

Though the exact age is not identified, it was undoubtedly after his thirties when Ramalingar finally left Madras for Chidambaram, and, after a certain period, settled in a hamlet known as Karuṅkul̲i near the present Vaṭalūr in the neighbourhood of Chidambaram. This place became the centre of his religious activities ever since. It is believed that Ramalingar had married before shifting to Karuṅkul̲i. Allegedly, his bride, Tan̲ammāḷ, was a daughter of his eldest sister. His marital life was a failure, although the particulars are not known. In Karuṅkul̲i, he composed numerous poems in praise of Naṭarāja and the poet-saints, which are collectively known as Nāyan̲ārs or Nāyan̲mārs, representative of the earliest phases of Tamil Śaivism.

In course of time, Ramalingar intuitively knew the Supreme to be immanent and yet indescribable beyond externalization or materialization. It could be emblematically represented in an amorphous form of, for example, flame. In his cult, a lamp lit and installed in the innermost portion of the sanctuary was not a substitute for a central *vigraha* (*mūlavar*) but an exemplification of the shapeless Infinite in the tentative form of flame. His unique religion of God as 'effulgence' (*cōti*, from Sanskrit *jyotis*) thus evolved, with light as the centre of ritual worship.

According to certain legends, Ramalingar did not cast his shadow on the ground. This indicates that he was endowed with a super-human body which was visible and, at the same time, transparent. The absence of a shadow can also be interpreted from the context of a cult centring on 'effulgence'. Interestingly, there are no extant photographs or portraits of this saint because he forbade people from taking his picture. Any attempt to photograph him allegedly resulted in failure.

Ramalingar was believed to be endowed with mystic power to heal the sick and even raise the dead. His miraculous deeds are, in many cases, conceptually related with 'deathlessness'. However, he did not readily perform miracles, particularly in public. Though the exertion of his *yogic* power was demonstrative of attaining his fulfilment (*siddhi*), and therefore, a requirement to attest his sainthood, it is indeed true that Ramalingar's image as a miracle man was not exceedingly remarkable during his lifetime except for the dramatic end of his vanishing into a void. Despite the intrusion of semi-mythical elements in his biography, his identity as a miracle man did not come to the fore: during his lifetime his reputation was that of a mystic.[7]

In the doctrinal aspect, Ramalingar placed significant emphasis on a kind of religious universalism in his specific terminology of *ca<u>n</u>mārkkam*, or *cutta-camaraca-ca<u>n</u>mārkkam* (exactly equivalent to Sanskrit *śuddha-samarasa-sanmārga*) in its full denomination, both of which are often translated as the 'Universal Religion' or 'Universal Brotherhood'. He also preached *cīva-kāruṇṇiyam*, compassion without distinction among all living beings. Ramalingar advocated non-violence, vegetarian diet, prohibition of animal sacrifice, and the abolition of discrimination by birth and others. His movement as a whole is known as the Ca<u>n</u>mārkkam movement.

ESTABLISHMENT OF THE THREE INSTITUTIONS AND HIS LAST YEARS

Ramalingar's ideals were crystallized into three distinct institutions founded successively during the last decade of his life, Caṅkam, Cālai, and Capai. In order to promote religious and social services, he launched an association in 1865 under the name of Camaraca-vēta-ca<u>n</u>mārkkac-caṅkam, and then renamed it as Camaraca-cutta-ca<u>n</u>mārkka-cattiyac-caṅkam in 1873 (usually, known as merely Caṅkam in its abbreviated form), which developed into Ramalingar (Irāmaliṅkar) Pa<u>n</u>ima<u>n</u><u>r</u>am, the Ramalinga Mission in English, in course of time. Without financially depending on others, the saint maintained this institution solely with the income gained from his writings and publications.

Thereafter, in quick succession, in 1867, immediately after the residents of Pārvatipuram, situated nearby, donated some land for construction, he built a house of charity known as Camaraca-cutta-caṉmārkka-cattiya-tarumac-cālai (the 'Sanctuary for Eternal Service') or Tarumac-cālai or even Cālai for short.[8] This was a facility in which free food was supposed to be distributed regularly to the needy or to those without refuge.[9] Announcements to notify people about the completion of the construction of Cālai were distributed widely. Meanwhile, through the activity conducted under the name of Caṅkam, the saint established a school, the Camaraca-vēta-pāṭacālai, to eradicate illiteracy and lack of education, though this attempt resulted in a failure.

After the establishment of the two institutions, an edifice was finally constructed to provide devotees a place for worship. This prayer hall, known as the Camaraca-cutta-caṉmārkka-cattiya-ñāṉa-capai (or simply Capai) referring to the 'Hall of True Wisdom of the Universal Brotherhood', was eventually completed in December 1871, about two years before his death. It was officially inaugurated in 1872. The completion of the Capai was publicized through many printed notices.

This building was specifically designed in the shape of full-blown lotus flower which provided expression to the human body as the abode of God.[10] It is also obvious that a lighted lamp (which is vulnerable, and therefore, should be guarded under mindful protection), evokes the image of 'life' dwelling in one's body as *jīva*; this is often associated in imagery with *dīpa* at the folk level of diction among the Tamils. Inside the structure of this Capai, there are seven curtains that conceal the light within. Behind all these curtain is a thick glass slab of about five feet tall in which a bright lamp is installed (Vanmikanathan 1980: 80). The curtains are indicative of seven powers with which one can unveil the seven secrets of the Lord (Annamalai 1988: 212).

The sacred fire in a lamp, symbolic of the Supreme was lit in the innermost chamber. Except for the lamp, nothing was installed inside the sanctum sanctorum (*garbhagṛha*). Ramalingar's notion of godhead is expressed by the term Great Effulgence (*peruñ-cōti*).

It gained its fruition by the construction of this magnificent hall.

Although this centre was stated to be used for many purposes including meetings of the devotees, religious discourses, investigations of herbal medicine, experiments of magical powers and others, no further details were reported. The fact that even at present, medicinal plants and materials are put on sale in front of the portals of the Capai reveals the association between Ramalingar with Tamil Cittars and their medicine (*citta-maruttuvam*).

In 1870, the saint shifted to an *āśrama* known as Citti-vaḷāka-māḷikai, or simply Citti-vaḷākam, located in Mēṭṭukkuppam, a hamlet about 4 km away from his headquarters in Vaṭalūr. In 1872, the Ca<u>n</u>mārkkam flag was hoisted in front of Citti-vaḷāka-māḷikai. The flag was two-coloured, yellow and white, the colour of the flame and purity, respectively. In 1874, at the age of fifty-five, Ramalingar died: more exactly, he disappeared into the void. He merged with the Infinite by undergoing the dematerialization process of the body. Thus he attained *citti* (*siddhi*).[11] Some biographies describe the demise as 'becoming one with flame'. Before his end, Ramalingar observed a fast, gave the final sermon, and eventually retired into seclusion in this *āśrama*. Thereafter, he vanished forever. In retrospect, it was the confinement in a room in his boyhood that led him to experience his first encounter with God as the Supreme Light of Grace. It is not coincidental that, to attain *citti,* he finally retreated into Citti-vaḷākam, in which a divine lamp had been lit several days before.

The symbolization of the Supreme as light has been maintained to date. A lamp forms the nucleus in the rituals of his followers even today. On the day of *Tai-pūcam* every year, a big lamp is lit on the top of the cupola of the Capai, which attracts the attention a considerable number of worshippers in and around Vaṭalūr and even in distant places.[12] Due to the unique mode of worship of the Absolute as the lighted flame, this God-oriented saint is familiarly known as Cōti-rāmaliṅka-cuvāmikaḷ.

Rules and procedures in conducting the worship in the Cattiya-ñā<u>n</u>a-capai were formulated by the saint himself during his lifetime, as stated in the following. A lamp with a glass container or a tin reflector should be installed in the innermost portion. Qualified persons of physical and mental purity should be selected to light the lamp outside the portals of the Capai. It is important to note that the brāhmaṇical dichotomy of purity and impurity inherent to one's birth is completely dismissed with the introduction of distinct criteria of eligibility to participate in the prescribed rituals. The lamp lit by the selected devotees should be brought into the sanctum by a juvenile less than twelve years or by an adult over seventy-two years of age.

The precinct should be cleaned regularly once in four days by the same category of devotees. Before entering, they should have a bath and wrap their feet in cloth. They clean the floor on their knees. When the lamp is installed, devotees should stand outside and chant in praise of God. People assembling for worship should first congregate outside the Capai and sing hymns. The sanctuary is closed to meat-eaters, who should stay away. Only those who refrain completely from eating meat, killing animals, and indulging in worldly desires are granted admittance to the hall to renew the wick of the divine light or to clean the precinct. However, there is no caste-oriented distinction either in the entry into the sanctuary or in worshipping from outside (Vanmikanathan 1980: 82–3).

Ramalingar's movement continues. An organization called Ramalingar Paṉimaṉṟam, responsible for matters related to publicization and social service, publishes his writings, establishes branches of the Caṅkam, and organizes many other operations centred on the Tarumac-cālai and the Cattiya-ñāṉa-capai.[13]

THE POETIC IMAGERY OF GOD AS GRACE-LIGHT

We now focus on the manner of his literary expression of God—not as a concrete figure of an icon (*arcā*) with well-defined attributes but abstractedly as the effulgent flame of a lamp. According to Ramalingar, the Absolute ought not to be referred to as a material object. It can only be provided a representation which indicates the divinity metaphorically. An often repeated *mantra* is believed to have been bestowed by the Almighty to Ramalingar. It is quite typical of his 'light-centric' mode of worship.

aruṭperuñcōti aruṭperuñcōti
taṉiperuṅkaruṇai aruṭperuñcōti[14]

O Great Effulgence of Grace! O Great Effulgence of Grace!
O Great Unique Immense Compassion! O Great Effulgence of Grace!

His novel representation of God figuratively as light, is reflected in the poetical creations of Ramalingar. His verses overflow with the imagery Grace-light (*aruṭ-cōti*) or the Great Grace-light (*aruṭ-peruñ-cōti*).

O lamp!
Thou hast lighted my heart
to remove the darkness of egoism
and to radiate the compassionate Effulgence.

(*Aruṭperuñcōti Akaval* 1495)[15]

In this poem from his *Aruṭperuñcōti Akaval*,[16] light emitted by a lamp (*viḷakku*), symbolic of the Divine Grace, illuminates the true Self and extends immense compassion to stray spirits. God and His impartial mercy are represented as a lamp and its luminosity, respectively. Hence, the concept of Grace and that of light are combined into one compound word *aruḷ-oḷi* that refers to the Light of Grace.

The Absolute for Ramalingar is not an entity totally free of qualities (*nirguṇa*) as typified in the neuter, impersonal *brahman* of the Advaitins, but personal God in the sense that He is omnipotent as well as omniscient and endowed with measureless auspicious qualities (*kalyāṇa-guṇa*). These include compassion, munificence, and magnanimity as proclaimed in the orthodox Tamil Śaiva theology.

Oh lamp of gnosis,
shining with a beauty possessed by none else,
Who, putting up with their thousands of misdeeds,
bestow grace on those who pay obeisance to You!
Oh glittering pure Gold of highest quality
Who shine on the left of Him
Who resides in illustrious O<u>ṟṟ</u>i,
Oh Vaṭivuṭai Māṇikkam! (*Tiruvaruṭpā* 1426)[17]

I called out to You:
'Oh Bestower of boons!
Exempting me from fasts, penances, etc.,
lighting up my mind with the lamp
of gnosis of Reality,
giving me the good ambrosia of union,
fulfilling all I had in mind,

bestow on me out of Your mercy,
the capability of exercising all the mystic powers'.
And You came and bestowed on me
the Effulgence of Grace!
Hallowed be Your magnanimity! (*Tiruvaruṭpā* 4664)[18]

In these stanzas in the vast collection of the *Tiruvaruṭpā* the Absolute—depicted as the generous forgiver of sins and misdeeds, the blissful bestower of boons and the glorious illuminator of the darkness of ignorance is intimately related to the concept of light.

As is eloquently proved by the same poetry presented above, a lamp (*viḷakku* in Tamil or *dīpa* in Sanskrit) and its associated attributes (light, glow, flame, splendour, luminosity) have had a positive implication throughout the spiritual tradition of South Asia, including Indian Zoroastrianism. A lamp or light in the Indian context is reminiscent of something enlightening, something to eradicate the sense of ego or something to burn accumulated sins. Flaming light has often been conceptually associated with the supreme knowledge dispelling illusion and ultimately resulting in release or salvation in the philosophical and theological treatises in classical and medieval India. In Vedāntic tradition, for example, *cit* or *jñāna*, ultimately synonymous with *brahman/ātman*, is characterized as self-luminous (*svaprakāśa, svayaṃprakāśa*, *svayaṃprabhā* or *svayaṃjyotis* in their terminology). Hindu philosophical conceptions defining the Supreme, namely benevolence, munificence, all-pervasiveness, formlessness, and sometimes even attributeless-ness (*nirguṇatva*), could also be alluded to with the help of the imagery of light.[19]

In Indian Christianity too, the *āratti* (in Tamil), which is the ritual motion of waving a lamp or lighted camphor in a plate often accompanied with singing in praise of God, has been rooted in ritual as one of the essential elements in religious service, as in the Hindu system of rituals in front of an image of a deity in temples and households.[20] This component is originally a derivative from its Hindu counterpart. It is commonly observed in Christianity worldwide, Catholic or Protestant, to symbolize God or the Holy Spirit in the form of light. The use of candles can also be interpreted in the similar context. It is not surprising that Ramalingar employed this pan-Indian or even universal image of a lamp and its effulgence to indicate the ultimate refuge and goal of the aspirants irrespective of their faiths.[21]

It is important to note that, though it may not form the sole imagery of the Supreme in his poetical works, the symbolization of God as light or luminosity is so prevailing that about half of nearly six thousand poems in the *Tiruvaruṭpā* collection is exclusively dedicated to *cōti*, the embodiment of God.[22] Saint Ramalingar's representation of God as effulgence, which can be traced back to his fundamental experience in his boyhood finally materialized as a shining lamp installed in the innermost chamber of the Cattiya-ñāṉa-capai in Vaṭalūr during his last years.[23]

The inseparable association of Ramalingar's teachings and his cult with a lamp or its radiance has been established and maintained to such an extent that books, booklets, brochures and many other publications about him, his belief, or his poetry always have the illustration of a lamp with its blazing flame. Considering this, it is unsurprising that he has been known as Tiruvaruṭ-pirakāca-vaḷḷalār (refers to Vaḷḷalār with Divine Grace-light) in an honorific title or, in its shortened form, Aruṭ-pirakācar (the One with Grace-light); the shortened form serves as an appellation of God.

As for Śiva, the *liṅga* is used to signify him; but Ramalingar employed a lighted lamp to denote the divinity while he was generally regarded as a Śaivite saint without reservation. He not only refused to endow God with polymorphic characterization but also, in all probability, consciously refrained from indicating Him with a gender distinction, although it is not deniable that he occasionally mentioned the Absolute under the particular name of *Civaṉ* (correspondent to Sanskrit *Śiva*) with the masculine suffix.

Another characterization of the Absolute in his poetry is found in the repeated emphasis on immanence. This theme crystallizes in poetic expressions, in a verse from the *Tiruvaruṭpā*:

Oh pure transcendent Being
Who dwelt within me,
and Who, after giving Your breast to this infant
who dwelt in the darkness of nescience of anything,
made a little wisdom accrue,
then, indwelling my consciousness,
made me cognizant of the Vedas—

(ordinarily) the subject of (laborious) study—
and the arts without any study whatsoever,
and, showing me the true sense of grace,
prevented me from going up the evil-thronging path
of religious sectarianism,
and directed me into the true universal path
of holy grace,
and, whenever I became confused,
exhorted me saying: 'Oh son, do not get confused,'
and rid me of all confusion! (*Tiruvaruṭpā* 3053)[24]

RAMALINGAR'S THOUGHT AND PRACTICES: THE RELIGIO-HISTORICAL BACKGROUND

Where can we trace the origin and significance of Ramalingar's representation representing the God as effulgence? Ramalingar recognized himself as being in the genealogy of Cittars in Tamil devotionalism. It was the Cittars who were inclined to represent the Divine as something dwelling within ourselves, although this parallelism can be observed more or less throughout the ages in the devotional literature of the Tamils. The immanence of divinity is illustrated in the poems composed by Civavākkiyār, one of the foremost Cittars in the early medieval period, most probably in the ninth century.[25] The verse runs as follows.

Millions and millions of people
have run all along
seeking, searching and looking for
the light that is within!
Getting completely exhausted
They die at last. (*Civavākkiyār* 3)[26]

It can be observed in the above poem attributed to this poet-saint that effulgence and immanence is already given explicit literary expression. It should also be noted that not only in the above-cited verses of Civavākkiyār but also in the bulk of poetic works written by Cittars, the Absolute, which ought to be omnipresent or all-pervasive theoretically, was preferably assumed to be immanent and above all radiant from within.

Some more aspects of the teachings and practises of Ramalingar shared by Tamil Cittars may be outlined as follows:[27]

1. advocacy of genuine devotion without discrimination by birth
2. objection to temple-oriented ritualism as obstacles in the pathway to God
3. critical attitude towards the established religious organizations
4. refusal of idolatry
5. lucid composition employing literary conventions of folk ballads
6. close affinity with Śaivism
7. sympathy for living beings, and emphasis on non-violence and vegetarianism
8. negative stance on the sexual rites of esoteric nature.

Cittars departed from the regular practice of Śaivism and Vaiṣṇavism, although they were accused of atheism and agnosticism by orthodoxy. Inarguably, the teachings and practises of Ramalingar coincided in many respects with those of Cittars who were historically an offshoot of Tamil Śaivism. It is true that Ramalingar identified himself in the lineage of Cittars as already explained (Francis 1990: 21). To provide a concrete example, his favourite term *camaracam*, derived from Sanskrit *samarasa*, which refers to 'harmony', 'unity', or 'equality' irrespective of faith and principles, was also used by his predecessors like Tirumūlar (the seventh century)[28] and Tāyumāṉavar (1604–61).[29] It is plausible that the latter, an immediate predecessor, inspired him in matters literary and spiritual.

Well-versed in the conventions and techniques of Tamil folk poetry and bhakti, Ramalingar excelled in lucid versification and paid tribute to God by expressing the overwhelming sentiments of his bhakti in plain diction like his predecessors in the Cittar tradition.[30] Non-violence was stressed by Saint Tāyumāṉavar as well (Sourirajan 1978: 30, 99). The concept *caṉmārkkam*, crucial to Ramalingar's philosophy, was already employed by Tāyumāṉavar centuries earlier (Sourirajan 1978: 38). The necessity of the reconciliation of Advaita (therefore Vedānta) and Śaiva-siddhānta was urged by Tāyumāṉavar (Varadarajan 1988: 210). Prior to Ramalingar, Tāyumāṉavar also composed devotional hymns following the patterns and conventions of folk ballads. He advocated universal love without distinction. The employment of imagery in the *akam* genre of the ancient Caṅkam corpus is commonly found both in Tāyumāṉavar and Ramalingar (Varadarajan 1988: 210). Tāyumāṉavar used the term *parañcōti*, indicating 'great light', to refer to Śiva (Sourirajan 1978: 23).[31] For this saint, as for Ramalingar, the flame was none other than an eternal symbol of God. These similarities cannot merely be a coincidence, and Ramalingar did directly refer to Tāyumāṉavar (Sourirajan 1978: 98).

Ramalingar was not an orthodox Śaivite. His initial aspiration and the movement led by him, which strictly opposed the existing religious establishments, provoked a strong antipathy among Śaivites, in particular the Śaiva-siddhāntins.[32] It was mainly a result of his critical attitude to the polarized sectarian identity among the Hindus and the unprecedented idea of God represented as a flame. This exemplification, in contrast to the conventional mode of representation of Śiva in the form of *liṅga* or an elaborate icon, was intended to avoid the difference between the two outstandingly influential schools, namely Vedānta and Śaiva-siddhānta, and synthesize both the tenets predominant in traditional Tamil thoughts (see Annamalai 1988: 111, 117). The verses from his *Aruṭperuñcōti Akaval* presented below provide a poetic expression to his full conviction that the Supreme as compared to the glow should transcend the established authorities of the Vedas, the Āgamas, and any other school of thought.

O absolute glow of gnosis!
Thou hast transcended the Vedas,
the elaborate Āgamas
and the eternal sound. (*Aruṭperuñcōti Akaval* 1543)[33]

The Boundless Benevolent *Cōti*
that graces the holy Hall (of wisdom)
is the source of the void of unique substance
beyond the realm of sectarian religions. (*Aruṭperuñcōti Akaval* 61)[34]

This representation of God without anthropomorphism helped emphasize the worship as being beyond the bipolar sectarianism ascribed either to Śaivas or Vaiṣṇavas. In fact, Ramalingar admired Śiva and Viṣṇu equally (Varadarajan 1988: 223), even though he took his place in the genealogy of Tamil Śaiva sainthood. However, what he termed as Śiva was not god in an ordinary sense with sectarian colouring, but something surpassing the realm of the Śaiva-Vaiṣṇava bigotry. The Absolute for him was sometimes *civam*, in the neuter, singular and without gender-related suffixation.[35]

There might have been another reason for the rejection of idol worship. In nineteenth-century India, deep-rooted practices observed among the Hindus, such as widow-burning, child marriage, prohibition of remarriage for widows, class discrimination, excessive ritualism, superstition, and worship of idols, incarnations, and local godlings, were condemned by the colonial authorities, whose spearheads included the Christian Missionaries. The employment of symbolic light, removed from visually anthropomorphic or even gender-based characterization of the Supreme, was convenient as well as powerful to change the hostile criticism against the Hindu idolatry and justify his own credo and cause. Judging from this, the movement, which became an ideological response and counter-offensive against European charges, proved to be strategic. Though no substantial evidence is available, it is possible from the historical context that the Islamic influence of iconoclastic rejection of idolatry also played a role.

At the same time, Ramalingar's approach implied his scepticism about the reform movements of the period led by the modernized, intellectual Hindus chiefly from northern India, who presented a formless, abstract God devoid of visual exemplification for personal worship. Ramalingar held that a visible object for ritual purposes is required to appeal to the mass and to retain their presence and faith within the Hindu fold.

Ramalingar's device for representing God as a flame, beyond name and form, was undoubtedly the product of an inner struggle to protect his devotion intact from the modernist attack. The reform he inspired can also be understood in this context. In reality, he proposed reforms that promoted the prohibition of animal sacrifice, the eradication of superstition, and the extermination of social prejudices and discrimination among the Hindus.

It is evident that, through his consistent activities of edification, Ramalingar endeavoured to surpass the multi-dimensional 'distinction'. First of all, he attempted to reconcile or even synthesize the discrepancy of the 'ultimate' (*-anta*) systems, Vedānta and Siddhānta. Second, he attempted to eliminate the distinctions between all living creatures on the earth by encouraging people to observe strict vegetarianism and non-violence. Third, he strove for the abolition of any external markings which discriminated among people.[36] This is well exemplified by the fact that he was always dressed in immaculate white with a very simple vestment to conceal his entire body except for his face, hands, and feet. He had no matted hair or saffron robes. This clothing unique to him, which hid the attributes of his individuality to an extreme, has its own significance.

RAMALINGAR AND MODERNITY

It is obvious from the foregoing discussion that Ramalingar's imagination of the Lord as light or flame is believed not to be his own invention but something inherited from his predecessors, who were known collectively as Cittars, particularly from Tāyumāṉavar in all probability. The imaginative representation of the Supreme as effulgence did not originate entirely with him. However, he was believed to be the first Cittar in the modern scenario who utilized the new devices of print and press in disseminating his messages. In spite of this, his unique and persistent manner of expression of God had an unprecedented significance, set in the context of the nineteenth-century India experienced under the British colonization.

It was the socio-cultural turmoil of the period that did not allow Ramalingar to remain as a quiet, introspective renouncer. His milieu in modern India somehow urged him to present himself as an active sage with a multifaceted identity. He was in reality an embodiment of the period. Since he was in pursuit of a spiritual goal, he established a religious organization to materialize his ideals in the social context. Further, the emergence of the print media and press during that period assisted him in his propagandist activities.

In the realm of theology, Ramalingar indulged in advocating the monotheistic principle. The truth is one, and, as a logical consequence, there should not be any discord or conflict in worshipping one and the same God. The ideal of religious co-existence was proclaimed by him as a natural extension of this view.

The Boundless Benevolent *Cōti*
has enlightened me

in the outset (of my enquiry) itself,
that caste, religion and creed
are all false. (*Aruṭperuñcōti Akaval* 211)[37]

Ramalingar's teachings and activities attracted many people from different religious or sectarian backgrounds including Christians, Muslims, followers of Śrī Aurobindo, advocates of integral yoga institutes, and many others. It is remarkable that, even during his lifetime, a considerable number of the sympathizers of his reform movement was in fact from non-Hindu communities. Many scholars have conducted comparative studies of this saint from different religious standpoints.[38] There are plenty of Christian devotees of Ramalingar. In this context, it can also be noted that a religious institution honouring universal God in the form of a flame was recently established by a well-known Roman Catholic entrepreneur in Tamil Nadu, in the vicinity of the ancient site of Māmallapuram. Perhaps this was done with expectation of inter-religious acceptability.

The characterization of the Supreme as flame, which did not allude to any particular sectarian faith, was initially an attempt to reconcile the different standpoints and consolidate them. In contrast to his original intention, but as an inevitable consequence, Ramalingar's universalistic ideal provided scope even for the self-justification of exponents of atheistic ideologies.

There is no concrete evidence that Ramalingar's religious thoughts, egalitarian ideals, and the social philosophy derived therefrom provided a perceptible influence on the emergence of Tamil anti-brahmin rage in the early twentieth century, during the initial phases of which an atheistic tendency prevailed. Although his influence may not have been immediate, and was limited mainly to the ideological sphere, in the course of time, the stimulus from this saint as a mentor developed and triggered the rationalistic Dravidian movement and its self-respect agitation (Thasarathan and Jaganathan 1990: 449). In the long run, his aspiration was partially (and much against his intention) brought to fruition in the formation of the political association known as DK (Tirāviṭar Kaḻakam) under the leadership of Tantai Periyār (E. Vē. Irāmacāmi Nāykkar, 1879–1973), a strict propagandist of atheistic rationalism, antagonistic to idolatry and brahmin-centred ritualism. Ironically enough, and quite indirectly, Ramalingar's universalism contributed to the emergence of powerful Dravidian political parties and the formation of their tactics.

Ramalingar's tenet, which might have been spiritual in essence and in origin, paved the way for the consolidated political movements with distinct factional claims. Unexpectedly, his inclusivist advocacy, undoubtedly derived from an egalitarian and philanthropic conviction, took an opposite course and, even in a roundabout way, inspired the advent of a vigorous 'sectarianism' in politics. It is a well-known fact that Tamil Nadu has continuously been under the regime of regionalist parties since 1967. It is indeed ironical that, being overshadowed by the new trend, Ramalingar's reform movement itself has remained inconspicuous, even stagnant, suffering discord within the body of devotees that has split them into conflicting groups.[39]

Another ironical fact in this context is that Ramalingar's long-fostered appeal for socio-religious reform failed to raise an echo from the depressed for their upliftment. His spiritual movement did not go together with the caste movement even of his own community. This distinguishes quite distinctly from, for example, Narayana Guru, his younger contemporary from Travancore, who advocated a universalistic principle inspired by the Advaitic monism initiated the upliftment of his own Īḻavar community. This difference may be partially attributed to a subtle difference in the composition of their constituencies. Compared with his Keralite counterpart, Ramalingar rallied diverse followers, which helped him exert widespread influence over varied communities. In spite of this, however, it can be stated that the awakening evoked by Ramalingar, failed overall, to win the support of the general public or to develop into a mass movement of comprehensive reform.

CONCLUSION

Ramalingar was a man of religion with multiple identities as repeatedly stated by Ma. Po. Sivagnanam (widely known as Ma. Po. Ci.), a twentieth-century historian with populist appeal (Sivagnanam 1987). On the one hand, Ramalingar was a renouncer and mystic *par excellence*, and on the other, a social reformer and philanthropist. He was a poet with unparalleled talent and creativity.

At the same time, he was also a *de facto* founder-director of his own religious institutions and a promoter skilled in organizing propaganda through his publications.

In this respect, he was indeed a very rare example among religious figures of significance in the period of 'Hindu Renaissance'. In case of these thinkers and men of religion, an incompatible identity either as renouncer or reformer was alternatively established. It is true that his contemporaries of the nineteenth and twentieth centuries such as Rammohun Roy (1772–1833), Debendranath Tagore (1817–1905), Dayananda Sarasvati (1824–83), Ramakrishna Paramahamsa (1836–86), Keshab Chandra Sen (1838–84), Sirdi Saibaba (1838?–1918), Annie Besant (1847–1933), Narayana Guru (1854–1928), Swami Vivekananda (1863–1902) and more recently, Ramana Maharsi (1879–1950). They were all to be exact, either renouncers or reformers: definitely not both. In contrast, Ramalingar was an exception; he embodied the twofold dimension in a single personality, though his influence was virtually limited to the Tamil-speaking area of southern India. He was undoubtedly a forerunner of the charismatic god-man of the following centuries, proficient in institutionalizing a body of devotees and strategically using the modern media.[40]

Ramalingar's foresight and uniqueness are a paradox. He attempted to reorganize Hindu ritual towards rationalization by abolishing excessive idolization. At the same time, he employed a symbolic object of worship simple and abstract, in order to meet the requirement of daily worship for ordinary Hindus. All these were interpreted as accommodations of a traditional religion at the dawn of the modern period. His universalistic ideal might have sent a coded message to his own people to join forces to overcome foreign rule and accusations.

However, in spite of the utmost use of print and press in his activities, the manifestation of his intense bhakti was virtually confined to a pre-modern framework following the folk patterns. In order to attain the depth of gnosis, he adopted radical mysticism. Ironically Ramalingar's inclination towards deeper mysticism paved the way to his deification to the extent that he became iconized in a personality cult as Caṉmārkkam. Thus, his orientation was split approximately into two in his dilemma between traditionalism and modernism. His twofold identity was none other than the self-contradiction he inevitably shouldered as a burden in the pursuit of his lofty ideals.

Ramalingar was at the vanguard in the age of reformation. As a pathfinder, he significantly contributed to enlightening the public and inspiring them to observe their own religious and social institutions with a new perspective, and he left precious lessons to those who followed his tracks. Regardless of whether he was successful, his challenge should be valued as a pioneering experiment in spirituality at the crossroads in the nineteenth century.

NOTES

1. The honorific 'irāmaliṅkar' in its Tamil transliteration is widely accepted by academics. However, I spell his name as 'Ramalingar' in accordance with the common practice among Tamil people. He used to be known as 'irāmaliṅkam' (popularly spelt as Ramalingam), the word ending in '*-m*' instead of the honorific suffix '*-r*' before he gained his reputation. Here, for the sake of convenience, I use 'Ramalingar' when even referring to him in his childhood.
2. The name 'Vaḷḷalār' is an honorific title referring to 'Munificent One', 'One of Boundless Liberty', or 'Magnificent One'. However, due to these appellations, he had to suffer the brunt of criticism from the theists of the existing religious sects. According to them, the title 'Vaḷḷalār' is applicable only to God, not to a human. Ramalingar himself, however, did not use this appellation on his own accord. In addition to this title, he was (and still is) often referred to as 'irāmalinka-cuvāmi' (or '-cuvāmikaḷ' with the honorific suffix). However, the saint himself did not allow this as stated above, for the reason that the Tamil word *cuvāmi*, from Sanskrit *svāmin*, ultimately represents God (Annamalai 1988: 18–19).
3. There exist inconsistent accounts in the minor particulars of his biography, while the outlines are more or less the same. Even the accounts of his life events provided by his institutions sometimes differ in detail from those provided by ordinary biographers. In this context, we depend on a comparatively standard account of his life without serious disputes. Some important dates are listed in Annamalai 1988: 209 (Appendix I). However, the dates provided are largely speculative.
4. The Tamil name of this place is Citamparam. However, as the spelling Chidambaram is commonly used.
5. Sivagnanam 1987: 19. 'Karuṇīkars' are a south Indian caste of village accountants. See *Tamil Lexicon*, p. 256.

6. The age difference between the two brothers is not provided in the biographies. However, legends exist that identify Capāpati as Ramalingar's eldest brother. There appears to be confusion among the traditions with regard to his childhood. A legend states that Capāpati left his brother in the care of Capāpati Mutaliyār in Kāñcīpuram.
7. For details about miracles believed to have been performed by Ramalingar, see Thurasiram 1980 (vol. I): 493–518. At the headquarters in Vaṭalūr, legendary stories on his miraculous deeds have been transmitted from one generation to the next by the volunteers and devotees, and are narrated to the pilgrims and visitors. I too heard about some of these from the volunteers.
8. The present structure of the Cālai was newly constructed in 1993 after demolishing the old and simpler building on the same site.
9. At present, *anna-dāna* is still firmly maintained as a central activity of the organization. According to the information obtained during my field research in August 2006, food is provided three times a day. More than thousand people sometimes, including school children from nearby schools, are fed every day. At present, in the Cālai, about ten workers are employed as cooks and helpers.
10. It is evident from the structure, particularly the uppermost portion of the dome, that the Cattiya-nāṉa-capai was designed after the model of the celebrated Kaṉaka-capai of the Naṭarāja Temple in Chidambaram.
11. In the terminology among the devotees, his birth was expressed by the term *avatāra* and his demise by that of *mukti.*
12. Devotees believe that he expired on the day of *Tai-pūcam.*
13. This isolated asylum is sometimes known not as Citti-vaḷākam but as Citti-viḷākam or Citti-viḷāka-māḷikai. The word *vaḷākam* meaning 'campus' or 'place' and the word *viḷākam* meaning 'surrounding area' can often be interchangeably used in Tamil.
14. Cf. Thurasiram 1980 (vol. II): 183.
15. For translation I referred to Swami Saravanananda 1989: 400. The original *akaval* poem is:
aruḷoḷi viḷaṅkiṭa vāṇava meṉumōr /
iruḷaṟa veṉṉuḷat tēṟriya viḷakkē /
16. The *Aruṭperuñcoti Akaval,* the 1596 line-long stanza and decade in *akaval* metre, presents the quintessence of his religious experience.
17. II.75 Vaṭivuṭai-māṇikka-mālai 41. For translation I referred to Vanmikanathan 1976: 278. 'Oṟṟi' in this context refers to the celebrated Śaiva Temple in Tiruvoṟṟiyūr. The original is as follows:
pōṟṟiṭu vōrtam piḻai ā yiramum poṟuttaruḷcey /
vīṟṟoḷir ñāṉa viḷakkē marakata meṉkarumpē /
ēṟṟoḷir oṟṟi yiṭattār iṭattil ilaṅkum uyir /
māṟṟoḷi rumpacum poṉṉē vaṭivuṭai māṇikkamē / (Ūraṉ Aṭikaḷ 1978: 250).

18. VI.86 Tiruvaruṭ-perumai 10. For translation I referred to Vanmikanathan 1976: 621. The original runs as follows:
viratamā tikaḷum tavirttumeyñ ñāṉa /
viḷakkiṉāl eṉṉuḷam viḷakki /
iratamā tiyanal teḷḷamu taḷittiṅ /
keṉkarut taṉaittaiyum purintē /
caratamā nilaiyil cittelām valla /
cittiyait tayaviṉāl taruka /
varataṉe eṉṟēṉ vantaruṭ cōti /
vaḻaṅkiṉai vāḻiniṉ māṇpē / (Ūraṉ Aṭikaḷ 1978: 887).
19. Cf. Swami Saravanananda 1989: 418. It is to be remembered here that the Tamil *cōti* embraces, in a word, all the above-mentioned concepts such as light, glow, flame, splendour and luminosity.
20. For details about the cultural adaptation by Christian missionaries that is generally known as 'acculturation', see Okamitsu 2006.
21. The multiple imagery of light observed in Indian religio-cultural traditions is suggested in Sourirajan 1978: 132–3.
22. Swami Saravanananda 1989: iii. The rest of the poems, approximately three thousand in number, are on many gods and goddesses worshipped traditionally.
23. The exact number of the poems is 5768 in 671 decades. Cf. Vanmikanathan 1980: 45.
24. V.1 Aṉpu-mālai 25. For translation I referred to Vanmikanathan 1976: 115–16. The original is as follows:
ētum aṟi yātiruḷil iruntaciṟi yēṉai /
eṭuttuviṭut taṟivuciṟi tēyntiṭavum purintu /
ōtumaṟai mutaṟkalaikaḷ ōtāmal uṇara /
uṇarvilirun tuṇartti aruḷ uṇmainilai kāṭṭit /
tītuceṟi camayaneṟi cellutalait tavirttut /
tiruvaruṇmeyp potuneṟiyil celuttiyum nāṉmaruḷum /
pōtumayaṅ kēlmakaṉē eṉṟūmayak kellām /
pōkki eṉak kuḷḷirunta puṉitaparam poruḷē / (Ūraṉ Aṭikaḷ 1978: 552).
25. Zvelebil 1973 (1): 81.
26. For translation I referred to Francis 1990: 23. The original poem goes as follows:
ōṭi ōṭi ōṭi ōṭi uṭkalanta cōtiyai /
nāṭi nāṭi nāṭi nāṭi nāḷkaḷum kaḻintupōy /
vāṭi vāṭi vāṭi vāṭi māṇṭu pōṉa māntarkaḷ /
kōṭi kōṭi kōṭi kōṭi eṇṇiṟanta kōṭiyē / (Māṇikkavācakaṉ 1995: 244).
27. These salient features have been found to be quite akin to that of Vīraśaivas or Liṅgāyatas in medieval Karnataka. It is not uncommon among many Śaivaite saints in the Tamil country. Civavākkiyār also opposed discrimination on the basis of birth (Francis 1990: 36).

28. Zvelebil 1973(2): 225.
29. Cf. Sourirajan 1978: 24, 35, 98, 254, 258 and 268. Tirumular, the author of the *Tirumantiram*, was regarded as a forerunner of Cittar (Raja and Mathialagan 1990: 328). For the controversy with regard to the date of Tāyumāṉavar, see Sourirajan 1978: 16–17. In this book, the author identified the period to be 1604–61 for reference to literary evidences, whereas M. Varadarajan attributes it to be 1705–42; however, no factual evidence is presented (Varadarajan 1988: 210). In this article, we temporarily follow the notion of the former. Majority of the scholars appear to prefer ascribing Tāyumāṉavar to the eighteenth century.
30. It is presumable that, after his death, Ramalingar discernibly influenced a patriotic poet of nationwide renown, Ci. Cuppiramaṇṇiya Pārati (widely spelt as Subramanya Bharati; 1882–1921) from Tirunelvēli, and, indirectly perhaps, contributed to the emergence of modern Tamil verse, although Ramalingar's literary expression of his religious inspirations was not restricted within the realm of poetry. Cuppiramaṇṇiya Pārati paid tribute to Tāyumāṉavar, but did say anything about Ramalingar and his influence (Sourirajan 1978: 99–100). It should be indicated here that there are scholars who understand Pārati in the lineage of Tamil Cittars (Ryerson 1998: 54–84; cf. Zvelebil 1973 (2): 221–2).
31. It is important to note that, according to Zvelebil 1973 (1): 75, Tirumūlar already called the Absolute 'light' or 'lustre'.
32. For some details of the lawsuit against him raised by Āṟumuka Nāvaḷar (1822–89) and others, see Meenakshi Sundaram 1965: 71–2 and Varadarajan 1988: 221–3.
33. For translation I referred to Swami Saravanananda 1989: 413. The original runs as follows:
vētamu mākama virivum parampara /
nātamuṅ kaṭanta ñāṉameyk kaṉalē /.
34. For translation I referred to Swami Saravanananda 1989: 17. The original goes:
camayaṅ kaṭanta taṉipporuḷ veḷiyāy /
amaiyun tiruccapai waruṭperuñ jōti /.
35. For the idea of *civam*, see Annamalai 1988: 116–17. Zvelebil indicates that the conception of *civam* prevails in the poems of Tirumūlar as well, who was the foremost of the earliest Cittars. See Zvelebil 1973 (1): 74–5.
36. For him, even the physical appearance attributable to the difference of sex or gender had no positive meaning. It is important to note that Saint Ramalingar is portrayed to be beardless without dispute. It appears that the distinction of sex or gender is only superficial and of relative significance for him (Cf. Swami Saravanananda 1989: 189–92).
37. For translation I referred to Swami Saravanananda 1989: 48. The original runs:

cātiyu matamuñ camayamum poyyeṉa /
ātiyi luṇarttiya varuṭperuñ jōti /

38. From the perspective of Christianity a notable example is T. Dayanandan Francis, a Protestant priest-scholar. More recently, Anand Amaladass, a Jesuit professor in Chennai, developed his interest in this saint. The list of scholars might be endless.
39. Vanmikanathan 1980: 83–4. According to my informants, the headquarters in Vaṭalūr came under the management of the Hindu Religious and Charitable Endowments Department of the state government, from which an Executive Officer is sent to administer the operations. At present, about twenty people are employed as the staff and paid at their secretariat.
40. Similarly, Satya Sai Baba (1926–), who has a typical god-man type of charisma of the twentieth century, does not prefer idols.

REFERENCES

Annamalai, Sp., 1988, *The Life and Teachings of Saint Ramalingar*, Bombay: Bharatiya Vidya Bhavan.

Francis, T. Dayanandan, 1990, *The Mission and Message of Ramalinga Swamy*, Delhi: Motilal Banarsidass.

Ganapathy, T.N., 1993, *The Philosophy of the Tamil Siddhas*, New Delhi: Indian Council of Philosophical Research.

Māṇikkavācakaṉ, Ñā. 1995, *Cittar Pāṭalkaḷ*, Ceṉṉai: Umā Patippakam.

Meenakshi Sundaram, P., 1965, *History of Tamil Literature*, Hyderabad: Marathi Sahitya Parishad.

Okamitsu, Nobuko, 2006, 'Senkyō to Chiiki Bunka: Minami-Indo Ichi Katorikku-kyōku ni okeru Shūkyō Girei (Mission and Local Culture: Religious Rites in a Catholic Diocese in Southern India)', Doctoral Dissertation submitted to Tohoku University.

Raja, P. and M. Mathialagan, 1990, 'The Cittar Movement in Tamil Literature', *Encyclopaedia of Tamil Literature*, vol. 1, Madras: Institute of Asian Studies, pp. 327–37.

Ryerson, C., 1998, *Regionalism and Religion: The Tamil Renaissance and Popular Religion*, Madras: Christian Literature Society.

Sivagnanam, Ma. Po. (tr. by Ganapathy, R.), 1987, *The Universal Vision of Saint Ramalinga (Vaḷḷalār Kaṇṭa Orumaippāṭu)*, Annamalainagar: Annamalai University.

Sourirajan, P., 1978, *A Critical Study of Saint Tāyumāṉavar*, Tirupati: Sri Venkateswara University.

Swami Saravanananda (tr.), 1989, *Arutperunjothi Agaval: Thiruvarutprakasa Vallalar*, Madras: The Ramalinga Mission.

Swami Saravanananda, 1998, *Saint Ramalingam: His Life and Teachings as Experienced from the Inner Divine Light*, Dindigul: Dayavu Nool Veliyeetu Arakattalai.

Thasarathan, A. and G. Jaganathan, 1990, 'Irāmaliṅkar Movement in Tamil Nadu', *Encyclopaedia of Tamil Literature*, vol. 1, Madras: Institute of Asian Studies, pp. 441–50.

Thurasiram, T.R., 1980, *Arutperun Jothi and Deathless Body*, 2 vols., Madras: The University of Madras.

Tiruvaruṭpirakāca Vaḷḷalār Aruḷiya Aruṭperuñjōti Akaval, (Perumāṉāriṉ Kaiyeḻuttup Patippu), Vaṭalūr: Vaḷḷalār Teyva Nilaiyam, 2004 (eṭṭām patippu).

Turaicāmip Piḷḷai, Auvai Cu., 1979–89, *Tiruvaruṭpā Mūlamum Uraiyum* (10 pakutikaḷ), Aṇṇāmalainakar: Aṇṇāmalaip Palkalaikkaḻakam.

Ūraṉ Aṭikaḷ (ed.), 1978, *Tiruvaruṭpā* (2 pakutikaḷ), Vaḷalūr: Camaraca Caṉmārkka Ārāycci Nilaiyam.

Vanmikanathan, G., 1976, *Pathway to God Trod by Saint Ramalingar*, Bombay: Bharatiya Vidya Bhavan.

Vanmikanathan, G., 1980, *Ramalingar*, New Delhi: Sahitya Akademi.

Varadarajan, M. (tr. E. Sa. Visswanathan), 1988, *A History of Tamil Literature*, New Delhi: Sahitya Akademi.

Zvelebil, K.V., 1973 (1), *The Poets of the Powers*, London: Rider and Company.

Zvelebil, K.V., 1973 (2), *The Smile of Murugan*, Leiden: E.J. Brill.

Postscript

When our three-year research project on bhakti movement in India which started in 2005, entered its third year in 2007, the organizer of this project, Iwao Shima, suddenly passed away (12 May 2007). We deeply regret his unexpected demise.

In the spring of 2005, Shima had conceived our research project on the historical development of the Bhakti Movement in India by inviting Japanese scholars specializing in fields related to this subject and organizing seminars for this project. Our academic works and seminars on bhakti made fairly good progress. When the project entered its final year, most of the paper drafts in this volume, were sent to him.

In order to follow and realize his academic plan of publishing a book on bhakti as the outcome of our research project, his two collaborators reorganized our research group and invited Kazuyo Sakaki, Yoshitsugu Sawai and Hiroshi Yamashita to join the editorial group and help in the process. Hiroshi Yamashita of Tohoku University took over the office work of our research group; Yoshitsugu Sawai of Tenri University organized subsequent seminars; and Teiji Sakata undertook the responsibility of editing and publishing this volume with the support of all the members of our research group and other related scholars. Moreover, the editing skills and efforts of Kazuyo Sakaki and Katsuyuki Ida proved invaluable. Masahide Mori of Kanazawa University, a close colleague of Professor Shima, kindly assisted us throughout the process of editing and publishing this book.

Let this volume embody our heartfelt gratitude to Iwao Shima.

EDITORIAL BOARD

Index

abhaṅg 199-201, 206, 210-11
abhayadāna 170
Abhinavagupta 117, 231-4
abhivyaktavāda 234
abhyāsa 135
abhyudaya 198
ācārya 81-2
acintyabhedābheda 239, 243
Acyuta 41
ādhāracakra 189-90
Advaita (school) 52-3, 70-1, 229, 276
Advaita (philosophy) 23, 30, 116, 222
advaitabhakti 198
ādhāra 137
Adhyātma Rāmāyaṇa 162, 252
advitīya 52
Āgama 51, 116, 277
agni 38, 118-19
agnikārya 119
Agnipurāṇa 175
Ahirbudhnyasaṃhitā 9, 77, 95, 99
ajapāgāyatrī 146
ajapājapa 146
Ajitāgama 117
Āḻvār 27, 51, 68, 81, 87, 183
amalatva 67
Amanaskayoga 133
Amaraughaśāsanam 133
Amṛtakuṇḍa 134
Amṛtānubhav 184
ānanda 8, 59, 67
anantatva 67
anna 45
annadāna 284
Aniruddha 84
antaḥkaraṇa 62, 154, 189
anubhāva 54, 58, 232-3, 235, 237-8
anugraha 39, 44, 103, 119, 225
anumitivāda 233
anurāga 72
anuyāga 49
apāna 138, 141, 144, 189-90
aparavidyā 24
apaśūdra 80, 85
Appaya Dīkṣita (Appayya Tīṭctar) 266
apramāda 76
apṛthaksiddha 52
āratti 273
arcā 80
arcana 119, 165
Arthapañcakam 78, 89
ārādhana 41, 60
āropasiddha 225
aruṭperuñcōti 272
Aruṭperuñcōti Akaval 272, 277, 279-80, 284
āsana 139
ascetic renunciation 113
āśrama 42
aṣṭāṅgayoga 137, 188
aṣṭādaśabhedanirṇaya 89
aśvamedha 117
atheist *see nāstika*
ātman 23, 52, 54, 56, 58, 60-9, 187-8, 192, 207, 273
ātmanivedana 166-7
Ātmasiddhi 76, 83
avatāra 202, 231, 254, 284
avidyā 37, 52-6, 63-4, 66-7, 72-3
Ayodhyā 253, 256-8, 261

Bābājī Raghavacaitanya 209
Bahinabai 201
Bengali Vaiṣṇava *see* Gauḍīya Vaiṣṇava
Besant, Annie 282
Bhagavat 114

Bhāgavata 45, 52, 70
Bhagavata dharma 197-8, 200, 205, 209
Bhāgavatapurāṇa 9, 26-7, 68, 95, 106, 115, 159, 197, 202, 223
bhagavanmaya 43
Bhagavadgītā 26, 46, 51, 60, 68, 70, 73, 80, 86-7, 103, 114, 151, 159, 164, 183-5, 187-8, 192, 198, 201, 223
Bhagavadgītābhāṣya 25, 51, 78, 80, 83, 95
Bhairavāgama 117
bhajana (*bhajan*) 165, 205-8
bhakta 35-8, 41, 44-5, 96, 113, 116, 120, 131-3, 197-8, 201-2, 205
bhakti 19, 23, 25, 27-8, 30, 35-8, 40, 44-6, 51, 58, 60, 63, 76-9, 81, 83-6, 88, 95-6, 105-7, 109, 113-20, 131, 149, 159-63, 166-9, 176, 183-6, 192, 197-206, 210, 213, 223-8, 230-1, 235-6, 243-4, 276
bhaktimārga 197, 200, 205
bhaktirasa 10, 232, 235-6, 238, 243
Bhaktirasāmṛtasindhu 30, 223-4
Bhaktisandarbha 224
Bhaktism 113-14, 124, 184
bhaktirūpa-upāsanā 225
bhaktiyoga 76, 83-7, 106, 186-7, 192
bhaktiśraddhāvrata 37
Bharata 231-2, 235, 238
Bhattacharyya, N.N. 131
Bhaṭṭa Nāyaka 233-5
Bhaṭṭa Lollaṭa 232-3
Bhaṭṭanārāyaṇa 115
bhāva 227, 229, 234-5, 240, 243, 247
bhāvabhakti 30, 228-31
bhāvanā 55, 71
bhoga 113
bhuktivāda 233
bhūtaśuddhi 132, 136, 141, 148
Bījak 213-15
Bījak Ṭīkā Manoramā 215
Bījak Pārakh-pradodhnī-vyākhyā 215
Bliss 60 *see also ānanda*
Brahmā 123
brahmacārin 119
brahmagranthi 140
Brahmasūtra 71, 80, 85, 110
Brahmasūtrabhāṣya 54
brahmavidyā 85
brahmavijñāna 54
brahman 23, 25, 28, 32, 40, 44, 52-6, 59, 61, 67, 69, 116, 168, 187-8, 191-2, 198, 207, 224-5, 231, 236, 272-3
brahmin 41, 52
Buddha 162, 178
buddhiyoga 105
buddhiviśeṣa 85
Buddhism 24, 168

Caitanya 27-8, 68, 72, 74, 184, 209, 223, 229
caitanya 52
cakra 137, 152, 191
Cālai 268-9, 284
Camaracacuttacaṉmārkkacattiyacciṅkam 268
Camaracacuttacaṉmārkkacattiyatarum-accalai *see* Cālai
Camaracavētacaṉmārkkacaṅkam 268
Camaracavētapāṭacalai 269
Cāṃgadevpāsaṣṭī 184
Caṅkam 268-9, 271
caṉmārkkam 270
Caṉmārkkam (movement) 268, 270, 282
Cāpai 268-71, 274, 284
Carman, John 19, 26-7, 31
Caturvarga-Cintāmaṇi 168
cetana 61
Chāndogyopaniṣad 85
Chidambaram 265, 267
Christianity 273
cit 273
Cittar 275-6, 279, 286
cittamaruttuvam 270
citti 270 *see also siddhi*
Civaṉ 274 *see also* Śiva
Civavakkiyar 275
consecratory ritual *see pratiṣṭhā*

coti 267, 279
court poet 159
cuttacamaracacanmārkkam see canmārkkam
Cuppiramaṇṇiya Pārati 286
Czerniak-Drożdżowicz, M. 35, 47

Dakṣiṇavibhāga 223
dāna 168-9
Dasgupta, S. 19-23, 26-7, 30-2, 74
Daśaratha 254, 257, 262
dāsya 166
Davis, R.H. 30
dehaśuddhi 132
Derret, J.D.M. 175
deśika 42
devatābhakti 115
Devī 121-2
devotee 39, 42, 116 *see also* bhakta
devotion 25, 40-1 *see also* bhakti
Devotionalism 113, 124, 275, *see also* Bhaktism
dhāraṇā 136, 142-3
dharma 46, 101-2, 185, 198
Dharmaśāstra 119, 123, 125, 169
dhātu 190
Dhavamony, M. 128
dhyāna 57-8, 65, 71-2, 82, 139, 186
dīkṣā 36, 120, 128
dīkṣita 118
dīpa 269, 273
disciple 36-7
Divine Grace 272
DK (Tiravitar Kalakam) 280
Dravidian movement 280
Dumont, L. 113-14, 126, 128
duṣkara 76, 84
Dvaita Vedānta 23

effulgence 265, 267, 271, *see also coti*
ekacitta 42
ekānta 49
ekāntin 42
ekatva 107
ekāyana 42
Eknāth 200-1, 209
emancipation 39, 79, 96, 107-8

faith 27, 29, 31
final liberation 113-15, 118, 120, 128, 192
folk tale of Candrahāsa 173

Gadyatraya 26
Garuḍapurāṇa 175
Gāthā 184
Gauḍīya Vaiṣṇava 223
Gītā see Bhagavadgītā
Gītābhāṣya see Bhagavadgītābhāṣya
Gītārthasaṃgraha 76, 185
Gītātātparya 95
Gītāvalī 252
God 113, 197, 270
god-man 282, 287
God-mysticism 24-5
Gonda, J. 100, 116, 131
Gopa 228
Gopī 224, 228
Gorakhbānī 133
Gorakhbodh 133
Gorakṣanātha 131, 133-4
Gorakṣapaddhati 133
Gorakṣasaṃhitā 133, 151
Gorakṣaśataka 133-4
Govind 204
Great Effulgence *see peruñ-cōti*
Gupta, Sanjukta 46, 104
guru 9, 38-9, 81, 118-26, 128, 135, 189, 225
gurubhakti 114-15, 119-20, 125
Gyāna Cauṁtīsā 213, 215-21

Hacker, P. 28, 70
haṃsa-mantra 145-6, 154
Hanumān 259-60
Hara, M. 114
Hari 44-6, 209, 259-60
Hari-kathā 208
Haṭhayoga 135, 137, 214
Haṭhayogapradīpikā 134
Heim, Maria 169
Hemādri 168

Hindu mysticism 26
Hindu Renaissance 282
Hindu Tantra 132
Hiraṇyakaśipu 162
Horse Sacrifice *see aśvamedha*
hṛdaya 189
Hṛṣīkeśa 46

iḍā 138, 145, 153, 188, 191
ignorance 37, *see also avidyā*
image 117
Indian mysticism 22
initiation 36, 42, 44
innate impression 54, 55
intuitive realization 57
irāmaliṅkar *see* Ramalingar
īśvara 28
īśvarapraṇidhāna 135

James, William 19
Jagadguru 30
Jagannātha 38
Jaiminibhārata 175
jaṅgama 119, 128
jālandharabandha 139, 144, 190
japa 49, 85
Jayākhyasaṃhitā 35, 38-9, 44, 98
jīva 132, 203, 225-6, 229, 237, 269
Jīva Gosvāmī 224
jīvanmukti 92, 132
jñāna 25, 30, 57, 67, 77, 96, 103-7, 116, 185, 201, 224-5, 229, 273
Jñāndev *see* Jñāneśvar
jñānayoga 76, 78, 83-4, 87, 104, 106, 185-7, 192
Jñāneśvar 184, 187-8, 192, 199-201
Jñāneśvarī 184, 187-8, 192
jñāna-viśeṣa 82
jyotiṣ 267
Jūlāhā 213

Kabīr 27, 184, 213-14, 221
Kālī 30
kaliyuga 206
kaivalya 79, 137
Kamban̲ 252
Kāñcīpuram 82, 266
kanda 138
karman 26, 53, 56, 63-8, 74, 77, 82-3, 88, 97, 103-7, 116, 118, 164, 185-6, 224
karmayoga 53, 62, 73, 76-9, 83-4, 87, 91, 102-3, 106, 185-7, 192
Karuṇīkar 265
kathā 160
kathākār see *kīrtanakār*
Kaula 120
Kavitāvalī 252
kāvya 159, 234, 240
Kāvyaprakāśa 235
Khecarīmudrā 144
kīrtana 163-4, 200, 205-8
kīrtanakār 207-8
knowledge 53, 55-6
Koskikallio, P. 175
kṛpā 120, 225
Kṛṣṇa 30, 107, 109, 223-6, 228-31, 235-7, 240-4
Kṛṣṇa-eroticism 28
kṛṣṇarati 241
Kṛttivāsa 252
kṣatriya 41
Kulārṇavatantra 120
Kulkarnee, N.H. 200
kumbhaka 143-4
Kumbhakapaddhati 143
kuṇḍalinī 138, 190-2

Lakṣmaṇa 257-8
Lakṣmī 44-5, 103-5, 108
Lakṣmī-Nārāyaṇa 44
Lakṣmītantra 35, 43-4, 86, 95
Laṅkā 259-61
letter of death 174
liberation 187
liṅga 117, 233, 274, 277
lokasaṅgraha 97
love 58, 62-4, 84

Madhva 23, 25, 68, 72, 74, 92, 95-101, 104-9, 183, 186-7, 192
Mahābhārata 95, 114, 159, 175, 251

mahāmudrā 139-40
Maharsi, Ramana 282
mahāśūnya 141
Mahāyāna Buddhism 132, 169-70, 213
mānavadharma 198
Maṇavāḷāmāmuni 75
maṇipūracakra 190
manonmanī 145
mantra 37-8, 41-5, 122, 124, 126, 145-6, 148, 225, 271
mantrajapa 143, 145-7
Manusmṛti 80
Marutūr 265
Mataṅgaparameśvarāgama 118
mārga 87
Mātṛceta 160
Matsyendranātha 131, 134
māyā 116, 187
meditation 10, 54-8, 188-92
Mesquita, R. 95
Mīmāṃsaka 235
Mithila 254
mokṣa 25, 30, 51, 53, 55-9, 62-8, 70-1, 74, 79, 95-6, 114, 165, 197
mudrā 139-40, 143-4, 189
mukti 113, 124
muktibhaj 118
mūlabandha 144, 189-90
Mumukṣuppaṭi 89
Muṇḍakopaniṣad 23
Murukan̲ 266-7
Muslim 280
mysticism 19, 23, 28, 31, 114
mysticism of introspection 24
mysticism of unifying vision 24

nādānusandhāna 140
Nakamura, H. 70-1
nāḍī 133, 137-40, 143-5, 147-8, 188, 191
namaskāra 117
nāmajapa 202, 210
nāmamantra 203
nāmasaṅkīrtana 202
nāmasmaraṇa 202-4
Nāmdev 27, 201
Nānak 27
Nārada 38
Nāradabhaktisūtra 163, 223
Nārāyaṇa 52, 70, 100, 104, 108
Narayana Guru 281-2
Nārāyaṇīya 98-9, 101, 103, 108, 110
nāstika 39
nāṭaka 234
Nāthamuni 70, 80
Nātha 131, 133, 184, 187, 191-2, 214
Nāthastotra 121
Nāthayoga 137-8, 141-3, 148
Nāthayogin 131, 134
nāṭya 240
Nāṭyaśāstra 232
Nāyan̲ār (Nāyan̲mār) 51, 267
nididhyāsana 104, 186
niḥśreyas 198
Nimbārka 183
nirākāra God 202
nirguṇa 52, 202, 209, 272
nirguṇabhakti 107
Nirgun-bhakti-sagar 215
nirvāṇa 39, 219
nirvāṇadīkṣā 42
niṣpatti 232
nityaparikara 224
niyama 135
non-violence 276, 279
nṛtya 237
nyāsa 122
nyāsavidyā 85-6
Nyāyasiddhāñjana 82, 84

offerings 31
Otto, Rudolf 19-22, 24, 26, 31

pādasevana 165
Padmapurāṇa 175
Padoux, A. 115, 128
pādukā 120, 123-4
pādukāmantra 124
Pāñcarātra 35, 46-7, 77, 82, 87, 98, 100-1, 108-10, 115
Pāñcarātrasaṃhitā 51
Pandharpur 201

Pāṇḍuraṅg 199
pañcatattva 113
parābhakti 52-3, 58-63, 65-8, 74, 84, 198, 203, 205
parajñāna 84
paramabhakti 84
paramārtha 54
Paramasaṃhitā 35, 47
Parameśvara 28
pāramitā 169
pariṇāma 168
Pārvatī Maṅgal 252
paryupāsana 166
Pātañjala yoga 132, 137, 139, 142, 148
Patañjali 135-6, 138
Pauṣkarasaṃhitā 35, 40, 43, 98
Periyapurāṇa see *Tiruttoṇṭarpurāṇa*
peruñcōti 269
phalabhakti 79
Piḷḷai Lokācārya 75, 77-82, 88-9
piṅgalā 138, 145, 153, 188, 191
Prabodhacandrodaya 159
practice 31
pradakṣiṇa 117
pradhāna 76
Pradyumna 84
Prahlāda 26, 28, 162
Prajāpati 123
prakāśa 121
prāṇa 137-8, 140-1, 144-5, 149, 190-1
praṇava 146
prāṇāyāma 132-3, 136, 139-48, 153
prapanna 38, 40, 43-6
prapatti 26, 35, 38, 40, 77, 79-82, 85-8, 106
prasāda 41, 95, 116
Prasad, R. C. 251
Prasādapratibhodbhavastotra 160
prasanna 46, 116
pratyāhāra 136
pratiṣṭhā 119, 122
praveśa 116
preceptor 38-9, *see also guru*
prema 28, 60
premabhakti 30, 228-9
prīṇana 60
prīti 58-60, 84
priya 59-60
Proudfoot, Wayne 19
pṛthak 84
pṛthagupāya 87
Pṛthivī 123
pūjā 31, 36, 41
pūraka 144
Purāṇā 159, 170
purification 132, 135-6, 139, 141, 143-5
puruṣa 136-7
puruṣakāra 81
puruṣayogyatā 238
putraka 36, 39, 42

Rādhā 225, 229-30, 240-1
Radhakrishnan, S. 198-9
rāga 60, 72
rāgānugā 230
rāgātmikā 228
Rāgānugābhakti 228
Raghuvaṃśa 159
Rahasyatrayasāra 86
Rāma 30, 251-64
Rāmacarita 159
Rāmdās 200
Rāmaiyā Piḷḷai 265-6
Ramakrishna Paramahamsa 282
Ramalingar 11, 265-83
Ramalingar Paṉimaṉṟam 268, 271
Rāmānand 184
Rāmāyaṇa 159, 251-3, 263
Rāmānuja 23-6, 51-7, 59-69, 71-3, 76-80, 82-3, 87, 92, 115, 183-7, 192
Rāmcaritmānas 162, 251-3, 262-4
Rāmlīlā 253
Rantīdeva 172-3
rasa 223, 231-6, 238, 240-1, 243
rati 229, 240, 243
Rāvaṇa 258-60
recaka 144
religion 27
Roy, Rammohun 282

Ṛgveda 214
rudragranthi 141
Rūpa Gosvāmī 30, 177, 223-4

sacrifice 43
saccidānanda 67, 231
Saddharmapūṇḍarīka 160
sādhaka 39, 42, 135
sādhanā 197, 203, 205, 210, 231
sādhanābhakti 30, 79, 226-7
sādhyabhakti 30, 85
saguṇa 30, 52, 202, 209-10
sahaja 131, 214
sahasrāra 142, 144
śaighrya 76
Śaiva 115, 122, 272, 277
saint 200, 202, 265
Śaiva scripture 116-17, 122, *see also* Āgama
Śaivasiddhānta 115-17, 124-5, 128, 267, 276-7
Śaivism 51, 70, 276
sākāra 202
sakhya 166
sākṣātkāra 54, 57, 108
Śākta 115, 118, 120-2, 124, 131
Śākta-Kaula 120, 148
Śākta scripture 124-5
śakti 44
Śakti 121, 125, 146, 190-2, 224
śakticālinīmudrā 144
Śaktimat 224
śālagrāma 175, 180
sālokya 96-7, 99, 107
salutation 117
samādhi 104-5, 136, 139, 145, 189, 208
sāmānyabhakti 226
samatva 198
samāvartana 123
samaya 43
samayajña 39, 42
saṃhitā 98
sāmīpya 96
Saṃkarṣaṇa 84
Sāṃkhya 103, 132, 148
Sāṃkhya-yoga 44
saṃnyāsa 103, 192
samyakdarśana 54
saṃyama 104-5
saṃyoga 232-3
saṃsāra 53, 56, 63-6, 68, 214
saṃtoṣa 135
saṅgasiddha 226
sanctuary 117
Śāṇḍilyasūtra 164, 179, 223
Śaṅkara 23-5, 28, 30, 51-7, 64, 67, 70-3, 82, 175, 184-7, 192, 223-4
Śaṅkuka 233
Sant 131
Śāntideva 160
sapramāda 76
śaraṇāgatabhūtaṃ 43
śaraṇāgati 105-7
Śaraṇāgatigadya 77, 91
śaraṇaṃ 46
Sarasvati, Dayananda 282
śarīra 61
śarīrātmabhāva 52, 61
sārūpya 96
sarvabhūta 198
śāstra 118
Śatapañcāśataka 160
ṣaṭkarmāṇi 137
sattva 136
sattvaśuddhi 135
satya 67
Satya Saibaba 287
Sātvatasaṃhitā 35, 38, 44, 98
sātvata 35
śauca 135
saukarya 76
sāyujya 96-7
Schrader, F.O. 100
science of *svara* see *Śivasvarodaya*
Sen, Keshab Chandra 282
serving *see sevā, sevana*
śeṣaśeṣībhāva 61
sevā 61, 225
sevana 164
Shima, Iwao 70, 183
siddha 102-3
Siddha 131

Siddhānta 278
Siddhasiddhāntapaddhati 133
siddhi 116, 210, 268, 270
Siṃhāsanadvātriṃśikā 167
Sirdi Saibaba 282
Sīta 251-64
śiva 119, 128, 278, 286
Śiva 30, 51, 114, 116-21, 124-5, 127, 148, 192, 203, 265-7, 274, 277
Śivasvarodaya 142
śivabhakti 114, 118
smaraṇa 164
sneha 60, 72, 96
soul-mysticism 24
Smith, W.C. 29
smṛti 57, 164, 186
śodhana 137
soma 45
śraddhā 35-7, 43, 45, 47, 114, 125, 169, 225, 244
śraddhābhakti 37
śraddhadhāna 45-6
śravaṇa 162-3, 178
Śrī 45-6, 81
Śrī Aurobindo 280
Śrībhāṣya 51, 53-4
Śrīvacanabhūṣaṇa 79-80, 89
Śrīvaiṣṇava 26, 29, 51, 75, 88, 90, 106, 276
Śrīvidyā 121
Śṛṇgeri 30
śrotriya 39
Stavacintāmaṇi 115-16
sthāyībhāva 232, 249
sthāyin 239, 243
story of Rantideva 171
stotra 125, 160
Stotraratna 77
śuddhi 137
śūdra 41, 80, 85, 92-3
Sufi 134
sukara 76, 79
sukha 59
śūnya 213
Supreme Light of Grace 270
Supreme Reality 121
suśaka 76
suṣumnā 137-8, 140, 144, 153, 188
Svacchandatantra 117-19
svadharma 198, 202
svādiṣṭhānacakra 190
svādhyāya 135
svakarman 53
svarūpaśakti 224, 231
svarūpasiddha 226
svarūpayogyatā 238
śvetadvīpa 41, 97, 108
Śvetāśvataropaniṣad 23
sympathy 27

Tagore, Debendranath 282
Tai-pūcam 270
Taittirīyopaniṣad 59, 231
Tamil Nadu 265, 280-1
Taṅka 57, 71
tanmayātmanam 43
Tantai Periyar 280
Tantrarājatantra 121
Tantrism 113-15, 123, 125, 131, 141, 148, 183-4, 192
tapas 123, 135, 139, 143, 154
Tāraka 136
tārakayoga 151
Tarumaccalai *see* Cālai
tattva 132
tat tvam asi 54
Tāyumāṉavar 276-7, 279
Teṅgalai 75, 88, 106, 184
Tēvāram 267
Tiruttoṇṭarpurāṇam (*Periya Purāṇam*) 266
Tirumūlar 276, 286
Tiruvaruṭpā 267, 272-5
Tiruvoṟṟiyūr 267
Tokunaga, M. 46-7, 105
Trika 118
Tukārām 27, 199-206, 209-10
Tulsīdās 251-3, 263-4
Tulple, S.G. 203
tyāga 103, 167, 169, 192

uḍḍiyānabandha 144, 190

Ujjvalanīlamaṇi 230
unio mystica 21
Underhill, Evelyn 19
upacāra 114
upanayana 123
upāsaka 37
upāsanā 25, 28, 54, 57, 71-2, 82, 84, 186, 225
upavāsa 85
upāya 81-2, 88
Upaniṣad 23, 25-6, 32, 45, 52, 57, 68, 71, 76, 183
upāyabhakti 85
Utpattivāda 232

Vaḍagalai 26, 75, 88-9
Vaikuṇṭha 97, 100-1
Vaiṣṇava 39, 115-16, 224-5, 251, 276-7
vaiśya 41
vajrāsana 189
vaidhibhakti 227-8
Vallabha 68, 72, 74, 183-4
Vaḷḷalār *see* Ramalingar
Vālmīki 252
vandana 166
Vārkarī 184, 205-7
varṇa 84-5, 198
vāsanā 54
Vasugupta 116
Vāsudeva 42, 45, 84, 223
Vaṭalūr 270, 274
Vātsya Raṅganātha 89
vedanā 57-8, 61, 71, 82, 186
Vedānta 23, 25, 32, 44-5, 51-3, 57, 68, 77, 85, 276-8
Vedānta Deśika 75-7, 82-3, 85-8
Vedānta salvationism 115
Vedāntasūtra 175
Vedārthasaṃgraha 51, 58, 61, 80
Veda 22, 60, 64, 71, 119, 277
Vedic asceticism 114
Vedic ritual 143, 148
Vedic ritualism 126
vegetarianism 276, 279
vibhāva 232-3, 235-7, 239-41, 243, 247
vibhāva 237, 243
vibhīṣaṇa 260
vidhi 227
vidhura 85
vidyā 53, 57-8, 66-7, 71, 122
vigraha 267
Vikrama 173
Vikramacarita 167
viḷakku 273, *see also dīpa*
vimarśa 121
vīrya 45
Viśiṣṭādvaita Vedānta 23, 70, 73
Viṣṇu 26, 28, 35, 37-9, 41-2, 44, 46, 51-2, 70, 95, 172, 175, 253-4, 259, 262, 264, 277
viṣṇugranthi 141
Viṣṇupurāṇa 26, 28
Viṣṇusmṛti 170
Viśvāmitra 254
Viṭṭhal 201, 205, 209
Vivekamārtaṇḍa 134
Vivekananda, Swami 282
vrata 36
vyabhicāribhāva 232-3, 235, 238
vyavahāra 54
vyūha 44, 98

White Island *see śvetadvīpa*
women 80, 85, 92

yāga 41, 103
yama 137
Yāmuna 52, 70, 76-8, 80, 83, 87, 183, 185, 192
yantra 126
Yatīndramatadīpikā 78-81
yoga 24-5, 30, 38, 54, 70, 103-5, 110, 135-6, 229
Yogabīja 153
Yogamārtaṇḍa 134
Yogasūtra 135
yogin 44, 122
yonisthāna 139
Yuktānanda, Swami 198

Zoroastrianism 273